Fig. 1

Fig. 2

Fig. 3

Fig. 4

Fig. 5

Fig. 6

Fig. 7

14

Fig. 8

Fig. 9

Fig. 10

Fig. 11

Fig. 12

Fig. 13

Fig. 14

Fig. 15

Fig 16

Fig. 17

Fig. 18

Fig. 19

Fig. 20

Fig. 21

Lebensmittel
Backwaren
Getränke
Frühstück
Öffnungszeiten

Bienes Dorfladen
Lebensmittel
Backwaren
Getränke
Frühstück

Fig. 22

Fig. 23

Fig. 24

Fig. 25

Fig. 26

Fig. 27

Fig. 28

Fig. 29

Fig. 30

Fig. 31

Fig. 32

Fig. 33

Fig. 34

Fig. 1
Agriculture, energy production, and natural habitat in rural areas around Nordhausen, Thuringia.

Fig. 2
Old farmhouses near the village of Qianshantou, Huangyan.

Fig. 3
At Huangyan's rural-urban interface, dilapidated rural houses, farmland, factories, and high-rise buildings coexist.

Fig. 4
A new apartment complex in central Huangyan.

Fig. 5
Commercial streets near the "Smart Molding Town" industrial area, Xinqian, Huangyan.

Fig. 6
Old village houses in the urbanized Xifan Village, Xinqian, Huangyan.

Fig. 7
An industrial zone for small enterprises, Huangyan.

Fig. 8
A modern organic vegetable farm in Beiyang, Huangyan.

Fig. 9
Organic artichoke production at a modern farm in rural Huangyan, targeting upper-middle-class urban consumers.

Fig. 10
A small town nestled in an area of intensive agriculture near Nordhausen, Thuringia.

Fig. 11
Spoil heaps from potash mining and gravel lakes characterize the landscape around Nordhausen.

Fig. 12
In rural Huangyan, water lilies cover a village pond used to grow duckweed.

Fig. 13
A modern farm in Huangyan practicing biodynamic agriculture.

Fig. 14
A "solar park" in the Nordhausen region.

Fig. 15
Beiyang, in the west of Huangyan, is characterized by agriculture.

Fig. 16
In Dashuxia Village, Huangyan, old village houses are being demolished to make way for new high-density residential areas.

Fig. 17
Forest dieback (as a result of climate change) is leaving bare slopes in the southern Harz region, near Nordhausen.

Fig. 18
A platform of a rural train station in the Nordhausen region.

Fig. 19
A restaurant and bowling alley in a small town in the Kyffhäuserkreis District of Thuringia.

Fig. 20
Agriculture and a village in the Nordhausen region.

Fig. 21
A residential house and derelict agricultural facilities on the shore of a lake, Nordhausen region.

Fig. 22
The declining number of village stores poses a challenge to maintaining essential infrastructure in the peripheral settlements around Nordhausen.

Fig. 23
The Village Elderly Care Center, built and financed by the Xifan Village Collective, offers all village elders free accommodation, food, and monthly "pocket" money.

Fig. 24
The construction of single-family homes is still in demand in the well-connected villages of the Nordhausen District.

Fig. 25
A small-town street in Stolberg, Nordhausen, with intact half-timbered houses.

Fig. 26
New housing construction in Shatan Village, Huangyan.

Fig. 27
An old village street in rural Huangyan.

Fig. 28
A village near an industrial area of Huangyan.

Fig. 29
The tangerine has become the emblem of Huangyan's agriculture, with orange mascots prominently displayed on every corner.

Fig. 30
A factory in Huangyan specializes in producing medical plastic containers, such as the components of COVID-19 self-testing kits.

Fig. 31
The molds designed and manufactured by this factory are used in global production chains for high-end plastic products.

Fig. 32
Production lines for low-cost products, such as Christmas baubles, extend to home workshops.

Fig. 33
Despite its dilapidated appearance, this small molding workshop is integrated into the same plastics production networks as modern factories.

Fig. 34
"Lan Mei Manor" agricultural leisure park attracts tourists to Beiyang Town.

Urban-Rural Assembly

A Handbook for Co-Visioning Interconnected Regions

Anke Hagemann
Ava Lynam
Gaoli Xiao
Wolfgang Wende
Li Fan
Sigrun Langner
Maria Frölich-Kulik
Laura Henneke
Lukas Pappert
(eds.)

jovis

Content

Urban-Rural Assembly: A manual

Anke Hagemann, Sigrun Langner, and Wolfgang Wende

In our era of planetary urbanization, the supply of resources and goods to cities is largely organized on a translocal (or even global) scale. At the same time, the recognition of planetary boundaries amid multiple global crises—such as climate change, public health emergencies, and socio-economic inequality—urges us to safeguard resources and return to more regional and circular systems of supply and consumption. To do so, we must overcome the "metabolic rift," the dissociation of production, consumption, and disposal that Karl Marx identified as part of the urban-rural divide almost 150 years ago. This "scaling down" of resource cycles brings us back to more classical city-hinterland relationships and accompanying discussions about self-sufficient regions. In efforts to advance regenerative supplies of energy, food, and building materials while mitigating climate change and preserving biodiversity, the territories of extended urbanization will become a central arena for future innovation. These include zones of agriculture, grazing, forestry, resource extraction, industry, and logistics, as well as watersheds, wetlands, and habitats for more-than-human species. Systems thinking across the urban-rural continuum is a prerequisite for sustainable transformation. We must understand the multifaceted interconnectedness *of* regions and *within* them to create visions for more resilient future development. These plans and visions aim to bridge the urban-rural divide and rethink heterogeneous physical landscapes as well as functional and social networks. They cannot be established and imposed solely from the top down but must be owned and supported by a critical mass of local actors willing to put shared ideas into practice in policy, administration, economy, agriculture, civil society, or everyday life.

The Urban-Rural Assembly project began in 2018 as a Sino-German research initiative by the Chair of International Urbanism and Design (Habitat Unit) at Technische Universität, Berlin, and the Faculty of Urban Planning at Tongji University, Shanghai. The aim was to address the polarization of a depopulating countryside vis-a-vis rapidly urbanizing metropolitan zones in close proximity. China can be seen not only as a forerunner in such "concentrated" forms of urbanization but also in experimentation with rural urbanization policies which have already been applied for several decades. Exploratory rural practices have taken shape in the hinterland of Huangyan—a city district in Taizhou, Zhejiang Province—, emerging from a well-established collaboration between Tongji University and the district government. Professor Guiqing Yang's sensitive approaches to revitalizing traditional Chinese villages and the "Rural Revitalization College" in Huangyan, where he shares his knowledge with policymakers and professionals, served as our starting point. Huangyan is a rapidly urbanizing district encompassing dense urban areas, intense industrial and agricultural production, and forested mountain regions. To broaden our grasp of the complex physical and socio-spatial transformations and potentials for future development in Huangyan, we turned our focus toward the region's dynamic urban-rural linkages to set up a common research project on "re-assembling" city and countryside. The term "assembly" refers here primarily to the processes (in industry or building) of putting pieces together to form an integrated, functioning system—essential when we look at resource flows or social inclusion across urban and rural territories. Likewise, the project "assembled" research from multiple disciplines to capture these complex dynamics; at the same time, "assembly" describes a gathering of people in a process of collective or democratic decision-making. The latter became a central element in our strategy of co-visioning and facilitating sustainable transformation in interconnected urban and rural regions.

Taking on board a number of disciplines and institutions, which integrate crucial and diverse perspectives, methodologies, and bodies of knowledge on rural-urban development, the Urban-Rural Assembly project secured funding on the German side from the Federal Ministry of Education and Research as part of the "Sustainable Development of Urban Regions" funding line. Two "Urban-Rural Living Labs" were defined within Huangyan District to focus on specific aspects and characteristic subregions while becoming more closely involved in local processes. During the main project phase (2020-2024), research teams engaged in extensive analyses from various perspectives: Bauhaus-Universität Weimar's Chair for Landscape Architecture and Planning observed the transformation of landscapes and traditional water systems, while the team at the Leibniz Institute of Ecological Urban and Regional Development in Dresden investigated the development and preservation of ecosystem services and biodiversity. At Technische Universität Berlin, the Chair of Circular Economy studied potentials for more circular material flows in agriculture, the China Center looked at mobility patterns and social inclusion, and Habitat Unit explored innovative socio-spatial practices at the urban-rural interface. All research activities were significantly and meaningfully supported by Chinese academic partners from the respective fields at Tongji University (Faculty of Urban Planning, including the Center for Ecological Wisdom), Shanghai University (Department of Architecture), and Zhejiang University (Institute of Landscape Architecture; Institute of Environmental Pollution Control and Treatment). This cooperation became especially salient during the COVID-19 pandemic.

Building on our accumulated shared knowledge of the region, we initiated a strategic planning process aiming to create a sustainable future vision for the Huangyan region and its sub-regions. This "co-visioning" strategy, arising from the German "Raumbild" approach to regional planning, involved a variety of local stakeholders from different sectors and levels of governance in the form of multi-actor workshops, which introduced novel formats and processes to the normally top-down oriented planning system in China. As the COVID restrictions allowed only very limited on-site activities before 2023, we tested the co-visioning methodology and tools in a German urban-rural region (Nordhausen, Thuringia) and later explored possibilities for adaptation in the Chinese context. In multi-actor workshops, diverse participants had a unique opportunity to openly discuss regional challenges, potentials, and future aims while contributing to a tentative vision for Huangyan. This vision is by no means comprehensive, complete, or agreed upon by everybody. Still, it is a co-produced, compelling statement toward more integrated, balanced, and sustainable development of an urban-rural region, including many innovative (and potentially pioneering) approaches and ideas awaiting first steps toward implementation. With the process itself pivotal to achieving local impact, the co-visioning planning methodology has been documented as an accessible guide to be distributed within China and internationally as a policy tool with the help of our project partners UN-Habitat and ICLEI Local Governments for Sustainability Southeast Asia.

This book highlights the transdisciplinary character of the Urban-Rural Assembly project. It is not a collection of lengthy scientific articles detailing our research results. Instead, it is intended as a handbook for researchers, practitioners, policymakers, or initiatives, providing practical guidance on how to understand, research, learn from, and co-vision urban-rural development. Thus, it aims to situate the Urban-Rural Assembly project within a wider context of global urban dynamics, multidisciplinary scholarship, urban and rural policies, empirical research practice, rural activism, and model cases in architecture, planning, and landscape urbanism. Condensed results, reflections, methods, and tools from the Urban-Rural Assembly project (found on pages with tinted paper) are accompanied by invited texts from esteemed colleagues who contribute valuable references and practices from China, Germany, and beyond. In addition to project collaborators and advisors, these include speakers from the international conference "StadtLand: From Thuringia to a Planetary Perspective," held in Apolda in 2023 and co-organized with Internationale Bauausstellung Thüringen.

The book is divided into four chapters: Chapter One provides contributions that help to "understand extended urbanization." It highlights the increasing relevance of looking at urbanization beyond classical understandings of cities, presents related policies in different parts of the world, and introduces the spatial dynamics in the Urban-Rural Assembly's project region, Huangyan. Chapter Two offers a wide range of methodologies and tools for "researching urban-rural dynamics" from diverse perspectives and reflects on the potentials and pitfalls of conducting research in an interdisciplinary and transcultural context. Chapter Three assembles best practice examples of rural regeneration and innovation from an international perspective, encouraging us to "learn from the hinterlands." Finally, Chapter Four presents various strategies and methods for planning urban-rural regions, including landscape-based and participatory approaches. It introduces and reflects on the concept of "co-visioning" urban-rural regions, elaborated and applied in the Urban-Rural Assembly project.

The editorial team would like to thank all authors for their contributions, all URA team members and partners for contributing their research work, knowledge, and advice, and the Federal Ministry of Education and Research for funding the Urban-Rural Assembly project, including this book.

Chapter 1: Understanding Extended Urbanization

Even in the contemporary era proclaimed as an "Urban Age," almost half of the world's population continues to reside in areas defined as "rural." These largely productive landscapes span vast portions of the Earth's landmass. However, in urban research and practice, the "countryside" has not yet received the attention it deserves as a provider of food, water, energy, biodiversity, and other resources for the benefit of urban dwellers. But if we are to address climate change and sustainable urban development from a more holistic perspective, it is essential to tackle the interrelationships and metabolisms between urban and rural areas. Chapter One examines both academic positions on "extended urbanization" and emerging international policy approaches to urban-rural linkages. It introduces China's strategies for rural urbanization and reaching out to hinterlands on a global scale. Finally, the chapter presents comprehensive research findings on the dynamic changes at the urban-rural interface in Taizhou-Huangyan, Zhejiang Province.

Fig. 1

Urbanization beyond cities

Anke Hagemann

Since the influential "State of the World's Cities" report by the United Nations was published in 2006, countless articles, books, and project proposals in the field of Urban Research and Design have opened with a statement such as, "more than half the world's population now live in cities." This assertion is intended to underscore the importance of a more intensive engagement with cities in an emerging "Urban Age." However, the question inevitably arises why we should focus so much on cities, when almost half the world's population still live in areas categorized as "rural?" Is the latter a realm that eludes the urban designer entirely? And how can we even draw such a clear distinction between the two?

Corresponding with the traditional European city model, the city is usually defined as a distinctive type of settlement that contrasts with other territories and settlement types located beyond its boundaries—usually defined as "rural" or "countryside." This city/non-city dualism has permeated Western urban theory since its emergence in the early twentieth century. However, in the second half of the twentieth century, scholars and planners have increasingly recognized that there is more than just the "city" and the "countryside." A diverse range of in-between and hybrid settlement types have emerged across the globe: small towns and large villages; suburbs, urban sprawl, poly-centric regions, and peri-urban landscapes. Since the 1980s, authors like Terry McGee, Bernardo Secchi, Paola Vigano, Thomas Sieverts, and Edward Soja have argued that contemporary urban realities can no longer be adequately described using the conventional concept of the city, which evokes specific associations of density, urbanity, and compactness. Instead, they have introduced programmatic concepts such as *Desakota*, *Zwischenstadt*, Exopolis, *Città Diffusa*, and the Horizontal Metropolis (see article by Andrea Palmioli on page 130).

The countryside, on the other hand, has long been defined in opposition to the city—as the outside, or simply everything else. Like the city, the countryside has become a blank canvas for the projection of various ideas and fantasies—whether as an underdeveloped hinterland and resource pool serving urban needs or as a pristine refuge from the industrial city with all its "evils" and hardships. These contradictory conceptions of the countryside—as both a "place of longing" and "the back of beyond"—are still prevalent today, perhaps most notably in the "back to the countryside" movement among well-educated urbanites, accelerated by digitalization and the COVID-19 crisis. This movement, which targets attractive locations with good mobility connections to urban centers, contrasts sharply with the increasing peripheralization of villages and small towns, which are losing both population and essential services and infrastructure while agriculture is being rationalized and scaled up. These trends are evident not only in Germany (and more broadly in Western societies) but also in China, as will be shown in this book.

The German Thünen-Institut classifies 91.3% of the country's land as "rural."[1] On a global scale, Nikos Katsikis calculates that urban settlements occupy only 3% of the Earth's surface, while the productive territories of the "non-city," intensively used by agriculture, forestry, and resource extraction, cover nearly 70% of the global landmass (see map on pages 58–59).[2] Despite the statistical significance of non-urban territories in terms of population and land surface, "the countryside is largely off (our) radar, an ignored realm," as star architect Rem Koolhaas states in his book *Countryside, A Report*.[3] This is the case not only in the design disciplines but also across urban social sciences, where "the hinterland question is today considered secondary or even irrelevant to the study of urbanization." However, in "the age of planetary urbanisation, this position is untenable: city/hinterland relations lie at the heart of the contemporary urban problematique."[4] Considering this, Neil Brenner and Nikos Katsikis advocate for an understanding of urbanization that goes beyond city growth: the urban sociologist Henri Lefebvre predicted as early as 1970 that urbanization would span the entire planet—encompassing both city and countryside. He conceived it as a comprehensive capitalist process that transforms contemporary society as a whole. Today, due to advanced globalization, we can clearly see that "urban" lifestyles are permeating all types of settlements across the world. As observed in rural Germany and China alike, traditional agrarian communities are being supplanted by a suburban workforce commuting to service or industry jobs in towns and cities. Modern farmers and their families also tend to prefer suburban houses and lifestyles; some market their produce over the internet or receive meal-kit deliveries for daily cooking.

Christian Schmid and Neil Brenner have expanded on Lefebvre's ideas when speaking of "planetary urbanization," which considers the multiple functional relationships between urban agglomerations and rural hinterlands.[5] These processes of urbanization now encompass the entire surface of the planet, even extending to wilderness and oceans. As a result, the "urban" can no longer be defined in contrast to the "non-urban," rendering the classical definition of the city obsolete. Instead, Brenner and Schmid emphasize the process of transformation and distinguish between "concentrated," "extended," and "differentiated" urbanization. Simply put, rather than focusing on "city-ness" and urban growth, one should aim to study the connections and spatial dynamics between concentrated and extended urbanization, shifting attention towards the various types of urbanized spaces beyond the classical city. These include the "operational landscapes" of industrial agriculture, resource extraction, and translocal infrastructures that supply urban agglomerations with food, water, energy, and raw materials.

Metabolic urbanism

This urban-rural metabolism has long been a crucial precondition for the development and growth of cities. It was, in fact, the surplus production of food through grain cultivation in the Neolithic age (around ten thousand years ago) that enabled the differentiated division of labor and, consequently, the evolution of early cities in the Near East.[6] The famous "Allegory of Good and Bad Government," a series of fresco panels in the town hall of Siena, Italy, shows the mutual exchange of city and countryside in an idealized way—as conceived in the fourteenth century. For a long time, the growth of cities had been limited by the supply capacities of urban hinterlands, maintaining a circular relationship with the surrounding countryside. Several hundred years later, it was not only the Industrial Revolution but also the Agrarian Revolution—marked by the mechanization of agriculture in the nineteenth century and breakthroughs in the development of artificial fertilizers around 1900—that facilitated the explosion of cities. This was further supported by the advancement of transport infrastructures, such as waterways and railways, which extended the supply reach of cities into remote hinterlands. The interplay between urban growth and the natural environment is deftly recounted in William Cronon's landmark book *Nature's Metropolis*, which tells the story of how Chicago became the largest trading hub for agricultural produce in the U.S. Cronon frames the city's explosion in the second half of the nineteenth century as a continuous metabolic exchange between Chicago and its extended periphery, describing how unprecedented growth was made possible through the restructuring of rural landscapes and the rationalization and up-scaling of agriculture: "'The cities have not made the country,' reflected one long-time resident of Chicago in 1893; 'on the contrary, the country has compelled the cities ... Without the former the latter could not exist. Without farmers there could be no cities.'"[7]

In the early nineteenth century, the German agronomist and economist Johann Heinrich von Thünen reflected on this interdependence in his treatise, "The isolated state with regards to agriculture and national economy." To explain why the intensity of agricultural production decreases with increasing distance from the agricultural market in cities, he developed an idealized model of a self-sustaining functional unit of city and hinterland. This model, which views the countryside as a resource pool serving the city, included production zones for all necessary primary resources, forming concentric rings around the urban core. Von Thünen allocated areas the central metropolis would need for a steady supply of vegetables, timber, dairy products, meat, and grain according to transportation requirements and land rents (Fig. 2).

A hundred years later, Martin Wagner, former director of Berlin's urban planning department, applied a similar model of concentric supply zones to Berlin. He envisioned the urban region as being able to supply itself circularly with basic food from its immediate surroundings. Like von Thünen, Wagner determined the required areas for producing vegetables, milk, and potatoes, calculating their distance from the city center based on the transportation needs of each respective product. Berlin's settlement areas, low-density garden cities, and industries would blend into its surroundings, forming a balanced metabolic exchange with rural Brandenburg, grounded in a planned economy, land collectivization, and advanced technologies.[8] His century-old ideas resonate with today's concepts of degrowth, self-sufficiency, and urban commons. Around the same time, Frank Lloyd Wright's famous vision of "Broadacre City" proposed a different approach, where the city dissolves completely, merging with the countryside into a decentralized, self-sufficient region—a patchwork of settlements and agriculture. In Broadacre City, every family would receive one acre (approximately 4,000 square meters) of land for subsistence farming, with these extended plots connected by a grid of streets for individual cars—a symbol of freedom at the time—and modern communication systems.

Such visions of self-sufficient urban-rural regions, which seem to recur over time, can also be seen as a response to the increasing dependency of cities on translocal economic networks and resource supplies. Faced with the technology-driven separation of city

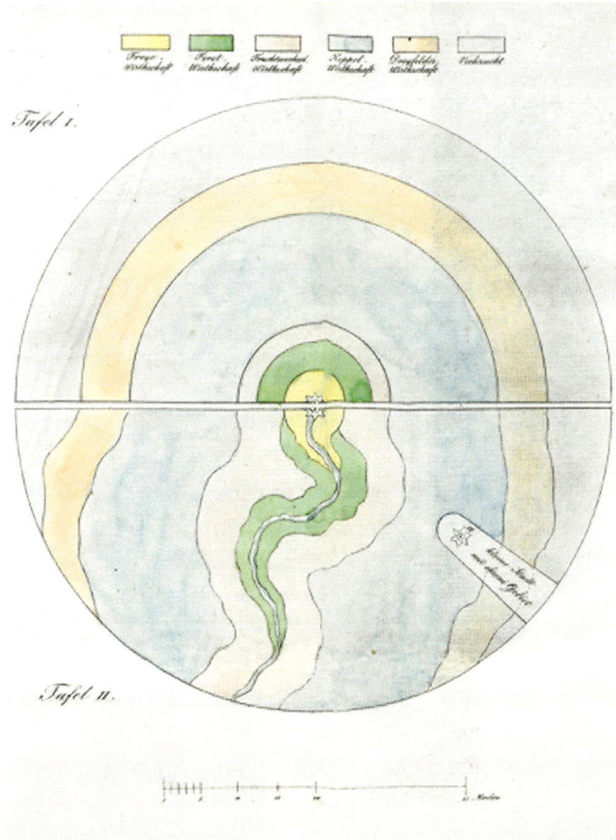

Fig. 2

and countryside under capitalism, Karl Marx already identified a "metabolic rift": agrarian soils were being depleted because they did not regain the nutrients exported to distant cities, while human excrement polluted urban waters. The translocal metabolism between city and countryside, as identified by Marx, and its negative ramifications have been the focus of an "Urban Political Ecology" movement in the social sciences since the 2000s.[9] This approach emphasizes that cities are produced and sustained through metabolic exchange processes that draw from "nature," and that these socio-natural processes are generally highly uneven and exploitative in character. However, the externalities are often invisible. The urban metabolism lens provides a useful counterpoint to the prevailing city-centric view of an "Urban Age," enabling us to understand urban and rural territories as highly interdependent, mutually produced spaces.[10]

Using world maps, Brenner and Katsikis draw our attention towards the "operational landscapes" beyond cities, which cover more than two-thirds of the Earth's landmass, highlighting the interconnectedness of these territories with cities on a global scale. Katsikis, accordingly, conceptualizes the entire globe as a town-country model reminiscent of Thünen's—a "Planetary Thünen Town."[11] The respective agricultural lands, forestry zones, mining areas, and infrastructural landscapes have been radically transformed in service of cities since early industrialization. Brenner and Katsikis observe that classical, contiguous urban hinterlands are entangled with more complex global supply networks, warning that these landscapes may be increasingly ecologically exploited, potentially becoming "sacrifice zones" for global capital.

Urban sustainability as a planetary task

This underscores the need to approach (urban) sustainability, ecological repair, and climate justice on a planetary scale. Hillary Angelo and David Wachsmuth have emphasized that cities alone cannot save the planet.[12] In the interview with Hillary Angelo in this chapter (see page 56), she argues that, despite the obvious functional and material entanglements between city and countryside, we remain stuck in urban-rural dualisms within academic disciplines, political governance, and spatial planning. However, in the face of the global climate crisis, we must re-connect city and countryside, building political coalitions across territories to create more sustainable and socially equitable urban-rural systems for food, water, and energy supply. In other words, the sustainability of cities should not rely on externalities occurring far afield—as is evident in the case of solar energy production or electric mobility, which depend on the exploitative extraction of mineral resources and the conversion of rural land into solar farms or industry parks (see "Solar Energy Supply Chain" on pages 62–63).

The case study presented by Hannes Langguth (see page 74) explores the translocal entanglements of such "green" industries, examining the intricate relationship between global production networks in the electric vehicle sector and the transformation of rural production sites. China has taken on an increasingly significant role in global green energy investment, with large-scale electric vehicle battery production becoming a desirable growth engine for peripheral regions in Europe. Langguth describes the emergence of new governance structures around these international investment projects and investigates how the formation of transnational spaces and borders impacts everyday life in the Thuringian countryside. Ultimately, this highlights the lack of a sensitive or sustainable integration of green technologies into urban-rural socio-spatial contexts.

The strong interconnectedness of cities and hinterlands worldwide must be considered in our approach to policy and spatial planning. For instance, in 2019, UN-Habitat launched a program aimed at strengthening urban-rural linkages (see interview with Remy Sietchiping and Grace Githiri on page 66). The program, which focuses on identifying specific challenges and demands in rural development, facilitates the exchange and collaboration of multi-level stakeholders from politics, planning, and civil society, thus advancing integrative concepts for urban-rural regions globally. Successful initiatives and best practices contribute to a compendium of case studies and the formulation of "Guiding Principles" and a "Framework for Action" to support regional actors elsewhere. Echoing Hillary Angelo, Sietchiping and Githiri underscore the importance of involving a wide array of stakeholders in promoting and shaping sustainable transformation.

One important actor within this UN network is China, which began shifting attention from rapidly growing megacities to rural urbanization in the early 2000s as a means of addressing the increasing territorial polarization between urban growth and rural decline. The revitalization of rural areas in Songyang County is a flagship project that has garnered international attention, largely due to the work of architect Xu Tiantian (see article by Eduard Kögel on page 182). In contrast, Elena Meyer-Clement (see page 82) introduces us to the more prevalent, mundane state policies of rural urbanization and their often drastic effects on rural settlements. Despite China's ongoing efforts toward integrated development, the dualism between city and country persists due to the binary household registration system ("Hukou") which distinguishes between urban and rural populations with little permeability. Strict, top-down land use regulations further complicate attempts to implement an integrated urban-rural planning approach.

The highly dynamic spatial transformation processes occurring in China position the country at the forefront of planetary urbanization, serving as a laboratory for addressing its significant challenges. To better understand the dynamics of extended urbanization in China and identify levers for sustainable regional development, the Urban-Rural Assembly research project has explored intricate, multi-scalar city-hinterland relationships in the urban region of Taizhou, Zhejiang Province. This research focused on a heterogeneous transition zone that encompasses dense urban and industrial neighborhoods, productive agricultural landscapes, and depopulating mountain regions, all connected by a river basin. Building on in-depth multi-disciplinary

The extent of Singapore's food supply, past and present

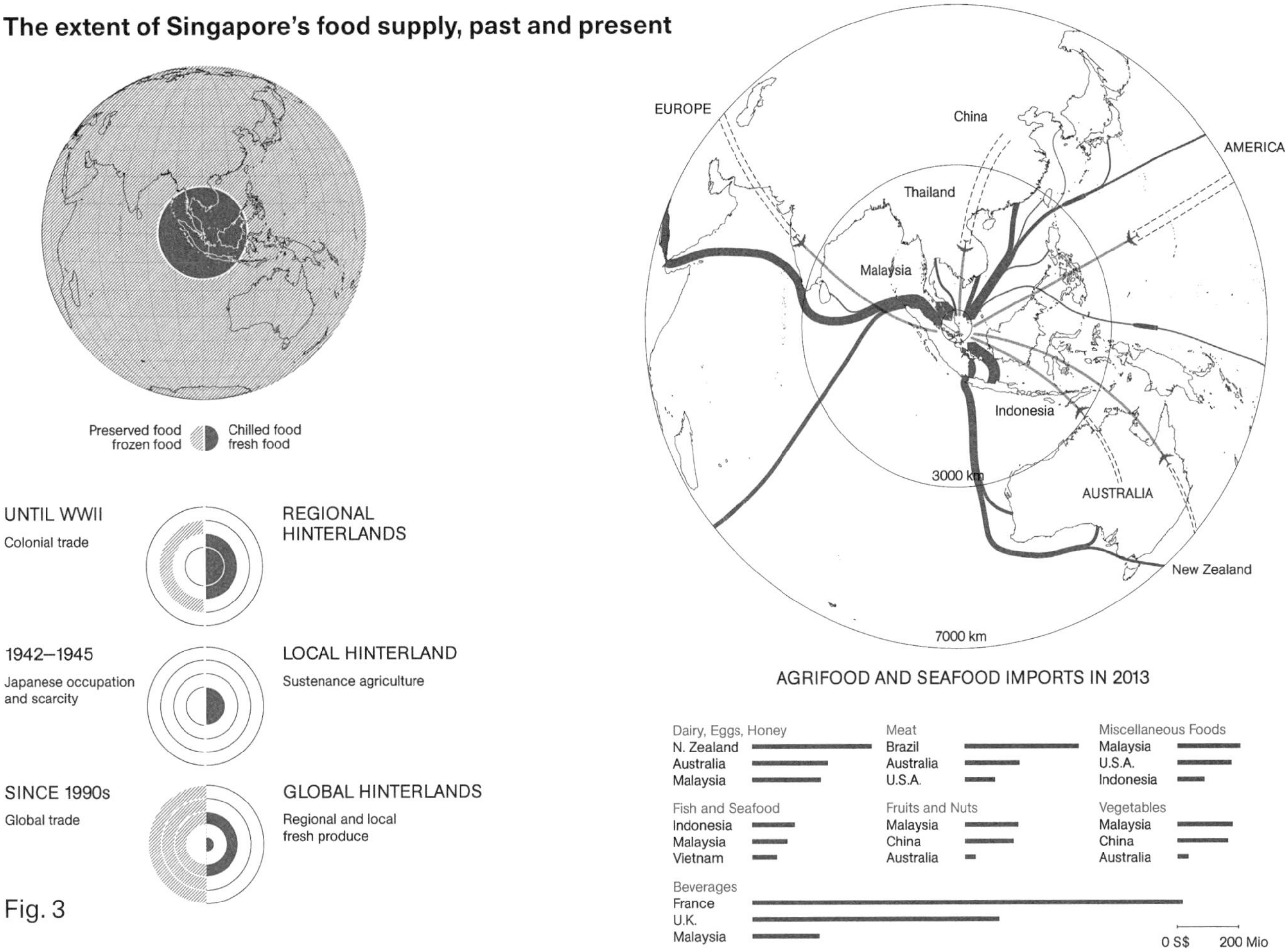

Fig. 3

analyses, the project initiated the collaborative development of integrated visions for regional transformation across both the city and the countryside. This chapter concludes with an article by the project's research teams, which characterizes the urban-rural region of Huangyan-Taizhou based on key research results from various disciplines (see page 90). These results include perspectives on landscape change, material flow in agriculture and industry, ecological transformation, and social mobility and innovation. By examining regional contexts and networks, the study avoids a rigid distinction between city and countryside, instead facilitating an understanding of both extended and concentrated urbanization through its underlying dynamics.

Innovation at the urban-rural interface

Facing urgently required transitions in food systems, energy production, the construction sector, and more—including the push for more regional, circular, and regenerative supply systems—we see non-city spaces emerging as crucial arenas for sustainable (urban) transformation. In their search for holistic strategies, urban scholars and practitioners must embrace this new field and develop the skills and tools necessary to engage with the landscapes of extended urbanization. They also must acknowledge the technological changes and innovations occurring in rural areas, often without their awareness. With his 2020 exhibition "Countryside: The Future" at the Guggenheim Museum in New York, Rem Koolhaas drew the attention of the architectural community to these unprecedented transformations: the digitalization and automation of agriculture, logistical landscapes and data storage, private investment in nature reserves, and repopulation of the countryside in select places. Additionally, more architects, urbanists, and planners recently rediscovered the planetary hinterlands and have turned towards a "new rurbanism"[13] and more territorial approaches to urban design.

Together with her team at ETH Zurich's Future Cities Lab in Singapore, Milica Topalovic has involved students in exploring and mapping the city-hinterland relationships and material flows that sustain the city-state of Singapore. This was done on all relevant scales—from the individual building to the globe—and

Fig. 4

across diverse fields, including food and water supply, construction materials (such as sand), labor migration, and industrial production. The study impressively illustrates the interdependence of cities and the wider territories of extended urbanization, along with the intricate infrastructures and logistics that bridge these distances.[14] Departing from a territorial approach practiced in ETH's Studio Basel for almost twenty years, Topalovic has shifted the focus towards rural development in teaching Urban Design at ETH Zurich. Architectural education serves as a relevant vantage point from which to rethink urban-rural relationships and envision sustainable transformations in rural land use, including agroecological changes. Her colleagues at EPFL Lausanne have extended this engagement with the "non-city" even further in their teaching and research, examining how ocean territories have been urbanized and operationalized—as can be seen in impressive mappings of the Barents Sea published by Harry Gugger, Nancy Couling, and Aurelie Blanchard.[15]

Innovative ideas and approaches to urban-rural development have also been tested beyond the academic field (see "best practice" examples in Chapter

Fig. 1
The countryside is functionally inextricably interwoven with urban centers through agriculture, energy production, or transportation infrastructure.

Fig. 2
The German agronomist von Thünen created a city-hinterland model of concentric rings with different types of agriculture to explain the decreasing intensity of land use with the distance from the central city.

Fig. 3
At ETH Zurich's Future Cities Lab in Singapore, Milica Topalovic and her team have been working with students to map the city-state's food and agricultural hinterland at regional and planetary scales.

Fig. 4
The atlas *Barents Lessons*, edited by Harry Gugger, Nancy Couling, and Aurélie Blanchard, maps the Barents Sea almost like an urban territory, crisscrossed by multiple shipping routes, cables, borders, or migratory birds. This is a section of a map that explores the ocean as a resource pool, including the potential for aquaculture or wind, geothermal, and tidal energy production.

Three of this book). The International Building Exhibition (IBA), for example, is an exceptional policy instrument in the German-speaking realm, exploring new and experimental models in spatial planning beyond the standard playbook. The IBA Thuringia (2012–2023) dedicated its ten-year activities to the topic of "Stadt-Land," developing manifold approaches to confront current challenges in rural German regions. Their pilot projects target, for example, the daily supply of remote villages, the revitalization of neglected tourist infrastructures and other vacant spaces, sustainable energy supply and climate mitigation in small town settings, and landscape transformation through soil-sensitive agricultural practices (see article by Marta Doehler-Behzadi on page 190).

Marta Doehler-Behzadi, former director of IBA Thuringia, suggests creating "multilandscapes instead of monofunctional acres," and calls for new visions of landscape design.[16] Acknowledging the vital role that productive landscapes play in the supply of urban centers and for sustainable transition, rural regions must develop unique qualities as livable (and indeed attractive) places for accommodating the roughly 43% of humankind who—at the time of writing—have not yet moved to cities. For Koolhaas, "the countryside must be rediscovered as a place to resettle, to stay alive; enthusiastic human presence must reanimate it with new imagination."[17] Architecture and urbanism can have significant agency in this imaginative transformation if they can look beyond the strict boundaries of the urban and take into account the manifold metabolic exchange processes that shape both the country and the city.

1 Patrick Küpper, "Abgrenzung und Typisierung ländlicher Räume," *Thünen Working Paper* 68 (2016): 27.

2 Nikos Katsikis, "Operational Landscapes and the Planetary Thünen Town," *Technosphere Magazine*, May 29, 2019, https://technosphere-magazine.hkw.de/p/Operational-Landscapes-and-the-Planetary-Thunen-Town-wEHRDNXmerHhSqB7jYXGuC.

3 Rem Koolhaas, *Countryside, A Report* (Cologne: Taschen, 2020): 2.

4 Neil Brenner and Nikos Katsikis, "Operational Landscapes: Hinterlands of the Capitalocene," *Architectural Design* 90, no. 1 (January 2020): 22–31.

5 Neil Brenner and Christian Schmid, "Towards a New Epistemology of the Urban?" City 19, no. 2–3 (May 4, 2015): 151–82.

6 Carolyn Steel, *Hungry City: How Food Shapes Our Lives* (London: Vintage, 2009). See also Sébastien Marot and Matthieu Calame, *Taking the Country's Side: Agriculture and Architecture* (Barcelona: Polígrafa, 2019).

7 William Cronon, *Nature's Metropolis: Chicago and the Great West* (New York: WW Norton & Co., 1992).

8 Joachim Trezib, "Das 'Neue Berlin II' von Martin Wagner: Modell einer Post-Wachstums-Ökonomie," *Arch+* 228 (2017): 82–89.

9 See, for example, Nik Heynen, Maria Kaika, and Erik Swyngedouw, eds., *In the Nature of Cities* (New York: Routledge, 2006).

10 Another perspective on translocal material flows—tested in research and teaching at TU Berlin and BTU Cottbus—is to study the spatiality of supply chains for basic consumer products, construction materials, or food. See: Anke Hagemann and Elke Beyer, "Globalizing Urban Research, Grounding Global Production Networks: Transnational Clothing Production and the Built Environment," *Articulo – Journal of Urban Research* 21 (January 31, 2020). See also: Anke Hagemann and Natacha Quintero-González, eds., *Feeding the City: Lebensmittelkreisläufe und die Produktion Städtischer Räume* (Cottbus: Brandenburgische Technische Universität Cottbus-Senftenberg, IKMZ – Universitätsbibliothek, 2021).

11 Nikos Katsikis, op. cit.

12 Hillary Angelo and David Wachsmuth, "Why Does Everyone Think Cities Can Save the Planet?" *Urban Studies* 57, no. 11 (2020): 2201–21.

13 *Arch+* 228 (2017), titled "Stadtland: Der neue Rurbanismus."

14 Milica Topalovic, Martin Knüsel, and Martin Jäggi, *Architecture of Territory – Hinterland: Singapore, Johor, Riau* (Zurich: ETH Zürich DArch, 2013), http://topalovic.arch.ethz.ch/materials/hinterland/.

15 Harry Gugger, Nancy Couling, and Aurélie Blanchard, *Barents Lessons: Teaching and Research in Architecture* (Zurich: Park Books, 2012). See also: Carola Hein, ed., *Oil Spaces: Exploring the Global Petroleumscape* (New York: Routledge, 2022).

16 Marta Doehler-Behzadi: "Stadt. Land. Stadtland: Plädoyer für eine neue territoriale Logik," in *StadtLand Perspektiven: Für eine neue Raumkultur*, ed., IBA Thüringen (Weimar: M BOOKS, 2023), 35–50.

17 Rem Koolhaas, op. cit.: 3.

Fig. 1

Connecting country and city in response to the climate crisis

Hillary Angelo, interviewed by Anke Hagemann

Anke Hagemann: Hillary, in several articles you have argued against the prevailing "city lens" and for "urbanization as a way of seeing" in urban studies. Why is it still so difficult to understand "city" and "countryside" as interconnected realms in research and practice?

Hillary Angelo: Let us first acknowledge that urban and rural space, or country and city, are always co-constituted and interconnected. Those interconnections include historical transformations—such as nineteenth-century enclosures of rural land that sent people to cities in need of waged labor across Europe—and the constant movement of goods, people, money, and services back and forth across urban and rural space in the twenty-first century. There is a long history of the study of these interconnections on the part of geographers and social scientists, from Marx's observations about the "metabolic rift" that industrial production created between country and city, to William Cronon's landmark *Nature's Metropolis*—a hinterland-focused history of the growth of Chicago.

However, despite this interconnection, there nevertheless remains little awareness and poor understanding of it in contemporary practice. Views of country and city have often been bifurcated, with their connections severed by the organization of scholarly disciplines and institutional structures of governance, planning, and politics. For example, in the social sciences, we have urban studies, a discipline interested in the production and transformation of cities (and, increasingly, how to make more "sustainable" urban environments). Meanwhile, rural sociology and agrarian studies are often concerned with many of the same issues (such as rural-to-urban migration, food systems, climate impacts, etc.), albeit from the opposite spatial perspective or vantage point. In policy—at least in the United States—we have municipal governments working hard to create sustainable cities when many of the issues they're dealing with transcend their jurisdictional authority, such as those related to spatially extensive water, transit, and energy infrastructure systems. In other words, even though country and city are highly entangled in material terms, it is often very difficult to work across these spaces and to hold them in one analytical frame, in part because of the organization of jurisdictions, disciplines, or issue areas. And, I would argue, the underappreciated

Planetary urbanization in the early 21st century: Concentrated and extended

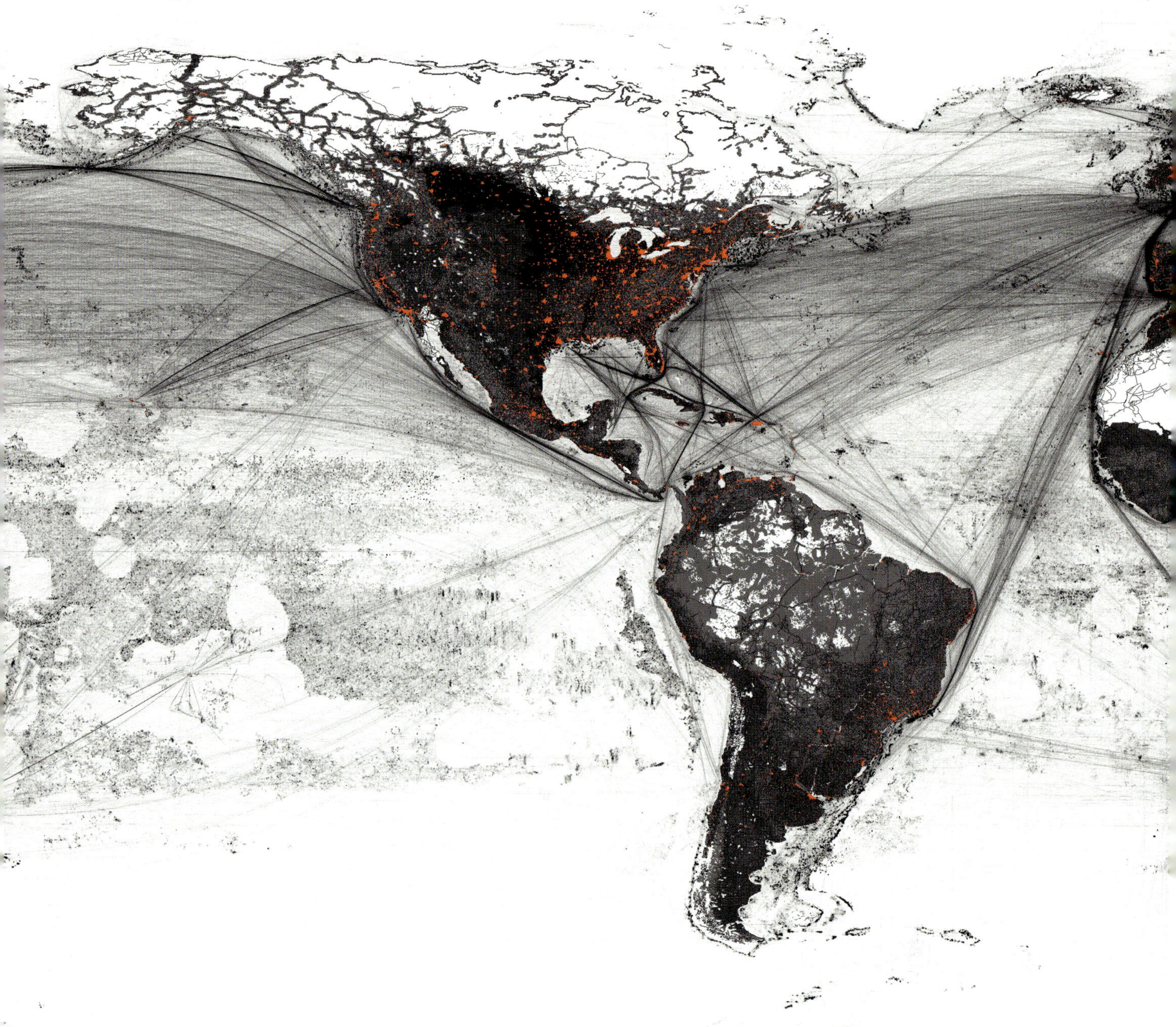

Fig. 2

The multitude of agglomeration zones of the planet are spread across the Earth's terrain. Settlement spaces, ranging from towns and cities to megalopolitan formations, concentrate population, economic activity, structures, and infrastructures in relatively condensed yet sprawling land areas. In total, these cover no more than four million square kilometers. However, this represents only one aspect of the landscapes shaped by the multiscalar and multivariate processes of urbanization. To sustain these densities, urbanization processes construct and transform a dense web of operational landscapes, including agricultural, grazing, and forestry landscapes alongside mining areas, fishing zones, and major land and marine transportation networks. This expansive network, shown as a dark background on the map, is estimated to cover roughly 100 million square kilometers of the planet's land surface, and extends into the air and sea. More than city—and often more-than-human—softscapes and hardscapes, they form the metabolic basis of planetary urbanization. *Map and text by Nikos Katsikis*

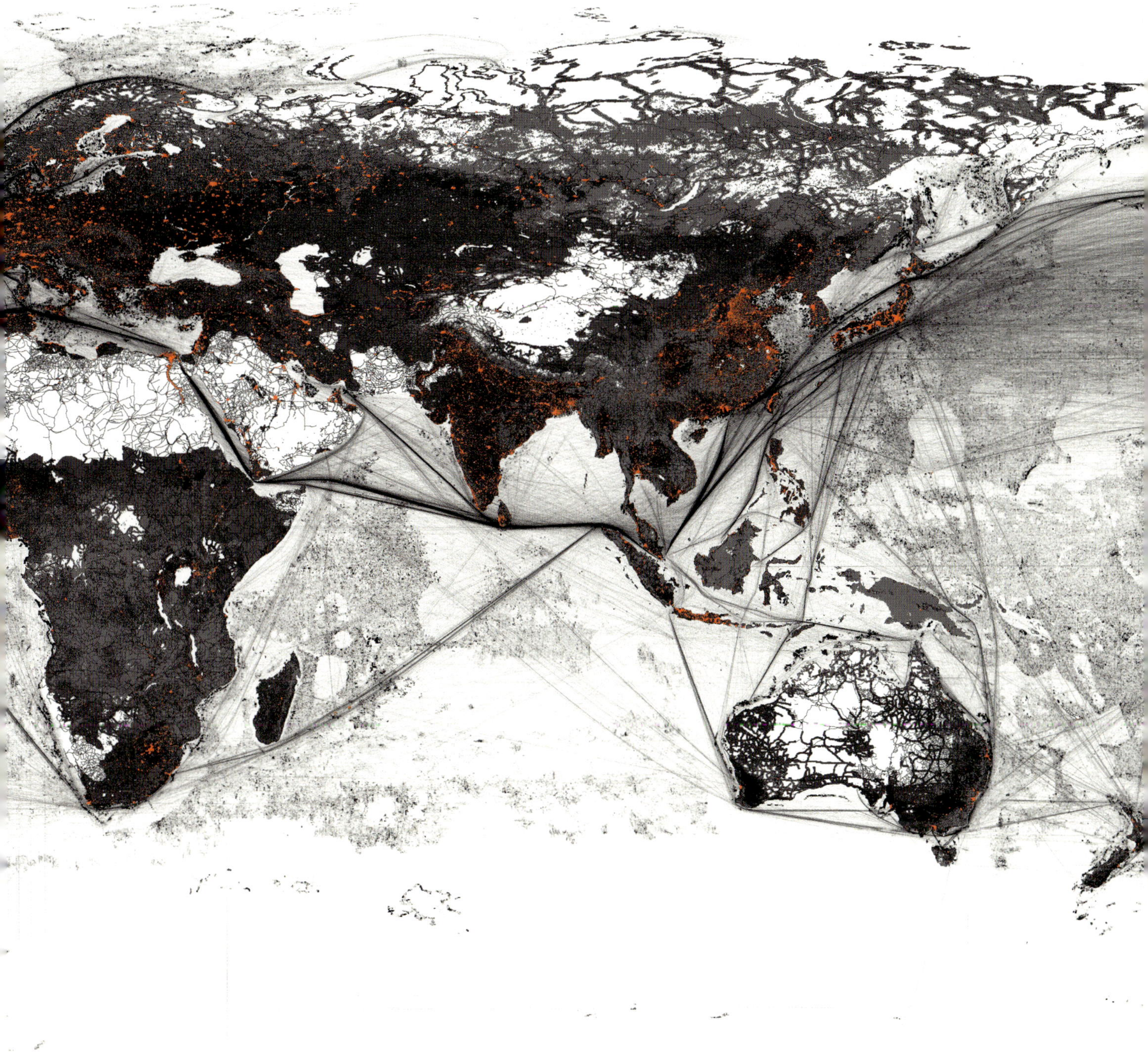

Urban agglomeration zones

Agricultural land (cropland, grazing land), forestry zones, mining areas, major fisheries

Transportation infrastructure (land, sea, air)

relationality of these issues becomes especially problematic in the context of climate change as we must transform infrastructural systems, remake the built environment, and build political coalitions across urban and rural space.

AH: How have scholars addressed this social and spatial relationality and the implications of such a view for planning, design, and policy *across* country and city?

HA: At least since the rise of industrial cities, scholars have made various attempts to develop effective analytic frameworks for thinking about "urban" and "rural" space together, as well as more diagnostic attempts to describe and intervene in these relations. Marx's idea of the metabolic rift was one of these, which fundamentally described a linear metabolism of raw materials coming into cities and waste flowing out (instead of a circular system). Another example is architect and urban planner Thomas Sieverts' conception of a *Zwischenstadt*,[2] or "in-between city," which refers to environments such as the Ruhr region of Germany that challenge notions of either urban or rural space.

One framework that has become particularly well known today (and which I've found useful) is Lefebvre's concept of "planetary urbanization."[3] Lefebvre used the phrase in the context of a historical argument about urbanization (soon to be) superseding industrialization as the process most responsible for the transformation of the planet. Today, most prominently for Neil Brenner and Christian Schmid, it has become a disciplinary intervention in urban studies—i.e., a call for urbanists to take urbanization as a process rather than the city as a site as the field's object of analysis.[4] Moreover, they present it as one that enforces a relational view across urban and putatively rural space.

Brenner and Schmid describe three mutually constitutive "moments" of urbanization: concentrated urbanization (the agglomerations we know as cities), extended urbanization (the "operational landscapes" often far beyond areas of population concentration and necessary for the agglomeration process), and differential urbanization (the ongoing capitalist "creative destruction" of configurations of society and space). In Nikos Katsikis' world map (Fig. 2), the cities or agglomerations appear in red and the operational landscapes in black. The latter depicts the totality of the used part of the planet, including agricultural lands, forestry zones, mining areas, and transport infrastructure. For scholars working in this tradition, the black on this map is just as "urban" as the red—these are two elements of the broader urban fabric (though I'll continue to refer to "urban" and "rural" space throughout this conversation for convenience).

This framework isn't perfect and has been the object of considerable critique. Some have argued that the name "planetary urbanization" itself continues to privilege urban agglomerations and centralities. It also raises questions about how other large-scale (i.e., "planetary") processes interact with urbanization, among other things.[5]

Critiques aside, what's most important here is the core insight that, if we are thinking about the transformation of either cities or rural environments as just one spatial context, we are missing a big part of the picture.

AH: How might this relational perspective on urban-rural territories change our approach to sustainable transformation in the face of climate change?

HA: As I said before, I have found that this kind of relational, processual view is especially important in the context of climate change and sustainability planning where we must transform infrastructural systems, remake the built environment, and build political coalitions across these spaces. For instance, bringing affordable, low-carbon energy to city residents requires massive changes to land and water far beyond cities where wind and solar farms are built. Creating more sustainable food and water systems in a climate-changed future involves changing patterns of urban consumption. Moreover, it involves remaking the broader food production and distribution, transportation, and hydraulic systems that bring resources into cities on regional, national, and global scales. And, we need to do this in ways that conserve water, reduce emissions, preserve habitat, and adapt to new patterns of heat and drought.

I want to use two examples from projects close to my research to illustrate what happens when we have a narrow view and how sustainability problems look different when we expand our frame. First, without a relational view of the sort I described above, there's a risk of creating what Samuel Mössner and Byron Miller have called—based on a study of Freiburg —"sustainability in one place."[6] They and others have shown how a dense, livable, walkable neighborhood may appear much less sustainable when taking a regional view or when considering the economic and racial dynamics of displacement.

Such elite green enclaves typically result in longer commutes with higher emissions for those displaced to cheaper peripheries. Meanwhile, wealthier residents of desirable "green" neighborhoods consume and travel more and have much larger carbon footprints.[7]

Depending on the geography, more vulnerable populations pushed to peripheries may also be exposed to increased environmental hazards, such as floods or wildfires.[8] In coastal Santa Cruz, California, where I live—as well as in many other places around the U.S.—there has been fierce local resistance to building dense, affordable housing on environmental grounds (i.e., in the interest of preserving green open space and other "natural" amenities), even though *not* building exacerbates each of these regional environmental problems.[9]

Second, there's the issue of new energy landscapes related to decarbonization. These require a new spatial organization of energy generation as we shift away from coal and oil (to wind and solar) and at the same time towards new geographies of extraction (such as the growing demand for mining lithium needed for battery storage). These energy-generating and extractive activities are often carried out quite far from cities but are intrinsically linked to the sites of urban concentration where most of this energy is consumed (Fig. 3). In the absence of a holistic, relational view of these systems, planning and discussion are often fractured across urban and rural space. For instance, I have been researching resistance to large-scale solar development in the Nevada desert in the United States (Fig. 4), where critics—including conservation biologists, residents, and local tribes—argue that old political economic and spatial patterns are being repeated in the use of public lands for renewable energy.[10]

Even though solar is an energy source that could be organized quite differently than nineteenth and twentieth-century systems—it can be small-scale as well as large and located on "disturbed" lands, in addition to those with relatively intact ecosystems—in the U.S., we're seeing energy development being pursued using the same old model. The government is lowering barriers for private development; renewables are being planned for centralized generation and long-distance transmission; and choices about siting reflect a binary understanding of society and nature. For the latter, policy and public debates often suggest that the only options are to preserve wild nature or instrumentalize it for "best" human use.

In addition, while critics of renewable energy are depicted in the mainstream urban media as NIMBYs ("Not In My Backyard") opposing progressive change, part of protestors' frustration is that they see these decisions being made in the absence of discussions of alternatives. These include reducing consumption, changing the distribution of costs and benefits (currently, benefits largely accrue in cities and costs in the countryside), or making different decisions about land use and environmental value in the context of biodiversity and extinction crises. Such issues concerning the spatial organization, political economy, and politics of renewables are raising fundamental questions such as: what is in the public good (i.e., the highest and best uses of these lands), who is the "public," and how are competing needs and desires to be adjudicated?

In both of these cases, we see forms of urban sustainability predicated on unsustainabilities elsewhere, which is what has led urban and environmental scholars to argue that we must "expand the frontiers of urban sustainability"[7] to encompass these kinds of relational inputs and impacts. Moreover, as the two examples above suggest, "expanding" the boundaries of sustainability thinking is necessary to adequately evaluate the actual sustainability of any climate solution *and* to facilitate proactive, progressive spatial planning and design.

AH: So, how must we change our thinking and practices for a more holistic understanding of urbanization and sustainability?

HA: I want to wrap up by offering three (working) principles for thinking relationally across urban and rural space based on the kind of research and rationale I've presented above. In doing so, I build on the work of scholars in agrarian and urban studies who are thinking explicitly across these spatial and disciplinary boundaries, developing arguments related to the themes I outline below.[11,12,13]

First, we need analytic and discursive relationality, rather than the dominance of one over the other. For example, from the perspective of cities, the "rural" too often appears simply as a site of extraction of materials for urban consumption, for the dumping of waste, or of agrarian lives rendered anachronistic or backwards by progressivist visions of urban futures. As an alternative to this, we'd ideally want a range of lives and livelihoods to be recognized as contemporary and legitimate.

Second, research and practice must be attuned to material relationality by focusing on the interconnected problems and processes linking urban and rural space. Examples include food produced in one place and consumed in another or energy grabbing for renewables in the countryside based on the need for affordable, low-carbon energy in cities.

Third, for policy, planning, and politics, we should strive to identify parallel and/or interconnected issues with potentially different articulations in each place. Climate adaptation to combat dangerous heat and sea level rise affects urban and rural communities in markedly different ways. For example, in cities, it takes

Solar energy supply chain

Mineral mining and processing
1. Polysilicon mining
2. Polysilicon processing plant

Manufacturing
3. Polysilicon production plant
4. Wafer production facility
5. Cell production facility
6. Panel production facility
7 "All-in-one" production facility

Distribution
8. Port
9. Retailers
10. Solar fields
11. Inverters
12. Cables
13. Batteries
14 Main electric grid
15 Household and industrial consumption

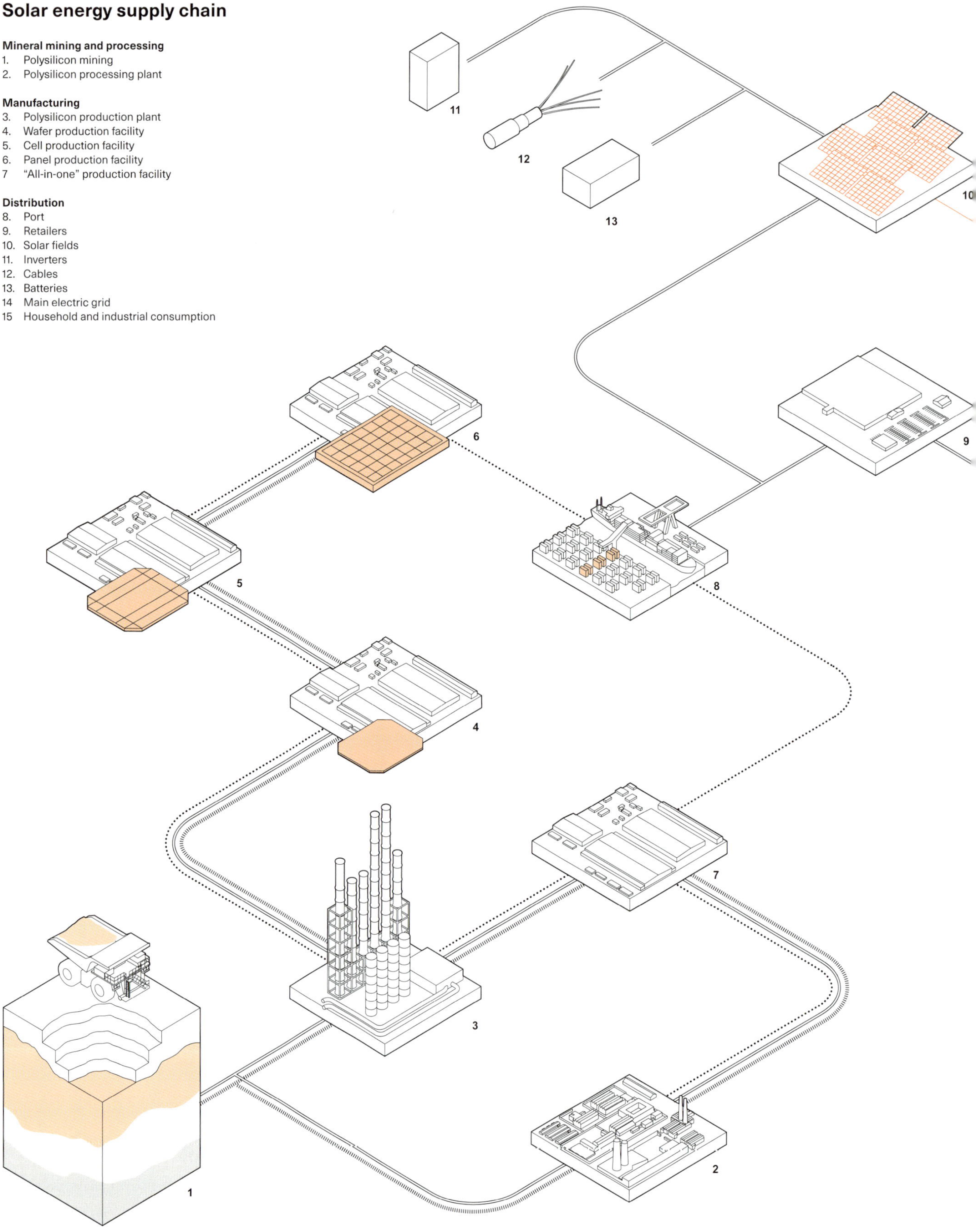

Fig. 3

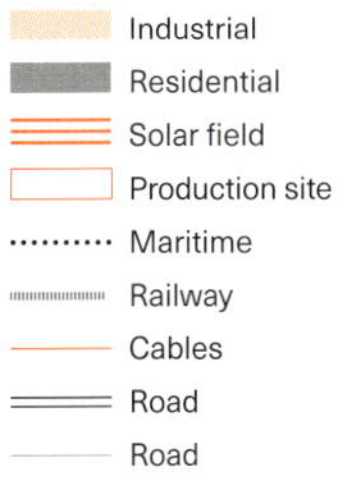

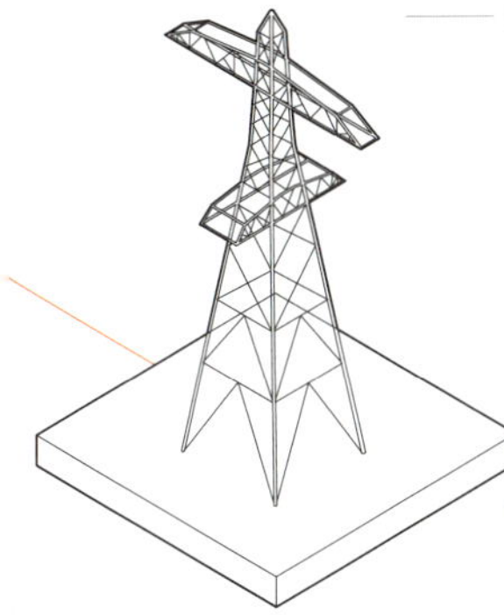

14

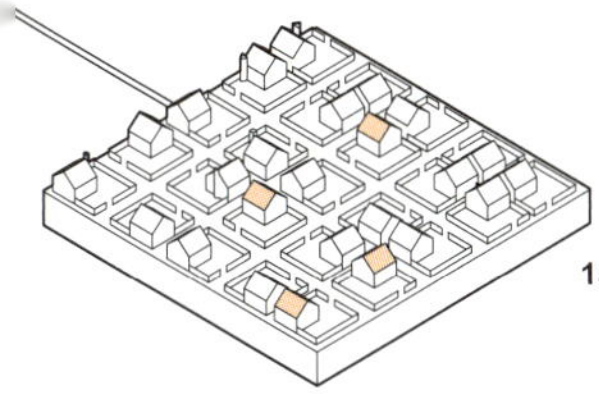

15

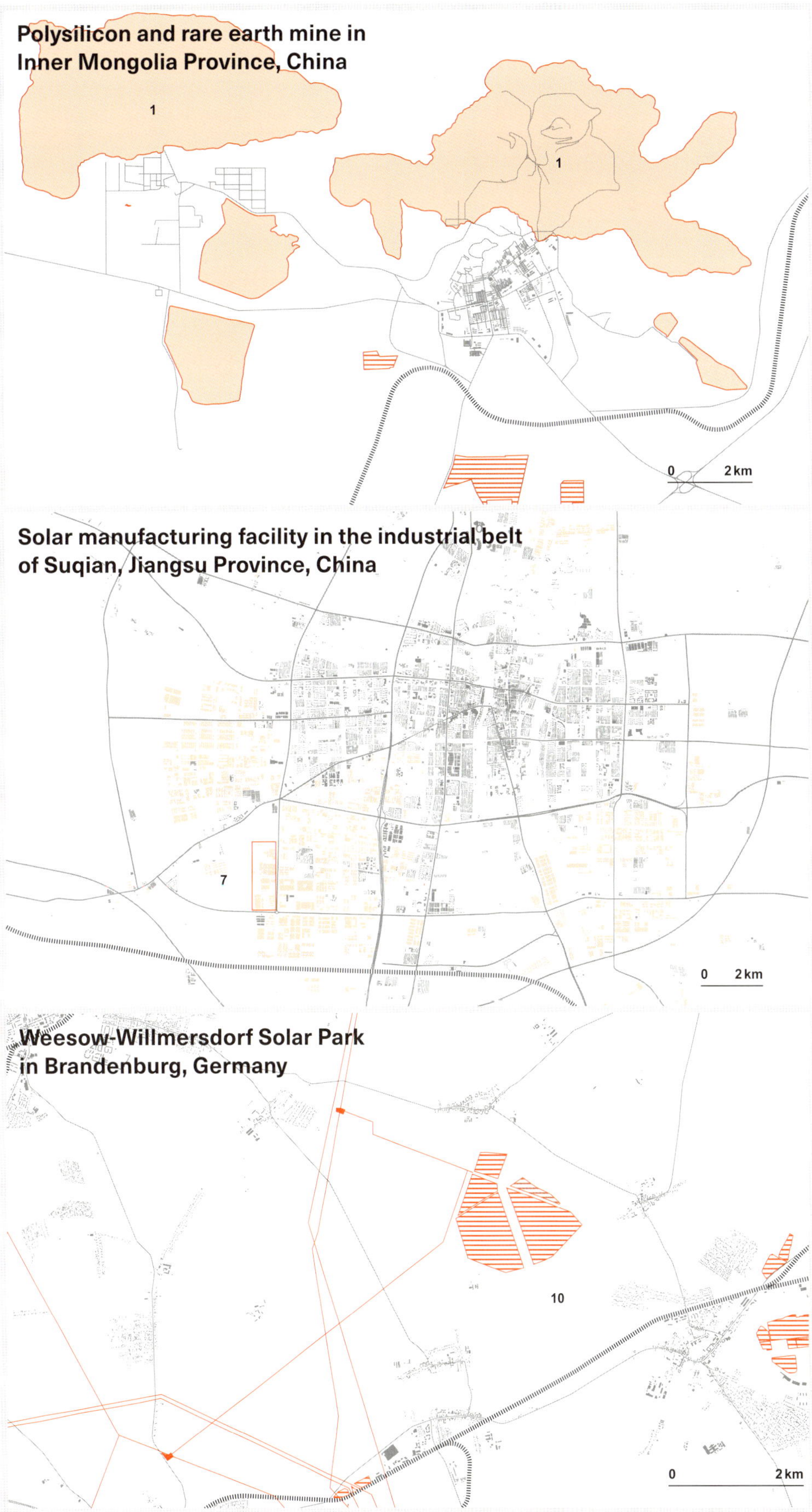

This diagram illustrates the complex production process of solar modules, which begins with the extraction of essential minerals like polysilicon **(1)** and their conversion into solar wafers **(2, 3)**. These wafers are then assembled into standardized solar panels through a multi-stage process **(4-6)**. Chinese companies are leading the way in optimizing this production line within a single integrated facility **(7)**. The rapid expansion of green energy projects in Europe is heavily reliant on the import of these advanced technologies **(8)**. Here, increasing amounts of agricultural land is being turned into solar parks **(10)**. This conversion, which offers the potential for substantial financial returns, is driven by low land prices, large parcels, and significant private investment.

the form of coastal adaptation against storm surge vulnerability; in rural Bangladesh, the main concerns are saltwater intrusion and its subsequent impacts on agriculture.[14] Decarbonizing energy production requires rethinking its infrastructure; this involves huge transformations of rural space as we shift from high-density, subterranean energy sources to low-density, land use intensive wind and solar.[15]

What could this mean in practical terms? For instance, how might a project like Urban-Rural Assembly integrate greater awareness of the regional and global relationality of these processes more explicitly in its work? One way might be to explicitly frame local interventions as responses to these global conditions. Another might be to trace, map, or visualize these interconnections from a specific place, as Fig. 3 models. However, a key question remains: what implications would such awareness have for local and regional planning efforts?

To enforce such a view in practice, the institutional, bureaucratic, and legal infrastructures that reproduce old, siloed thinking would have to be reworked in confronting climate change. It is for this reason that

Fig. 1
Solar Park Weesow-Willmersdorf, rural Brandenburg, as shown in Fig. 3 (bottom right).

Fig. 2
Nikos Katsikis's mapping of the planet's operationalized landscapes was part of his doctoral dissertation at Harvard University's Graduate School of Design and has received widespread attention.

Fig. 3
The supply chain for solar energy production (from resource extraction and solar parks in rural settings to urban energy consumption) was traced and mapped by David Bauer, Santiago Martinez Murillo, Yuliya Navatskaya, and Joseph Smithard as part of the publication *Power, Flows and Transformation* by David Bauer and Philipp Misselwitz (eds.) (JOVIS, in publication).

Fig. 4
Industrial solar farm near Primm, Nevada. The profit-oriented exploitation of desert land in the course of a solar land rush has provoked local criticism and resistance.

interdisciplinary environmental study programs are becoming more common in universities. Outside of such institutions, many environmental laws, structures of land use planning, and public agencies could be reconstructed to facilitate the kind of multi-spatial, relational types of planning and policy that climate adaptation and the pursuit of sustainability require. Transforming such structures moves beyond simply visualizing things differently (though this is an important starting point). It requires leveling out the existing "imperialism" of urban thought and practice to create holistic public discussion around these issues. This agenda dovetails with the work of political movements with broader interests in a "just transition," or ensuring systemic changes in response to climate crises are fair and inclusive.

In conclusion, we live in a world with very high levels of interconnection across country and city but with relatively low scholarly, policy, or public attention to that fact. From my perspective, responding to climate change and building truly sustainable environments requires focusing on relational interconnections. This means seeing local planning and design issues as part of one larger whole—conceptually, materially, and politically—as we work to transform infrastructural systems, remake the built environment, and build political coalitions across urban and rural space.

1 Hillary Angelo, "From the City Lens toward Urbanisation as a Way of Seeing: Country/City Binaries on an Urbanising Planet," *Urban Studies* 54, no. 1 (January 2017): 158–78.

2 Thomas Sieverts, *Cities without cities: an interpretation of the Zwischenstadt* (Routledge, 2003 [1997]).

3 Henri Lefebvre, *The Urban Revolution* (Minneapolis: University of Minnesota Press, 2003 [1970]).

4 Neil Brenner and Christian Schmid, "Towards a new epistemology of the urban?," *City* 19, no. 2-3 (2015): 151–82.

5 For a review, see Hillary Angelo and Kian Goh, "Out in space: Difference and abstraction in planetary urbanization," *International Journal of Urban and Regional Research* 45, no. 4 (2021): 732–44.

6 Samuel Mössner and Byron Miller, "Sustainability in one place? Dilemmas of sustainability governance in the Freiburg metropolitan region," *Regions Magazine* 300, no. 1 (2015): 18–20.

7 David Wachsmuth, Daniel A. Cohen, and Hillary Angelo, "Expand the frontiers of urban sustainability," *Nature* 536, no. 7617 (2016): 391–93.

8 Miriam Greenberg, et al., "Relational geographies of urban unsustainability: The entanglement of California's housing crisis with WUI growth and climate change," *Proceedings of the National Academy of Sciences* (2024).

9 Miriam Greenberg, "The Progressive Disjuncture on Land Use and Housing: Learning from the Leftmost City," *New Labor Forum* 30, no. 3 (2021): 56–64.

10 Hillary Angelo, "Boomtown: A Solar Land Rush in the West," *Harper's Magazine*, January 2023, accessed October 25, 2024, https://harpers.org/archive/2023/01/boomtown-beatty-nevada-solar-farms-death-valley/.

11 Swarnabh Ghosh and Ayan Meer, "Extended urbanisation and the agrarian question: Convergences, divergences and openings," *Urban Studies* 58, no. 6 (2021): 1097–119.

12 Levi Van Sant, Taylor Shelton, and Kelly Kay, "Connecting country and city: The multiple geographies of real property ownership in the US," *Geography Compass* 17, no. 2 (2023): e12677.

13 Hillary Angelo, Kian Goh, and Kasia Paprocki, "Rural-Urban Entanglements: Toward Intellectual and Political Solidarities in a Climate Changed World," working paper (2024).

14 Kasia Paprocki, *Threatening dystopias: The global politics of climate change adaptation in Bangladesh* (Ithaca: Cornell University Press, 2021).

15 Matthew T. Huber and James McCarthy, "Beyond the subterranean energy regime? Fuel, land use and the production of space," *Transactions of the Institute of British Geographers* 42, no. 4 (2017): 655–68.

Fig. 1

Connecting horizons: Empowering communities through urban-rural integration

Remy Sietchiping and Grace Githiri, interviewed by Anke Hagemann

Against a backdrop of accelerated and ever-expanding urbanization around the globe and its associated fundamental strain on our planetary boundaries, national, regional, and local representatives from politics, planning, and civil society are working worldwide on the reintegration of urban and rural areas. The "Urban-Rural Linkages – Guiding Principles and Framework for Action" program was initiated by UN-Habitat and later acknowledged in the 2019 UN-Habitat Assembly resolution.[1] It contributes to an exchange of these regional initiatives within the framework of an international learning network and provides concrete pathways for integrated urban-rural development. Remy Sietchiping and Grace Githiri promote and coordinate the program in the UN-Habitat head office.

Anke Hagemann: What are the challenges concerning the transformation of urban and rural regions from a global perspective and why is it necessary to establish guiding principles for integrated urban-rural development?

Remy Sietchiping and Grace Githiri: "Leave No One Behind" is one of the central commitments unanimously adopted in 2015 by United Nations member states as a universal value and principle of the 2030 Agenda for Sustainable Development. The "New Urban Agenda"—an action-oriented and people-centered document—was adopted the following year, taking up this demand and translating it into concrete instruments for actors to localize the promises in *all* territories of human settlements. However, in most contexts, the UN global goals are insufficiently met by the outlined governance approaches as there persists a distinction between urban and rural development policies.

Urbanization is a strong transformative force reshaping the world's urban and rural landscapes. As a driver of development and poverty reduction, it can bring prosperity to many regions. However, the forces of urbanization have also led to numerous challenges while creating new forms of social and spatial inequality, unsustainability, polarization, and divergences in development between urban and rural areas. Thus, there is an urgent need to promote sustainable and integrated growth of cities and territories. Above all, rural areas face neglect in various forms, such as inadequate investment in infrastructure, limited job opportunities,

Fig. 2

challenges in agriculture sectors and livelihood opportunities, inadequate healthcare, and limited access to training and funding. This neglect naturally varies by region and country, with some governments formulating rural development policies while others face more significant challenges. Examples can be found in remote developing regions with limited basic services and in depopulating areas in developed countries. To tackle this problem, a comprehensive approach is needed with targeted investments in infrastructure, healthcare, education, agriculture, and job creation. This should be implemented alongside an improved understanding of the continuum between urban and rural areas to achieve more balanced and equitable development.

AH: Do we need a different approach to governance and planning?

RS, GG: Yes, integrated urban and rural development requires a different approach to spatial planning and governance to account for the unique needs and dynamics of both urban and rural areas. Key points of an integrated approach include recognizing the interdependence between urban and rural economies, optimizing resource use across different areas, promoting economic diversification to create jobs in urban and rural communities, and reducing disparities to ensure social inclusion and equitable, resilient, and sustainable development for all. A suite of planning, financing, and governance instruments and arrangements must be developed and used by all levels of government, stakeholders from urban and rural areas, and experts from various disciplines.

AH: Urban scholars claim that city-hinterland relationships have gained a planetary dimension today—see Hillary Angelo's contribution to this issue. How can transnational links between (rural) resources and (urban) consumption become more sustainable?

RS, GG: Globalization is complexifying the relationship between resources, production, and consumption within the urban-rural continuum. Many resources that fuel cities come from rural areas but travel long distances to meet urban needs. This has implications for sustainability; for instance, transporting resources from rural

Fig. 3

to urban areas requires adequate infrastructure and services, sufficient energy, and the management of emissions. Therefore, reducing these distances could lower emissions. Moreover, extracting rural resources unsustainably to meet urban demand can degrade ecosystems through issues like deforestation, soil erosion, and groundwater depletion. Also, urban waste like plastic and sewage can end up back in rural areas through rivers and landfills if not properly managed, placing a disproportionate burden on rural communities. To improve urban-rural linkages for sustainability, we must reduce resource transportation distances, implement more sustainable resource management in rural areas, and find ways for cities to better manage their waste to mitigate impacts on rural environments.

AH: What is the UN-Habitat program on urban-rural linkages aiming at and what does it comprise?

RS, GG: Together with more than 130 partner institutions, including urban, rural, and regional development experts, representatives of national and subnational governments, development partners, think tanks, academics, and international organizations, the specific Guiding Principles were developed.[2] This is based on the premise that urban and rural areas should no longer be treated as separate entities in the elaboration of regional development plans and governance strategies. Instead, it is about strengthening the multiple potentials that arise from the synergy of urban and rural areas. Leaving no one behind, even in peripheral rural areas, is a promise that the program aims to fulfill through the targeted strengthening of regional cycles and interrelationships along the entire urban-rural continuum. The aim is to develop pragmatic strategies and propose a framework for action to support regions and their decision-makers in identifying and strengthening place-specific urban-rural relationships.

The joint initiative agreed upon ten guiding principles and an actionable framework with eleven areas addressing the most important tangible and intangible interrelationships in the urban-rural continuum. Proposed actions include designing locally anchored, place-specific interventions while promoting financially inclusive, participatory development approaches and utilizing evidence-based data.

Fig. 4 & 5

With the help of the jointly established guiding principles, national, sub-national, and local decision-makers are to be made aware of all dimensions of sustainable urban-rural development—in particular, the associated economic, ecological, and social implications arising from it. Overall, the urban-rural linkages program offers a wide range of concrete instruments and working materials to support member states and partner institutions in implementing their respective activities.[3] For example, this includes a priority-setting toolkit to identify urban-rural relations in different geographical contexts and assess specific challenges, opportunities, capacities, stakeholders, and development gaps. Over fifteen countries across Africa and Latin America have been supported by UN-Habitat in integrating urban-rural linkages in their policy processes. Moreover, a guide was developed to assist policymakers at the national level in considering urban-rural relations in the design of national urban policies.[4]

AH: Can you give examples of best practices in different parts of the world that can serve as models for other regions?

RS, GG: Since the launch of the Urban-Rural Linkages Initiative, UN-Habitat has collected and curated over sixty international case studies in a growing compendium showcasing region-specific experiences and inspiring practices from different countries.[5] These include efforts to realize integrated governance and coordination among different levels of government, prepare integrated spatial development plans, strengthen local food systems, invest in infrastructure (such as transportation, digitalization, and utilities), promote economic activities and job opportunities (in both urban and rural areas). They also include the integration of environmental considerations and ecosystem services, social policies, and the exchange of knowledge and skills between urban and rural communities.

For example, the area of Aburrá Valley, Colombia, has formulated a planning strategy to address unplanned urbanization that is advancing over the hills and water basin in the region. This has resulted in ten municipalities being reunited to jointly manage urban-rural planning, environmental issues, and mobility. Similarly, Niger State in Nigeria has recently implemented the rural access and mobility project to improve transport conditions and bring sustained access to the rural population. This has benefitted more than 700,000 people, among them farmers, resulting in improved access to farm inputs, increased school enrollment, and reduced post-harvest losses, among other benefits.

AH: What role has China played in the program so far and can the country become a pioneer in progressive urban-rural development in the future?

RS, GG: China's rapid urbanization has brought economic growth but also created rural-urban development challenges. Issues include a widening income gap between urban and rural residents and a lack of infrastructure and services in rural areas. The government has launched various initiatives like the "Rural Revitalization Strategy" (2018) to address these issues through improving rural incomes, infrastructure, and living standards. Thus, China has made progress in urban-rural development while demonstrating its ability to implement large-scale policies and achieve ambitious goals. However, there are concerns about the implementation and sustainability of related projects. Therefore, more holistic reforms may be needed to truly promote balanced urban-rural development in China and overcome challenges including income inequality, environmental sustainability, and preserving cultural heritage in the face of rapid urbanization.

Fig. 6

By continuously refining their strategies, adopting sustainable practices, and promoting inclusive growth, China has the potential to become a pioneer in progressive urban-rural development. The country's experience and lessons learned from its ongoing processes of urbanization can provide valuable insights for other countries facing similar challenges.

One outstanding and inspiring practice is the "acupuncture" strategy aimed at revitalizing rural communities in Songyang County, which faces issues of economic decline and outmigration of young people. The approach involved minimal architectural interventions in villages to create public spaces and stimulate rural economic development. Local communities were engaged from the beginning in defining public programs tailored to the context and needs of each village. The county government funded the projects while the villages themselves raised additional funds. Interventions included renovating abandoned buildings, upgrading traditional production facilities, and constructing new public facilities. Their impacts have been positive, including increasing village populations as young people return, boosting tourism, higher incomes for villagers, and restoring village identity and community spirit. The architectural acupuncture strategy demonstrates how small-scale, community-led revitalization efforts can make a difference in rural areas (see article by Eduard Kögel on page 182).

The Songyang County People's Government has maintained a strong partnership with UN-Habitat since 2019. At that time, the two organizations signed a letter of intent establishing their collaboration on issues of mutual interest. A key focus of this cooperation has been sharing Songyang's inspiring practices to strengthen urban-rural linkages with a global audience. To do so, it has co-hosted UN-Habitat's biannual forums on these linkages for the past three events. By hosting these forums, Songyang County has provided stakeholders with an opportunity to see "ground truths" firsthand and learn from successful initiatives. This hands-on learning experience has generated significant interest from international participants and supports UN-Habita's goal of sharing promising practices to be replicated elsewhere. The county has also contributed case studies to UN-Habitat's compendiums on this topic, highlighting its rural revitalization efforts.

Fig. 7

Fig. 1
The pilot shelter project Kalobeyei new settlement in Turkana, Kenya, represents UN-Habitat's continuous efforts to support integrative rural housing for vulnerable communities with an area-based, sustainable approach.

Fig. 2
UN-Habitat supports economic empowerment through job creation in rural areas: Women in the Kalobeyei settlement (Turkana, Kenya) produce renewable energy briquettes (2018).

Fig. 3
Nyabigufa Bridge is one of several new infrastructures in Kigoma Region, Tanzania, that improves farmers' access to urban centers, as featured in the third "Compendium of Inspiring Practices on Urban-rural Linkages" (2023).

Fig. 4 & 5
The FoodLAND (Food and Local, Agricultural, and Nutritional Diversity) research and development project has set up multi-actor centers of innovation for urban and rural food systems in selected African countries, such as the Food Hubs in Nakaseke, Uganda.

Fig. 6
Songyang County, China, has co-hosted UN-Habitat's biannual International Forums on Urban-Rural Linkages since 2019. Here, stakeholders from around the world could experience successful initiatives on the ground and learn from them.

Fig. 7
In South Darfur, Sudan, collaborative strategies were applied to inform durable solutions for displaced communities across the urban-rural continuum. An inclusive approach brought together local authorities, affected communities, and international actors (2021).

AH: How can scientific research foster an integrated and more sustainable urban-rural development?

RS, GG: The science-policy interface is crucial here. Research generates data that inform evidence-based decision-making by analyzing trends and patterns. This helps to uncover the interdependencies between urban and rural areas by studying resource flows. Additionally, it promotes innovation by exploring new technologies and solutions, providing insights to support policy development and implementation. Finally, research can facilitate stakeholder engagement and capacity building through participatory approaches, as can be seen in the Urban-Rural Assembly project. However, to be effective, scientific study must be multidisciplinary, involving experts from various fields to ensure research findings manifest as practical actions.

AH: Why are participative and co-creative processes so crucial in achieving these aims?

RS, GG: Participative and co-creative processes involving local communities and stakeholders are essential for achieving integrated and sustainable urban and rural development. They enable inclusive decision-making that considers the needs of all parties, empowering local communities by giving them ownership, tapping into local knowledge and expertise, fostering collaboration for innovative solutions, building trust through transparency, and generating context-specific outcomes that are more likely to succeed. This stakeholder participation contributes to more sustainable, equitable, and resilient urban and rural areas overall.

AH: What have you learned from accompanying the Urban-Rural Assembly project and the planning activities in its living labs in Taizhou/Huangyan, China?

RS, GG: UN-Habitat has gained valuable insights from the Urban-Rural Assembly project. Its collaborative nature has provided hands-on learning opportunities drawing from Germany and China. The "living lab" approach in particular allows the project team to test ideas in real-world settings and obtain feedback from communities, demonstrating the wealth of knowledge and practical experience they possess to inform development strategies. Providing citizens with a voice and role in decision-making helps to ensure projects meet actual needs and are sustainable. Another key lesson was realizing the need for integrated approaches, in contexts where the independent operations of government institutions can hinder progress. An integrated approach bridging sectors like agriculture, infrastructure, and education is necessary to address complex urban-rural challenges. This was possible through the immersive planning approach. Finally, international collaboration was particularly fruitful, where exchanging ideas with partners from diverse contexts sparked creative solutions. Through these exchanges, the Sino-German consortium has been able to draw on varied experiences and perspectives to develop innovative but practical recommendations.

1 United Nations Human Settlements Programme (UN-Habitat), "Implementing the New Urban Agenda by Strengthening Urban-Rural Linkages – Leave No One And No Space Behind" (Nairobi, 2017).

2 United Nations Human Settlements Programme (UN-Habitat), "Urban-rural Linkages: Guiding Principles," accessed January 26, 2024, https://unhabitat.org/urban-rural-linkages-guiding-principles.

3 United Nations Human Settlements Programme (UN-Habitat), "Urban-Rural Linkages Handbook," accessed January 26, 2024, https://urbanpolicyplatform.org/download/urban-rural-linkages-handbook/.

4 United Nations Human Settlements Programme (UN-Habitat), "National Urban Policy Guide: Mainstreaming Urban-Rural Linkages in National Urban Policies," accessed January 26, 2024, https://unhabitat.org/national-urban-policy-guide-mainstreaming-urban-rural-linkages-in-national-urban-policies.

5 United Nations Human Settlements Programme (UN-Habitat), "Compendium of case studies for the implementation of the urban-rural linkages: Guiding principles (URL-GP) and framework for action," 1st edition, accessed January 26, 2024, https://unhabitat.org/compendium-of-case-studies-for-the-implementation-of-the-urban-rural-linkages-guiding-principles.

Fig. 1

Networked peripheries: China's green energy frontiers and urban-rural reconfiguration in Europe

Hannes Langguth

The EU's green transition has ignited a significant transformation in sparsely populated and—as most would call them—peripheral or rural sites of Europe. Large-scale renewable energy projects increasingly manifest as urbanizing frontiers of transnational capital, serving Europe's urban centers at the expense of ever-expanding operational landscapes worldwide. They can take the form of offshore and onshore wind farms, solar photovoltaic and solar thermal technologies, green hydrogen and hydropower plants, or battery manufacturing and storage facilities. In this context, East Asian (particularly Chinese) firms play a central role: first, European countries currently rely on numerous Chinese green technologies and their associated know-how and resources to meet the EU's climate neutrality goals; second, Chinese firms are increasingly investing in renewable energy projects and related infrastructure throughout Europe. Thus, this article assesses the background of Chinese investments in green energy projects in Europe in the context of China's global infrastructure-led development. It then takes the recent development of large-scale Chinese facilities for the manufacturing of electric vehicle (EV) battery cells—so-called "gigafactories"—as an entry point to trace the changing nature of marginal territories in Europe. Finally, it focuses on a specific case study in peripheral Thuringia, Eastern Germany, to delineate the multi-scalar reconfiguration of urban-rural relations and its local implications on everyday lives.

China's global infrastructure-led development

Recent Chinese investments in large-scale renewable energy projects in Europe represent a new era of geographical expansion and spatial restructuring. These factors have underpinned China's transition towards capitalistic production from the late 1970s to the present day. The first phase of developmental expansion was characterized by China's enormous investments in domestic infrastructure, coupled with the establishment of Special Economic Zones from the 1980s to the early 2000s. The second phase was defined by the aftermath of the 2008 global financial crisis when China experienced an abrupt 30% decline in its export rates and had to literally reinvent its economic power.

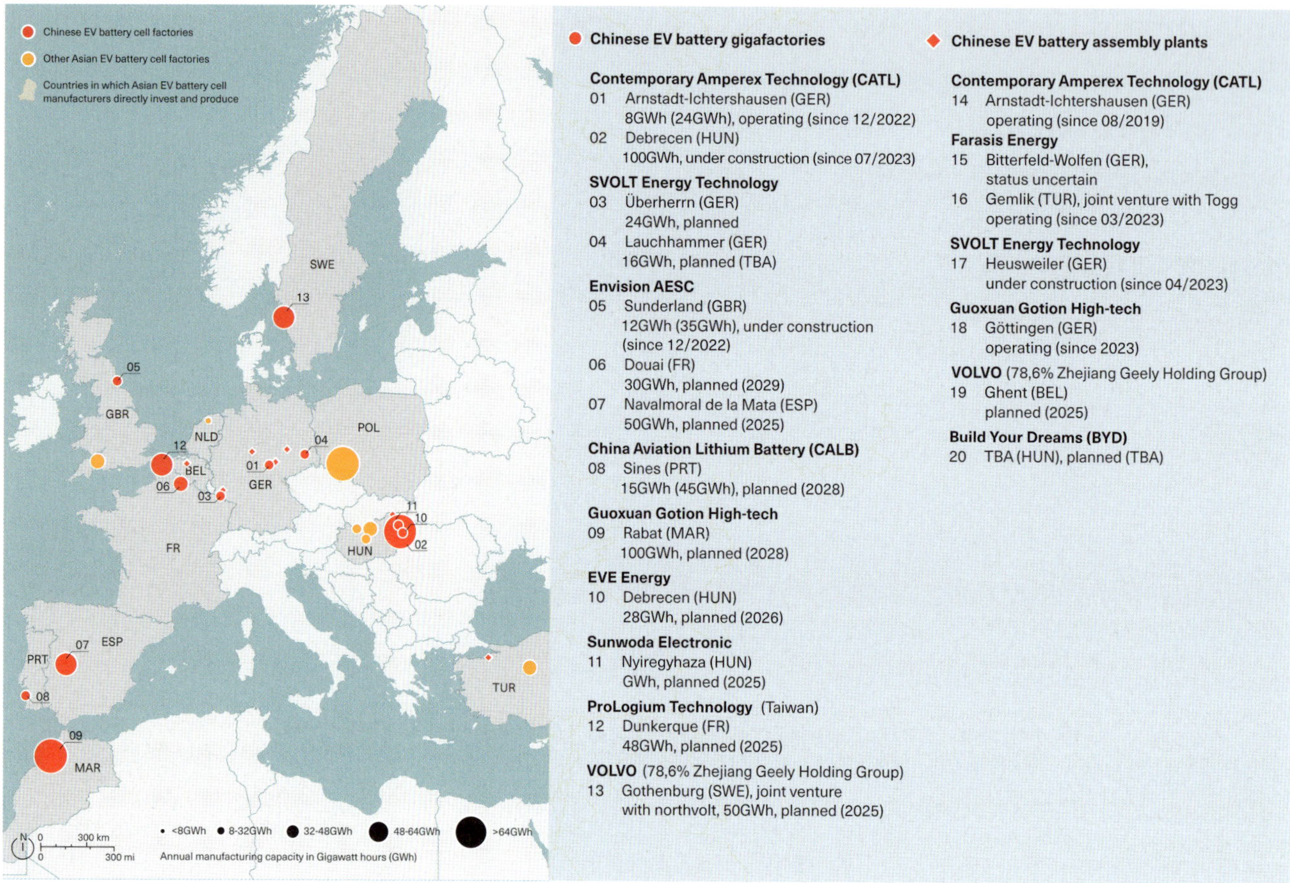

Fig. 2

The Chinese government reacted promptly by adopting a range of monetary policy measures, including a US$586 billion infrastructure fund—one of the first truly large-scale fiscal responses to the crisis worldwide.[1] This included major investments particularly focusing on domestic urban infrastructure; however, the subsequent post-2008 construction boom of roads, airports, and residential complexes ultimately led to an oversupply and the emergence of "ghost cities" across China. This refers to vacant neighborhoods and sometimes entire cities that were built but never inhabited—the result of China's reliance on housing as an investment strategy.

The third phase of expansion aimed at deploying large-scale infrastructure developments beyond mainland China, perhaps best exemplified by China's Belt and Road Initiative (BRI). Launched by Chinese president Xi Jinping in 2013, the BRI is today grouped around six main economic corridors involving 146 countries at the same time spanning land and maritime routes across six continents. Following China's thirteenth "Five-Year Plan (2016-2020)," the Chinese government granted numerous loans and exported massive amounts of building materials and labor to establish new infrastructure projects. These included new railways, ports, submarine and telecommunication cables, airports, power plants, energy grids, and urban housing complexes on a worldwide scale. Such a comprehensive overseas infrastructure portfolio associated with the BRI has served China as a "spatial fix": facilitating the geographical expansion of capital flows to secure economic growth and address its domestic overaccumulation crisis while strengthening economic relations with Southeast Asia, Central Asia, and Europe.[2]

However, China's infrastructural expansion corresponded with the broader global phenomenon of "infrastructure-led development" at the time. Emphasizing state-led spatial planning, it was especially adopted by the World Bank as the primary strategy to face the global economic crisis.[3] Fueled by cheap capital and low interest rates, the core pillar of this unprecedented global development approach is the increase of cross-border connectivity between sites of resource extraction and modes of production and consumption. This was underpinned by the provision of global access

Fig. 3

Fig. 4

to cheap labor and favorable regulatory environments. The concept of "the production of a constantly widening sphere of circulation, whether the sphere itself is directly expanded or whether more points within it are created as points of production" was predicted by Marx and signals the expansionist nature of global capital that facilitates infrastructure-led development.[4]

In the latest phase of infrastructural expansion of recent years, China has shifted its global economic engagement towards targeted investments in key technologies and the green energy sector. At the UN General Assembly (UNGA) in September 2021, Xi Jinping announced that China would now support the production of green and low-carbon energy worldwide. Looking to Europe, this applies to the production of renewables—for example, in the case of the state-owned company China Three Gorges' (CTG) large engagement in wind and solar farms in Portugal, Spain, and Germany—and to increasing capital flows in Europe's clean technologies. Of particular interest here are EV battery cells and battery systems dominated by Chinese enterprises through processes of manufacturing, research, and recycling.

Peripheral Europe as territories of transnational connectivity

Despite global restrictions imposed by the COVID-19 pandemic, including the disruption of supply chains, extensive travel bans, and increasing uncertainty in overall manufacturing capacities, China's outbound investment in the EU's EV industry has recovered rapidly since 2020. It has since become the mainstay of the country's economic engagement in Europe. Here, 13 Chinese gigafactories play a key role in the manufacturing of EV battery cells located in eight EU countries (Fig. 2). This includes either announced, planned, or already implemented projects by firms including Contemporary Amperex Technology (CATL), SVOLT Energy Technology, China Aviation Lithium Battery (CALB), Sunwoda Electronic, Envision AESC, EVE Energy, the Taiwanese ProLogium Technology, and VOLVO—the latter of which is to a large extent owned by China's Zhejiang Geely Holding Group. In addition, seven Chinese EV battery component manufacturing sites are currently planned or in operation.

With the recent surge of Chinese investment in Europe's EV industry, peripheral and rural sites have become a particular focus of development. Due to their sheer size and favorable subsidies, gigafactories and their associated infrastructure (manufacturing, research, logistics, and recycling) are projected to be located in regions away from urban centers. The majority are previously "left-behind places" that have witnessed processes of peripheralization over previous decades, such as outmigration, an aging society, and lacking public services.[5] This applies to deindustrialized and socio-economically hard-hit regions of post-Soviet states in Central and Eastern Europe (CEE), including Eastern Germany, as well as economically weak regions in Southern Europe or Northern England. However, across nearly all of these regions, recent Chinese large-scale projects in the EV industry fuel the delusions of grandeur of politicians, allowing them to promote a future economic transition based on EV-related green and clean technologies. Recent Chinese investments in the production of EV battery cells are therefore seen as a key driver for future developments in these places.

However, in the wake of such pioneering spirit, it is worth taking a closer look at the state actors involved in these projects. The first ever Chinese gigafactory was inaugurated in Europe in January 2023. It was located in the industrial park "Erfurter Kreuz" on the northern outskirts of the small Thuringian town of Arnstadt in Eastern Germany. Representatives of the Thuringian state government almost single-handedly enabled the investment and its implementation. Despite escalating geopolitical tensions between the German nation state and the Chinese government, the Thuringian government was remarkably dedicated to attracting regional investment. This commitment can be evidenced by the substantial concessions made to the Chinese investor CATL, including adjustments in energy costs and the facilitation of skilled labor recruitment. A different case is Hungary, which has pursued an extraordinarily open policy towards Chinese investment at the federal level for more than a decade, becoming the most significant BRI-related EU partner for China in the process. Today, in eastern Hungary—particularly the Debrecen region—, a noticeably large number of new Chinese projects in the EV industry are currently being implemented, including another CATL gigafactory three times larger than the one in Thuringia.

Current large-scale green projects, such as those in Thuringian Arnstadt or Hungarian Debrecen, are used by national or sub-national states to strategically open up to multilateral investments. These initiatives integrate regions into far-reaching territories of China's infrastructure-led development. However, this equally aligns with other global expansion initiatives; for instance, in the case of Germany's recent Memorandum of Understanding (MoU) to join the US-led project of the India-Middle East-Europe Economic Corridor

Fig. 5

Fig. 6

(IMEC). Such opportunistic interactions between political systems sought to harness the dynamism of globally connected infrastructure and emerging markets in a multipolar world order. Thus, it characterizes the "twenty-first-century infrastructure state," which "seeks to mobilise *foreign* capital [...] in order to undertake infrastructure projects that enhance *transnational* connectivity."[6] But how exactly does this manifest across affected regions and how do physical (infra)structures manifest spatially on site? Moreover, how does everyday life transform in the context of these fluid urban-rural continuums? Finally, how can we adequately interrogate the multi-scalar dynamics of these new interconnected peripheries?

Urban-rural reconfiguration and everyday geographies of the twenty-first-century infrastructure state

As their operational context largely transcends their immediate spatial environment, gigafactories are mostly built in remote island-like locations. As newly constructed infrastructure, they are located somewhere on

Fig. 7

the edges of existing industrial parks or cleared land. This is also the case in Thuringia, where CATL has just completed a 540-meter-long, 220-meter-wide industrial complex on a newly developed 74-hectare site. It is deeply embedded in a supraregional—even global—network of flows and goods as it is well connected with nearby highways, freight transport, and logistics hubs. This ensures CATL can guarantee the import of lithium from—for instance—the Australian Pilgangoora mine, or the supply of cobalt and nickel from the Chinese mining company Ganfeng Lithium Co. Ltd. In addition, CATL's recent investments in the wider region have strengthened connectivity; for example, through new logistics sites in Erfurt-Vieselbach (Thuringia) and Magdeburg-Sülzetal (Saxony-Anhalt)—the latter of which provides direct access to the port of Hamburg via inland waterways.

However, while the new gigafactory and its logistics facilities increase the proximity of global production chains, they also lead to new relative distances, especially on a local scale. Thousands of people work in windowless, oversized stalwart structures in a relatively monotonous environment. Like in Arnstadt-Ichtershausen,

Fig. 1
Workers from a Chinese machine supplier en route to their shift to set up manufacturing lines at the new CATL battery cell factory, Arnstadt-Ichtershausen.

Fig. 2
An overview of Chinese and other Asian EV battery cell factories, currently in planning, under construction, or implemented in Europe and neighboring countries.

Fig. 3
Construction site of a CATL battery cell factory on the northern edge of Arnstadt, Thuringia.

Fig. 4
Construction site of the new CATL factory and its gargantuan windowless "cleanroom" for manufacturing battery cells.

Fig. 5
The traditional café and restaurant "Waffelstübchen" in Arnstadt town center has become a popular eatery for CATL workers since being taken over by a Chinese family in 2021.

Fig. 6
A bus from a Romanian transport company is chartered by a Chinese agency to transport CATL workers between their homes and the new battery cell factory, Arnstadt-Ichtershausen.

Fig. 7
Most apartments in this housing block, owned by the Arnstadt housing association and located east of the town, are rented to Chinese CATL workers.

most laborers originate from China and stay temporarily to help set up manufacturing lines. They mostly now live and work close to highways but don't have cars. Their apartments are located, for instance, in previously abandoned blocks on the outskirts of the town or in reused former countryside properties and hotels located in nearby villages. To get to these residences, they either walk past roaring trucks to one of the rare bus stations (to catch one of the even rarer connections), or they use buses chartered by Chinese agencies. Both choices highlight the remoteness workers are exposed to on these new gigafactory working "islands."

Spatial distance is just one obstacle that is hard for these Chinese workers to overcome; another is the differences in culture. For the majority of Chinese workers, their employment at these new gigafactory sites is just a stopover on their way to subsequent career placements elsewhere. The orchestration of their daily affairs, encompassing interactions with local authorities, running errands, and securing accommodation, is predominantly delegated to personnel agencies. Agencies headquartered in major cities such as Shanghai, Ningde, or Frankfurt am Main exert significant influence over the daily lives of individuals situated in these remote locales. A subset of workers aspires to an extended stay, accompanied by their families. This inclination often manifests in the form of new restaurants in the town center, open to the public but predominantly frequented by Chinese migrants. Moreover, food outlets establish independent Chinese food supply networks without the involvement of the other local residents.

These are only some of the numerous examples illustrating how the localization of new gigafactories removes global borders and redraws them on a local scale. Moreover, it demonstrates how new global connectivity for especially economic actors reinforces separation from others. Thus, in- and outflows of commodities, goods, finance, people, and know-how can decisively transform formerly "left-behind places" into new peripheral centralities associated with the boom of the global EV industry.[7] Within global production networks and supply chains, these regions are integrated into extensive metabolic systems that enable the green transition in the world's urban centers, often at the cost of continually expanding operational landscapes and environmental destruction elsewhere.[8] Thus, they not only become interlinked with China's globally networked infrastructure-led development but also manifest as new geographies of extended capitalistic urbanization, including ever-changing and multi-scalar processes of centralization (connectivity) and peripheralization (exclusion) within affected peripheries. Future research should interrogate these dialectic geographies of the twenty-first-century infrastructure state and undertake multiscalar inquiries that are both grounded and transcend state boundaries.

1 Ho-fung Hung, ed., *China and the Transformation of Global Capitalism, Themes in Global Social Change* (Baltimore: Johns Hopkins University Press, 2009).

2 David Harvey, *The Limits to Capital* (New York: Verso, 2018).

3 Elia Apostolopoulou, "Tracing the Links between Infrastructure-Led Development, Urban Transformation, and Inequality in China's Belt and Road Initiative," *Antipode* 53 (2021): 831–58.

4 Karl Marx, *Grundrisse: Foundations of the Critique of Political Economy* (Harmondsworth: Penguin Books, 1973).

5 Andrea Fischer-Tahir and Matthias Naumann, *Peripheralization: The Making of Spatial Dependencies and Social Injustice* (New York: Springer Science & Business Media, 2013).

6 Seth Schindler, Jessica DiCarlo, and Dinesh Paudel, "The New Cold War and the Rise of the 21st-Century Infrastructure State," *Transactions of the Institute of British Geographers* 47 (2022): 331–46.

7 Nicholas A. Phelps, Paul J. Maginn, and Roger Keil, "Centring the periphery in urban studies: Notes towards a research agenda on peripheral centralities," *Urban Studies* 60 (2023): 1158–76.

8 Neil Brenner and Nikos Katsikis, "Operational Landscapes: Hinterlands of the Capitalocene," *Architectural Design* 90, no. 1 (2020): 22–31.

9 Roger Keil, "Extended Urbanization, 'Disjunct Fragments' and Global Suburbanisms," *Environment and Planning D: Society and Space* 36, no. 3 (2018): 494–511.

Fig. 1

The politics of urbanizing the Chinese countryside

Elena Meyer-Clement

One of the most outstanding characteristics of China's urbanization process is the dominant role of the state—or, more precisely, the "party-state"—as the spheres of the ruling Communist Party and state are hardly distinguishable. Thus, in the following article, "state" and "government" always refer to the close affiliation of party and state. However, the state is a conglomeration of various actors with often differing interests. Moreover, during the rapid social and economic developments of the last decades, political goals shifted and institutions evolved. This chapter provides an overview of the changing political strategies of central and local government actors in China's urbanization. It focuses on urbanization dynamics in rural and semi-urban areas since the beginning of the economic reform period in the late 1970s, and it distinguishes between two major phases characterized by different policy environments and different institutional relationships between central and local governments. One of the most salient differences between these two periods is the role city governments have played in urbanizing their rural hinterlands. A third phase may also be evolving, stemming from 2014 when the central government published its first genuine urbanization policy and (re)centralized the political regulation of urbanization. However, it is not yet foreseeable how far centralized control can affect the well-established strategic behavior of local governments in the context of China's ongoing urbanization process.

Rural industrialization and in situ urbanization

In the late 1970s, before China introduced the first far-reaching policies to gradually dismantle the planned economy, the country had experienced twenty years of very low urbanization rates, if not "de-urbanization."[1] The political leadership under Mao Zedong had installed strong restrictions against rural-to-urban migration, primarily to ensure food supply and high standards of social welfare for urban workers and to support the country's industrialization with agricultural surplus. Moreover, during the highly ideologized periods of the "Great Leap Forward" (1958-1961) and the "Cultural Revolution" (1966-1976), millions were "sent down" from cities to the countryside. Statistical data relating to China's urbanization should be treated with

Fig. 2

caution—not least because definitions of urban and rural populations have changed several times. However, the general picture is still revealing; the population census of 1964, which had applied a very narrow criterion for urban population, accounted for an urbanization rate of 18.3 percent. In contrast, the following census of 1982 counted all residents living in administratively defined urban areas as "urban," thus including populations from the rural surroundings of cities. Nonetheless, it still calculated an urbanization rate of only 20.9 percent.[2]

Several institutions built during the Maoist period to regulate population mobility continue to take effect in China's urbanization to this day. A particularly prominent one is the household registration system, also known as the "Hukou" system. Instituted in 1958, this system divided the population into "agricultural" and "non-agricultural" households and evolved into a kind of internal passport system within China's national boundaries, creating enduring structures of discrimination for rural migrants in China's cities.[3] Others include the bifurcated bureaucratic organization of urban and rural areas, which encompasses a land system that distinguishes between collective property rights of rural land and state ownership of urban land.

In the late 1970s, reformers made the far-reaching decision to maintain the administrative differentiation of land, people, and bureaucracies. However, the early reform period also witnessed several significant administrative and economic changes that started to dismantle the socialist market economic system. One of the most notable consequences in the countryside was a surge of industrialization and in situ urbanization. According to Chinese official data, between 1983 and 1996 the number of market towns (*zhen*) grew from 2,968 to 18,171 while the number of county cities rose from 142 to 445.[4] As elsewhere in the world, migration (much of it unregistered) has been the primary driver of urbanization in China. However, the rapid growth of small towns was still remarkable, prompting several scholarly investigations into China's "rural urbanization."[5]

Some scholars suggested historical and cultural explanations for this development, citing the continuity of rural characteristics and urban-rural interconnections

Fig. 3

in Chinese urbanization.[6] Others compared the Chinese case to urbanization processes elsewhere, characterized by the persistence of rural practices alongside emerging urban activities, such as in regions known as *Desakota* (composed of the Indonesian words for "town" and "village").[7] However, both explanations failed to fully explain what occurred in many of China's rural and semi-urban regions in the 1980s and 1990s. Most importantly, the crucial role of state institutions and local governments acting as entrepreneurs in these processes sharply contrasted with urbanization processes elsewhere.[8]

The causes of rural urbanization in the early reform period stem from a combination of socialist legacies and specific political-economic conditions. The rural agricultural collectives of the Maoist period had been dismantled and rural markets were emerging, both favoring industrial developments. This was spurred by the support and entrepreneurial initiatives of local governments, which had been granted more decision-making power over their budgets.[9] Additionally, for ideological reasons, central policies still favored small-town development over large-city growth. Migration restrictions gradually loosened for small towns but remained in place for large cities. Meanwhile, the criteria for designating towns were lowered.

State-led urbanization: Demolition and resettlement

In the second half of the 1990s, rural enterprises lost their competitive position in the rapidly developing national economy. Around the same time, a shift in urbanization processes in rural and semi-urban areas toward more city-centered initiatives occurred. This shift was connected to changes in the political-economic structures that effectively altered power relations and interests among local governments, ultimately strengthening the role of city governments in urbanization.

In 1994, a reform of the tax system completely overhauled the fiscal relationship between the center and the localities, leaving local governments with only a fraction of the previous tax income. Around the same time, the nascent urban land market yielded increasingly higher land use fees that soon became an important source of local government income.[10] By maintaining

Fig. 4

the system of state ownership of urban land and designating municipal governments as the representatives of the state in land deals, the central government consolidated the monopolistic position of municipal governments in the land market. The result was a local "land revenue regime,"[11] under which revenues from land development, construction, and real estate came to dominate local growth strategies. Between 2004 and 2013, land sales alone accounted for half of local government revenue.[12] These developments were accompanied by a newfound political appreciation for urbanization. In the tenth "Five-Year Plan" (for the years 2001–2005), the center officially acknowledged urbanization as a driver of modernization. Thus, in the following years, urban ideals fueled the imaginations of policymakers nationwide.[13]

The vibrant urbanization that emerged within this political-economic landscape has been described as "state-led" and "land-based." State-led urbanization emphasizes the monopoly of state actors in the land market and state control over land use planning and regulation; land-based urbanization describes local governments' fixation on land deals, urban development, and real estate projects that often overlook population demand. The process usually involves the expropriation of village land (for its conversion into urban land, whose use rights can be traded on the land market), the demolition of villages, and the resettlement of the village population. Resettlement, in turn, involves housing construction elsewhere, creating a whole "economy of demolition and resettlement."[14] Among the most noticeable excesses of this form of urbanization are the violent land grabs that made land conflicts the most common source of mass protests and citizen discontent,[15] as well as the many "ghost cities" built solely for the appreciation of land rents and urban imagination.

Since the end of the 1990s, government efforts to regulate these processes have intensified, along with centralized monitoring and supervision of land use changes. Most significantly, in 1998, the central government implemented quotas for land designated for agricultural and construction purposes nationwide and introduced the national "red line" of 1.8 million mu (about 120 million hectares) of farmland as a bottom line that must be protected. Interpretations of the

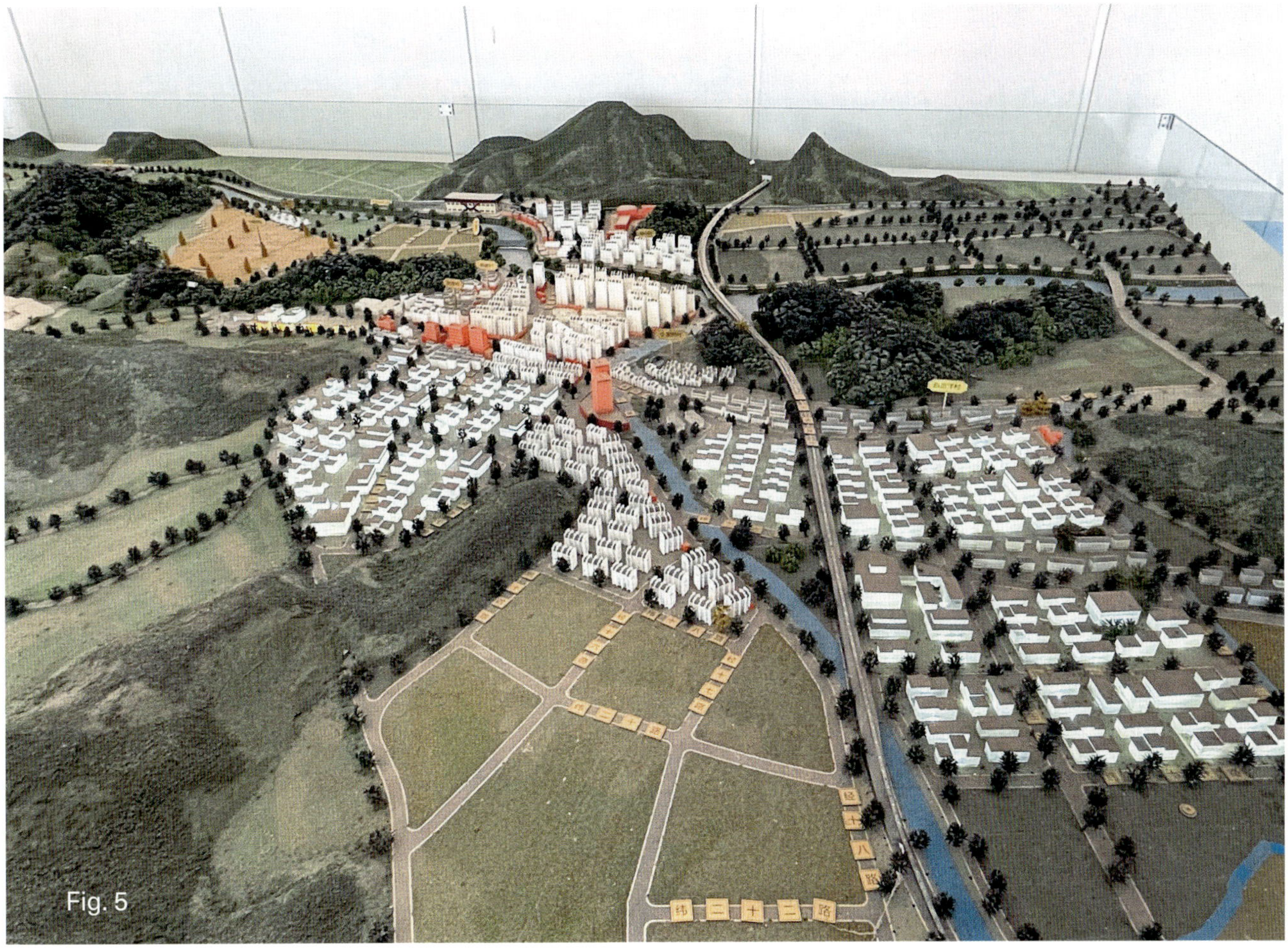
Fig. 5

Fig. 1
As agricultural land is strictly protected from changes in land use, the demolition of villages is a fundamental means of obtaining land for urban expansion, as can be seen at the urban fringes in Huangyan (2024). The construction of streets is usually the first step for revaluing land.

Fig. 2 & 3
To save building land, particularly in more remote areas, local governments merge villages into larger communities, substantially changing the living conditions of villagers and the appearance of the countryside.

Fig. 4
In rural Huangyan, the populations of remote villages are relocated to “land-saving” multi-story residential blocks.

Fig. 5
This model, displayed in the town hall of a local government in Huangyan (2023), illustrates future plans for concentrating rural settlements to enhance land use efficiency.

“public interest” that permitted the expropriation of village land became stricter while particularly valuable “basic farmland” could not undergo land use changes without central government approval. Additionally, villagers’ legal rights to their land were strengthened and compensation entitlements increased.

Municipal governments responded by adapting their urbanization strategies to the increasingly regulated environment. Their strategies have included finding new justifications for converting farmland into building land and reserving as much land as possible on the outskirts of cities for later development. The new justifications for farmland occupation and village demolition must closely align with current national policies; prominent examples include the creation of “university towns” and “smart” or “green” city districts.[16] While such politically recognized urban expansion can bypass building restrictions on farmland, it still may violate the allocated local quota of protected farmland. However, increasing the amount of farmland elsewhere in the administrative territory of cities, which includes surrounding rural counties, can resolve this issue. As a result, the merging and demolition of villages before reclaiming village land as farmland has become a popular means of saving building land and acquiring more farmland.[17] In this quota game that allows city governments to pursue further urban development, village populations are often relocated en masse to "land-saving" multi-story residential blocks.

The reported problems of this (local) state-led approach to rural urbanization have been manifold. They range from corruption and low-quality construction to a lack of service infrastructure and social problems associated with adapting to new lifestyles. Nonetheless, the overall approach aligns closely with national policies. Notably, the large-scale rural development program titled "Building a New Socialist Countryside," launched in 2006 in a campaign-like manner, promoted the construction of new residential complexes as a means of modernizing rural life.

A new phase of rural urbanization under centralized control?

After the leadership turnover in 2013, new policies aimed to address some of the problems associated with state-led village modernization and urbanization. The so-called "new-type urbanization" promised a shift from "land-based" to "people-based" urbanization, promoting several policies to improve city life and officially integrate rural migrants into the cities. It also criticized the indiscriminate replication of urban models in rural settings and advocated for the development of more villages and towns with special cultural and historical features. The "Rural Revitalization Strategy", which supplanted the "New Socialist Countryside" as the state's rural development program in 2017, shares similar objectives. It frames rural development as a combination of modernization and the preservation of traditional rural values and practices. In addition to promoting large-scale commercial agriculture and urbanization, for example, it also emphasizes the importance of family farms and the preservation of rural cultural heritage.

The extent to which these policies will alter the dynamics of urbanization through village demolition and resettlement remains uncertain. The institutional structures that make local government budgets dependent on land development under the constraints of land use efficiency have not changed. Concrete land use policies continue to advocate for reductions in rural building land utilizing population resettlement, and neither grassroots initiatives of development nor land use planning that depart from local government interests stand much of a chance of implementation.[18] Under these conditions, tourism development has become a much sought-after variant of rural urbanization. Programs like the "beautiful village" combine resettlement and village redevelopment with promises of income for local governments while showcasing the implementation of policies like sustainable development and cultural heritage protection.

Essentially, rather than working towards ending prevalent local resettlement practices, the current policies instead increase hierarchical government controls over land use changes and population mobility. At the national level, the current urbanization policy delineates different types of urban agglomerations for different regions. Moreover, reforms of the *Hukou* system introducing general rules for population settlement based on city size ended the decentralized character of migration policies that allowed cities to define their own rules. One of the aims of these reforms is to steer the population towards smaller cities and towns. While strict controls on population growth apply to the largest cities, smaller cities and towns have to absorb large numbers of rural populations. Furthermore, bans for designating new towns and cities installed in 1997 and 2002 to counter the city-building frenzy at the time have been removed.

This new push for "rural urbanization" has a completely different character from its precursor of the 1980s and 1990s. It primarily entails state-led urbanization, which persists in resettlements and the reduction of housing land in rural areas to enhance land use efficiency from the state's perspective. The vested interests of local governments in generating income from land development remain unchanged and continue to underpin these activities; however, it appears that the central government aims to channel more of these efforts toward the development of small cities, market towns, and rural areas.

Rural urbanization and the state

Urbanization in the rural peripheries of China's urban agglomerations has taken various forms since economic reform policies dismantled rural collectives and gradually introduced markets for land use rights. The role of the state has been particularly prominent, not only as a regulator of these processes but also as a market-based entrepreneur. However, the role of different state actors in China's urbanization has varied. The entrepreneurial activities of rural governments still played a significant role in the urbanization processes that emerged during the early stages of the economic reform process. Their localized character earned them the term "rural urbanization." Since the end of the

1990s, municipal governments have become major players in urbanization processes in the rural peripheries. Their hunger for building land resources has had a huge impact on the development of land use and living conditions far into the countryside. However, in recent years, the central government has increasingly intensified its attempts to regulate these processes. Simultaneously, it shares with local governments an interest in increasing state control over rural development; thus, in the foreseeable future, we can expect urbanization through resettlement and the restructuring of villages to continue. This trend is likely to further weaken the influence of villages over local land use changes, with potentially unpredictable consequences for village life.

1 Barry Naughton, *The Chinese Economy: Adaptation and Growth*, 2nd ed. (Cambridge, MA: The MIT Press, 2018).

2 National Bureau of Statistics of the People's Republic of China (NBS), 年度数据 (*Annual data*), accessed March 30, 2024, http://data.stats.gov.cn/easyquery.htm?cn=C01.

3 Dorothy J. Solinger, *Contesting Citizenship in Urban China: Peasant Migrants, the State, and the Logic of the Market* (Berkeley: University of California Press, 1999).

4 National Bureau of Statistics of the People's Republic of China, op. cit.

5 Gregory Eliyu Guldin, ed., *Farewell to Peasant China: Rural Urbanization and Social Change in the Late Twentieth Century* (Armonk, NY: M. E. Sharpe, 1997).

6 Hsiao Tung Fei et al., *Small Towns in China: Function, Problems and Prospects* (Beijing: New World Press, 1986).

7 Terry G. McGee, "Urbanisasi or Kotadesasi? Evolving Patterns of Urbanization in Asia," in *Urbanization in Asia: Spatial Dimensions and Policy Issues*, eds. F. J. Costa et al. (Honolulu: University of Hawaii Press, 1989), 93–108.

8 Kam Wing Chan, "Fundamentals of China's Urbanization and Policy," *The China Review* 10, no. 1 (2010): 63–94.

9 Jean C. Oi, "Fiscal Reform and the Economic Foundations of Local State Corporatism in China," *World Politics* 45, no. 1 (1992): 99–126.

10 Christine P. Wong, "Paying for Urbanization in China: Challenges of Municipal Finance in the Twenty-First Century," in *Financing Metropolitan Governments in Developing Countries*, ed. Roy W. Bahl et al. (Cambridge, MA: Lincoln Institute of Land Policy, 2013), 273–308.

11 Shaohua Zhan, "From Local State Corporatism to Land Revenue Regime: Urbanization and the Recent Transition of Rural Industry in China," *Agrarian Change* 15 (2015): 413–32.

12 Christine P. Wong, op. cit.

13 You-tien Hsing, *The Great Urban Transformation: Politics of Land and Property in China* (New York: Oxford University Press, 2010).

14 Op. cit.

15 Sally Sargeson, "Violence as Development: Land Expropriation and China's Urbanization," *The Journal of Peasant Studies* 40 (2013): 1063–85.

16 Fulong Wu, *Planning for Growth: Urban and Regional Planning in China* (London: Routledge, 2015).

17 Lynette H. Ong, "State-Led Urbanization in China: Skyscrapers, Land Revenue and 'Concentrated Villages'," *The China Quarterly* 217 (2014): 162–79.

18 Elena Meyer-Clement, "Rural Urbanization under Xi Jinping: From Rapid Community Building to Steady Urbanization?" *China Information* 34, no. 2 (2020): 187–207.

Fig. 1

Understanding urban-rural transformation in Huangyan-Taizhou

Laura Henneke, Maria Frölich-Kulik, Hongqing Li, Ava Lynam, Kateřina Marečková, Lukas Pappert, Gaoli Xiao, Suili Xiao, Zheng Yang, Yulin Zhang, and Yuqi Zhang

Fed by several springs in the lush, steep hills of its western hinterland, Huangyan's landscape is shaped by the meandering Yongning River (Fig. 1) and an extensive network of manmade waterways, reservoirs, and ponds. These waterways are the lifeblood of the region. Weaving their way through a mosaic of agricultural fields and rural settlements, they enrich the soils of the plains before flowing through increasingly dense urban areas—where industrial activities thrive along the riverbanks—and finally emptying into the East China Sea.

Huangyan is a district of Taizhou, a prefecture-level city located in Zhejiang Province on the southern reaches of China's Yangtze River Delta. The region has experienced dramatic and rapid urbanization since the country's economic reform in 1978 when Zhejiang Province emerged as a pioneer in China's market-driven economy, becoming a hub for successful private enterprises that were deeply integrated in global markets. This economic dynamism has greatly enhanced the region's appeal, attracting a diverse workforce and inviting migration from far and wide. The influx of people seeking jobs and opportunities has driven rapid urbanization across the province, transforming its cities into thriving centers of economic activity. Huangyan is administratively defined as an "urban" district and encompasses dynamic industrial clusters as well as dense residential and commercial districts. However, it is equally characterized by its distinctly rural landscapes made up of wooded mountains and remote villages.

The following text is a portrayal of the urban-rural region of Huangyan-Taizhou. Assembled by the interdisciplinary Sino-German research team of the Urban-Rural Assembly project, it draws on perspectives from urbanism, landscape architecture, circular economy, ecology, and sociology. This portrait lays out the region's urban-rural dynamics and the challenges Huangyan is currently facing, covering economic activities, migration and social inclusion, landscape and ecosystem transformation, material flows, along with planning and land management. In order to study these ongoing and complex processes of rural-urban transformation, Urban-Rural Assembly researchers collected and analyzed data in two selected "Urban-Rural Living Labs," Beiyang and

Fig. 2

Xinqian, both situated at Huangyan's urban–rural interface zone. While Beiyang is primarily characterized by agricultural activities and represents the relatively "rural" part of Huangyan, Xinqian is comparatively more urbanized, defined by its long-standing molding industry and densely populated workers' neighborhoods.

Economic activities

"We produce 70,000 plastic bottles per day. One third is sold in China, two thirds overseas." Interview with the owner of a plastics company in Xinqian

Huangyan is known for several distinctive "urban" and "rural" industries, including garment and plastic production, as well as watermelon seed and tangerine cultivation. The garment industry was most active in the 1980s and 90s before plastic production became a pillar industry in the late 90s. Today, the plastic industry—and plastic mold production in particular—has driven the emergence of many private companies of varying sizes and technological standards. The molding industry involves precision manufacturing to produce detailed molds from blocks of steel, which shape plastic materials for a wide range of applications, including automotive, medical, and consumer goods, and packaging. Over time, the molding industry in Huangyan has developed a highly productive and profitable translocal network with intimate connections to global production lines, supplying China and other world regions with diverse everyday plastic products, such as the Monobloc chair, sports water bottles, or litter bins (Fig. 4). It is in this context that the "Smart Molding Town" was developed: a modern multi-functional industrial park located in Xinqian, designed to expedite the region's industrial upgrading process. To date, more than 130 large modern factories have settled in the Smart Molding Town, alongside recreational spaces and housing. While large-scale factories in Huangyan are usually concentrated in industrial zones, various steps of the production line extend into rural or urbanizing villages, which operate smaller-scale factories and household workshops. In some cases,

Fig. 3

Fig. 4

Fig. 5

assembly processes take place in living rooms or in communal courtyards between houses, integrating industrial activities into the daily lives of villagers (Fig. 5).

In the agricultural sector, Huangyan's economic activities range from traditional small-scale subsistence farming to modern large-scale enterprises. Some of these enterprises are conventional, while others are dedicated to producing and shipping organic food, or oriented towards agritourism. Together with vegetable cultivation and rice farming, tangerines are perhaps Huangyan's most prominent agricultural product, having been widely planted in the region since the third century. The local government, recognizing tangerine production as an important part of the region's agricultural heritage and a staple of Huangyan's brand, has taken measures to support the industry through promoting agritourism (Fig. 6), providing technical services and introducing financial incentives. However, challenges persist due to the decreasing profitability of the agriculture sector, deteriorating climate conditions, restrictive land use policies, and a lack of farmer participation in governance.

Huangyan's fast-track urbanization has led to extensive land use changes, marked by a shift from agriculture to industry and from rural to urban. Despite receiving varying levels of compensation, many farmers who lost their land have also lost their livelihoods and consequently their everyday practices. In addition, a significant number of these farmers lack the necessary skills to participate in or benefit from other industries, leaving them at a disadvantage in the rapidly changing socio-economic landscape. The pace of industrial and urban growth also threatens biodiversity and ecosystems, considerably disturbing the water network and leaving formerly important cultural landscapes in crisis. Local governments and academic actors have already started to acknowledge these challenges. We are now seeing a shift towards a stronger sense of cultural heritage that, at the same time, prioritizes economic and environmental sustainability in new visions for the region by aiming to implement more circular, socially inclusive development pathways for the future.

Fig. 6

Social fabric, mobilities, and migration patterns

> "If I have a headache or cold, I usually just buy some medicine from the pharmacy. For more serious illnesses, I would have to go back to my hometown for treatment." Interview with a migrant worker

Huangyan's urban-rural interfaces are characterized by socio-economic inequalities, varying levels of social inclusion and exclusion, and uneven distribution of public services, particularly for marginalized migrant workers and their families. The successful local molding industry has driven a significant population inflow to Huangyan, primarily workers from less economically developed domestic provinces, with a diverse "floating population"[1] arriving in and around industrial agglomerations. The employment and investment opportunities offered by the dynamic nature of the region's economic development have encouraged both locals and migrants to engage in formal and informal translocal economic networks and production lines. At the same time, many skilled workers are moving out of Huangyan toward more developed and urbanized regions.

While Huangyan's well-developed physical infrastructure facilitates the daily movement of various social groups, commuting patterns and the ways people use various spaces for their daily activities reveal challenges for social and spatial inclusion.[2] These issues pertain to income and employment, family structure and livelihoods, migration backgrounds, consumption and recreation, alongside institutional factors such as access to housing, education, and social services. Some migrants who came to Huangyan have established successful businesses, achieved high positions, upgraded their skills within local industries, and developed strong social and professional networks. Many others, especially low-skilled workers, face significant challenges, such as poor employment and housing conditions and harsh work-life balances resulting in very limited ability to establish and maintain social networks. While there have been efforts to improve institutional exclusion through reforming the *Hukou*[3] (household registration) and education systems, unequal accessibility

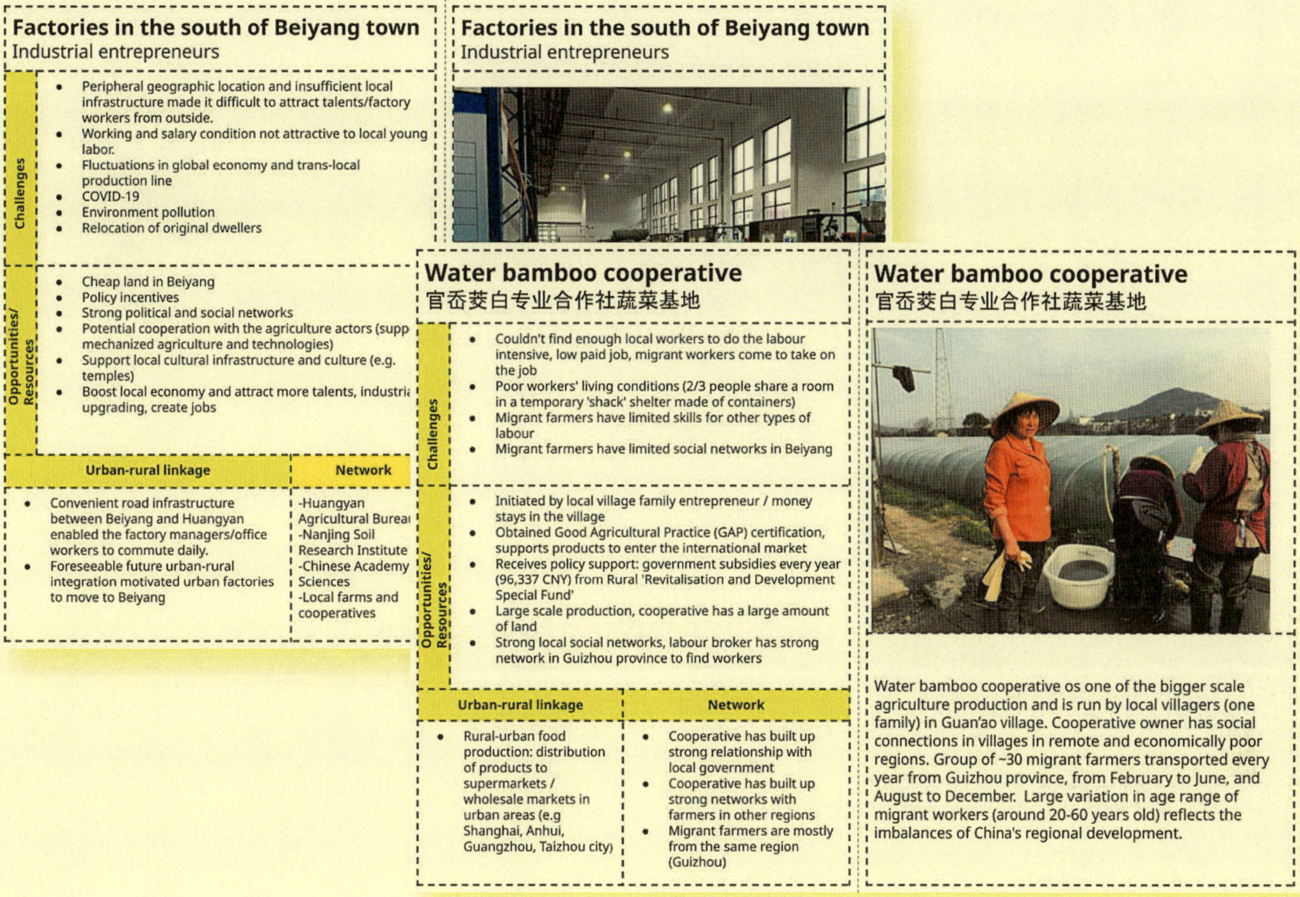

Fig. 7

to social and public services between migrant and local populations persists.

Interactions between local and migrant social groups are often limited, especially in smaller towns and rural areas of Huangyan such as Beiyang. Here, an expanding industrial zone and rural tourism—as well as increased possibilities of finding affordable rental housing—bring more people and greater opportunity to the area. However, labor-intensive work in farms or factories, coupled with a lack of urban amenities and entertainment, still drive many young laborers to seek out desirable job prospects and lifestyles in more urbanized regions, thus creating a "left behind" population of elderly and children. In Xinqian, agglomerations of molding factories, well-developed public infrastructure, and a vibrant urban environment offering convenient services and entertainment making it a more attractive destination for incoming migrants of various skill levels. However, many maintain a weak sense of belonging or place attachment to the local area, even when they have lived there for many years. Ultimately, those with more financial or social capital typically find it much easier to settle down.

Land management and zoning policies

"Making use of the rural homestead land is our number one priority now. We are trying to reduce scattered rural houses by compensating with urban apartments." Interview with a Huangyan planner

China's dual land system creates a distinct separation between urban and rural areas, with urban land owned by the state and rural land collectively owned by village communities. This also applies to Huangyan, where rapid urbanization over the past two decades has transformed extensive agricultural and forest land into urban and industrial built-up areas, raising concerns about food security, social justice, and environmental sustainability. To address these concerns on a national level, China has enacted stringent land policies to safeguard basic permanent farmland and establish ecological protection zones, which local governments are required to implement. In Huangyan-Taizhou, a land use plan released in 2022 (referred to as "Three Zones and Three Lines" in Chinese)

Fig. 8

delineates clear spatial boundaries between urban construction areas, farmland, and ecological protection zones. However, the design and application of centralized policy—often implemented without careful consideration of local contexts—have led to numerous problems, particularly in rural areas experiencing population and economic decline.

One major conflict lies in the pragmatic designation of basic permanent farmland in Huangyan, which, in some cases, is encroaching on land with a different actual use, or, in other cases, allows little to no space for further urban development. As Elena Meyer-Clement describes in her article (see p. 82), the concentration of village populations in new high-density housing estates is another strategy that enables the transformation of village land into farmland in exchange for more intensive urban construction. The exploitation of rural land for urban expansion prevents sufficient land being allocated to meet the housing demands of rural inhabitants. Moreover, such rigid land use designations can significantly hinder the development of modern agriculture, tourism, and industries in rural areas. In the western part of Huangyan, for example, where livelihoods are heavily dependent on rural tourism, ecological preservation efforts have led to the forceful closure of many rural homestays and other tourism-related businesses, contributing to the hollowing-out of villages. In areas where agricultural and industrial practices are established, many entrepreneurs are confronted with strict land use regulations that hamper their everyday business operations. The profitability of agriculture is additionally undermined by policies prohibiting flexible land use for constructing warehouses, food processing workshops, or tourism facilities.

This has created a critical dilemma in terms of achieving a balanced, equitable process of urban-rural development, since the modernization of agriculture and rural industries is pivotal for enhancing the rural economy. In tackling these challenges, social actors in Huangyan demonstrate a highly adaptive attitude. Temporary container structures for housing are constructed on farmland, which can be easily demolished during inspections (Fig. 8). Tourism or industrial operators have quickly shifted to more profitable businesses, such as watermelon or

Adjusting the course of Yongning River

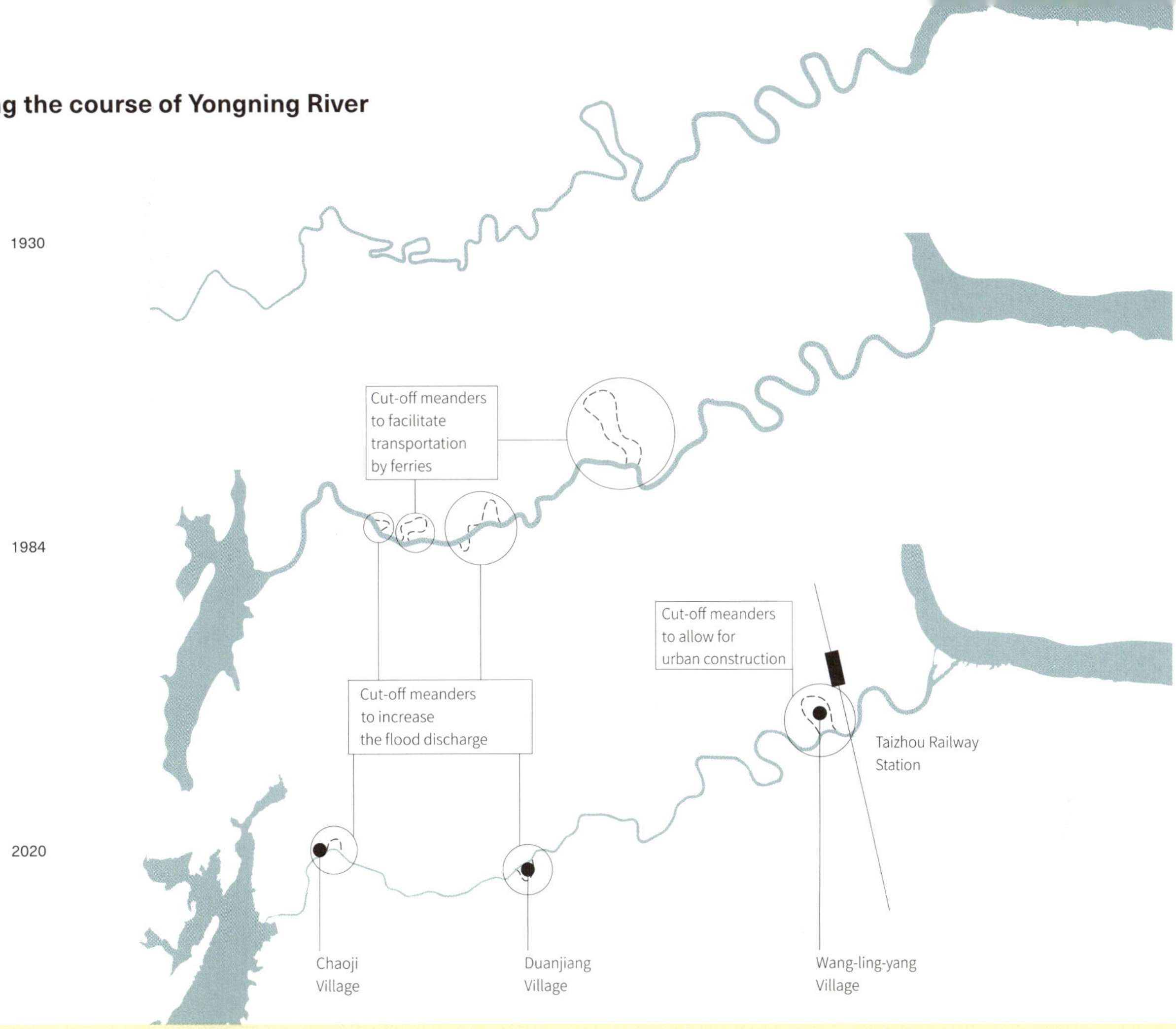

Fig. 9

tangerine cultivation, that are supported by the government. However, not all social groups possess the same level of agency or bargaining power. Vulnerable groups, such as people with lower socio-economic status—including the elderly, migrant workers, and women—face greater obstacles in adapting to displacement from their homes, lifestyles, land, or sources of income. Throughout the Urban-Rural Assembly research phase, it became clear that ensuring land development policies are tailored to local conditions (and adaptable to changing circumstances) and could significantly improve efforts to balance food security and ecological conservation with housing and construction demands. Such an approach requires greater coordination between the interests and needs of numerous local stakeholders, and between top-down and bottom-up planning.

Water systems and landscapes along the Yongning River

"The Changtan Reservoir rarely discharges water into the Yongning River as it did in the past. This makes the river narrower and shallower." Interview with a Huangyan resident

The landscape of Huangyan-Taizhou is defined by the Yongning River. Its water intimately shapes urban and rural spaces, influences ecological dynamics, and is inextricably linked to settlement development and economic structures. With a significant impact on everyday practices, it is embedded in cultural memory. Historically, the Yongning was a tidal river system meandering across the entire plain. There were pontoon bridges and numerous ferries distributed along the river that enabled trade and exchange across the river plain regardless of tidal levels. The water system of the Yongning River was characterized by winding rivers and ancient canals that were closely interwoven with the settlement structures. An ingenious system of ditches and ponds provided the villages with water for drinking, washing, and irrigating the fields. Inherent to this system of water management were culturally significant sites, such as temples (see Fig. 9 on p. 166). Today, everyday water-related practices remain ubiquitous, but their hydrological

Fig. 10

Fig. 11

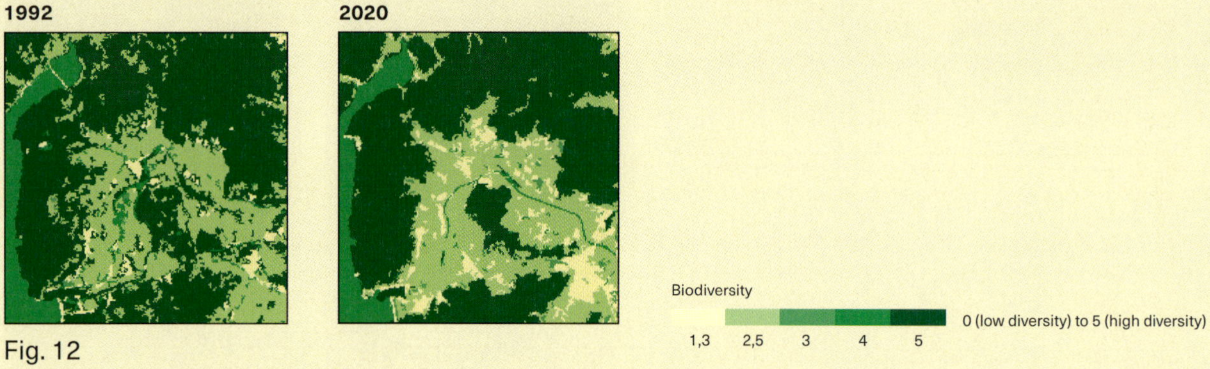

Fig. 12

and ecological context has changed dramatically in a very short time frame due to alterations to the river system (Fig. 9): in 1964, the Changtan Reservoir was constructed upstream to supply the region with drinking water, and in 1994, the Great Yongning Sluice was built at the river's estuary. These modern interventions have eliminated the river's interaction with currents and tides, making it inaccessible to shipping. To meet the water demands of residential areas and industries, the reservoir captures runoff from over half of the basin's area and only opens the sluices in extreme cases to "flush" the riverbed, resulting in a significantly reduced water flow. This, combined with pollution from industrial and agricultural activities, has led to severe environmental degradation in the estuary area.[4] Although various measures are being taken to improve water quality, the lack of adequate infrastructure for sustainable water management in industry, agriculture, and settlement areas continues to impact water quality significantly.

Despite the low water quality, the waters in and around the Yongning River are actively used for everyday practices (Fig. 11): laundry is washed in the morning, fishing enthusiasts hope for a good catch along the river, and people can be seen carrying water from the river, canals, ponds, and ditches using large buckets and shoulder poles to reach their homes and smallholdings. These everyday practices show how traditional ways of using water have always been—and still are—core to local life in Huangyan. Although the water quality today suffers greatly owing to its disconnection from the original hydrodynamic processes described above, there is nonetheless great potential in the remaining water structure elements. The challenge for the future is to develop and manage a continuous, interconnected, and accessible blue-green network operating across different scales, ensuring that it provides multiple ecosystem services, preserves cultural and natural heritage, and fosters social gathering places.

Urban-rural ecology and land use change

"While in some areas along the river we see an unchecked spread of alien invasive species such as Canadian goldenrod, other sections are used

Energy potential of crops and livestock on an ecological farm in Huangyan

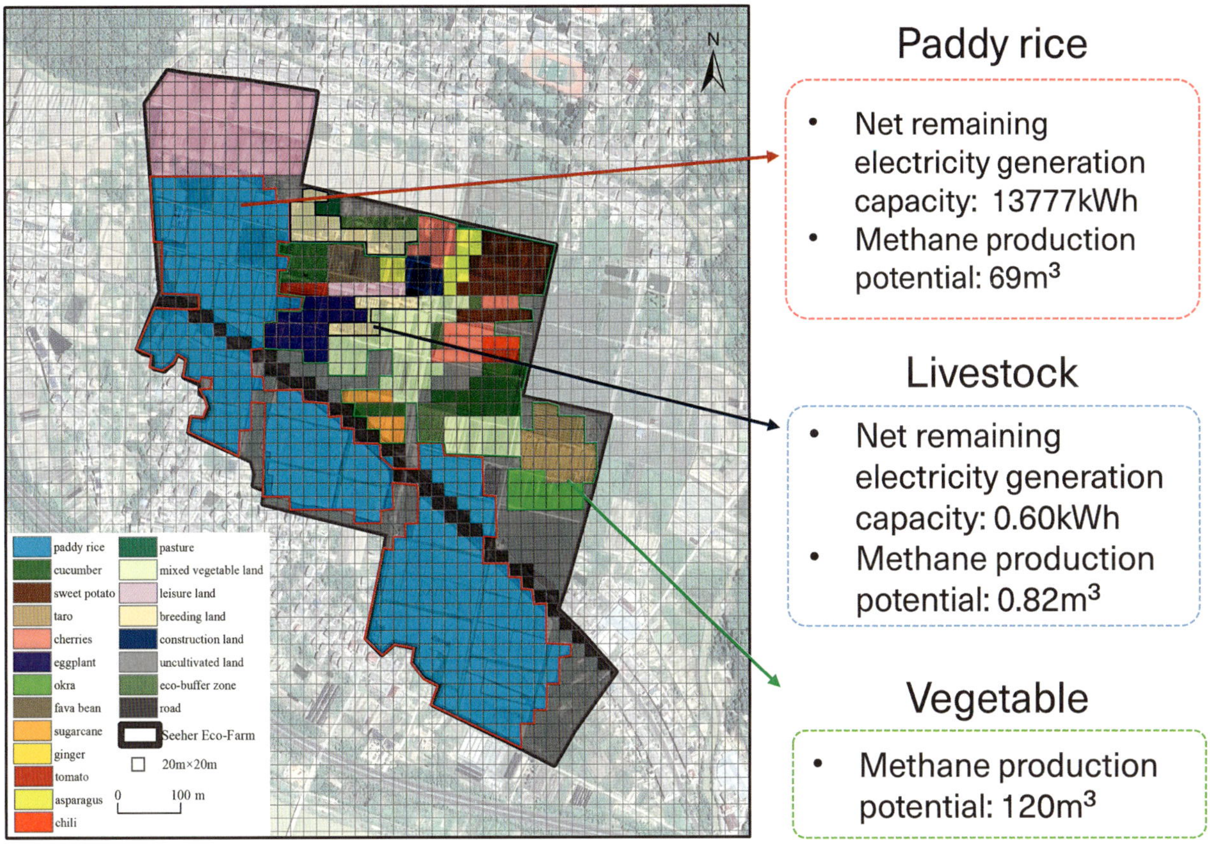

Fig. 13

for thriving vegetable gardens." Interview with a village river manager

Ecosystem services are the benefits that humans receive from natural ecosystems, including provisioning resources like food and water, regulating climate and disease control, supporting nutrient cycling and soil formation, and cultural values such as recreation and spirituality. An analysis of land use change and its impacts in Huangyan showed a general decline in ecosystem services due to rapid urbanization processes over the past three decades, despite sporadic improvements. While forest remains the dominant form of land cover, the reduction of forest cover was undoubtedly a significant factor contributing to the decline in Huangyan's ecosystem services. The primary reason was urbanization and the associated expansion of built-up areas, as well as the increase in cultivated land. Between 1992 and 2020, Huangyan saw its built surface expand from 3 to 13% of the total land cover.[5] Such changes in land use patterns have a direct impact on landscapes, ecosystem services, and biodiversity. Many smaller habitats and biotopes were eliminated by the expansion of urban and agricultural areas, resulting in a wide-spread homogenization of the landscape and its habitats (Fig. 12). This, in turn, led to the isolation of previously linked ecosystems and biodiversity hotspots, as well as the reduction of recreational and flood retention areas.

There has also been a decline in terrestrial insect populations in Huangyan, mainly caused by habitat loss, chemical pollution (e.g., through pesticide use), and the effects of climate change. Despite the protection of ecological zones designated by strict top-down land use policies, gaps remain in the protection of species and their distribution. For example, several habitats of the Golden Kaiser-i-Hind—a butterfly which has been identified as a national priority for conservation—are not included in the network of protected areas, despite being adjacent to currently protected areas. The existing ecological protection network should be maintained and expanded to secure and restore more habitats and thereby protect various endangered and rare species. Lush green spaces in Huangyan's urban and peri-urban areas can fulfil multiple functions here: they can serve as refuges for wildlife and reconnect ecosystems and biodiversity hotspots; they can mitigate the heat island effect, reduce

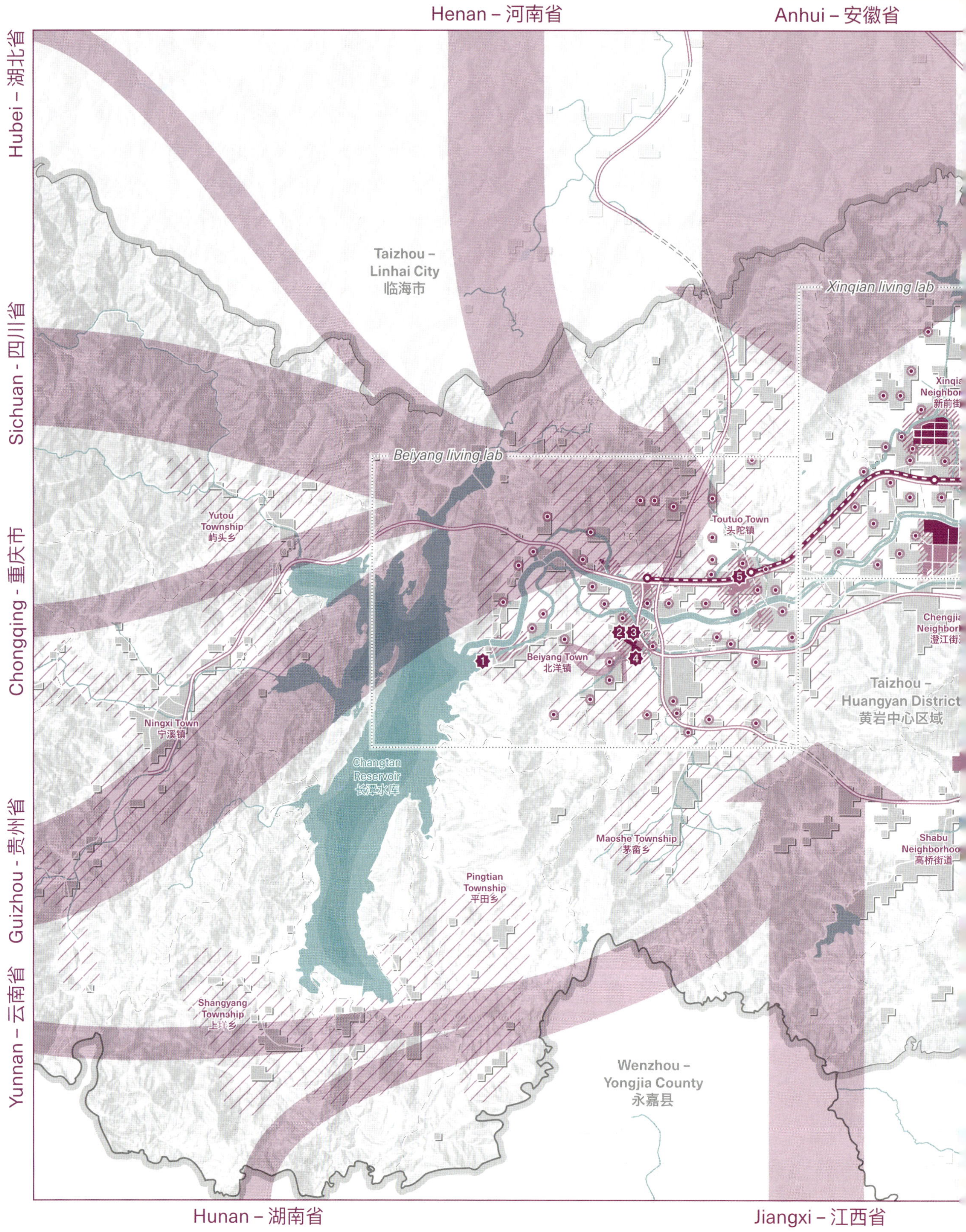

Henan – 河南省
Anhui – 安徽省
Hubei – 湖北省
Sichuan – 四川省
Chongqing – 重庆市
Guizhou – 贵州省
Yunnan – 云南省
Hunan – 湖南省
Jiangxi – 江西省
Taizhou – Linhai City 临海市
Xinqian living lab
Beiyang living lab
Yutou Township 屿头乡
Toutuo Town 头陀镇
Beiyang Town 北洋镇
Ningxi Town 宁溪镇
Changtan Reservoir 长潭水库
Taizhou – Huangyan District 黄岩中心区域
Maoshe Township 茅畲乡
Pingtian Township 平田乡
Shangyang Township 上垟乡
Wenzhou – Yongjia County 永嘉县
1
2
3
4
5

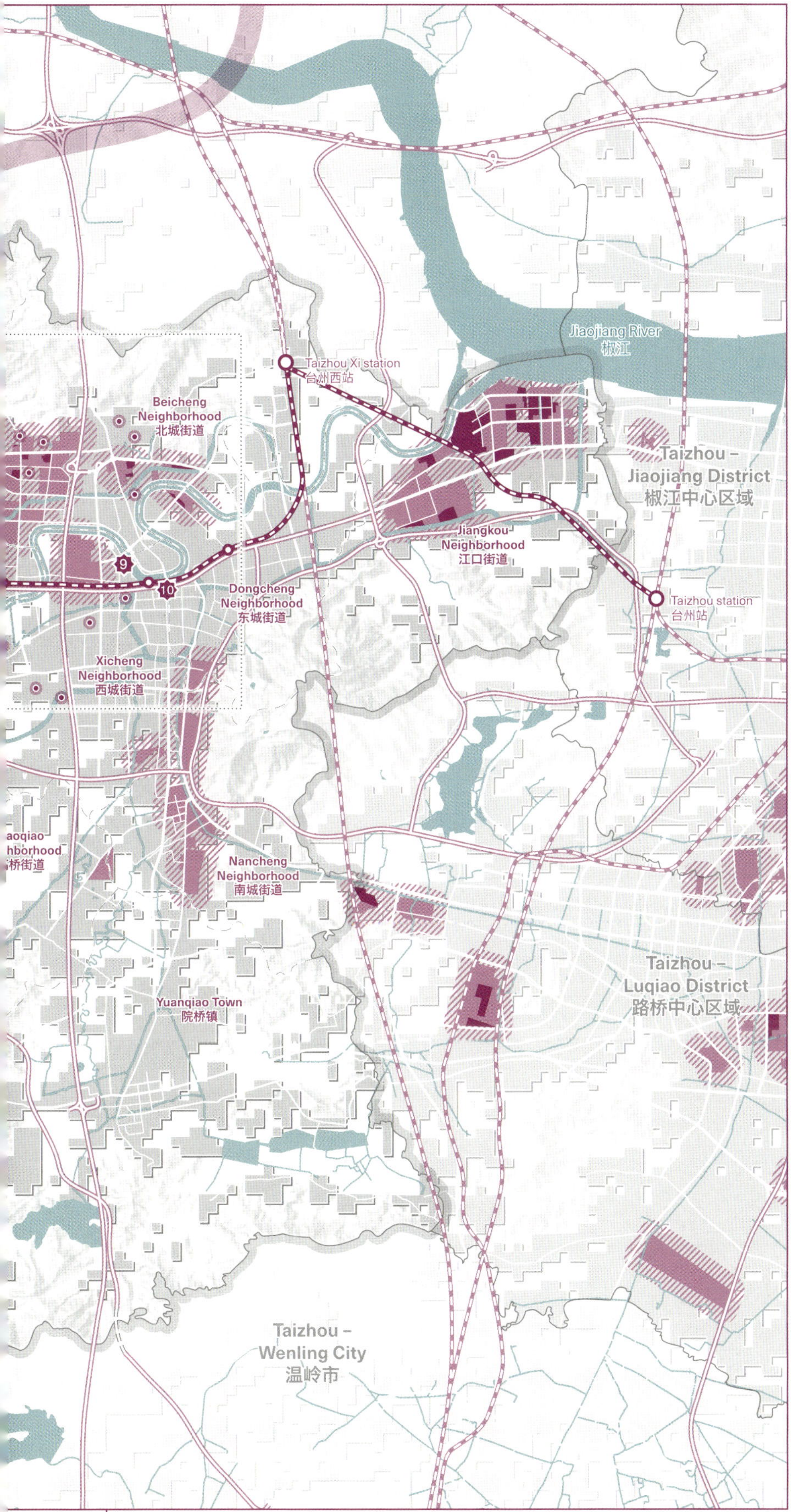

Socio-spatial fabric and migration patterns

Economic opportunities in Huangyan-Taizhou draw in a diverse "floating population," fostering translocal social and economic networks. Many incoming migrant workers and their family members live in villages or dorms in and around industrial zones. Mental mapping (see p. 164) conducted in both living labs revealed sites of social significance and daily mobilities of migrant workers in local neighborhoods and across rural and urban regions in Huangyan, including patterns of exclusion.

- Industrial zones until 2010
- New industrial zones (from 2010 to 2021)
- Neighborhoods around industrial zones
- Tendencies of aging population
- Remaining village structures in the Urban-Rural Living Labs
- Important social spots near living labs (based on interviews).
  1) Changtan Reservoir
  2) Cultural hall Beiyang Town
  3) Temporary market Beiyang Town
  4) Green spaces along canal
  5) Toutuo town center
  6) Xinqian night market
  7) Tianyoucheng shopping mall
  8) Green space near Lucheng residential complex
  9) Yongning Park
  10) Wuyue Square
- Light rail connections (planned / under construction)
- Origins of floating population in Taizhou
- Highways
- Railways
- Water bodies, rivers
- Settlement areas
- Streets
- Administrative borders – neighborhoods
- Administrative borders – districts
- Administrative borders – Huangyan District

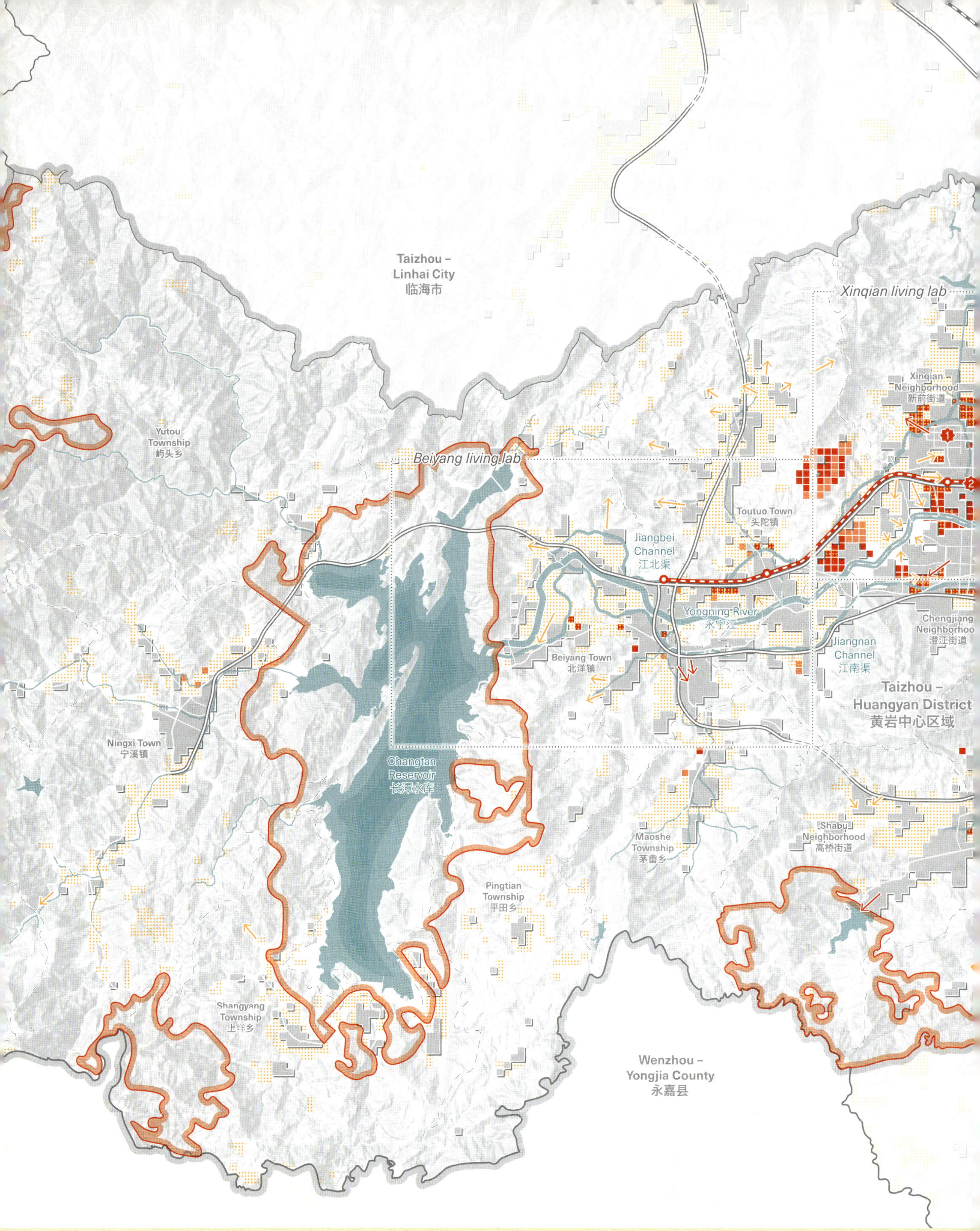
Taizhou –
Linhai City
临海市
Xinqian living lab
Xinqian Neighborhood
新前街道
Yutou Township
屿头乡
Beiyang living lab
Toutuo Town
头陀镇
Jiangbei Channel
江北渠
Yongning River
永宁江
Chengjiang Neighborhood
澄江街道
Jiangnan Channel
江南渠
Beiyang Town
北洋镇
Taizhou –
Huangyan District
黄岩中心区域
Ningxi Town
宁溪镇
Changtan Reservoir
长潭水库
Shabu Neighborhood
高桥街道
Maoshe Township
茅畲乡
Pingtian Township
平田乡
Shangyang Township
上垟乡
Wenzhou –
Yongjia County
永嘉县

Urban development and land management

In Huangyan-Taizhou, a land use plan released in 2022 (referred to as "Three Zones and Three Lines" in Chinese) delineates clear spatial boundaries for urban construction areas, farmland, and ecological protection zones to address raising concerns about food security, social justice, and environmental sustainability. However, the rigid frameworks behind these land use plans cause multifaceted challenges to urban development planning and the ability to implement multi-functional land use concepts.

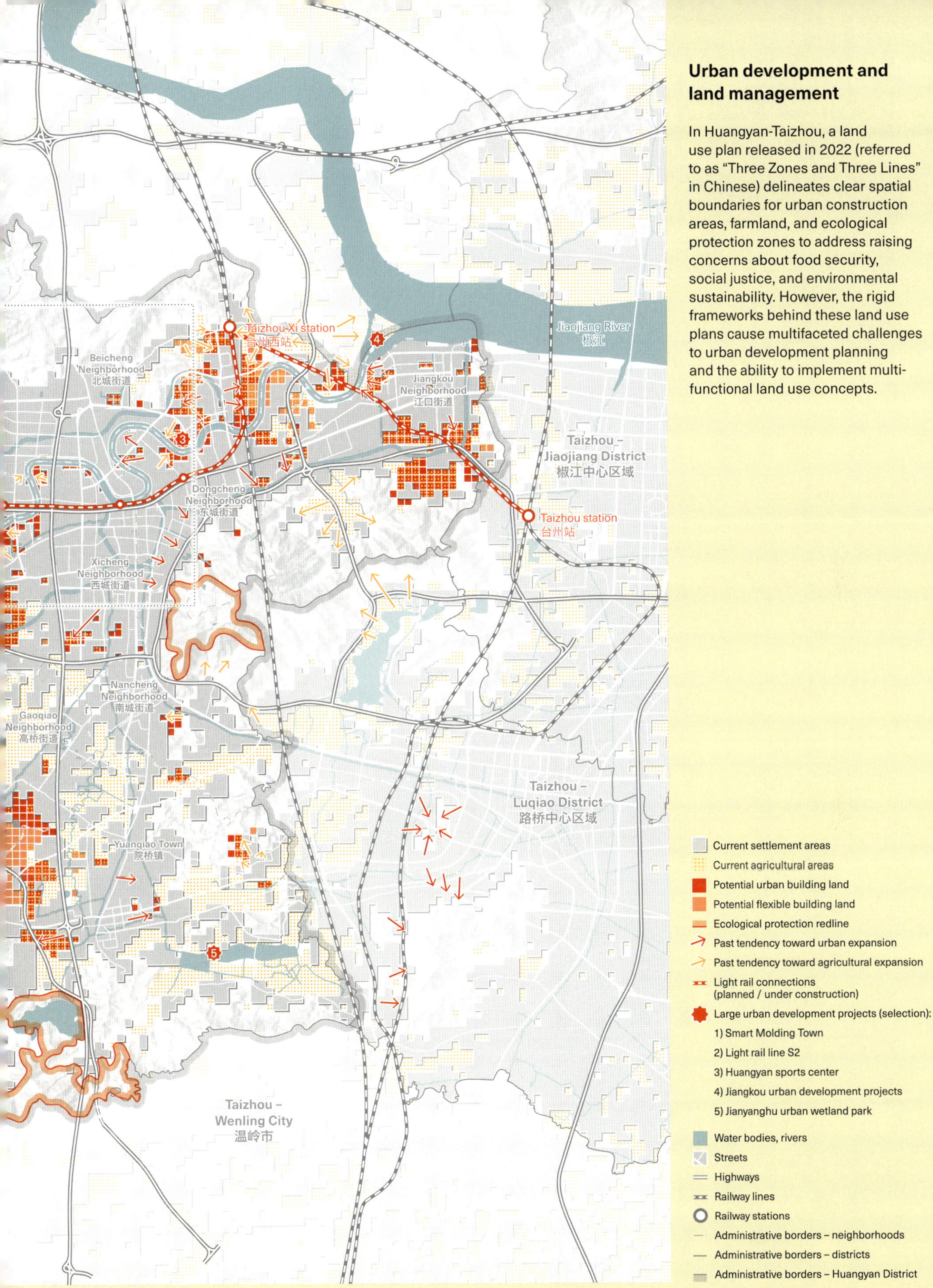

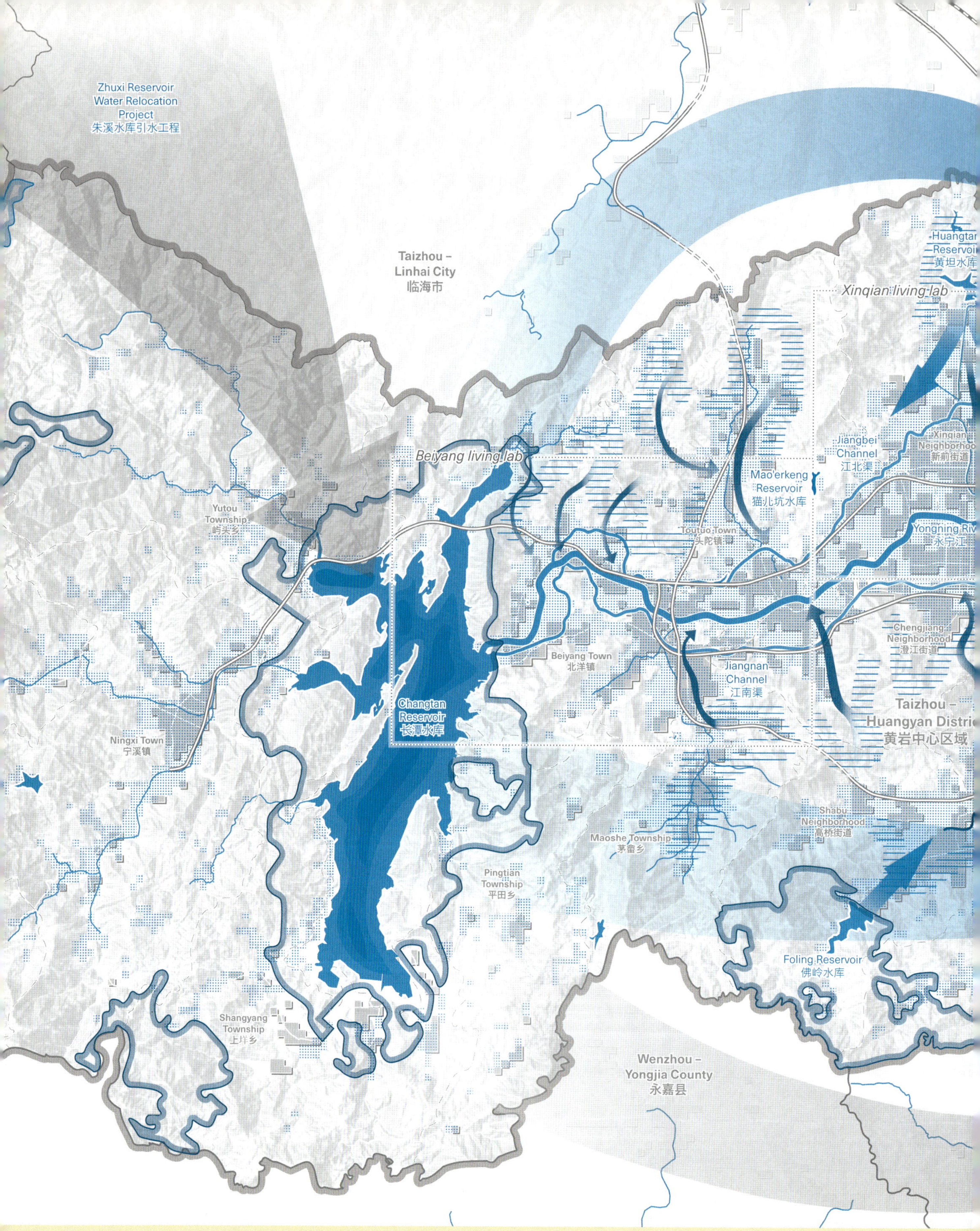

Zhuxi Reservoir
Water Relocation
Project
朱溪水库引水工程
Taizhou –
Linhai City
临海市
Huangtan
Reservoi
黄坦水库
Xinqian living lab
Beiyang living lab
Jiangbei
Channel
江北渠
Xinqian
Neighborhoo
新前街道
Mao'erkeng
Reservoir
猫儿坑水库
Yutou
Township
屿头乡
Toutuo Town
头陀镇
Yongning Riv
永宁江
Beiyang Town
北洋镇
Chengjiang
Neighborhood
澄江街道
Jiangnan
Channel
江南渠
Changtan
Reservoir
长潭水库
Taizhou –
Huangyan Distri
黄岩中心区域
Ningxi Town
宁溪镇
Shabu
Neighborhood
高桥街道
Maoshe Township
茅畲乡
Pingtian
Township
平田乡
Foling Reservoir
佛岭水库
Shangyang
Township
上垟乡
Wenzhou –
Yongjia County
永嘉县

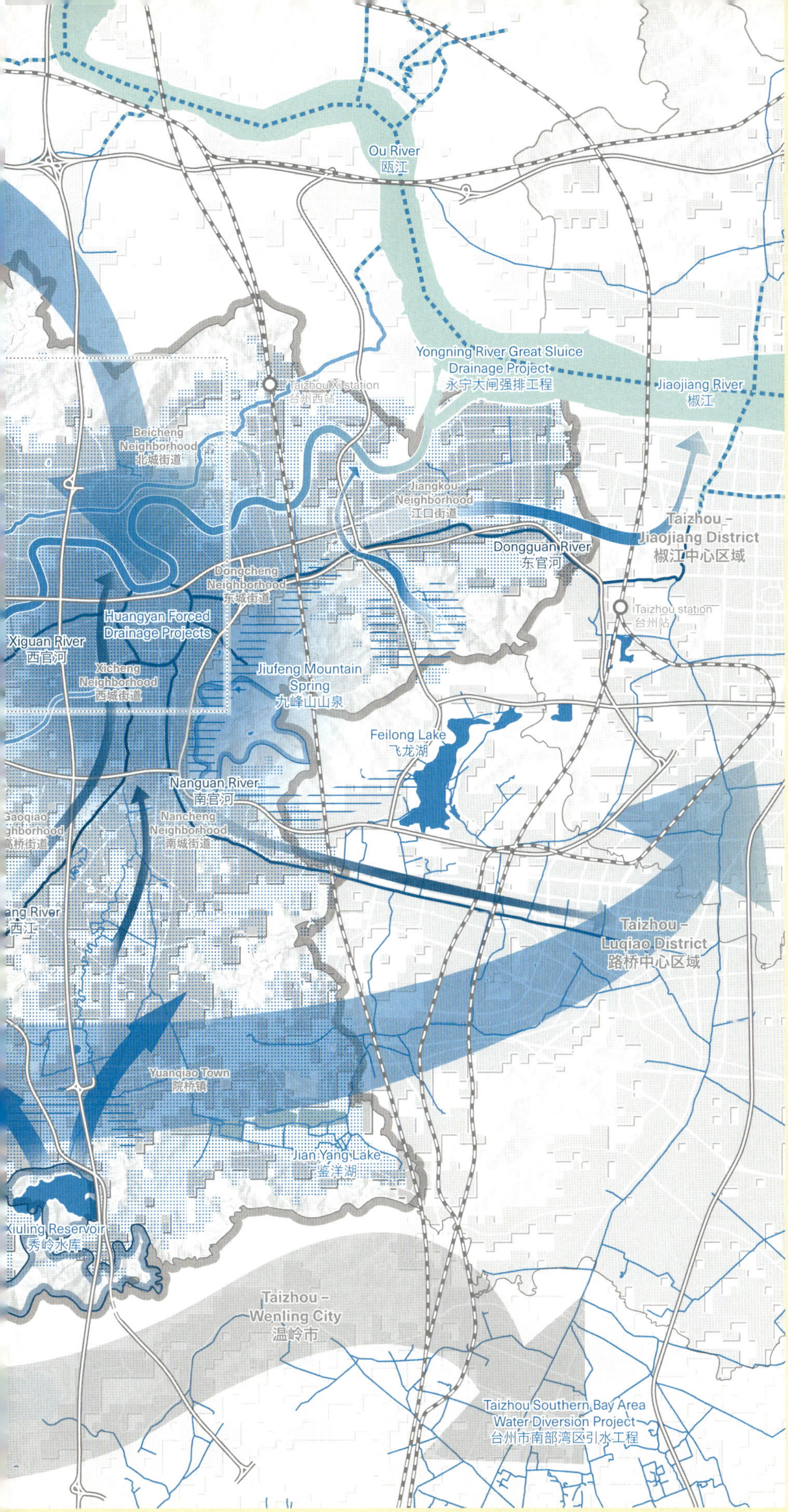

Water systems and landscapes along Yongning River

In the past, the Yongning River basin, which once followed natural water cycles, and traditional water infrastructures efficiently supported agricultural irrigation and domestic supply. However, hydrologic patterns in Huangyan have been significantly altered by the construction of the Changtan Reservoir in the west and Yongning Sluice at the river's estuary.

- Water bodies (fresh water)
- Water bodies (salt water)
- Tidal river network (transition between salt and fresh water)
- Main canals for drainage and agri water supply
- Ancient canal system (based on Huangyan County map, 1930)
- Non-tidal river (fresh water) and agri water supply
- Agri-supplementary / industrial water supply
- Water relocation
- Domestic water supply of Taizhou's urban districts
- Ecological protection redline
- Waterlogged area & pump drainage project
- Low flood protection
- Mountain edges (areas of increased water pollution)
- Settlement areas
- Streets
- Highways
- Railways
- Administrative borders – neighborhoods
- Administrative borders – districts
- Administrative border Huangyan District

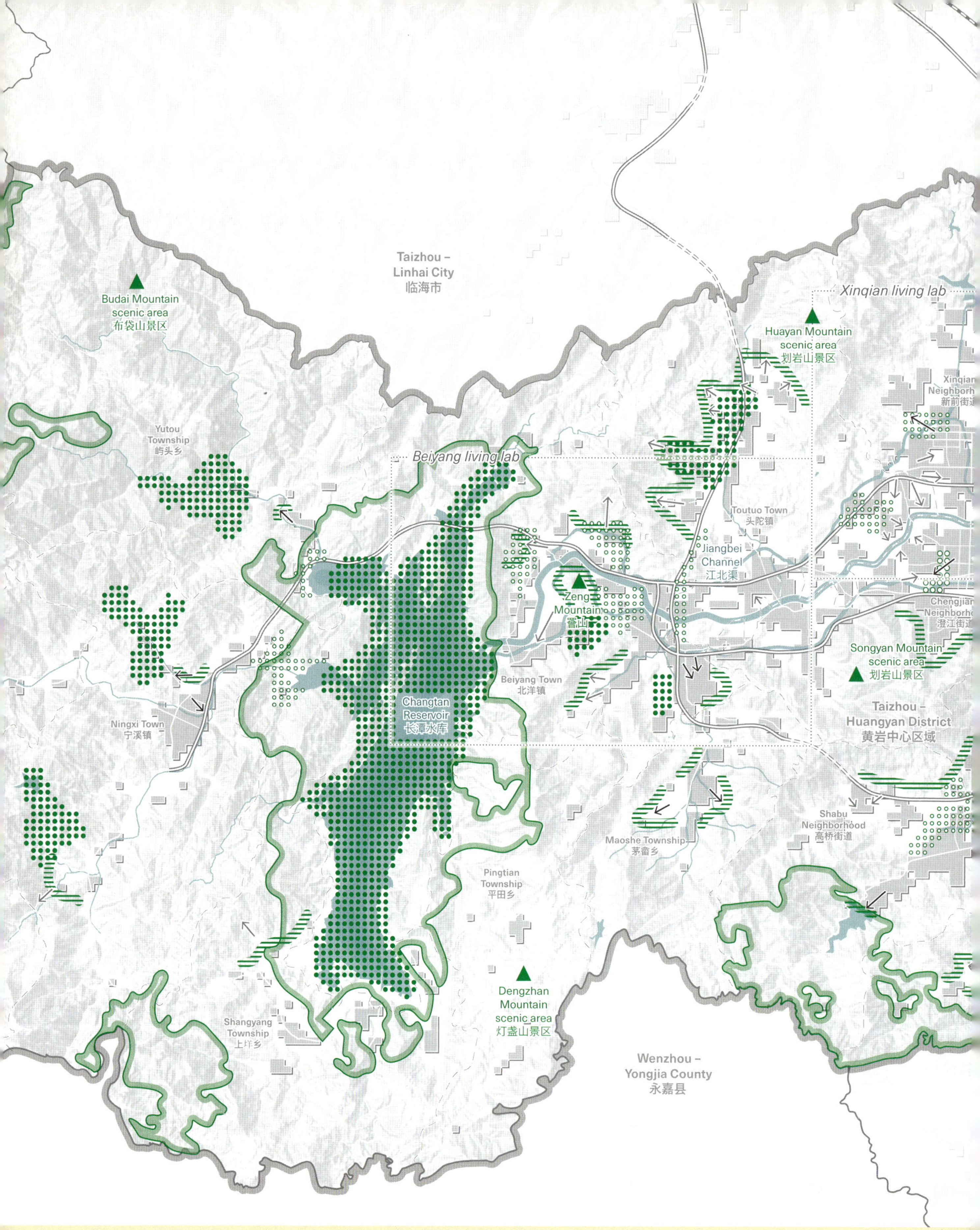

Taizhou –
Linhai City
临海市
Budai Mountain
scenic area
布袋山景区
Xinqian living lab
Huayan Mountain
scenic area
划岩山景区
Yutou
Township
屿头乡
Beiyang living lab
Toutuo Town
头陀镇
Jiangbei
Channel
江北渠
Zeng
Mountain
Beiyang Town
北洋镇
Changtan
Reservoir
长潭水库
Songyan Mountain
scenic area
划岩山景区
Taizhou –
Huangyan District
黄岩中心区域
Ningxi Town
宁溪镇
Shabu
Neighborhood
高桥街道
Maoshe Township
茅畲乡
Pingtian
Township
平田乡
Dengzhan
Mountain
scenic area
灯盏山景区
Shangyang
Township
上垟乡
Wenzhou –
Yongjia County
永嘉县

Urban-rural ecology and land use change

Between 1992 and 2020, Huangyan saw its built surface expand from 3 to 13% of the total land cover. Agricultural land use expanded accordingly. Such changes in land use patterns have a direct impact on landscapes, ecosystem services, and biodiversity. While biodiversity in new settlement areas has declined sharply, a certain increase can be observed in the mountain areas.

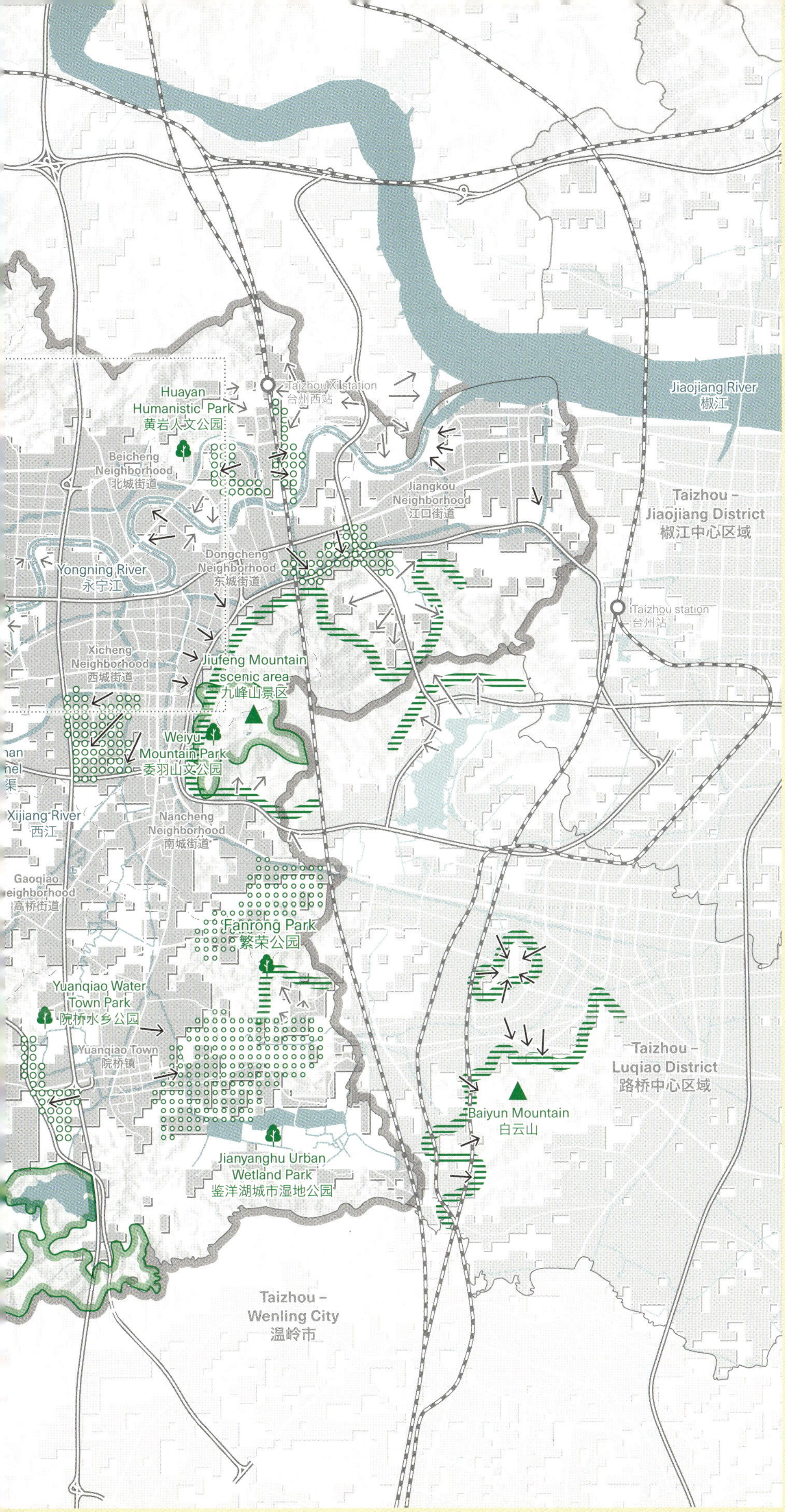

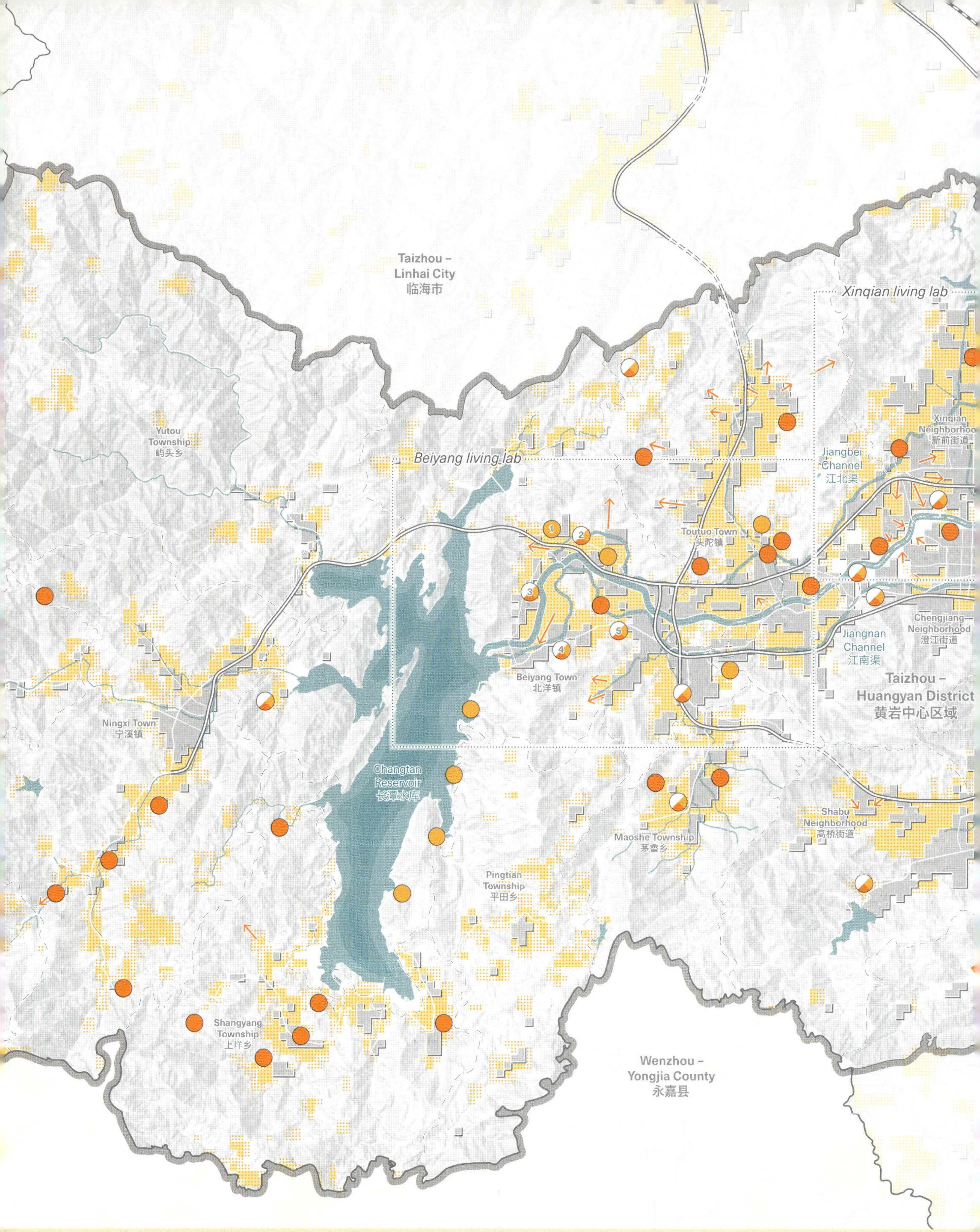
Taizhou –
Linhai City
临海市
Xinqian living lab
Beiyang living lab
Yutou
Township
屿头乡
Xinqian
Neighborhoo
新前街道
Jiangbei
Channel
江北渠
Toutuo Town
头陀镇
Chengjiang
Neighborhood
澄江街道
Jiangnan
Channel
江南渠
Taizhou –
Huangyan District
黄岩中心区域
Beiyang Town
北洋镇
Ningxi Town
宁溪镇
Changtan
Reservoir
长潭水库
Shabu
Neighborhood
高桥街道
Maoshe Township
茅畲乡
Pingtian
Township
平田乡
Shangyang
Township
上垟乡
Wenzhou –
Yongjia County
永嘉县

Agricultural production and food supply

Agriculture plays a strong role in Huangyan's economy. It includes large commercial farms for urban and supra-regional supply, as well as traditional and small-scale subsistence farming. The region is well known for its tangerine orchards, which are widespread in Huangyan.

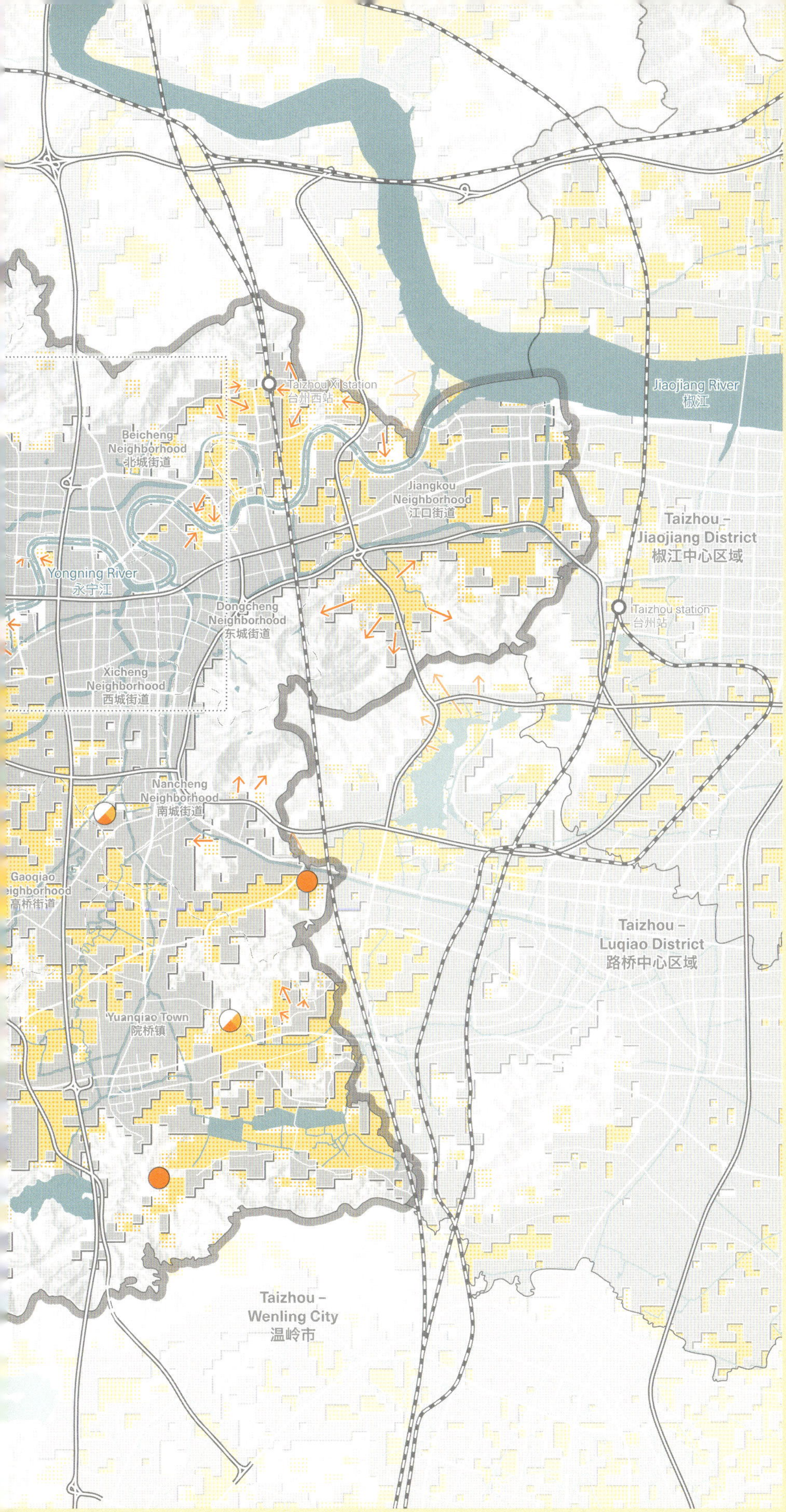

- Agricultural production (predominant land use)
- Agricultural production (partial land use)
- Agricultural land use expansion (comparison of land use data from 2015 and 2019)
- Orange farms (selection)
- Other single-crop farms (selection)
- Multi-crop farms (selection)
- Farms in Beiyang living lab (selection):
  1) Water bamboo cooperative
  2) Xihe Farm
  3) Lvwochun Farm
  4) Lan Mei Tian Yuan Farm
  5) Sino-German Farm
- Local food markets in Xinqian living lab (selection):
  6) Qianshun fresh supermarket
  7) Yuxia agricultural trade market
  8) Xinqian trade market
  9) Zhengbin supermarket
- Water bodies, rivers
- Settlement areas
- Streets
- Highways
- Railways
- Administrative borders – neighborhoods
- Administrative borders – districts
- Administrative borders – Huangyan District

pollution, beautify the environment, and enhance well-being and a sense of belonging for residents.

Material cycles and potential for a circular economy

> "We hope that new composting technology can be brought to our farm. It would make our composting more efficient and help us use less external organic fertilizer, making our farm more sustainable." Interview with a farmer in Beiyang

Working toward a circular economy is essential for the sustainable development of urban-rural regions. Essentially, circularity takes the form of minimizing waste and maximizing resources through recycling, reusing, and regenerating materials. This process creates a closed-loop system between urban and rural areas, reducing environmental impacts and increasing sustainability. In the urban-rural region of Huangyan, key areas of interest for the Urban-Rural Assembly project included resource management and conservation, with a particular focus on natural resources such as water, biomass, and soil. In the agricultural region of Beiyang, we investigated nutrient cycles and the material flow characteristics of farms using different cultivation methods.[6] While conventional farming methods usually rely on chemical inputs, ecological cultivation emphasizes farming in harmony with the environment to maintain biodiversity; meanwhile, organic cultivation strictly avoids synthetic chemicals and genetically modified organisms, focusing on natural processes to enhance soil health and crop yield. Analysis has shown that the theoretical nutrient requirements of organic farms are slightly higher than those of ecological farms. In contrast with an organic farmer in Beiyang, who does not use any external fertilizers, the owner of an ecological farm shared that their operation depends heavily on external organic fertilizers due to the lower efficiency of their composting process. Additionally, the ecological farm grows a greater variety and volume of crops than the organic farm, thus necessitating the use of more fertilizers.

Further research into waste-to-energy options in Huangyan has shown that organic farms have the

greatest potential for biogas production (Fig. 13). Sugarcane bagasse was found to be the most suitable waste from all of Beiyang's major crops (vegetables, citrus fruits, rice, water bamboo, and sugarcane), though rice residue is also a sound option due to the sheer size of the area under cultivation.

The transition to a circular economy in Huangyan entails several challenges, primarily the lack of understanding and support among the local population. Many residents are unaware of what a circular economy involves and its benefits, leading to resistance or apathy toward initiatives aimed at waste reduction, recycling, and other sustainable practices. Additionally, the region struggles with insufficient infrastructure for waste management and recycling. However, effective circular economy practices require robust systems for the segregation, collection, and processing of recyclables and compostables. Moreover, economic incentives and policies to promote circular practices are limited in Huangyan. Without financial benefits or regulatory requirements, businesses and individuals are less likely to adopt sustainable practices over traditional methods. Implementing

- Potentials
- Biodiversity increase
- Yongning River Greenway
- Local water flows
- Blue-green infrastructure potentials
- S2 light rail
- Villages
- Ecological protection redline
- Challenges
- Lack of green spaces
- Ageing population in villages
- Lack of connections to neighborhoods
- Moderate biodiversity decrease
- High biodiversity decrease
- Forest edges at risk from urban development
- Significant water pollution in the Yongning River
- Water bodies
- Streets
- Highways

Challenges and potentials for future development

Maps of the Beiyang (left) and Xinqian (right) living labs summarize research findings and field observations relevant to planning.

Fig. 14

circular economy principles often demands new technologies and innovative approaches to material reuse and resource regeneration. Difficulties the Huangyan government faces in terms of accessing, developing, or adopting these technologies include high costs, skills gaps, or a lack of local innovation ecosystems. Finally, effective circular economy practices must be integrated throughout the supply chain, requiring coordination and cooperation among various stakeholders, including suppliers, manufacturers, consumers, and waste managers. Disruptions or inefficiencies in the supply chain can significantly hinder the transition to circular practices. Addressing these challenges requires concerted efforts to raise awareness, develop supportive infrastructure, create economic incentives, foster technological innovation, and ensure supply chain integration.

The need for integrated and collaborative strategies

These perspectives on various aspects of Huangyan's urban-rural development—gathered by the Urban-Rural Assembly project—reveal significant challenges to sustainable development. As detailed above, these include intensive land use changes (a result of the dramatic increase in built-up areas), a reduction of arable land, displacement of local communities, and serious environmental impacts such as soil erosion, water pollution, flooding, and loss of green space. This transformation presents major threats to biodiversity and livelihoods across villages and urban centers, which is only compounded by unequal agencies among social groups. Concurrently, the urgency to implement sustainable solutions has become more pronounced as climate-related threats intensify in China's coastal regions, including typhoons, heatwaves, and droughts. Research has also revealed multiple interdependencies between concentrated and extended forms of urbanization in the region: flows of water, nutrients, and people circulate across diverse territories, creating complex links between urban and rural settlements, as well as industry, agriculture, and socio-ecological landscapes.

However, despite conflicting interests between economic prosperity and environmental sustain-

Fig. 15

Fig. 1
The banks of Yongning River are used for sports and recreation, with tangerine-shaped lanterns lining the Green way.

Fig. 2
The urban fabric of central Huangyan encompasses dynamic industrial clusters as well as dense residential and commercial districts.

Fig. 3
Many businesses in Xinqian are part of the plastics production network. This one is offering a variety of plastic pellets sold in bags of twenty-five kilograms.

Fig. 4
Robots in this factory mold 70,000 plastic water bottles per day.

Fig. 5
Villagers in Huangyan play an instrumental role in global production lines by assembling industrial products in household workshops.

Fig. 6
Citrus orchards are a dominant feature of the landscape along the Yongning River, and the tangerine has become the mascot of Huangyan.

Fig. 7
Socio-spatial profiles were created to reveal the diversity of actors in Huangyan's social fabric.

Fig. 8
The former site of an orange farm's storage house, demolished by the government due to its location on the designated permanent basic farm land.

Fig. 9
Yongning River has been transformed from a meandering tidal river into an almost stagnant body of water.

Fig. 10
Thriving vegetable gardens along the riverbanks are maintained by the residents of nearby dwellings.

Fig. 11
Village ponds still play a vital role in the villagers' everyday life but are often polluted.

Fig. 12
Change of biodiversity potential in Beiyang Town between 1992 and 2020.

Fig. 13
Energy potential analysis of products from an ecological farm in Beiyang.

Fig. 14
Rural setting in western Huangyan.

Fig. 15
Commercial street in Xinqian.

ability, these interconnected challenges also point toward future potential, through adopting a territorial perspective that works to ensure more inclusive, climate-friendly, and circular forms of development. For example, dispersed water systems and biodiversity hotspots could be reconnected into an integrated blue-green network that mitigates climate-related risks, raises living quality, and fosters rural eco-tourism (see challenges and potentials maps on pages 110, 111). This offers the possibility of creating inclusive public spaces—e.g., at village ponds—while promoting local heritage and a sense of identity, incorporating participatory planning processes to meet both urban and rural social needs. Local organic agriculture initiatives offer another starting point for integrating circular economic practices in the field of advanced composting, soil regeneration, and biogas production. In turn, these operations could function as best practice models and training centers for other interested farms.

Attempts have already been made to enhance rural development and strengthen urban-to-rural tourism in Huangyan, through several small and medium-sized university-led revitalization projects run in historical villages and small towns across the region (see article by Guiqing Yang on page 214). However, many tourism-oriented projects in Huangyan have limited impact in halting the damaging effects of rapid urbanization and the decline of rural villages, with such revitalization initiatives often being largely decorative in nature. Solutions must go beyond superficial revitalization efforts and focus on sustainable practices that balance environmental, social, and economic priorities. By fostering common understanding and close coordination among all stakeholders, and embracing innovative, territorial perspectives, Huangyan can work toward a more resilient future. This will require bold policy shifts that prioritize long-term socio-ecological resilience, ensuring that both rural and urban areas can thrive in the face of rapid urbanization and climate-related risks.

1 In the Chinese context, the term "floating population" refers to people who migrate from other regions without changing their official household registration (*hukou*). These migrants move temporarily in search of work, education, or other opportunities, but do not have the same legal rights and access to public services as registered residents.

2 Ava Lynam, Fengqing Li, Gaoli Xiao, Liyuan Fei, Huang Huang, and Lukas Utzig, "Capturing Socio-Spatial Inequality in Planetary Urbanisation: A Multi-Dimensional Methodological Framework," *Cities* 132 (2023): 104076.

3 Since 1958, the *hukou* household registration system has categorized the population into two distinct groups: "agricultural" and "non-agricultural" households, perpetuating enduring structures of discrimination for rural migrants in China's cities (see article by Meyer-Clement, p. 84).

4 Sigrun Langner, Yuting Xie, Maria Frölich-Kulik, Yuling Zhang, and Karl Beelen, *Between Land and Water* (Berlin: JOVIS, forthcoming 2025).

5 Suili Xiao, Till Fügener, Wolfgang Wende, Wentao Yan, Hui Chen, Ralf Uwe Syrbe, and Bing Xue, "The Dynamics of Vegetation and Implications for Ecosystem Services in the Context of Urbanisation: An Example from Huangyan-Taizhou, China," *Ecological Engineering* 179 (2022): 106614.

6 Julia Santolin, Oliver Christopher Larsen, Albrecht Fritze, Bing Xue, Zheng Yang, and Vera Susanne Rotter, "Reaching China's Fertilizer Reduction Goals through Nitrogen and Phosphorus Recovery: A Substance Flow Analysis Case Study." *Journal of Material Cycles and Waste Management* 26 (2024): 3650–64.

Chapter 2: Investigating Urban-Rural Dynamics

To effectively study complex urban-rural linkages involving flows of people, natural resources, commodities, and information, researchers must employ a variety of methods in different combinations to support data collection and analysis. This becomes even more complex when working in an international research constellation. Chapter Two critically reflects on experiences of conducting research at rural-urban transitional zones within and beyond the Urban-Rural Assembly project. The contributions present innovative methods and tools that have been developed, applied, or experimented with across disciplinary, geographic, and cultural boundaries. They offer practical guidance on how to study urban-rural regions comparatively and facilitate meaningful dialogue among various actors. Ultimately, the chapter underlines the need for a diverse and integrative research approach to support the development of impactful strategies for sustainable rural-urban transformation.

Fig. 1

Conducting collaborative research across borders and disciplines

Sigrun Abels, Anke Hagemann, Ava Lynam, and Gaoli Xiao

As our world faces escalating geopolitical tensions, the imperative for international cooperation to contend with interconnecting global issues becomes even more pronounced. Critical challenges require a collective sense of responsibility and integrated strategies with the ability to translate solutions across national borders. Planetary urbanization and its close interaction with climate change—as both a cause and a lever for mitigation—is one of these challenges (see interview with Hillary Angelo on page 56). Thus, we must urgently foster collaborative efforts for sustainable transformation across national borders involving politics, business, and civil society. Universities—as important voices in civil society and educational institutions for future generations—have a particular role to play. This includes comprehensive, interdisciplinary knowledge production on sustainable urban transformation and transformative practical approaches delivered through multi-stakeholder efforts as more viable development pathways.

In this context, collaborations between universities from different countries and cultures are vital and enriching since they facilitate the international exchange of knowledge and practical experience of strategies for sustainable transition. At the same time, they may come with substantial differences in values, expectations, and approaches. The political framework for international cooperation across some global regions has become increasingly difficult in recent years. This is especially the case for Sino-German university cooperation. The call for greater expertise on China has been heard frequently and loudly in Germany and Europe for some time now, appealing for more dialogue and cooperation to take place on an equal footing. There have been equally amplified demands in the opposite direction, calling for greater competition with—and increased distance from—China.[1] As the multiple challenges of rapid urbanization and rural decline converge in China, there is an intensified need to work together to develop pioneering sustainable and integrated development approaches with potential for application elsewhere.

As an introduction to Chapter Two, this article reflects on several challenges related to conducting research in complex urban–rural settings while transgressing political systems, cultures, disciplines, and the limits of academia. The contributions in this chapter

Fig. 2

present methods and practical tools from various disciplines that confront these challenges in order to conduct sensitive and impactful collaborative research on rural–urban dynamics. Additionally, the authors discuss the preconditions of transdisciplinary research and reflect on the imbalances of intercultural fieldwork. The following five points synthesize some key issues and learnings concerning research across borders and disciplines. Alongside referring to the chapter's individual contributions, they are complemented by experiences from the Urban-Rural Assembly project.

Fig. 1
Various methods were employed in the Urban-Rural Assembly project to integrate local knowledge into the interdisciplinary Sino-German research framework.

Fig 2
The Urban-Rural Assembly team organized a Sino-German intercultural exchange in Xinqian village square, featuring Easter egg painting and traditional Chinese paper cutting, as a step toward fostering local trust and understanding.

1. Seeking mutual ground in international research constellations

Contributions to this chapter indicate that strong, mutually beneficial, and trusting relationships with academic partner institutions are an essential prerequisite for good collaboration. This is stressed by Ya Ping Wang (see article on page 122) in his discussion of conducting comparative urban research across seven African and Asian countries. As an exchange taking place between national research teams on an equal footing, the project aimed to avoid the dominance of research partners from Western countries, which often results in a mono-directional transfer of knowledge. However, such balanced cooperation is not typically the norm; in the case of the Urban-Rural Assembly project, funding was limited to the German side of the consortium, challenging the ability of the Chinese partners to engage productively in the research cooperation. The team addressed this by seeking mutually beneficial opportunities for collaboration; for instance, through publishing co-authored articles and conference papers or joint teaching initiatives. The project was able to navigate this imbalance with trust which had been established through long-standing partnerships with Chinese partner universities. This facilitated access to fieldwork, local networks, and sensitive data—not to mention assistance with visa applications and navigating complex political tensions.

2. Managing multi-directional communication

Complex international, interdisciplinary, and transdisciplinary research frameworks confront research teams with multiple challenges of communication, translation, and mediation. Language barriers are the first difficulty—not just between researchers of different nationalities but between local languages and dialects, as is the case in the Chinese context. In their article, Gaoli Xiao, Ava Lynam, and Yuqi Zhang (see page 150) reflect on communication challenges faced during fieldwork in Huangyan for the Urban-Rural Assembly project. Here, language constraints impacted the extent to which foreign researchers could build local relationships and many nuances in data collection were inevitably "lost in translation." Fostering effective collaboration in this context required creative and flexible solutions, as well as mutual support across the international research team. Culturally sensitive communication is another precondition for successful collaboration. To this end, efforts to understand local cultural codes using clear and transparent communication should be the starting point for building trust among research institutions, as well as bridging relationships with local authorities and other key decision-makers.

Another crucial challenge is establishing a common understanding among research teams from different disciplines or academic cultures. Finding shared definitions for key terms and concepts—such as "neighborhood" and "informal housing" (as reported by Ya Ping Wang), or "living lab" and "urban–rural linkages" (as in the case of the Urban-Rural Assembly project)—is an important foundation for research collaboration. To this end, the Urban-Rural Assembly team explored the use of a bilingual (English–Chinese) glossary as a working document. This supported a shared understanding of research terminologies, policies, and planning approaches for urban–rural development across the multi-disciplinary Sino-German consortium (see "Urban-Rural Assembly Glossary" on page 177). In contrast, the "Horizontal Metropolis" project presented in Andrea Palmioli's article (see page 130), created its own terminology and visual language as part of a long-term international research network focusing on morphological urban comparison across Europe, the US, and China. Moreover, a transdisciplinary research approach (as presented by Jue Wang on page 142), which aims for greater stakeholder involvement and research-by-design, faces the additional challenge of translating ideas and concepts between academic and non-academic contexts, as well as facilitating productive discussions between actors from different sectors, hierarchies, and social groups (see point 5).

3. Working with comparative and multi-disciplinary research frameworks

Starting from the hypothesis that comparative research can be a powerful tool to understand global urban (and rural) regions,[2] the projects featured in this chapter have developed individual methodologies and frameworks for researching patterns and dynamics of urbanization in different locations involving multiple disciplines. The "Horizontal Metropolis" research protocol presented by Andrea Palmioli offers a rigorous, multi-scalar framework for studying, comparing, understanding—and, ultimately, re-designing—hybrid urban-rural morphologies across global regions. Ya Ping Wang also highlights the importance of implementing clear frameworks when comparing urban areas in diverse cultural contexts. However, he emphasizes the need to consider their distinctive political situations and socio-economic backgrounds.

The Urban-Rural Assembly project intentionally combined research perspectives from the disciplines of planning, technical, social, and natural sciences, to effectively study complex urban–rural dynamics involving flows of people, circulations of natural resources and materials, and landscape transformations. A diversity of methods and tools for data collection and analysis, as well as inter- and transdisciplinary dialogue, are presented in this chapter in the form of a "toolbox" (see "Tools for researching urban–rural transformation" on page 158). However, integrating these different disciplines in a joint research process—finding a common language and assembling diverse types of data, such as soil samples, interviews with migrant workers, and land use maps—posed an ongoing challenge throughout the project, as did the task of establishing a collaborative planning process. These negotiations required constant efforts of translation, a high degree of coordination across the team, and creativity with discursive formats.

4. Striving for transdisciplinarity

Transdisciplinary research goes beyond interdisciplinarity by integrating not only knowledge from different academic disciplines but also local insight, community expertise, and stakeholder perspectives.[3, 4] Moreover, with the aim of applied, transformative research,[5] academic knowledge is intended to be handed over to local stakeholders to initiate sustainable change at ground level. The Sino-German project on sustainable rubber cultivation in Xishuangbanna, China—presented in this chapter by Jue Wang—integrated different scientific disciplines (such as social and environmental science, agriculture, and ecology) while focusing on the involvement of diverse stakeholders (such as local farmers, practitioners, governments, and NGOs). Various methods were employed to meaningfully involve participants, ensure active listening, and support shared decision-making processes. These strategies aimed to facilitate local stakeholders to "identify sustainability problems, take ownership of them, and become more engaged in producing lasting solutions" (see page 149). Similar aims were pursued in the Urban-Rural Assembly project through the integration of living labs (see "Urban-Rural Living Labs" on page 174) as locally-embedded research anchors from which to engage with local stakeholders.[6] Through a series of multi-actor workshops, a broad spectrum of participants from academia, administration, politics, business, and civil society were assembled to discuss local issues and challenges, with a view to co-developing sustainable future visions for urban–rural development (see "Multi-actor workshops" on page 175). Both projects developed strategies and tools that support communication between scientific and non-scientific parties—such as an explanatory video documentary (see "Film for transcultural communication" on page 178), with the primary aim of increasing the accessibility of workshop procedures in the Urban-Rural Assembly project.

Other formats targeted particular groups; to enhance communication between science and policymaking, a series of online dialogues focused on topics identified as critical to local development—such as the circular economy, ecological restoration, and social inclusion—were facilitated by an international NGO (ICLEI: Local Governments for Sustainability). These dialogues brought international and Chinese academics and policymakers into contact, ultimately aiming to inform policy-related research and enrich its impact on local policy-making. Besides local officials, experts, and entrepreneurs, the research team also sought opportunities for exchange with neighborhoods and residents on the ground during fieldwork (see article by Gaoli Xiao, Ava Lynam, and Yuqi Zhang) (Fig.1). In addition, a Sino-German intercultural event, involving a local school, was organized in a village square in Huangyan, which helped to increase the project's visibility and build local trust (Fig. 2).

5. Transferring concepts and approaches

International and intercultural research projects also aim for the transfer of knowledge, concepts, and transformative approaches between different cultural, political, and socio-economic contexts. Even though we face similar challenges in terms of climate change and sustainability, it is important to reflect on the degree to which Western planning concepts can and should be adapted for other global contexts—or vice versa.[7, 8] Similarly, Ya Ping Wang poses the question of whether Chinese urban planning approaches can be transferred to other countries in the Global South, where the economic influence of China has been steadily growing. He highlights the risks of making "quick and direct transfers or copying ... specific practices or policies from one system to another." Rather, he emphasizes the need for a multi-directional learning process to "broaden the knowledge base for theoretical development, as well as new innovative urban policy design" and to find more tailored local solutions to similar problems (see page 129). The "Horizontal Metropolis" research and design approach builds on a common morphological language that can be applied to any type of urban-rural sprawl, with the aim of making physical patterns and dynamics comparable around the globe. Though stemming from Western European approaches to urbanism, it highlights the similarities of contemporary urbanization patterns, such as "Desakota" in Southeast Asia and "Zwischenstadt" in Germany. The continuously expanding application of the framework and its dissemination through major exhibitions contributes to the acceptance of diffuse types of urbanization—not just as an incidental phenomenon but as a predominant model.

Questions of comparability and transferability were also inherent in the Sino-German Urban-Rural Assembly project. In addition to twoUrban-Rural Living Labs in Huangyan, a third in Thuringia, Germany, was integrated as an initial testing ground for the project's participatory planning strategy during the travel restrictions caused by the COVID-19 pandemic. Applying the principles of the German "Raumbild" approach for strategic and collaborative vision building (see article by Lukas Pappert and Maria Frölich-Kulik on page 286) raised critical questions concerning the suitability, relevance, and adaptability of the approach within the Chinese context. More specifically, this related to the feasibility of an international research team implementing participatory workshops in the context of a top-down governance system in China. Indeed, the selection of appropriate venues for events, the content of discussions, and the invite list all had to be approved by the local government. Despite these limitations, the multi-actor workshops opened a lively dialogue among stakeholders from different administrative sectors, stimulating broad exchange about topics rarely addressed during everyday work. Similarly, Jue Wang reports that in their Sino-German project in Yunnan Province, certain local stakeholders were initially hesitant about the participatory research process. However, after careful steps were taken to establish trust-based engagement, they even saw potential in applying similar tools in future projects.

Lessons learned

The contributions in this chapter underline the challenges that arise in international collaborative research as it attempts to bridge various gaps: between languages and cultures, academic disciplines, academics and non-academics, and different political contexts. Concurrently, they show the value of international academic collaboration and establishing dialogue between science and policy while securing the engagement of local actors when developing integrated solutions to critical global issues. In our efforts to achieve more sustainable urban–rural development, we must pay special attention to how knowledge transfer operates in multiple directions. Such awareness is key for fostering lasting cooperation, local acceptance, and resilience to changing conditions. Productive collaborations involving a variety of actor groups require active steps to establish balanced partnerships, support sensitive communication with mutually understandable terms and concepts, integrate methodologies from various disciplines, and adapt knowledge and ideas to local situations and needs. Ultimately, this demands continuous attention and efforts from all partners to support a meaningful collective learning process.

1 Sigrun Abels and Christian Bode, "Aktuelle Herausforderungen für deutsch-chinesische Hochschulkooperationen," in *Handbuch China-Kompetenzen*, eds. Gabriele Thelen, Helena Obendiek, and Yinchun Bail (Bielefeld: Transcript Verlag, 2022), 51–68.

2 Jennifer Robinson, "Thinking cities through elsewhere: Comparative tactics for a more global urban studies," *Progress in Human Geography* 40, no. 1 (2016): 3–29.

3 Antonietta Di Giulio and Rico Defila, *Transdisziplinär und Transformativ Forschen: Eine Methodensammlung* (New York: Springer Nature, 2018).

4 Julie Thompson Klein, "Prospects for Transdisciplinarity," *Futures* 36, no. 4 (2004): 515–26.

5 Agnes Förster, "Alle wollen wirken: Transformative Forschung trifft Stadtentwicklung," *pnd – Planung Neudenken* 1 (2022): 43–69.

6 Ulf Hahne, "Reallabore. Katalysator für die Nachhaltige Stadt- und Regionalentwicklung," *Raumplanung* 200, no. 1 (2019): 50–55.

7 Ananya Roy and Aihwa Ong, eds., *Worlding Cities: Asian Experiments and the Art of Being Global* (Malden and Oxford: Wiley-Blackwell, 2011).

8 Vanessa Watson, "Seeing from the South: Refocusing Urban Planning on the Globe's Central Urban Issues," *Urban Studies* 46, no. 11 (2009): 2259–75.

Fig. 1

Fig. 2

From South to South: Comparative urban research and knowledge transfer

Ya Ping Wang

In 2016, UN-Habitat published the "New Urban Agenda"—a framework for action aspiring to readdress how cities and human settlements are planned, designed, financed, developed, governed, and managed.[1] It offered a series of principles for more sustainable pathways to global urban development to be implemented at a local level. However, are there any universally applicable planning, design, finance, and management systems for all countries to follow? Most urban researchers and policymakers tend to view cities in a framework familiar to their training and experience from their home country. They sometimes think they may have found the best solution for the sustainable development of future cities and aim to influence urban planning and development in other countries. This can be observed in the case of China, where politicians and academics are keen to offer successful Chinese lessons and methods to other developing countries.

China has made huge progress in urbanization in the last forty years and is now home to many of the world's largest cities; its urban population has grown from less than 20 percent in the 1980s to 65 percent in 2023.[2] A significant proportion of Chinese people have experienced an unprecedented improvement in their living standards and quality. Many have given up their simple and dilapidated shelters in traditional villages and moved into apartments in high-rise residential buildings, typically grouped into various-sized housing estates in cities and towns. China's experience in industrialization and urban transformation is also an important part of the Chinese style of modernization and a driving factor in its "Global Development Initiatives." In the last ten years, China's industrial development and investment have had an important impact on urbanization processes in Asian and African countries. This is particularly evident in major cities along the routes of the Belt and Road Initiative—China's worldwide infrastructure development strategy launched in 2013. Concurrently, Chinese researchers and experts have begun to play key roles in many international organizations, which will no doubt leave important marks on global urban development policies. But how suitable is the Chinese urban experience to other countries? Could other cities replicate Chinese urban planning and development practices? What lessons can China learn from other rapidly urbanizing countries? These ambitions of transferring development ideas between contexts with different political and cultural systems emphasize the significance of cross-country comparison in urbanization processes.

I started my research career with a PhD project on a comparative analysis of urban land use planning systems in China and Scotland with case studies focusing on Xi'an and Edinburgh.[3] This was in the late 1980s, when China had just opened its doors to the world and was very enthusiastic to learn from other countries. Over the years, my research has largely focused on urban changes in China but always with a comparative lens.[4] In recent years at the University of Glasgow, I led a major international comparative study on "Sustainable, Healthy, and Learning Cities and Neighborhoods" (SHLC).[5] China, as an example of a fast-growing economy, is one of seven case study countries included in the project. In this short article, I will introduce the comparative methods we used in this project, reflecting on the values and challenges in cross-country knowledge transfer. The following sections include a brief introduction to the SHLC project, the research methods used, and some of our main findings—which I hope shed some light on the questions raised above.

A cross-country comparative study on urban neighborhoods

Sustainable cities depend to a considerable extent on the resilience of their population, developed through access to resources related to health and learning. Equally, quality healthcare and education depend on the sustainable development of cities and the neighborhoods within them. Yet, recent global urban policies for developing countries tend to operate at a general level and are mainly focused on the conditions of slum areas. Aside from slums or informal settlements, there are many other types of urban neighborhoods emerging in fast-growing cities, some more sustainable than others. Based on this assumption, the SHLC project aims to conduct systematic and comparative research on the formation and differentiation of neighborhoods in urban areas across Africa and Asia, with the aim of addressing challenges associated with urbanization and large-scale rural-to-urban migration. Within Africa and Asia, we recognize the diversity of these countries regarding economic development, regional characteristics, cultural and historical background, level of industrialization, and urbanization. Therefore, our research framework divided countries into two broad categories: fast-growing and emerging economies (BRICS countries of South Africa, India, and China) and others (Rwanda, Tanzania, Bangladesh, and the Philippines). To achieve a better understanding of regional complexities in urbanization, we selected two cities in each case study country: one large city or the capital, and one regional city. In each case study city, we identified and categorized all sorts of neighborhoods into five types of socio-spatial structures, ranging from slums to rich residential areas or gated communities. This research design (Fig. 2) allowed for comparative analysis from several dimensions: within a country and region, between countries and continents, between different economic development levels, and (most importantly) between types of cities and neighborhoods.

Region	Country	Case study cities
Africa	South Africa	Cape Town (parliamentary seat, capital); Johannesburg (GCR) (major city region)
	Tanzania	Dar es Salaam (national city and financial center); Dodoma (new national capital city)
	Rwanda	Kigali (national capital); Huye (regional city)
South Asia	India	Delhi (national capital); Madurai (regional city)
	Bangladesh	Dhaka (national capital); Khulna (major regional center)
East Asian	China	Chongqing (national city in the west); Datong (regional city, inland and north)
	Philippines	Manila (national capital); Batangas (regional city)

Fig. 3

The core SHLC project included four common "Research Task Packages" of data collection and analysis, implemented in each case study city by the country research team:

The first package examined the relationship between urbanization, migration, economic development, and sustainability in the case study cities. We reviewed planning and urban development policy documents over the last twenty years, examining key ideas and policies that shaped the delivery of public services, especially education and healthcare.

The second focused on emerging patterns of neighborhood/community distribution in the cities. We employed quantitative spatial analytical methods (GIS and satellite image analysis) and field investigations to

Fig. 4

explore how the socio-spatial structures of cities have changed in relation to rural-to-urban migration and to reveal emerging social-spatial stratification.

The third involved detailed neighborhood-level research. First, we categorized neighborhoods in each city into five economic and wealth groups: low-income (including slums), lower middle-income, middle-income, higher middle-income, and high-income neighborhoods (including gated and privileged communities). We then carried out a comprehensive audit of housing, living conditions, and public service provision in one to three typical neighborhoods in each category. We also conducted face-to-face questionnaire interviews with a random or stratified sample of households in these neighborhoods. This household survey covered the socio-economic and demographic profiles of populations living in different types of urban neighborhoods. Moreover, it analyzed their experiences concerning health, education, neighborhood facilities, governance, economic opportunities and income, and the impacts of the COVID-19 pandemic. Finally, we organized focus group discussions with resident representatives in one neighborhood of each category to capture views and opinions about these communities, in addition to needs concerning health and education issues.

The fourth brought early findings together to develop an integrative and comparative analysis, highlighting similarities and differences between case study countries and cities.

Similar trends but different paths of urbanization

The SHLC study identified some common urbanization trends across these countries in Asia and Africa, including fast urban population growth caused by inward migration from rural areas, increased residential and building density in existing urban neighborhoods, a significant proportion of informal and spontaneous residential development, and limited provision of public services. In terms of health and education, a large proportion of urban residents are dependent on the private sector in most cities (apart from in China). In most African and Asian countries, slums (or informal, unregulated, unplanned, squatter settlements or colonies) can be found in various parts of the cities. Moreover, the decline of old public housing areas

Fig. 5

has been observed.[6,7] In all case study cities, people live in unique spatial environments consisting of a variety of neighborhoods, such as informal/unregulated/unplanned settlements of various types including slums, urban villages, townships, relocation settlements, privately constructed housing areas (either by commercial firms or individual families), gated or semi-gated communities of the rich, tenement and high-rise condominium/apartment block estates of the middle class, state-provided low-income settlements, and civil servant housing estates.

Very different paths of urbanization have also been observed between cities; for example, South African cities often exhibit serious inequality as a result of early apartheid policies and race segregation. Rich and middle-class white neighborhoods stand in sharp contrast to townships and emerging large-scale informal settlements of predominantly black and low-income communities. Contrastingly, cities in Tanzania and Rwanda have experienced extensive urban sprawl in their largest cities as a result of rapid economic growth, international trade, freedom of population movement, and lenient land use planning and building regulations. Huge areas of suburban rural land were designated for housing development, with landowners dividing their land into small plots and selling them to individuals to build detached houses. However, these "planned" settlements are often left without adequate infrastructure, such as surfaced roads, sewage, or drainage systems.

Urbanization in Asia shares some similarities with African cities, including private ownership of urban and rural land, small plots and family-organized construction, no large and commercially built housing estates, and very basic planning—all with varying degrees of informality. There are also very important differences. African urbanization is characterized by the horizontal expansion of individual family houses at very low density; in Asia (apart from China and some Chinese communities located in other Eastern Asian countries), new urban development is dominated by the construction of apartments in small tenement buildings. For example, Dhaka and Khulna in Bangladesh experienced rapid suburban expansion and inner area redevelopment characterized by the subdivision of family-owned land into plots and the construction

Fig. 6

Fig. 7

of individual multi-floor apartments. These were organized by either the original landlord or small housing cooperatives of middle-class families.

Comparison with China

As highlighted in Fig. 7, there are many differences in urban development between China and other countries, especially African countries. Through the SHLC project, I had a particular interest in finding out how Chinese urban villages compare with slums found in other developing countries. Policymakers in China often view urban villages in a very negative way. In the Chinese context, these are typically neighborhoods built on rural land now absorbed by cities and housing low-income communities. Often associated with unhygienic and overcrowded living conditions, poverty, crime, and backwardness, they are seen as a transitional stage towards modernization and full-scale urbanization, eventually replaced by professionally designed and constructed high-rise housing estates. However, the SHLC study shows that Chinese urban villages are very different from slums in other Asian and African

Fig. 1
Large high-rise housing estate in Datong, China.

Fig. 2
Selective rebuilding and urban intensification in Khulna, Bangladesh.

Fig. 3
Selection of different types of cities within case study countries for comparative analysis of neighborhoods.

Fig. 4
Recently built informal housing (COVID-19 settlement) in Cape Town, South Africa.

Fig. 5
Middle class, family-built suburban housing in Dar es Salaam, Tanzania.

Fig. 6
High-rise housing estate and community service center (*shequ*) in Datong, China.

Fig. 7
Middle-class housing as a result of plot-based redevelopment in Dhaka, Bangladesh.

Fig. 8
Comparing features of urban development across case study regions of China, South Asia, and Africa.

	China	South Asia	Africa
Initial focus of urban development	Mainly land use and property-focused urban development	Mainly resident-led urban development with some larger commercial projects	Mainly family and resident-led urban sprawl and development
Primary form of development	Modern multi-story buildings and tower blocks, homogeneity and uniformity	Mainly low-rise residential buildings with diversity in design and construction	Horizontal and low-density sprawl, simplicity, diversity, and flexibility
Urban-rural relations	Toward conurbations, metropolitan areas, and clusters of cities and towns; some degree of rural decline	Large-scale urban expansion in major cities and the creation of urban villages	Urban and rural segregation, urbanization of poverty
Main driving force and decision-making	Planner/architect and government official decisions; economic and political solutions	Landowner and individual middle-class family decisions, market solutions	Ordinary family/people's choice; market solutions and cultural continuation

Fig. 8

countries, where considerably worse living conditions were observed and residents face very different social, economic, political, and environmental challenges. We found that Chinese urban village development is actually very similar to the overarching processes of urbanization in countries like Tanzania and Bangladesh, where land is divided into small plots and construction of housing is organized primarily by individual families rather than large property developers. However, the large-scale commercial high-rise housing that has dominated China's urban development in the last thirty years has not been reproduced on a large scale in cities in the other countries we studied.

In China, urban development projects are initiated by the government (politicians and planners) and property developers. Housing estates are constructed before the arrival of people, while in other countries people arrive before housing construction. Not many governments in Asia and Africa have the political will and economic power to nationalize land for large-scale, professionally planned housing development, apart from limited areas in city centers. There are always questions over the long-term future of large-scale construction of high-rise and high-density residential estates in China; for example, whether the huge amount of expensive concrete buildings are assets or liabilities for future generations. With the current slowing of the urban property market and declining birth rate and total population, the voices posing such questions will become louder and clearer. If Chinese development practices are still in doubt, we need to think very carefully about the impact and suitability of these approaches to modernization in other countries.

Challenges and merits of comparative urban research

It has been long recognized that cross-country comparative urban research can lead to fresh, exciting insights and a deeper understanding of urban social, economic, and environmental issues proving central concerns in different countries.[8,9] It can also improve urban policy-making and practice by pointing to possible new directions that policymakers may not previously have been aware of. The SHLC project, funded by the UKRI (UK Research and Innovation) with eight international partners and led by the University of Glasgow, promoted productive research exchanges across case study countries. The South-South comparative framework allowed equal partnership between teams and shared responsibility and ownership in research design. As all case study citics undergo fast urbanization, the research teams can observe and learn from different global contexts with similar urban issues. The most interesting and important part of the project was to allow all researchers from case study cities to participate in fieldwork in other cities. This avoided the tendency of researchers based in Western countries to lead and tell researchers in developing countries what they should do. On a personal level, the project and its findings have changed some of my previous ideas about density, high-rise development, sustainability, and urbanization. Moreover, they have questioned my understanding of what a "good city" or a "good neighborhood" is, and how we should research our cities and plan their futures.

Conducting international comparisons also presents many difficulties. Language is the first; hence, finding the right collaborators in each country is very important. SHLC was lucky to have research teams who speak English in each of the case study countries. Even so, there remain disparities over the meaning of key terms or concepts in urban research. For example, the term "neighborhood" is an ambiguous and debatable concept. In China, it could refer to a newly built housing estate or an urban village; in other countries, it could be an informal settlement or colony (as in India). Therefore, we must allow for flexibility in defining comparable spatial and social units in practice. Moreover, a lack of comparable data could be another major challenge. Official statistics could be collected at different times with different definitions as not every country has the same data collection framework.

More importantly, cities, neighborhoods, and urban problems are embedded in each country's socio-economic, political, cultural, historical, and environmental context. Urban problems in neighboring countries which share some common history and regional cultural values—such as India and Bangladesh, or Tanzania and Rwanda—could be easily compared and analysed. Comparative urban studies in countries located far apart or with very different historical, cultural, and political systems—such as China and India—are more difficult. In such cases, similar urban problems could result from very different causes and policies. This does not mean we should avoid comparison. If the comparative study is well designed, there are always many lessons to be learned and the rich knowledge gained from very different contexts could lead to innovative ideas. When conducting comparative urban research, I always follow a clear framework. For similar countries with comparable stages of development and shared heritages or political systems, a comparative study can focus tightly on key research topics. Contrastingly, for very different countries, to achieve an in-depth understanding of the urban problems and issues we must first pay particular attention to each national and local socio-economic, political, historical, cultural, and environmental context.

Considering the challenges raised above, cross-country comparative studies should not aim for quick and direct transfers or copying of specific practices or policies from one system to another. Multi-country comparisons should be pursued to broaden the knowledge base for theoretical development, as well as new innovative urban policy design. Moreover, comparative case studies should be viewed as experimental labs for idea and policy testing. It is unlikely that professionally planned, designed, financed, and constructed cities and housing estates in China will become a dominant urban development paradigm for other developing countries soon. They lack the strong political will of the government, state ownership of land, and willingness of people to move to such high-density areas. It is also equally unlikely that China will adopt the flexible and family-led form of African urbanization. However, lessons from other countries can help Chinese policymakers reflect on their model of development in view of long-term sustainability. Ultimately, well-designed comparative research frameworks involving in-country partners and a mutual understanding of each other's cities are essential in finding tailored and effective solutions to our common global urban problems.

1 United Nations Human Settlements Programme, "The New Urban Agenda," *World Cities Report 2016* (United Nations, 2016), 175–95.

2 National Bureau of Statistics of China, *Annual Data on Population*, accessed March 29, 2024, https://data.stats.gov.cn.

3 Ya Ping Wang, *A Comparative Study of Urban Land Use Planning Systems in Scotland and China: with case studies in Edinburgh and Xian*, PhD Thesis, Heriot-Watt University, Edinburgh, 1991, http://hdl.handle.net/10399/2117.

4 Ya Ping Wang, *Urban Poverty, Housing and Social Change in China* (London and New York: Routledge, 2004).

5 The SHLC project resulted in a large number of reports and other publications which are accessible on the project website: https://www.centreforsustainablecities.ac.uk/. SHLC data has been published by the UK Data Service at ReShare and can be accessed and downloaded from the ReShare website: https://reshare.ukdataservice.ac.uk/855998/.

6 David Everatt, Halfdan Lynge, and Caryn Abrahams, *Neighbourhood Characteristics and Inequality in the City of Johannesburg* (SHLC, 2023), https://www.centreforsustainablecities.ac.uk/research.

7 Ivan Turok, Justin Visagie, and Andreas Scheba, *Neighbourhood Matters in Cape Town* (SHLC, 2023), https://www.centreforsustainablecities.ac.uk/research.

8 Jennifer Robinson, ed., *Comparative Urbanism: Tactics for Global Urban Studies* (Hoboken, NJ: Wiley, 2022).

9 Arnold J. Heidenheimer, Hugh Heclo, and Carolyn T. Adams, *Comparative Public Policy: The Politics of Social Choice in America, Europe and Japan* (New York: St. Martin's Press, 1990).

Fig. 1

Fig. 2

Applying the “Horizontal Metropolis” framework in the Yangtze River Delta

Andrea Palmioli

Over the past four decades, the Yangtze River Delta has undergone significant urbanization and industrialization, transforming it into a mega-urban region encompassing Shanghai and the provinces of Jiangsu, Zhejiang, and Anhui. These areas are interconnected through economic, social, and infrastructural networks and are characterized by high levels of economic integration, extensive transportation systems, a shared environmental heritage, and multifunctional rural areas. As of 2023, the Yangtze River Delta accounts for a substantial portion of China's land area, population, and GDP, making it one of the world's largest conurbations facing unique challenges. These include environmental sustainability, urban sprawl, and the need for coordinated governance across different administrative areas. The urban expansion of the Yangtze River Delta has escalated market demand in sectors like food production and industry, impacting both agricultural lands and rural communities. A rural-to-urban shift in the region has emerged as a paradigmatic example of the intricate interplay between urban expansion and rural environments (Fig. 1 and 2). This shift, marked by urban migration and challenges, such as depopulated “hollow villages,” has prompted new policies to adopt rural revitalization strategies, blending rural progress with urban advancement and leveraging digital technology. In this context, the significance of the “Horizontal Metropolis” research protocol becomes apparent. The concept of “horizontality” is adopted to envision complementarity or interdependence between different parts of the territory,[1] operating in practice through localized urban design interventions interlinking and rebalancing cultural, economic, environmental, and social capitals between rural-urban realms.

Dealing with these variegated forms of entanglement necessitates an actionable framework to enhance the living conditions and spatial networks in the region, thereby informing more effective rural-urban development strategies. The following sections unfold in three parts: first, it will trace the historical evolution and theoretical underpinnings of the Horizontal Metropolis research protocol's, offering insights into its genesis and intellectual framework; second, the discussion explains the protocols application, systematically exploring its tools, steps, and objectives to understand urban-rural interplay; lastly, it advances a new perspective on the integration and re-envisioning of rural spaces within the Yangtze River Delta, advocating for holistic strategies to bridge the rural-urban divide in the research methodologies of urban design.

The genealogy of the Horizontal Metropolis research protocol

The urbanization process is commonly interpreted as a departure from the traditional equilibrium between rural and urban landscapes. This shift, often deemed a byproduct of modernization, is becoming manifest in urban sprawl. The dissolution of this equilibrium has been perceived as haphazard and unstructured, resulting in scattered fragments without coherence. Contrasting this perspective, certain urban economic and geographical studies in Italy have emphasized the evolution of society and territories as a continuous, fracture-free transformation[2] resulting in a new mode of "diffuse urbanization."[3] This complex type of urbanization lacks the density and intensity typical of metropolitan cores, instead spreading over wider territories. It encompasses a network of small and medium-sized urban centers surrounded by less densely built-up areas, integrating both residential and productive activities and serving a significant portion of the population within their ecosystems.

The evolution of these studies is embedded in a broader context of European research in urbanism that investigates the intermingling of rural and urban settings, as expressed in concepts like Italy's "Diffuse City," Germany's "Zwischenstadt," and Flanders' "Radiant Periphery," along with McGee's "Desakota" in Asia.[4] The acknowledgment of the "diffuse urbanization" represents a shift from traditional theories of urban sprawl towards a refined comprehension of urban dispersion alongside rural-urban land use dynamics and its management strategies. Based on this theoretical groundwork, Paola Viganò and Bernardo Secchi initially developed the Horizontal Metropolis concept in 2011 as a territorial vision for Brussels and Flanders, transcending traditional demarcations between urban contexts and rural landscapes.[5] The vision recognized the intricate web of relationships among mid-sized cities in the larger metropolitan area, emphasizing a landscape not limited by administrative boundaries but shaped by topography, where urban, agricultural, and open spaces are interwoven. Moreover, it encouraged ecological coexistence and diversity within a dynamic, integrated rural-urban continuum. The approach has developed into an action-oriented research protocol, culminating in the "Horizontal Metropolis: a Radical Project" exhibition in urbanism, presented as a collateral event at the Venice Architecture Biennale in 2016.[6] The initial exhibition covers five case studies of diffuse urbanization in Venice, Boston, Valais, Lausanne, and Hangzhou, with Hong Kong also featured in a follow-up exhibition in 2021. Developed out of this earlier stage and case studies, the research protocol has been applied in the Yangtze River Delta, proposing five rural-urban visions encompassing Shanghai, Suzhou, Hangzhou, Ningbo, and Nantong. The research outcomes have been showcased in the exhibition "Horizontal Metropolis Yangtze River Delta: Entangling Capitals"[7] (Fig. 4). This new exhibition expands the Horizontal Metropolis concept by introducing the notion of "capital entanglement," inspired by the quantum physics phenomenon of entanglement linking particles across spatial divides. It underscores the importance of examining spatial dynamics across scattered or non-coherent territories in an interconnected manner, offering a pathway to a more comprehensive understanding of socio-spatial relations within the realms of urbanism, political science, and social sciences.[8]

Applying the research protocol in the Yangtze River Delta

The exhibition aimed at devising comprehensive design practices for non-centralized spatial structures by creating a direct linkage between the initial regional analyses and broader, future-oriented urban strategies. It was organized into three fundamental parts: "Traditions, people and places,""Measures," and "A radical project." "Traditions, people and places" bridged theoretical interpretations of "diffuse urbanization" through a series of video interviews by scholars (e.g., John Friedman, Terence McGee, Francesco Indovina, Andrea Branzi, Thomas Sieverts, Marcel Smets, Bernardo Secchi) with tangible contexts described through fieldwork expeditions conducted in each case study area. These were characterized by a combination of ground-level observations, annotative mapping, and spatial sampling (e.g., flora, building typologies), engaging interviews with local inhabitants, and drone recordings (Fig. 3). All these tools aimed to capture a reliable understanding of each milieu, including the everyday spaces, prevailing lifestyles, and productive activities within these regions. Ultimately, they endeavored to link long-term territorial development with contemporary landscapes.

The section "Measures" sought to comprehend the spatial characteristics of the selected territories through an examination of their measurements, consistency,

Rural settlement growth in the Yangtze River Delta

Fig. 3

Fig. 4

and rationalization. It aimed to identify transforming structures emerging from historical settings (e.g., increase of built-up areas, rectification of the irrigation system). Three different territorial frames (50 by 50 kilometers, 10 by 10 kilometers, and 3.2 by 3.2 kilometers) (Fig. 5) were utilized to sample each territory and to identify distinct morphological characteristics at these different scales. The first, a mesoscale of 50 by 50 kilometers (Fig. 6), captures large-scale systems, landforms, and ecological dynamics, enabling an understanding of the territorial structures and their historical legacies. The second is a more detailed scale of 10 by 10 kilometers, which captures the urban dimension where environmental and built structures exhibit more complex interactions to provide a nuanced understanding of the urban fabric, collective spaces, and forests. The third scale, 3.2 by 3.2 kilometers (Fig. 7), deliberately refers to Frank Loyd Wright's "Broadacre City" (1932)—a territorial vision of dispersed urbanization that was similarly adopted in visions by the Atelier international du Grand Paris. The overall cartography, regardless of the adopted scale or representation, contributes to the description of five main territorial aspects: urbanization, water (i.e., hydrological) networks, mobility infrastructures, productive landscapes, and forests. Additionally, thematic maps at various scales covered specific topics, such as flooding scenarios, spatial distribution of place names, and diachronic urban sprawl.

In a practical sense, the series of mappings derives from the "Latin square," a method initially proposed by Ronald Fisher in 1925. Originating from the field of combinatorial mathematics, it is characterized by a matrix with an equal number of rows and columns, where each cell has distinct features. In urbanism, the Latin square can be utilized as a tool for spatial sampling and analysis to obtain a representative sample of an entire urban region. It facilitates the identification of patterns and relationships between different urban features, aiding in more informed decision-making.

The data revealed in each sampling describe the physical form of the analyzed case studies. This corpus of descriptions helps to identify the spatial characteristics and their resilience to short-term changes. It serves as a foundation for the development of strategic visions for territorial metamorphosis and is intended to support the process of adapting or modifying dispersed and intermingled spaces in rural-urban contexts. Ultimately, statistical data for each territory showcase comparable information, such as demographics, the extent of built-up areas, and energy consumption, along with the GDP per capita (Fig. 8). These key figures help to compare the different territories and identify distinctive characteristics, dynamics, differences, and commonalities.

Within the section "A radical project," highly interpretive visions of the Horizontal Metropolis were developed, elaborating on the capabilities of diffuse territories through axonometric representations and physical models (measuring 3.65 by 3.65 meters). Here, contexts, themes, and hypotheses have been explored through the identification of "figures of space" (urban-territorial structuring devices) and "socio-spatial prototypes" (spatial adaptations within both urban and open spaces). From this identification and the interaction and replication of these elements, new "design rules" were formulated which inspired the development of strategic scenarios. "Figures of space" are extracted from the context and are essentially structures with specific morphological characters, which reveal or construct relationships among different elements and help to articulate spaces. These figures can act as connectors, like canals, civic streets, or rivers, strengthening the connectivity and accessibility of each place. Additionally, they can incorporate

Framing of sampling areas in Nantong Prefecture

Fig. 5

Productive landscapes in Nantong Prefecture

Fig. 6

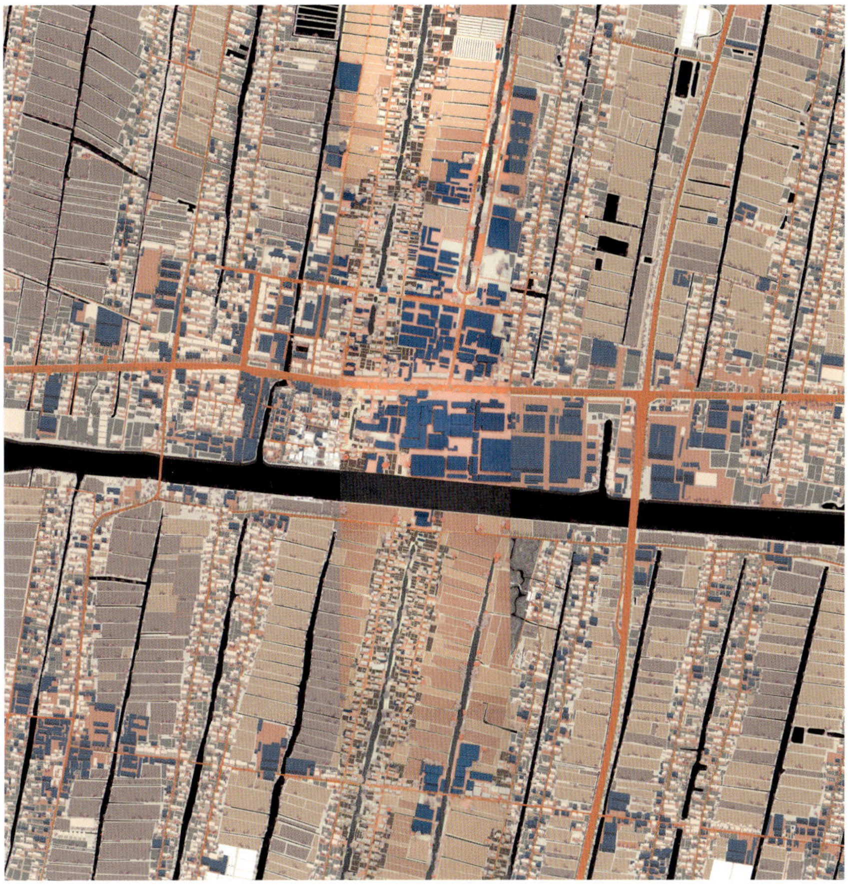

Fig. 7

0 km 3.2 km

landscape components, such as cultivated land systems or elements of ecological corridors. These devices or elements lend coherent structure to the Horizontal Metropolis and define a new spatial synthesis. The figures which result from the selection of spatial elements belonging to different systems (like water systems, landscapes, mobility infrastructures, etc.) are then recombined into new hybrid configurations; for example, by integrating water management, rural infrastructures, and built settlements (Fig. 9). They serve a dual purpose: symbolically encapsulating complex realities and acting as cognitive tools to bridge conceptual understanding with imaginative explorations. This dual functionality facilitates a deeper comprehension of the spatial dynamics, even in contexts where they are not directly measurable.

"Socio-spatial prototypes" are developed based on the identified figures, aiming to explore how design interventions can be replicated in similar spatial contexts. These spatial prototypes suggest guidelines for spatial coexistence between different elements (such as natural features and structural components). For instance, in the vision for Nantong prefecture in China, the approach diversified monofunctional cropping areas by integrating wetlands and floodable zones. Residential spaces have been merged with cultural centers, smart working spaces, and public facilities (Fig. 10). This broad set of interventions has been specifically applied in the design strategies detailed in corresponding maps. The visions were represented in physical models measuring 3.65 by 3.65 meters and scaled at 1:877 (based on the dimensions of Wright's famous Broadacre City model), which translates the entire range of interventions into a tangible territorial representation of the Yangtze River Delta Horizontal Metropolis (Fig. 11). These models offer a comprehensive view of the various urban and landscape environments, showcasing settlements, productive areas (like industrial and agricultural zones), and natural terrains (including forests, meadows, and rivers). Through this detailed vision, the models effectively demonstrate the organizational principles underlying diffuse urbanization.

Finally, the whole set of research outputs, including recordings, maps, statistical data, project drawings, and physical models, is compiled into atlases with

Statistical key figures in comparison

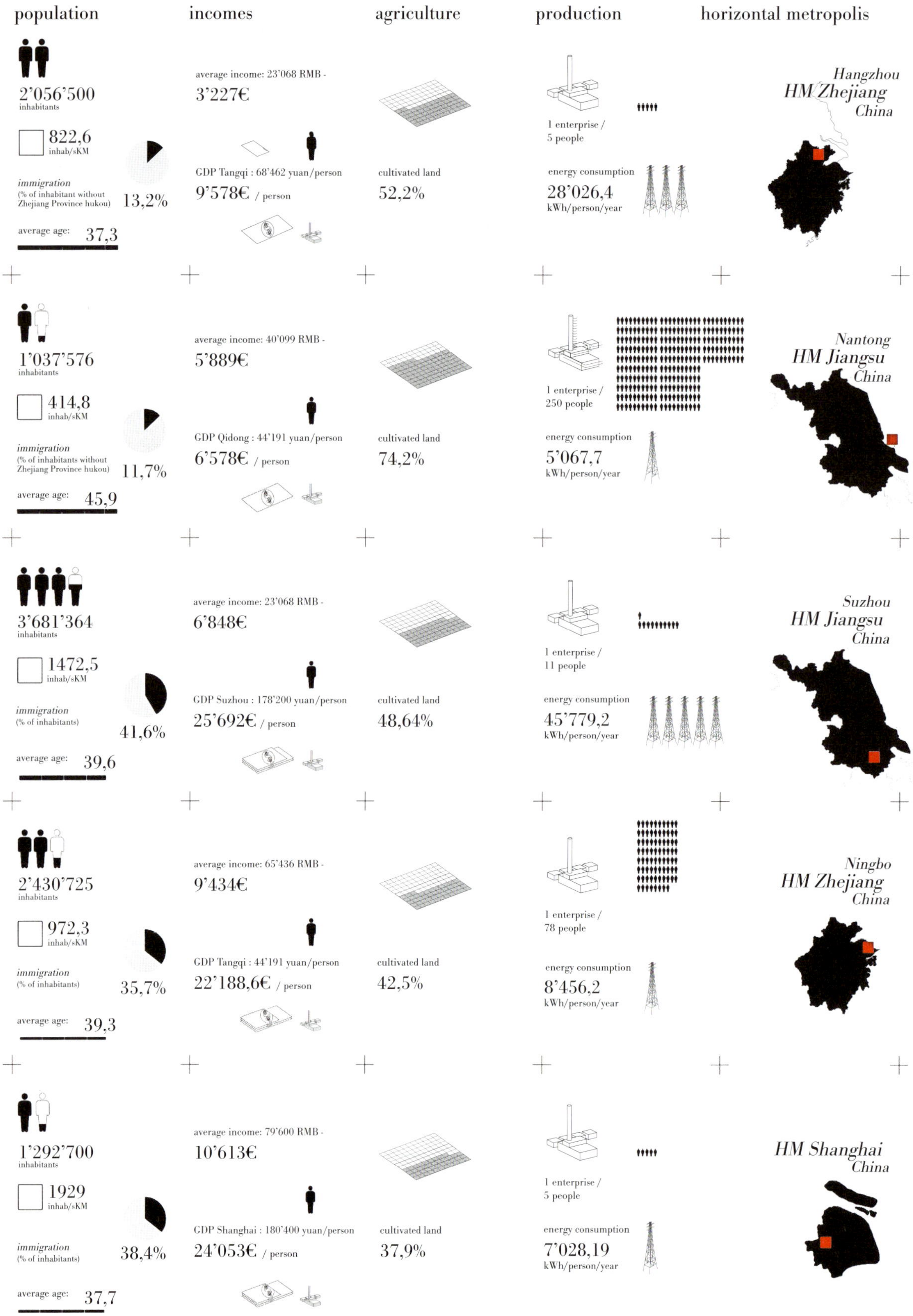

Fig. 8

"Figure of Space": design interventions in Tianfen Village

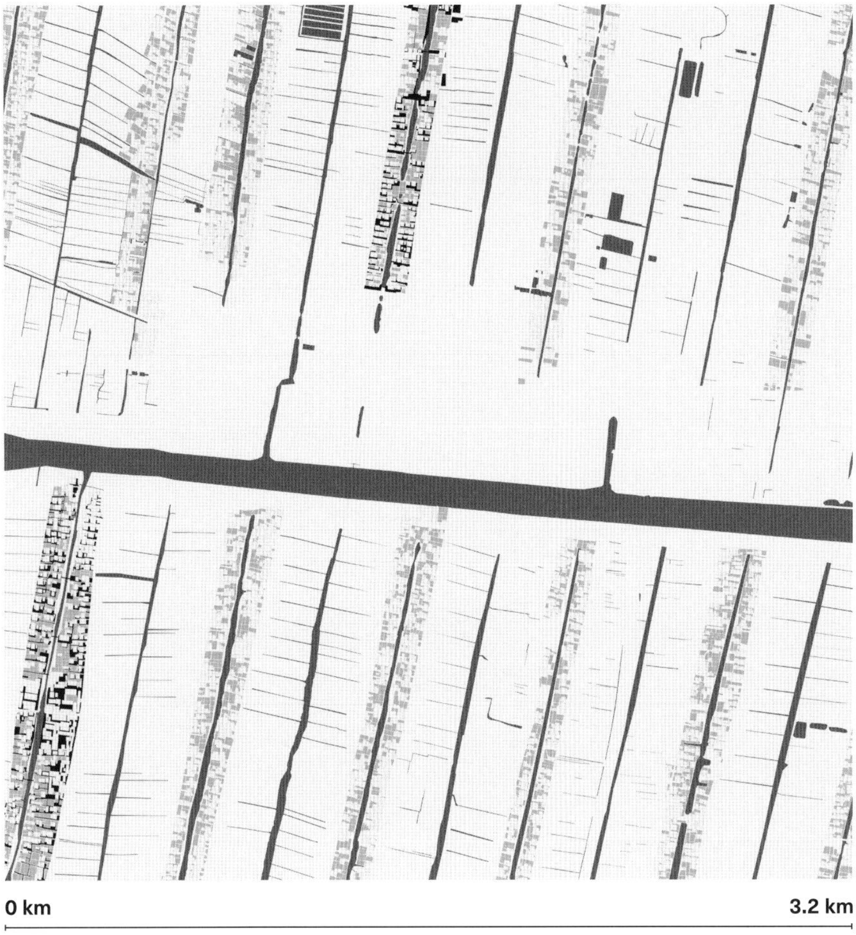

Fig. 9

one dedicated to each case study. An atlas serves as a detailed compendium, outlining hypotheses for the future development of territories under the Horizontal Metropolis research protocol. The creation of an atlas, along with a comprehensive database for the new territorial visions in the Yangtze River Delta, plays a crucial role for several reasons: firstly, each project within the atlas highlights evolving issues or areas of interest, showcasing the dynamic nature of collective spaces and their perceptions; secondly, an atlas offers a platform to assess the coherence of various projects, evaluating them in quantitative and functional (alongside morphological and cultural) perspectives; thirdly, it serves as a strategic tool, detailing the specific characteristics of a territory and informing the selection of actions within implementation strategies; fourthly, the atlas emphasizes the inertia of spatial elements, vis-à-vis more dynamic aspects such as technological development and migration. This inertia endures through the physical legacy of several generations that are utilized and interpreted in various ways. Essentially, the atlas acts as a platform, linking different interventions and fostering connections between projects.

Re-envisioning the "constitutive outside"

As Paola Viganò underscores, the Horizontal Metropolis research protocol establishes a comprehensive framework encompassing analytical mapping, statistical analysis, and design strategies.[9] Notably, distinguished by its adaptability, a protocol deliberately avoids the rigidity or extensive detailing of case-specific techniques or procedures which mainly characterize a research methodology. The research protocol pursues two main objectives: firstly, to advocate for a "non-selective design" in spatial planning, and secondly, to foster a vision of "territorial metamorphosis." The concept of "non-selective design" denotes a strategy that avoids giving precedence to—or excluding—any specific elements or areas in urban and rural development projects. It seeks to integrate a diverse array of spatial, social, and ecological factors, aiming for a comprehensive and cohesive transformation across urban and rural landscapes. Accordingly, a "territorial metamorphosis" implies an extensive reconfiguration of a territory's structure and functions beyond mere changes or transformations that might be partial or specific.

Fig. 10

Fig. 1
Drone shot of Tianfen Village in Nantong Prefecture, located in southeastern Jiangsu Province, China.

Fig. 2
Aerial view of the main canal connecting Nantong City to Lvsigang Town, part of a vital water transportation network stretching from the Yangtze River to the East China Sea.

Fig. 3
Growth of settlement areas officially defined as "rural" in the Yangtze River Delta, 1980-2018.

Fig. 4
The "Horizontal Metropolis" exhibition in Hangzhou showcased the Yangtze River Delta visions, including an atlas, model, and video for each case study.

Fig. 5
This map of Nantong Prefecture shows the framing of the 50 by 50, 10 by 10, and 3.2 by 3.2 kilometer sampling areas, which were applied in each case study.

Fig. 6
Mapping of productive landscapes in Nantong Prefecture within a 50 by 50 kilometer frame.

Fig. 7
A strategic intervention in Tianfen Village (Nantong Prefecture) was showcased in a model covering 3.2 by 3.2 kilometers. A strip-shaped physical model was inserted into an axonometric drawing.

Fig. 8
Comparison of statistical key figures from case studies in Yangtse River Delta.

Fig. 9
"Figure of space": Diagrammatic mapping of strategic interventions in Tianfen Village (a 3.2 by 3.2 kilometer frame).

Fig. 10
Physical model depicting design interventions in Tianfen Village.

This overhauled transformation is characterized by a continuous transition, serving to properly capture the nuanced interactions between change and continuity within rural and urban landscapes, as envisaged by the research protocol.

Ananya Roy introduces the concept of "constitutive outside" to describe the rural as an integral element shaping the urban landscape.[10] In doing so, Roy highlights the interconnectedness and interdependence between urban and rural spaces. In an era of planetary urbanization, acknowledging the role of rural areas in defining urban spaces becomes essential for devising comprehensive strategies for these intertwined spaces.[11] Applying the Horizontal Metropolis research protocol in the Chinese context re-envisioned the current understanding of rural-urban dynamics by examining the Yangtze River Delta, a region where urbanization is deeply intertwined with historical agrarian legacies and rural landscapes. The research findings underlined the interdependence of rural-urban spaces, which is key to addressing the complexities of present-day urban landscapes. The Horizontal Metropolis Yangtze River Delta established a foundational contribution to challenge the conventional notion that the "urban" exists in isolation from its rural surroundings. It has stressed the need to integrate the rural-urban continuum in urban studies and regional policies, advocating for the role of urban and territorial design as an enabler of new collective imaginaries for the future of rural-urban metropolises.

This research was made possible through the support of the National Natural Science Foundation of China (NSFC), under the General Grant with Approval Number 42071190, to whom we extend our deepest gratitude.

1 Paola Viganò, "The Horizontal Metropolis: A Radical Project," in *The Horizontal Metropolis Between Urbanism and Urbanization*, eds. Paola Viganò, Chiara Cavalieri, and Martina Barcelloni Corte (Cham: Springer International Publishing, 2018), 1–9.

2 Giorgio Fuà, "L'industrializzazione nel Nord Est e nel Centro," in *Industrializzazione senza fratture*, ed. Carlo Zacchia (Bologna: Il mulino, 1983), 7–46.

3 Chiara Barattucci, "Italian Neologisms to Name Diffuse Urbanization. Relationships between Specialised Language and Urbanism Actions," *Journal of Urbanism: International Research on Placemaking and Urban Sustainability* 0, no. 0 (2022): 1–14.

4 Martina Barcelloni Corte and Paola Viganò, eds., *The Horizontal Metropolis: The Anthology* (Cham: Springer International Publishing, 2022).

5 Bernardo Secchi and Paola Viganò, *Antwerp, Territory of a New Modernity* (Amsterdam: Sun Publisher, 2009).

6 The "Horizontal Metropolis: A Radical Project" was exhibited previously at EPFL University of Lausanne (2015), the Venice Biennale of Architecture (2016), at Brussels Bozar with specific reference to the Flanders region (2018), at Shenzhen Bi-City Biennale (2019), and the Hong Kong City Gallery focusing on Hong Kong rural territories (2021). "Hong Kong Horizontal Metropolis," last modified June 3, 2024, https://hkhm.org.

7 The exhibition, curated by Andrea Palmioli and Paola Viganò, was first exhibited at Hangzhou West Railway Station from November 18 to December 10, 2023. "Horizontal Metropolis Yangtze River Delta: Entangling Capitals," last modified June 3, 2024, http://www.hmyrd.org/.

8 The analogy with quantum entanglement offers a novel perspective on state power and social relations by suggesting that these forces can extend beyond physical boundaries in a manner akin to entangled particles in quantum physics. Entangled particles maintain a connection despite the distance, implying that actions affecting one particle can instantaneously influence the other, regardless of the space between them. Similarly, state influence and social dynamics can manifest across spatial divides, challenging the traditional notion of territory as strictly geographically bounded. This perspective encourages a deeper analysis of how state power and governance operate and interact across and beyond territorial limits, recognizing the complex, interconnected nature of political, social, and spatial phenomena. Daniel Neep, "State-Space beyond Territory: Wormholes, Gravitational Fields, and Entanglement," *Journal of Historical Sociology* 30, no. 3 (2017): 466–95.

9 Chiara Cavalieri and Paola Viganò, eds., *HM the Horizontal Metropolis: A Radical Project* (Zurich: Park Books, 2019).

10 Ananya Roy, "What Is Urban about Critical Urban Theory?" *Urban Geography* 37, no. 6 (2016): 810–23.

11 Neil Brenner, *Implosions / Explosions: Towards a Study of Planetary Urbanization* (Berlin: JOVIS, 2013).

Fig. 1

Fig. 2

Facilitating stakeholder participation in land use planning: Lessons from a transdisciplinary Sino-German project

Jue Wang

The development of sustainable land management strategies depends on various and heterogeneous stakeholders from multiple disciplines and positionalities, in addition to their knowledge of local issues. It is therefore currently widely accepted that land use planning requires a careful evaluation of multiple stakeholder interests and influences in the decision-making process to facilitate negotiations, reduce conflict, foster mutual learning, and increase buy-in for decisions made.[1] Compared with "inter-disciplinarity" and "multi-disciplinarity," the concept of "transdisciplinarity" is interpreted as a crossing of boundaries between scientifically trained individuals and non-scientists, as well as going beyond conventional research to the implementation of solutions.[2] Within such an approach, appropriate methods must be carefully developed or adapted to safeguard participation and integrate various stakeholder perspectives. These include "stakeholder analysis"—a constructive approach to understanding stakeholder needs, interests, and interrelations—and "stakeholder participation"—a process in which stakeholders are empowered to take an active role in decision-making.

Stakeholders are individuals, groups, or organizations that can affect—or are affected by—a decision or action, both positively and negatively.[3] For a research consortium, this includes both scientific stakeholders from the research project and non-academic stakeholders. Stakeholder analysis generally consists of four main steps: identifying the issue, identifying stakeholders, investigating stakeholder interests, and investigating stakeholder interrelations.[4] While a range of tools for each step can be applied to gain a holistic understanding of stakeholders in the system, a tailor-made approach is necessary to adapt to the real-world complexities of their interactions.

Reed defines participation as "... a process where individuals, groups, and organizations choose to take an active role in making decisions that affect them."[5] Stakeholder participation is now seen as essential in many research projects to generate more effective solutions and create ownership of project outcomes. There are several degrees of participation, ranging from passive to active forms, with many methods and techniques available depending on project objectives.[6,7] The methods chosen depend on several factors, such as the

Fig. 3

degree of participation, types of stakeholders, local conditions, and available resources.[8,9] Moreover, triangulation of methods is necessary to meet multiple demands in projects involving various stakeholders during different phases.

This article presents a case study of transdisciplinary land use planning using the Sino-German Sustainable Rubber Cultivation in the Mekong Region (SURUMER) project as an exemplar, summarizing the tools and experiences involved while offering lessons for future research.

A multi-stakeholder process toward sustainable rubber cultivation in Xishuangbanna

Xishuangbanna, in China's Yunnan Province, is one of the world's richest biodiversity regions and is also known as the "Indo-Burma hotspot." In recent decades, the rapid expansion of rubber plantations has positively contributed to local economic development; however, it has also caused environmental degradation and vulnerability in local livelihoods. SURUMER intended to develop an integrative, applicable, and stakeholder-validated concept for sustainable rubber cultivation in Xishuangbanna (Fig. 3). The goal was to transfer scientific concepts into practical land use solutions to be achieved jointly by scientists and various stakeholders.

The SURUMER project included various scientific disciplines (such as social science, environmental science, agriculture, and ecology) and heterogeneous society groups (such as Non-Governmental Organizations (NGOs), local governments, villagers, international organizations, state farms, and businesses) as part of a typical transdisciplinary consortium in which actors cooperate across geographical, professional, and cultural boundaries. It was carried out in China, where decision-making processes are strongly top-down with limited stakeholder participation. The experiences gathered from the project provide meaningful insights into how transdisciplinary project management could take shape under diverse social and cultural contexts. SURUMER consisted of nine research subprojects structured in three main project phases: Phase I included land use assessment; Phase II covered modeling trade-offs and synergies between alternative land uses; Phase III included valuation of acceptance of

Stakeholder analysis

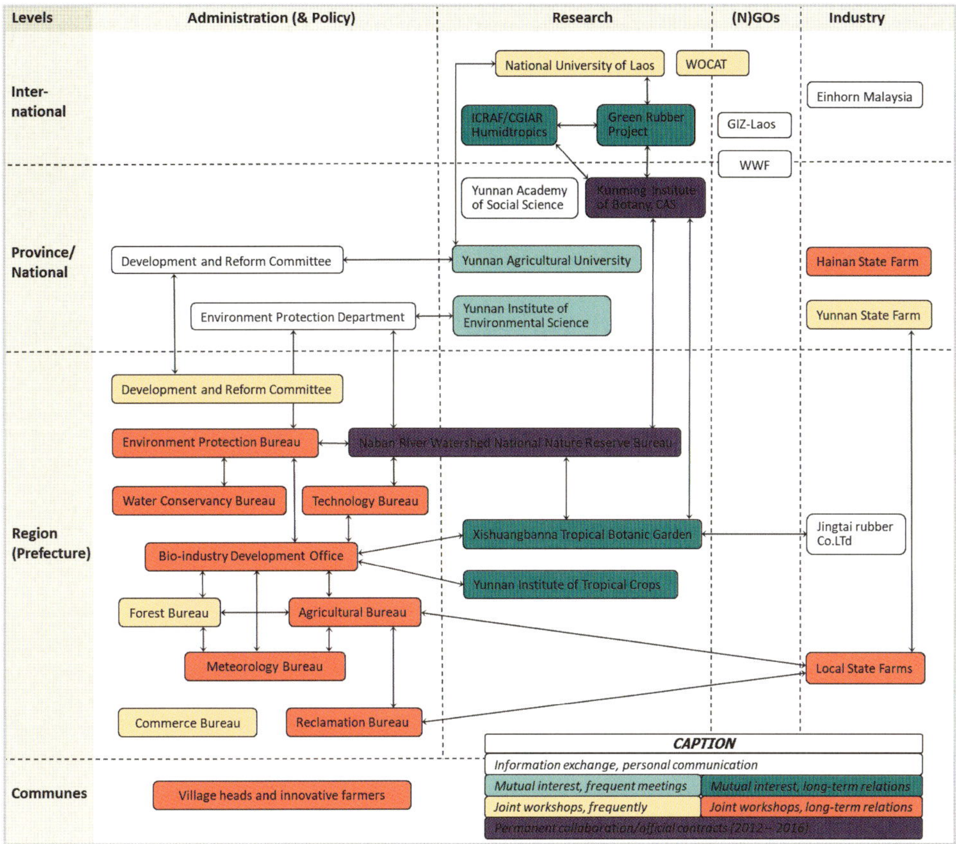

Fig. 4

solutions. Knowledge transfer and communication processes were fundamental principles of the project.

Analyzing stakeholder interests, networks, and interactions

As a first step, gaining in-depth knowledge about the local context can identify the most relevant stakeholders for involvement. In SURUMER, local actors were asked about land use problems and objectives. The results highlighted a need to further clarify identified problems, a process which lasted for the entire project duration. This included participatory rural appraisals and a series of multi-actor workshops.[10] To achieve a deeper understanding of our findings, the reasoning behind actor perceptions of issues was further explored, for instance, regarding the commonly identified theme of "water issues": while farmers were most concerned with drinking water quality, managers primarily foregrounded environmental degradation. Therefore, allowing this dialogues became a window for scientists to comprehend local conditions in more depth and encouraged practitioners to exchange perspectives.

The second step involves identifying stakeholders to stimulate communication across actor groups and disciplines. In SURUMER, important decision-making groups were identified using the "snowball" technique, which involves bringing in further stakeholders through networking. Researchers and their local partners first brainstormed a list of groups affected by decision-makers of regional land use development; representatives of these groups were then asked to confirm and modify the list. Three groups were identified: regional decision-makers (administration, institutes, and enterprises) with a central role in shaping land management; farmers, as the direct users of the land; and actors at the provincial level (policymakers, institutes, and NGOs) who govern the broader policy setting. Stakeholder roles in the research and implementation of the project were evaluated to develop a more sustainable concept for rubber cultivation.

A further step of identifying stakeholder interests could deepen the understanding of their needs and enhance their motivation to improve the situation. In SURUMER, we asked stakeholders about their views on other stakeholder opinions. Such approaches may

Fig. 5

Fig. 6

be particularly important and effective for topics in which people feel more comfortable talking about others rather than about themselves. In addition, stakeholder interests and expectations were obtained by scoring methods: stakeholders valued a series of land use measures by expressing their subjective preferences ("wishes") and their predictions based on experience ("assumptions") as indicators of the likelihood of implementation. The scores of wishes and assumptions can be seen as stakeholders' votes for these scenarios, from which relevant strategies could be developed for the most favorable scenario for the majority to increase implementation acceptability. This helped researchers target the critical issues among many research topics and set priorities linked to practitioner needs and interests.

Moreover, exploring stakeholder networks and interactions is vital in providing clues for more successful implementation. In SURUMER, formal hierarchies among actors were well known, while informal decision-making structures required more exploration. Qualitative methods—such as in-depth interviews—were applied, in which interview partners were asked to self-assess their relations with proxy indicators. These included official status, reputational influences, decision-making abilities, and communication patterns among actors. Participants were also asked about their views on other stakeholders as part of a crosscheck. With roles, functions, and networks more clearly illustrated and understood (Fig. 4),[11] implementation was expected to be more plausible in labor and task division and therefore more likely to lead to sustained effects.

Methods aimed at meaningful stakeholder participation

The overall goal of stakeholder participation in SURUMER was to build an ongoing dialogue to enhance communication among stakeholders and develop sustainable land management strategies for implementation. Over thirty scientists were involved in the project, with approximately half directly interacting with non-academic stakeholders during field research, focus group discussions, workshops, and meetings (Fig. 1,2,5,6). Approximately five provincial and twenty

Phased application of participatory methods

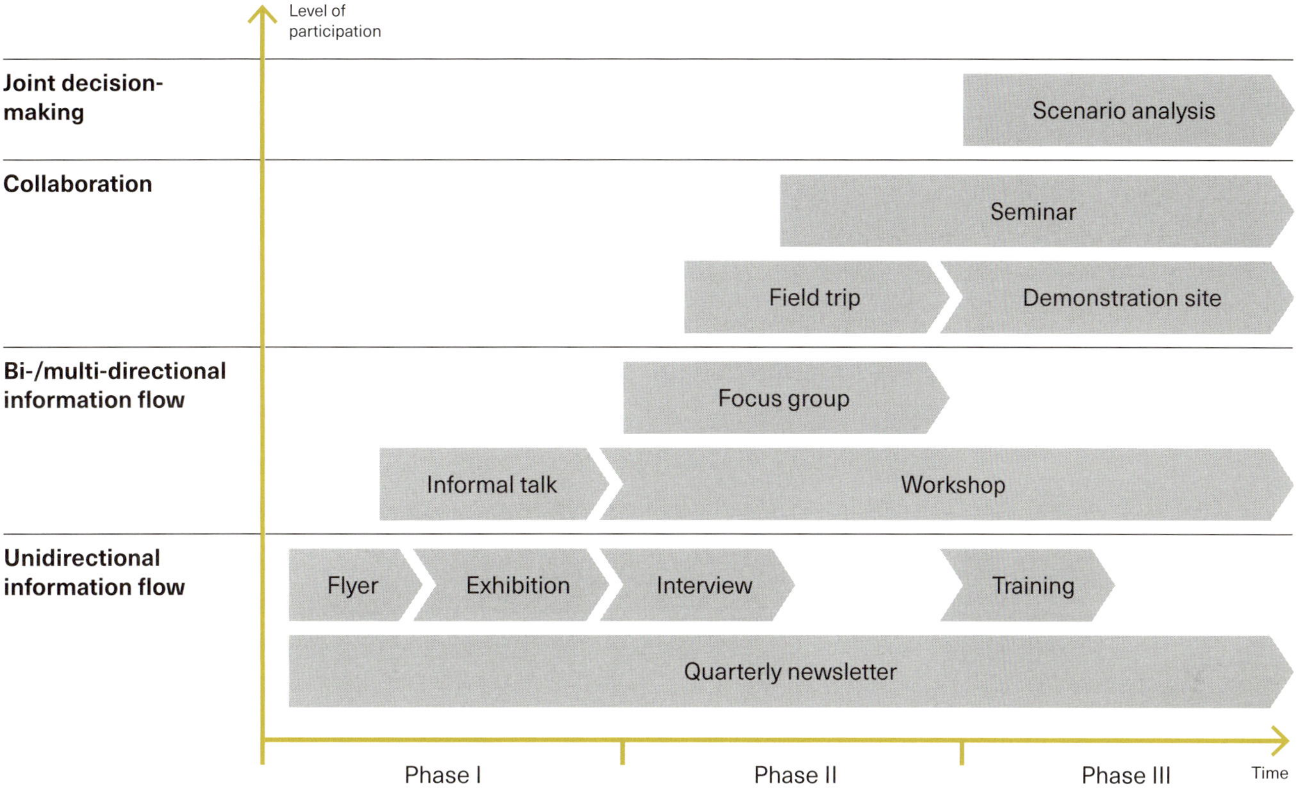

Fig. 7

regional decision-makers alongside ten village heads were consistently involved in dialogue during these events.

Fig. 7 summarizes the methods applied during the project with gradually intensified participation. Methods for passive participation are noted at the bottom of the figure; flyers, newsletters, a small exhibition, and field trips were used to introduce the project to practitioners in the first instance. Such methods were then continuously applied throughout the project as primary communication channels among stakeholders. Moving towards higher levels of participation, consultation methods—informal talks and meetings—enabled stakeholder identification, providing an overview of key issues and stakeholders at the beginning of the process. Open, semi-structured, and in-depth interviews were used as consultation tools to collect stakeholder ideas, while a series of workshops relating to key topics gradually gained further depth and provided platforms for science-practice interaction and joint decision-making. Practical and action-oriented learning measures were also implemented, with indoor activities (e.g., focus groups and workshops) supplemented by outdoor

Fig. 1
Researchers learn about land use issues in Xishuangbanna, Yunnan Province, through field trips with local stakeholders.

Fig. 2
Stakeholder workshops were held to promote transdisciplinary dialogue on sustainable land management strategies.

Fig. 3
Rubber plantations in Xishuangbanna have expanded over recent years, with varied impacts on local economies, livelihoods, and the environment.

Fig. 4
Analysis of networks and relationships among diverse stakeholders engaged in the SURUMER project.

Fig. 5
Village heads were consistently involved in participatory events such as focus group discussions.

Fig. 6
Interviews with local farmers revealed key concerns about income generation and water supply.

Fig. 7
Overview of participatory methods used in SURUMER, illustrating a gradual increase in participation levels.

activities (e.g., field excursions and on-farm demonstrations). Moreover, participation techniques were chosen to correspond to the varying needs and communication patterns of each stakeholder group: an exhibition, open interviews, and a training unit for farmers; in-depth interviews, field trips, workshops, and scenario discussions for regional decision-makers; and newsletters, meetings, and workshops for provincial decision-makers.

Looking back at the participatory process after the project, it was clear that diverse stakeholders learned to listen to each other, gradually coming to understand differing viewpoints through repeated interaction. Scientists also changed their attitude toward communication with local stakeholders, moving from relative indifference to more active listening to farmer problems and perspectives. Efforts were made to phrase topics in similar wording to those of local stakeholders, supported by visualization techniques and stories[12] to facilitate a better understanding of scientific terms. Ultimately, non-academic stakeholders adapted to the participation approach and increasingly became open to interaction. One indicator exemplifying this was when a local partner expressed they would like to apply the collaborative methods to other projects in the future. This suggests a lasting positive impact in terms of changing attitudes toward participation and related behavior in the long term.

Experiences and lessons learnt: Accommodating difference

Complex multi-stakeholder decision-making processes consist of several dimensions: a large number of stakeholders with different interests, varying influences in the decision-making process, and multiple levels in which decision-making processes take place. In each dimension, there are possibilities for conflicting viewpoints, bringing increased complexity to the process when these factors interact with one another. For example, a specific strategy favored by one stakeholder group may be considered unacceptable to others. In SURUMER, farmer interests largely involved income generation and water supply, whereas actors in management positions emphasized sustainability on a regional scale. Conflicts can exist among varying interests that must be adequately addressed to implement an enhanced land use strategy. However, the experiences gained from SURUMER illustrate how differences do not have to lead to conflicts—with the right approach, there can be buffer zones for negotiation, accommodating the coexistence of different interests. Stakeholder analysis is an invaluable tool allowing this type of negotiation by contributing towards mutual learning and understanding between stakeholders.

Meaningful stakeholder participation is not only about obtaining resources or support from local actors; its promise lies in its potential to co-produce higher-quality decision-making and solutions through increased involvement. Within these processes, stakeholders actively participate in decision-making within the framework of a research project by defining problems and objectives and generating knowledge and information. This can promote solutions that often achieve higher acceptance among those who implement land use changes. In SURUMER, practitioners expressed their needs and negotiated with researchers relating to how they would like to be involved in the process and the information they wanted to receive. To some extent, the practitioners led the dialogue, highlighting how the methods deployed supported increased ownership of the overarching process.

In China, the government administration makes land use decisions formally within a hierarchical system. In this context, local stakeholders may view participation as "unnecessary," believing their voices will not be heard and decisions will be made from the top down. Our experiences in SURUMER showed high participation levels were not necessarily better than lower participation intensity. Instead, participation intensities may suit different stakeholder groups, resources, and local conditions. For instance, while a workshop series was suitable for in-depth discussions with key decision-makers on progressively focused topics, larger-scale surveys could broadly capture opinions from farmers, including marginalized people. In this case, there were dynamic levels of higher or lower engagement in the participation process; therefore, it is vital to identify the optimal form for different stakeholder groups rather than only striving for the highest. In the Chinese context, it proved helpful to start with more passive forms of participation at the beginning to engage with local stakeholders and develop more active forms later on, after trust had been built.

The SURUMER approach was designed with a high level of flexibility to match the complex project context and meet the demands of different stakeholder groups. For instance, while the project aimed to develop scenarios in a participatory way, it was notably difficult to discuss scientific scenarios with local stakeholders. This was due in part to insurmountable gulfs between the academic language of modelers and practitioners, as well as between scientific scenarios and reality for non-academic stakeholders. Instead, the team discussed expectations with stakeholders in more detail that could be translated and integrated into modeling. Another example was that we noticed stakeholders with higher positions often dominated workshop discussions while those with lower positions seldom contributed. From this observation, we learned it is better to invite workshop participants with similar positions to ensure all are heard equally. Finding ways to improve such situations requires patience with a deep and reflexive appreciation of how change occurs, in addition to considering the roles of researchers and practitioners. Continuous adaptation of the participatory approach throughout the entire process helps fulfill stakeholder needs more adequately, builds trust among them, and contributes to keeping research focused on local needs.

To conclude, the SURUMER project illustrated how developing sustainability solutions for land use planning requires intensive and effective communication with various stakeholders to integrate scientific and local knowledge. The overall experience shows how, within transdisciplinary projects, the foundation for effective interaction among stakeholders is based on understanding and empathy. This requires a willingness to communicate among stakeholders, work across disciplines and cultures, and contribute enough time to participate. In this respect, dedicating more space and time for meaningful stakeholder analysis and participation is vital, ideally initiating contacts at the very beginning and steadily building trust and networks among actors throughout the process. A flexible, tailor-made approach to transdisciplinary communication is key so researchers and practitioners can better identify sustainability problems, take ownership of them, and become more engaged in producing lasting solutions.

1 David W. Cash et al., "Knowledge Systems for Sustainable Development," *Proceedings of the National Academy of Sciences of the United States of America* 100 (2003): 8086–91.

2 Julie T. Klein, "Prospects for Transdisciplinarity," *Futures* 36 (2004): 515–26.

3 Edward R. Freeman, *A Stakeholder Approach to Strategic Management* (Mansfield: Pitman, 1984).

4 Robin Grimble, *Stakeholder Methodologies in Natural Resource Management* (Chatham: Natural Resources Institute, 1998).

5 Mark S. Reed, "Stakeholder Participation for Environmental Management: A Literature Review," *Biological Conservation* 141, no. 10 (2008): 2417–31.

6 Jules Pretty, "Participatory Learning for Sustainable Agriculture," *World Development* 23, no. 8 (1995): 1247–63.

7 Diane Warburton, *Participatory Action in the Countryside: A Literature Review*, (Countryside Commission, 1997), sharedpractice.org.uk/Downloads/Participatory_Action_Review.pdf

8 Mark S. Reed, op. cit.

9 Gene Rowe and Lynn J. Frewer, "Public Participation Methods: A Framework for Evaluation," *Science, Technology, and Human Values* 25, no. 1 (2000): 3–29.

10 Participatory rural appraisal is an approach which aims to incorporate the knowledge and opinions of rural people in the planning and management of development projects and programs, including techniques such as transect walks, wealth ranking, social mapping, focus group discussions, and semi-structured interviews. Nammalvar Narayanasamy, *Participatory Rural Appraisal: Principles, Methods and Application* (Los Angeles: SAGE Publications, 2009).

11 Figure based on: Jue Wang and Thomas Aenis, "Stakeholder analysis in support of sustainable land management: Experiences from southwest China," *Journal of Environmental Management* 243, (2019): 1-11.

12 A series of assumptions of possible future scenarios described to stakeholders using everyday language.

In the field: Researching China's urban-rural hinterlands

Gaoli Xiao, Ava Lynam, and Yuqi Zhang

The majority of research on urban and rural development in China still follows an urban-rural dichotomy, resulting in a gap in understanding the unique socio-spatial practices and power dynamics at urban-rural transitioning zones. Through agriculture-to-industry transformation, social interactions and spatial configurations in these areas become particularly intricate due to the cohabitation of urban dwellers, kinship-based rural communities, and a significant influx of migrant workers. This complexity requires researchers to engage with their social and spatial surroundings with great sensibility and flexibility. Political constraints, ethical considerations, field access, language barriers, socio-cultural nuances, and the preparedness of local interlocutors to engage in research all pose challenges for researchers in their everyday field activities.

Guided by an inter- and transdisciplinary, international, and practice-oriented research design, researchers in the Urban-Rural Assembly project frequently encountered these challenges in the field in Huangyan, a secondary city district in the Yangtze River Delta. During their trips to the urban-rural hinterland, the project's researchers navigated issues of positionality and intercultural differences, building trust and safeguarding their duty of care with participants and managing boundaries between professional and personal life. To critically reflect on these experiences, we conducted two focus group discussions with researchers from the Urban-Rural Assembly project who carried out fieldwork at Huangyan's rural-urban interface. In this article, we discuss some of the main challenges encountered during and after their time in the field, sharing learnings that may be valuable for other empirical research on rural-urban transformation within similar intercultural, transdisciplinary research frameworks.

Positionality and bias

Ethnographers and anthropologists have reflected on their inevitable subconscious biases when conducting qualitative research and producing narratives about so-called "alien" communities.[1] When interpreting the social world, researchers are, to some extent, subjective and influenced by their socio-cultural backgrounds.[2] Similarly, when collecting data, power imbalances

Fig. 2

between researchers and participants influence what stories are told and in which manner. Especially in development studies, critical scholars have long reflected on research frameworks in which the researcher (from the Global North) holds authoritative positions over the "researched" (in the Global South), establishing an inequitable power dynamic that has the potential to marginalize the perspectives of those under study.[3] Therefore, acknowledging and mitigating the researcher's biases is crucial for achieving a collaborative, ethical, and nuanced understanding of the research subject.

In the Urban-Rural Assembly project, the question of positionality arises already during the initial phase of research design. Though initiated under a collaborative framework of Chinese and German universities, only the German side secured funding. This imbalance skewed the conceptualization and design of the research toward the German context before being introduced to the Chinese "case study region." Integral to the project are real-life living laboratories from which to conduct intensive field research and develop practical strategies to support more sustainable rural-urban development. However, problems and possible solutions were identified and developed primarily from a "German lens," which may not fully apply to the Chinese context. Such structural challenges were often mentioned by researchers who conducted fieldwork in Huangyan:

> "When I was doing fieldwork in Huangyan, I sometimes felt as if I was imposing a certain value on my interlocutors and influencing their way of thinking. For example, the idea of, 'sustainable transformation,' is core to our research design. However, for most people I interviewed, this concept is not yet on their agenda or everyday life. I found it difficult to frame interview questions that do not bring up a certain perspective or positionality." Chinese researcher employed by a German university

In response to this challenge, researchers adapted how they framed questions and applied terminologies to better align with the local context. For example, rather than asking whether a villager considers "sustainability" in their daily activities, researchers posed more practical questions regarding the reasons behind certain practices

Fig. 3

(e.g., washing clothes in the river or planting vegetables on the riverside). Consequently, greater emphasis was placed on uncovering the underlying reasons behind practices that might be considered environmentally harmful by researchers but not perceived as "problematic" by locals. This approach allowed a deeper understanding of how villagers perceive their relationship with the ecological environment. Moreover, researchers iteratively refined the research framework in response to challenges identified by local residents. This adjustment facilitated a mutual learning process: researchers gained grounded insights into how locals navigate their self-identified challenges, while local residents had an opportunity to learn from perspectives informed by academic training. This approach echoes Haraway's suggestion to regard research participants as "knowledgeable experts" in their own right and underscores the importance of gaining insights into everyday experiences without presuming definitive interpretations.[4]

Researchers from the Urban-Rural Assembly project discussed how interpreting their subject from a different socio-cultural lens can offer an outsider's perspective which could add richness to observations. However, it also risks reinforcing socio-cultural biases, potentially leading to selective data collection and analysis based on the value systems of the researcher. To be more mindful of how this may impact findings, reflections on the researcher's background and context of the investigation were included when writing up results. In doing so, researchers aimed to remind readers—as well as themselves—that "how they 'write up,' their findings is never a purely neutral matter."[5]

Access to the field and gaining trust

Ethnographers commonly stress that the challenge of gaining access to informants determines who is interviewed and who is not, thereby influencing the quality of data collected.[6] Accordingly, the international and transdisciplinary nature of the Urban-Rural Assembly project significantly impacted researcher access within the field. Researchers from the German side heavily relied on partner institutions in China to legitimize their fieldwork through key social and political actors, with relationships with Chinese partners decisive for administrative access, networking, and operations in the field.

This also meant that the expectations or motivations of each partner institution could influence what kind of field access they facilitated. Acknowledging that engagement with foreign institutions might bring risks to local project partners in a politically sensitive context, Urban-Rural Assembly project members decided to compromise their research agenda in certain cases. This was intended to build trust and seek common ground with partner institutions by identifying mutually beneficial research frameworks and goals. When organizing participatory workshops in Urban-Rural Living Labs, researchers invited participants through government officials, despite the risk of selection bias and involuntary participation due to top-down power dynamics and hierarchies. This decision was based on the understanding that a local meeting organized by foreign researchers with open invitations to local participants may bring potential trouble to Chinese academic partners who had provided invitations to access the field. This, to some extent, compromised some fundamental principles of participatory processes; however, researchers remained reflective about how a flexible approach to the research agenda could potentially affect data quality.

In the field, researchers found that those who stand out as being foreign can change the dynamic of interactions with local actors. On one hand, foreign researchers often raised curiosity, which increased chances for interactions. Moreover, the possibilities of bias increased as field informants sometimes selectively portrayed positive images of their contexts. On the other hand, where people held skeptical attitudes towards foreigners due to increased government emphasis on national information security, it was observed that the presence of foreign researchers may have contributed to decreased interaction.

In addition, researchers noted how outward appearances can be integral in gaining trust:

> "I felt sometimes when I went to interview government officials, some of them were not taking me so seriously. Maybe it's because of my age or gender or what I wore. But I think it's a really important thing for us to keep in mind as researchers, especially in a country like China, where everybody pays a lot of attention to your appearance." Chinese researcher employed by a German university

> "When approaching villagers, we tried to dress in a more everyday manner and needed to use colloquial language to try to communicate as kindly as possible. If we dress too formally, people may not be very open. But when facing government officials (such as village secretaries), we often needed to act professionally and formally to help us be better received and obtain more useful information." Chinese researcher from a Chinese university

This illustrates how age, gender, and choice of clothing affected the ability of researchers to gain trust with different types of actors, necessitating a flexible approach to adjusting their appearance where possible to fit more comfortably into various field environments.

Language and data quality

Language barriers were a prominent constraint to field research for the Sino-German team working across three languages. When conducting interviews, non-Chinese speaking researchers highly depended on their Chinese colleagues for translation support. In addition, the diversity of regional and local dialects in China further complicated the translation process. To some extent, this also introduced bias in data collection, in cases where the selection of research participants depended on the ability to communicate in the same regional dialect:

> "I realized most of the people I talked to were those who could speak Mandarin because I was just incapable of chatting in the local language. So what happens in the end is that the people who speak Mandarin are more present in my research results, which should be considered as bias." Chinese researcher employed by a German university

Researchers realized that, in some situations, live translation during interviews could not only slow down or interrupt the conversation but also reduce the richness of information gathered. To better support one another during the interview process, roles were divided among Chinese and non-Chinese-speaking researchers. While one researcher focused on detailed participatory observation and visual documentation, the other maintained the flow of the conversation. The observations made by non-Chinese researchers complemented findings and helped reduce the bias of local researchers who may overlook aspects they are well accustomed to.

> "As a foreign researcher, it's important to recognize that it just won't be possible to reach the same level of richness when it comes to expression in language terms during the empirical data collection. So, you need to balance it with other supporting methods to triangulate and cross-reference the data." Non-Chinese researcher employed by a German university

Fig. 4

Taking a flexible and contextual approach to translation proved necessary while conducting fieldwork in a context where a wide variety of actors are encountered. For instance, with government officials or village leaders, researchers carried out formal interview procedures with informed consent, addressing predetermined interview questions with real-time translation. However, when interviewing villagers or migrant workers in casual or spontaneous settings, researchers often chose not to interrupt the natural flow of the discussion for translation. Instead, they conducted a recap session between researchers immediately after the interview to translate and document the data as accurately as possible.

Balancing fieldwork and the researcher's personal life

Given the nature of social and ethnological research, the sense that "data is everywhere and emerges all the time" led URA researchers to continue conducting observations, interviews, and spontaneous conversations during off-duty hours, often leading to exhaustion. Moreover, in Huangyan's rural-urban transition zone, informality plays a major role in the local socio-cultural context. Personal contacts are highly valued and expected to be made through intensive networking activities. In this context, researchers found it challenging to navigate building close social connections with participants while maintaining professional distance. For example, in some cases informants shared intimate details about their personal lives and struggles during interviews, leading to a natural attempt to form a personal relationship with the researcher, even if they had been clear about their intent. Some researchers encountered a dilemma: while they had encouraged informants to share, they later found it uncomfortable to continue engaging when the field investigation was over and wanted to handle the situation ethically.

> "A contact I made wrote to me even after one year, just wanting to chat and talk about their children. And it feels very unnatural to not respond because at one point I was asking them intimate details about their life. So, I felt pressure on some level to engage

with these topics again because I'm the one who brought them up in the first place." Non-Chinese researcher employed by a German university

Fig. 5

Fig. 1
A researcher chats with a migrant worker while washing clothes in the river next to the village's industrial zone.

Fig. 2
Conversation between researchers and a group of village neighbors during a transect walk.

Fig. 3
Co-producing mental maps with a migrant factory worker.

Fig. 4
View of a factory zone in Xifan Village, where researchers collected detailed empirical data.

Fig. 5
A researcher joins a village elder in assembling plastic products.

This reflection resonates with what ethnographers see as a significant power imbalance between researchers and subjects: the ability of the researcher to leave the field and return to the everyday academic world.[7] It also speaks to Oakley's argument that maintaining a sense of detachment while informants share personal experiences reinforces and perpetuates inequalities between researchers and participants.[8] Following this line of thought, Irwin argues that cultivating subjective, intimate, and emotionally close relationships with participants in the field—superficially at least—seems to offer a potential remedy to the inequalities entrenched in traditionally masculine scientific approaches which encourage objectivity, distance, and rationality.[9]

However, situations arose where URA researchers decided that such a close relationship was not necessary or it was unethical to develop either intimate or inauthentic friendships with field informants. For instance, several informants were eager to display hospitality toward researchers by acting as local tour guides, offering gifts, and extending invitations for dinners and leisure activities. Some of these advances were accepted to build local relationships; however, researchers increasingly felt a sense of "social debt," with their research agenda becoming subtly steered toward participants' own interests. For example, some expressed hope that researchers could leverage the government or other powerful institutions to address their concerns. This prompted researchers to think about how to better navigate research boundaries and manage the expectations of local actors that they may not be able to fulfill.

In Huangyan, there was often no need to repeatedly clarify intent when engaging with individuals familiar with social research or those with academic backgrounds, such as local officials, civil servants, and entrepreneurs. Owners of small businesses were often willing to provide information, but may also wish to leverage the researcher, especially foreign researchers, to advertize their businesses. However, villagers or migrant workers with limited knowledge of academic research sometimes misunderstood the reasons for being approached. Through these experiences, researchers reflected on the need to more sensitively develop relationships with field informants with what may be expected in mind, to protect both themselves and their participants from over-investing time, resources, and emotions. They learned that special attention must be paid to the cultural context and social background of people they approach, such as gender, age, socio-economic situation, and professional or educational background, as well as their motivations for engaging.

Ways forward

The above reflections from the Urban-Rural Assembly project show that conducting social science field investigations at the rural-urban interface in China is not an easy task for both Chinese and non-Chinese researchers, especially given its political sensitivity. While partnerships with local institutions are vital for accessing the field, indirect access could also influence what kind of data could be collected. Moreover, complexities of bias permeated every stage of the empirical research process, presenting issues that demanded more attention to developing culturally sensitive approaches. During field investigations, researchers learned that carefully adapting appearances, attitudes, and methods based on specific contexts are all important steps for gaining trust. To overcome language constraints and bias, researchers found they could better support one another by playing different roles in the data collection process.

One of the greatest challenges was finding ways to contextualize research ethics while maintaining careful consideration for any possible risks introduced to field informants and researchers themselves. The reflections of the URA research team challenge the idea of a universalized approach to ethics. They support the idea that ethical standards within formal research protocols require adjustments to specific situations of "when", "where", and "how" an interaction occurs between the researcher and participants, as well as in which social, cultural, and political context the investigation is embedded.[10] This duty of care is especially important when navigating intimacy and professional and personal boundaries in relationships made in the field.

Ultimately, the issues faced by researchers of the Urban-Rural Assembly project in the field revealed power dynamics between the "Global North" and the "Global South," the "researcher" and the "researched," and the "global" and the "local," which may significantly impact data collection, analysis, and dissemination of findings. This reflects ongoing academic debates on how to most ethically and effectively approach research projects that integrate an international framework. Paying special attention to how the framework came into being and how it impacts the research process and outcomes may help to better address ethical concerns, both with participants in the field and within the research team.

With special thanks to our focus group participants Li Fan, Xiaoxue Gao, Huang Huang, Laura Henneke, Zheng Yang, Yulin Zhang, and Haoxun Zhang.

1 James Clifford and George E. Marcus, *Writing culture: The poetics and politics of ethnography* (Berkeley: University of California Press, 1986).

2 Thomas Gary and David James, "Reinventing Grounded Theory: Some Questions about Theory, Ground and Discovery," *British Educational Research Journal* 32, no. 6 (2006): 767–95.

3 Gabriel Bamana, "Doing Ethnography beyond China," *New Directions in Africa–China Studies*, (2018): 118–30.

4 Donna Haraway, "Situated Knowledges: The Science Question in Feminism and the Privilege of Partial Perspective," *Feminist Studies* 14, no. 3 (1988): 575–99.

5 Paul Atkinson, "Ethics and Ethnography," *Twenty-First Century Society* 4, no. 1 (2009): 27.

6 Martyn Hammersley and Paul Atkinson, *Ethnography: Principles in practice*, 3rd ed. (London: Routledge, 2007).

7 Gesa Kirsch, *Ethical dilemmas in feminist research: The politics of location, interpretation, and publication* (Albany: State University of New York, 1999).

8 Ann Oakley, "Interviewing Women: A Contradiction in Terms," *In Doing Feminist Research*, ed. Helen Roberts (London: Routledge, 1981), 30–61.

9 Katherine Irwin, "Into the Dark Heart of Ethnography: The Lived Ethics and Inequality of Intimate Field Relationships," *Qualitative Sociology* 29, no. 2 (2006): 155–75.

10 Paul Atkinson, "Ethics and Ethnography," *Twenty-First Century Society 4*, no. 1 (2009): 17–30.

Fig. 1

Tools for researching urban-rural transformation

Zheng Yang, Yulin Zhang, Maria Frölich-Kulik, Suili Xiao, Gaoli Xiao, and Ava Lynam

This contribution sheds light on the key methods used by the Urban-Rural Assembly research team to study urban-rural relations in the case study region of Huangyan-Taizhou. Our toolbox of research methods brings together social, technical, landscape, and ecological perspectives. The interdisciplinary research framework formulated by the project incorporated a blend of qualitative, quantitative, and mixed-method approaches to support each other when interpreting the complex spatial and temporal dynamics of urban-rural transformation. In terms of data collection, the team used tools such as literature reviews and document analysis, questionnaires, sampling and laboratory analysis, semi-structured interviews, participant observation, digital ethnography, and remote sensing. Data analysis tools included landscape mapping, material flow analysis, grid-based data analysis, actor-network mapping, Location-Based Services data analysis, Normalized Difference Vegetation Index analysis, and socio-spatial profiles. Presented in the following pages as a toolbox comprising bite-sized descriptions, these approaches have been richly applied in the Urban-Rural Assembly project. Some are commonly used methods while others have been developed and customized for our specific needs. However, each tool provided unique insights, leading to a multi-perspective recognition of the complex dynamics associated with urban-rural change.

Bringing such a diverse array of methods together from divergent disciplinary approaches increased the complexity of our research design. Thus, the Urban-Rural Assembly team promoted multi-actor dialogue through Urban-Rural Living Labs, focus group discussions, multi-stakeholder workshops, films, and the Urban-Rural Assembly glossary. While the team still faced challenges in trans- and interdisciplinary communication, these platforms helped to develop an integrated research framework through which diverse methods seek to complement one another to form the basis of a more holistic understanding of rural-urban dynamics. In turn, an interdisciplinary research toolbox holds the potential to lay the groundwork for developing more balanced, inclusive, and sustainable urban-rural transformation pathways.

Fig. 2

Data collection

Semi-structured interviews

Yuting Xie, Zhelei Miao, Jing Jin, Xiangning Chen, and Peiwen Huang

Semi-structured interviews are a widely applied qualitative research method wherein the interviewer poses a series of questions without adhering to a rigid structure.[1] This encourages naturally flowing conversation and provides in-depth insights into the perspectives of participants. In Huangyan, our research team applied this method to investigate human-water relations, complementing macro-scale spatial insights gained from mapping and nuanced, human-scale information derived from observation (Fig. 2).

Through this method, we gained rich, descriptive insights from various types of local residents regarding challenges they face in their daily lives and their future visions concerning human-water interactions. The interviews revealed that industrialization processes spurred by the establishment of the Smart Molding Town in Xifan Village have resulted in the degradation of the traditional ditches and ponds system, which held significant local cultural value and was embedded in collective memory. Interview partners offered insights about the agricultural activities supported by the water system and the impact of the diversion of the main river in Houyanghuang Village. We also learned how the development of a commercial street in Yuxia Village exacerbated a disconnection between residents and the traditional water lanes. Detailed semi-structured interviews with local residents supported the development of planning strategies that aim to optimize the human-water relationship for the benefit of diverse local needs, such as the restoration of pond and ditch systems and the promotion of small businesses to reactivate water lane spaces.

During our interview process, we occasionally faced language barriers, especially with elderly people only speaking in local dialects. In these cases, identifying an appropriate local translation partner was essential for capturing the richness of language and ensuring these distinct perspectives were included.

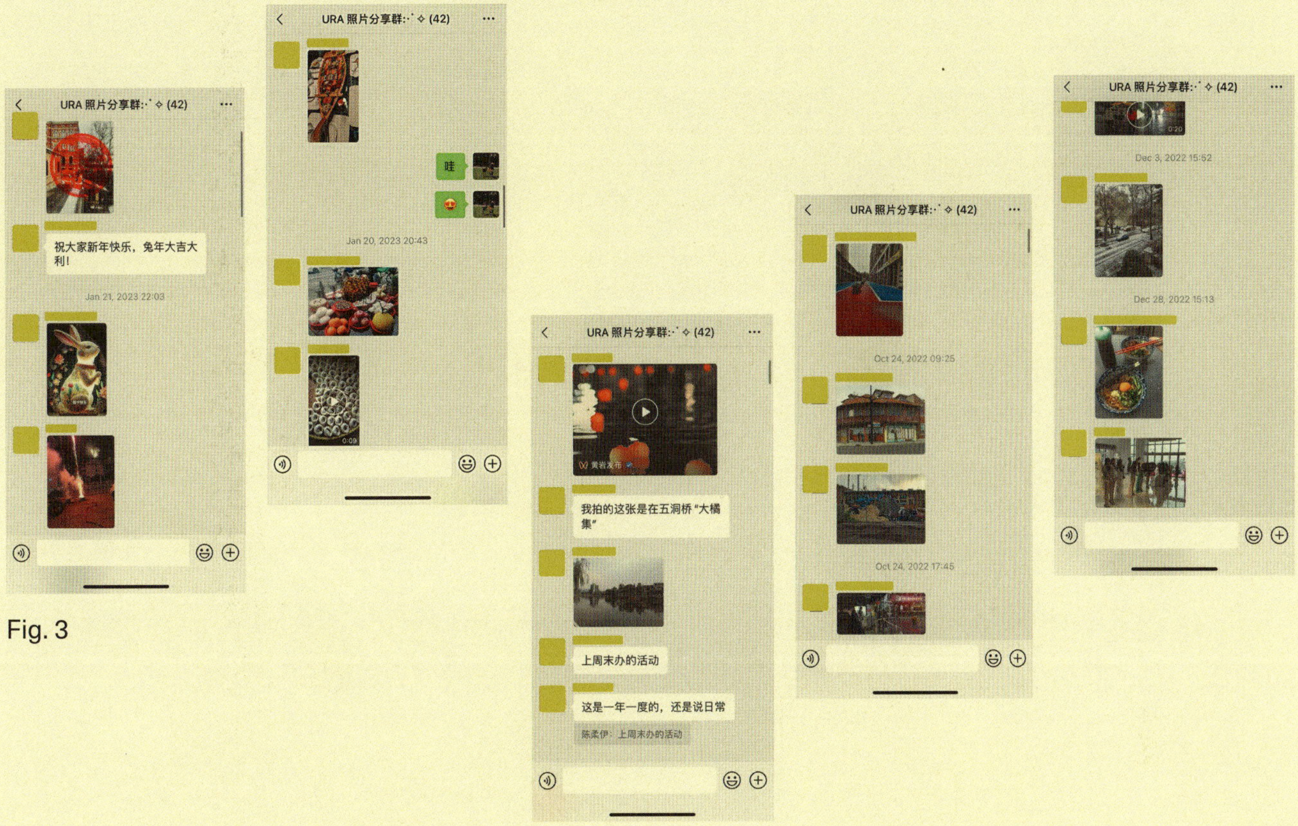

Fig. 3

Digital ethnography
Gaoli Xiao, Kit Braybrooke, and Ava Lynam

Digital ethnography extends traditional on-site ethnographic approaches into digital spaces—such as social media and online communities—through observation, participation, and analysis of online activities.[2] During the COVID-19 pandemic, when physical field visits were not possible, digital communication became essential for the Urban-Rural Assembly project due to its reliance on local knowledge of urban-rural transformation. In 2022, we set up a photo exchange via a WeChat group (Fig. 3), the most common Chinese social media app. Participants in China and Germany, including researchers and local actors in our field site of Huangyan, were invited to share visual materials (photos, videos, and stickers) from their daily lives and engage in informal chats.[3]

A series of calls related to a weekly theme, including: "places you like to spend leisure time," "your favorite green spaces," and "a place with a special memory." The choice of images allowed researchers to identify significant cultural sites, public spaces, and places carrying special meanings, as well as their use at different times of day. The diverse activities shared included children playing in the park, villagers washing clothes at the riverside, urban festivals, COVID-19 test sites, and religious practices in temples. We also gained insights into issues prioritized by local residents. For instance, when a group member shared a photo of the Changtan Reservoir with a low water level, this sparked a lively discussion on local environmental concerns.

Digital ethnography allowed us to build rapport with field informants and gain impressions of local socio-spatial practices, all while overcoming travel restrictions and time and cost constraints. However, we also faced challenges when forging trust with participants, encountering language barriers, and mitigating biases in content sharing. In addition, we considered the ethical risks of the photo exchange regarding its potential to visualize inequalities among participants.

Fig. 4

Biomaterial sampling

Zheng Yang and Hongqing Li

Biomaterial sampling is a key method for collecting biomass and soil data in the study of urban-rural transformation processes, providing detailed insights into the environmental impacts of these changes.[4] This approach involves the meticulous collection of samples from various urban and rural areas, followed by thorough laboratory testing to assess soil composition, nutrient content, and quality of biomass. Researchers in the Urban-Rural Assembly project applied this method by collecting samples of crop residues and soil in Beiyang—one of the project's living labs in Huangyan—for analysis (Fig. 4). The aim was to understand local crop bioenergy potential, nutrient cycling potential, and soil biodiversity. This enabled us to assess potentials for circular economies in agricultural production by capturing nutrient profiles in agricultural outputs, the energy potential of biomass residues, and the feasibility of nutrient recovery. By measuring factors such as soil pH, organic matter, and heavy metal content, researchers were able to evaluate the impact of different types of agricultural cultivation on the soil and the potential for nutrient cycling in agricultural production. Biomaterial sampling also helped to reveal shifts in vegetation types and densities in Beiyang, which is indicative of land use changes as urban expansion in the area increases.

Although precise and reliable, this method requires representative sample collection and involves high costs for advanced laboratory equipment. Moreover, variations in laboratory analysis standards across different countries can lead to inconsistent results, presenting a challenge to comprehensive comparative studies. These challenges underscored the necessity of contextualizing and standardizing interpretations of our laboratory results.

Fig. 5

Participant observation
Ava Lynam

Participant observation is a common qualitative method in which researchers immerse themselves in real-life research contexts to study social phenomena or cultural behaviors. In Huangyan, our research team used participant observation to study interactions between social practices and physical spaces firsthand as rural-urban transformation takes place. In this highly dynamic environment, ample empirical observations from the ground were essential to supplement remote or static methods. Participant observation also allowed foreign researchers to support colleagues carrying out interviews by documenting detailed contextual observations.

Several walks were taken through villages to identify key areas for observation. Researchers then attempted to organically join in the everyday activities of villagers to observe the use of space by different social groups. This included interactions between migrant mothers and their children in a village square, the use of street sides by mobile vegetable vendors at different times of day, and communal activities relating to the assembling of plastic products by local elderly people (Fig. 5). Observations were recorded in field notes capturing the context surrounding interviews and documenting physical space in great detail, key in the development of socio-spatial profiles (see toolbox entry on socio-spatial profiles).[5]

It is important to acknowledge that, despite best efforts, researchers may inadvertently transpose biases onto observations, potentially leading to misinterpretation. For instance, after observing the living conditions of some migrant workers, the researchers assumed there may be more discontent than was later expressed in interviews. We also considered potential differences in observations from a cultural insider (local) or outsider (foreign researcher): while the former will pick up on many more cultural cues and meanings, the latter may sometimes benefit from a more detached perspective and notice different details. Therefore, we made sure to complement observations with interviews for verification and always reflect on the positionality of the researcher.

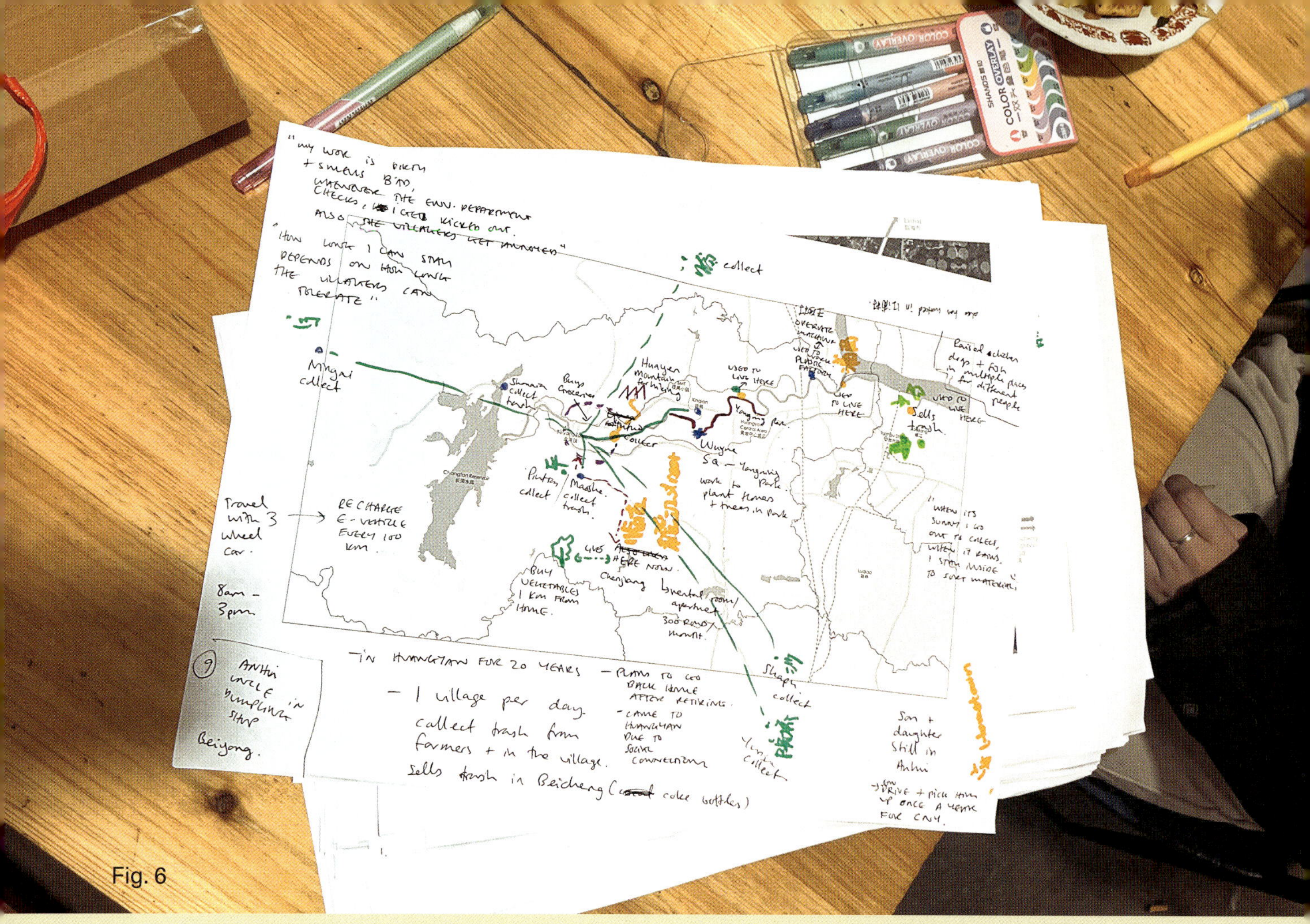

Fig. 6

Mental mapping
Yuqi Zhang, Ava Lynam, and Gaoli Xiao

While pivotal to Huangyan's economic advancement, migrant workers grapple with significant structural and everyday challenges. To understand their mobility patterns and socio-spatial practices, researchers from the Urban-Rural Assembly project experimented with mental mapping—cognitive maps drawn to capture research participant's perception of their everyday spatial environment.[6] These maps aim to visualize how people navigate, behave, interact, and experience space. Researchers used mental mapping to identify daily routines and meaningful places for migrant workers and local residents, incorporating physical environments (such as local landmarks, everyday commutes, and mobility beyond immediate surroundings) and social practices (such as non-spatial attributes and emotional associations with places) (Fig. 6). While participant-drawn maps capture more nuanced and direct cognitive spatial representations, we primarily used the researcher-drawn approach to make it more accessible to those less comfortable reading maps or translating mental perceptions of space into drawings.

We brought base maps prepared at neighborhood and city scales while conducting interviews. Posing concrete questions such as "where do you live/work?" and "how do you commute to work?", we encouraged the participant to identify locations on the map. With open-ended questions, such as "where do you spend your free time?" and "how could your living environment be improved?", we tracked perceptions and narratives of place expressed by different social groups. Paying particular attention to inequalities between migrant communities and local villagers, the mapping process enabled the comparison of mobility patterns and areas where they typically spend their time. Thus, mental mapping proved an effective tool to gain impressions of how different types of people experience the "right to the city" and the role of space and place in their lives.

Despite concerns that participants may feel intimidated when presented with a map, the interview-guided mapping process served as an

Fig. 7

Fig. 8

interactive tool to facilitate discussions and create a more informal atmosphere. We found it effective if researchers assumed different roles—e.g., interviewer, translator, or note-taker/mapper—to allow conversations to flow naturally while mapping. However, our results were influenced by our subjective spatial interpretation, which could lead to inaccuracies or bias.

Questionnaire surveys
Suili Xiao

Questionnaires are commonly used in quantitative and qualitative research to elucidate people's motivations or perceptions about a given topic, often using a social survey design. In the Urban-Rural Assembly project, we employed questionnaires to collect data that investigated the demand and preferences for recreation and ecosystem services among different social groups in Huangyans. We paid particular attention to cultural ecosystem services, "the non-material benefits people obtain from ecosystems through spiritual enrichment, cognitive development, reflection, recreation, and aesthetic experiences."[7] We designed a questionnaire with thirty-six questions related to themes such as "habits of using blue-green space," "preference for different landscape elements and recreational activities," and "suggestions for improving services and management of blue-green spaces."

During our field trips, we went to cultural halls in villages to talk with different types of local people, recording answers using the questionnaire (Fig. 7, 8). We conducted further surveys online by circulating our questionnaires on WeChat, a highly popular social media app in China. The data we collected has supported a comparative analysis of the demand for ecosystem services in Huangyan. For example, the top three reasons for not visiting blue-green spaces are: "there are mosquitoes and bugs," "no time," and "too far away, no convenient transport." This enables us to propose targeted ecosystem interventions that are more likely to respond to local needs and be well used by different social groups.

Socio-cultural landscape mapping of the Yongning River, Huangyan

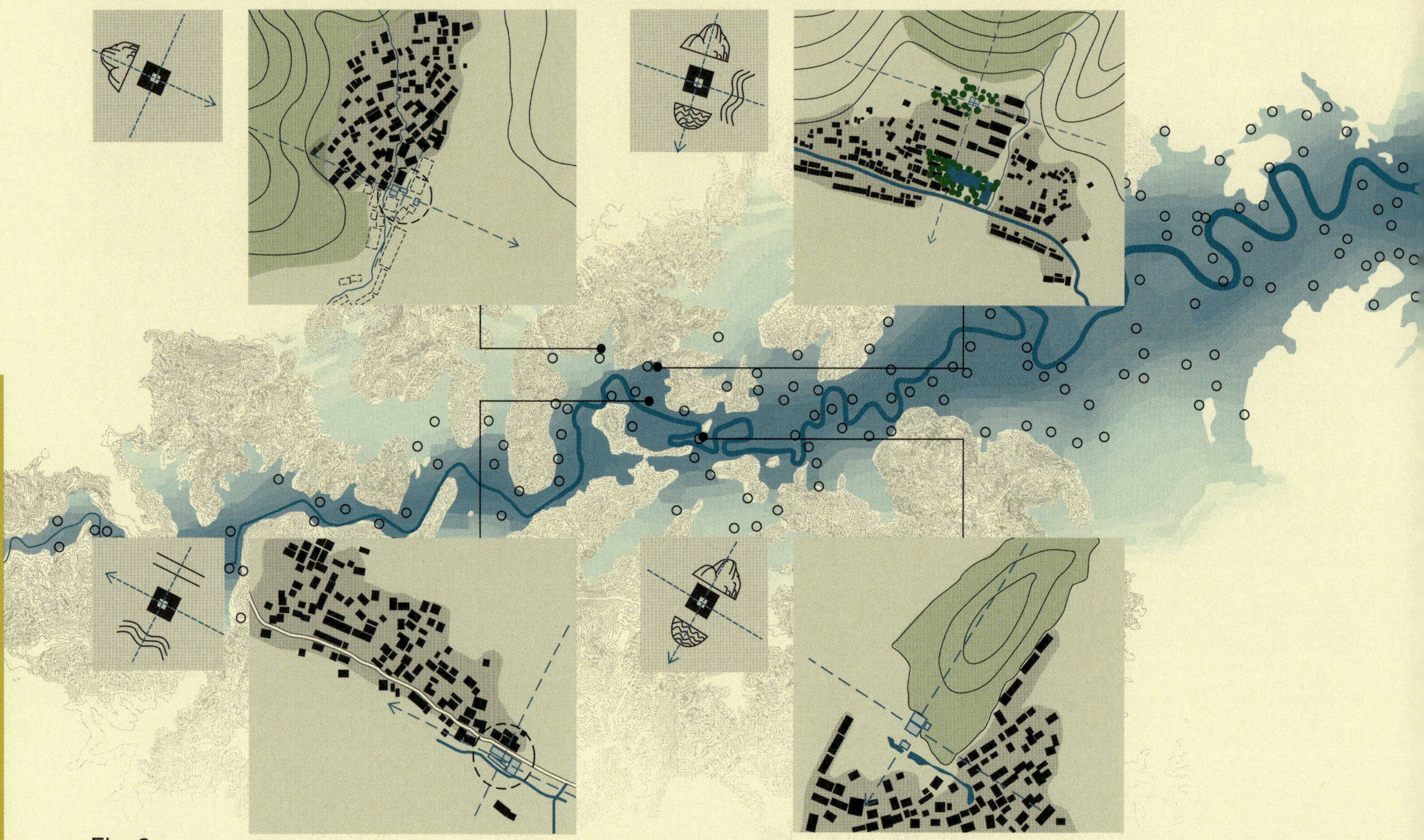

Fig. 9

Data analysis

Socio-cultural landscape mapping

Yulin Zhang

Urbanization is a multifaceted process resulting in far-reaching physical and social impacts on rural landscapes. To understand the dynamic and complex interplay between urban and rural areas, it is important to study the cultural and historical aspects of landscapes, as well as their material features. Within the Urban-Rural Assembly project, we used socio-cultural landscape mapping as a tool to visualize and analyze urban-rural transformations (Fig. 9). Through this method, we traced the trajectory of landscape changes and captured both the physical environment (such as water bodies, topography, land use, and settlement structures) and cultural patterns (for instance, in beliefs and social practices demonstrated in Fengshui in site selection and architectural layout design).[8] We used this mapping method to translate data gathered from various sources including interviews, archives, satellite imagery, planning documents, and photographs into a visual framework, offering a context-sensitive portrayal of rural-urban landscapes. This framework then helped us to envision potential future development pathways together with local stakeholders.

By layering different types of social and spatial information, socio-cultural landscape mapping can support the interpretation of interdependencies and connections between natural and social processes in an integrated manner. This helps to decode the underlying structures of the landscape through a visual medium. The mapping process also comes with challenges, such as gaining access to accurate and up-to-date data and the difficulty in visualizing in-depth social context on a map, which may limit the representativeness of mapping outcomes.

Normalized difference vegetation index change 1992–2020, Huangyan

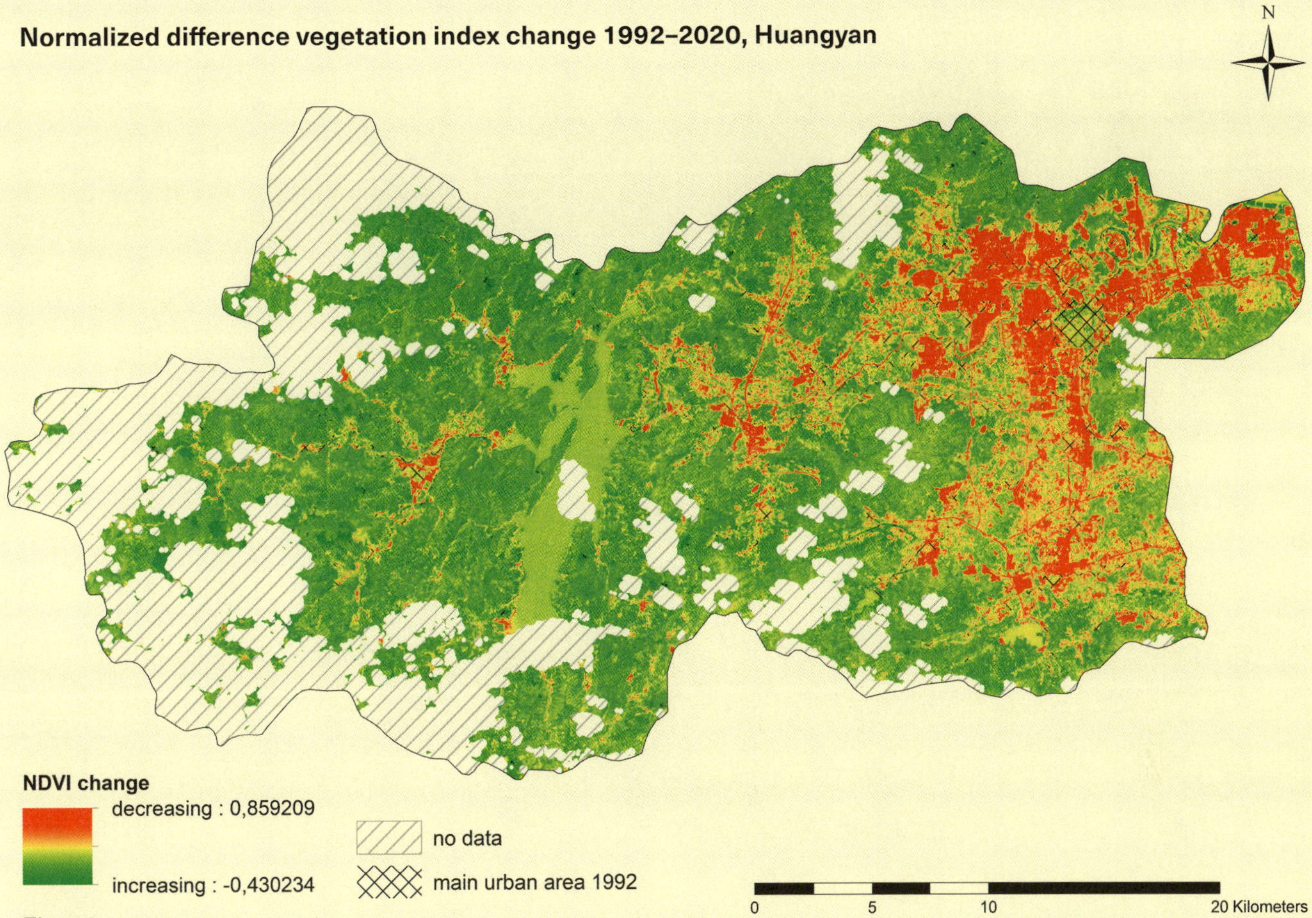

Fig. 10

Normalized Difference Vegetation Index
Suili Xiao, Alexander Maximilian Haase, and Wolfgang Wende

Urbanization often leads to changes in land cover and vegetation structures, particularly at the edges of cities or urban-rural interfaces. To understand the extent to which urban expansion has influenced the quantity and quality of local vegetation in Huangyan, we used the Normalized Difference Vegetation Index. This index is an indicator of the greenness of vegetation and is closely linked to the analysis of vegetation density and productivity.[9] It is widely used for evaluating greening trends and assessing greenness exposure for health benefits in urban and rural areas by analyzing the mean vegetation index over time.[10] The Normalized Difference Vegetation Index operates by analyzing the ratio of reflected red light and near-infrared radiation captured in satellite images, serving as an estimate of photosynthetic activity and the existence of green vegetation. Through the measurement of the disparity in reflected red and near-infrared light using satellite sensors, we can generate images illustrating areas abundant in greenery relative to those with less vegetation. We conducted comparisons of these images across various time periods to track alterations in land cover and vegetation structures resulting from urbanization in our study region. Throughout the analysis, precautions were taken to account for non-vegetated surfaces, such as concrete or water bodies, to prevent misinterpretation of the results.

In Huangyan, we used the Normalized Difference Vegetation Index to calculate and map changes in the quantity and quality of vegetation at the urban-rural interface area over thirty years. As an indicator of the biomass, condition, and density of vegetation, the index was particularly useful for our analysis and assessment of ecosystem potential in Huangyan, as well as their contributions through ecosystem services. Only through the Normalized Difference Vegetation Index analysis were we able to recognize the high degradation of vegetation in the local area, especially in dense urban areas (Fig. 10). While the index is highly useful for large-scale desktop studies of landscape transformation, we also required

Suggestions for ecological restoration in Beiyang Town

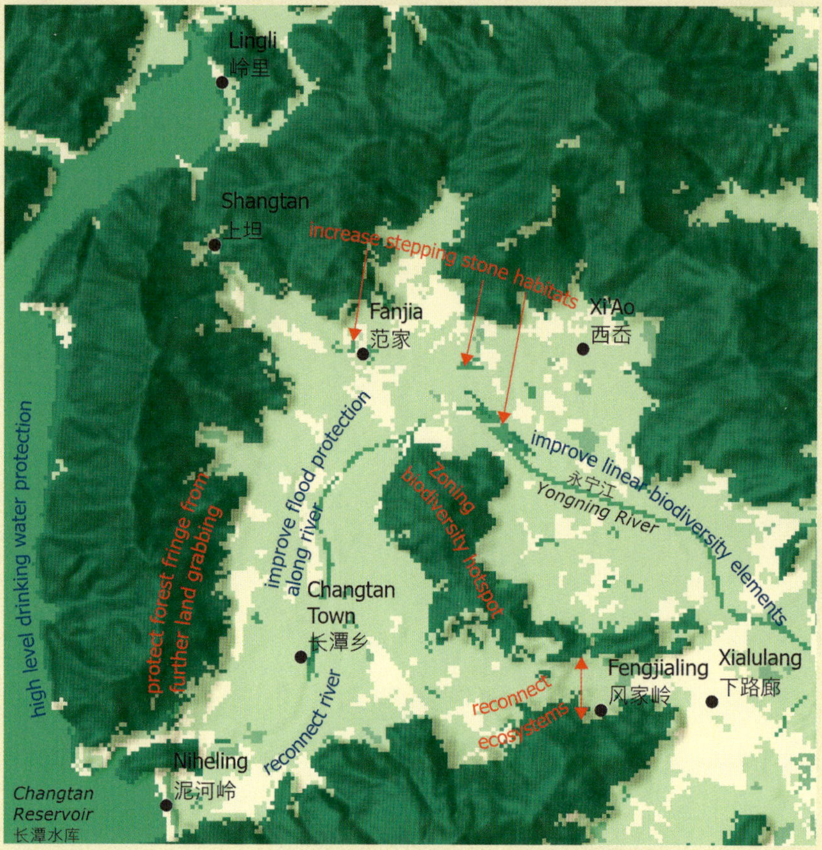

Fig. 11

supplementary methods such as interviews, questionnaire surveys, and field observations to support a greater understanding of the drivers and impacts behind the identified changes.

Building on the findings from the Normalized Difference Vegetation Index analysis and other biodiversity assessment tools, we proposed several restoration measures in Beiyang, Huangyan. This aimed to assist in the design of sustainable development pathways in the region over the coming decades.[11] These measures include, for example, protecting the Changtan Reservoir, reconnecting linear biodiversity elements, expanding waterside habitats, and enhancing overall flood protection (Fig. 11).

Actor-network mapping
Huang Huang

Actor-Network Theory—developed by sociologists Michel Callon and Bruno Latour—is often used to guide analytical approaches to mapping complex relationships between actors in a socio-spatial setting.[12,13] It explores interactions between actors with different resources and levels of power and how they shape social processes. Actor-Network Theory-informed actor-network mapping considers both human "actants" (such as authorities, residents, or developers) and non-human actants (such as land, built environment, water, heritage, globalization, or intercity competition). It can help to reveal how actors mobilize to take part in a network and influence others' decisions. In urban studies, Actor-Network Theory is commonly used to guide the analysis of interests and motives of human and non-human actants and the tactics they use to exercise or resist power in urban spaces.[14]

Our research team used Actor-Network-Theory-guided actor-network mapping to analyze complex

Mapping of actors and networks in Huangyan

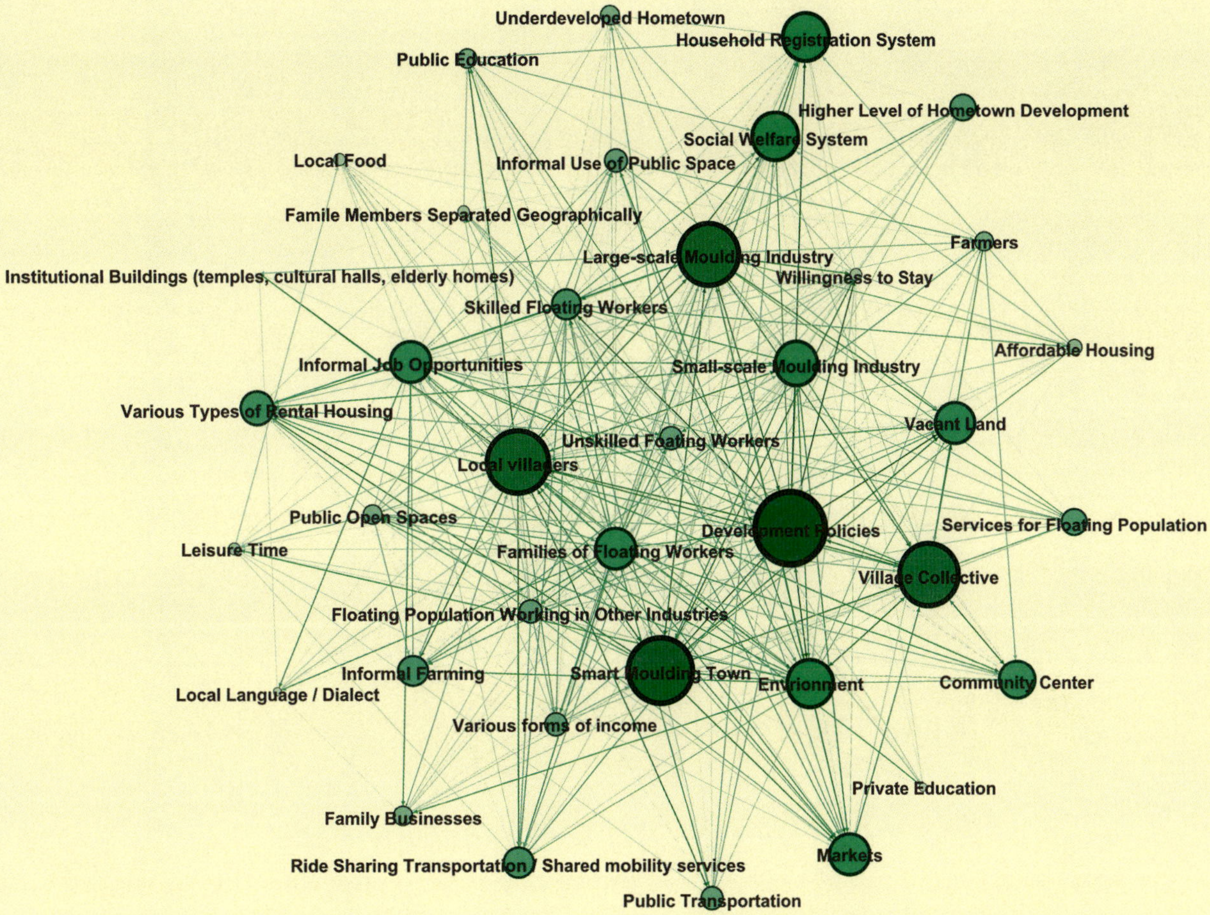

Fig. 12

rural-urban transformation processes involving variegated social relationships, resources, and forms of mobility. Semi-structured interviews and participant observation were conducted in Huangyan to collect the motivations, constraints, reactive tactics, and meanings behind the actions and relationships of different actors. Actants influencing local rural-urban transformation were identified and their relationships were subsequently categorized according to the level of impact observed between them. The actor networks were later visualized using “Gelphi” software.

Analysis of these actor-network maps allowed for the identification of factors of inequality among stakeholders of different levels of power during the rural-urban transformation process. For example, this map (Fig. 12) shows relationships among actants in the Smart Molding Town industrial zone and surrounding villages, revealing which assume dominant roles in shaping the local transformation process. Through this mapping, we could observe clear differences in influence among migrant workers and local villagers. Moreover, we identified development policies as the most influential actant as they directly restrained or enabled different development routes. Meanwhile, villagers and village collectives also played a key role due to their dominant votes on the use of collective lands.

Operationalizing Actor-Network Theory for actor-network mapping can be challenging as there is no fixed route to practice in the literature. Researchers relied on subjective judgment for interpreting actants and relationships among them, which also involved an abstraction of social dynamics. Furthermore, it is impossible in practice to exhaustively identify all possible actants involved in a transformation process.

GIS grid-based data analysis identifying local crops

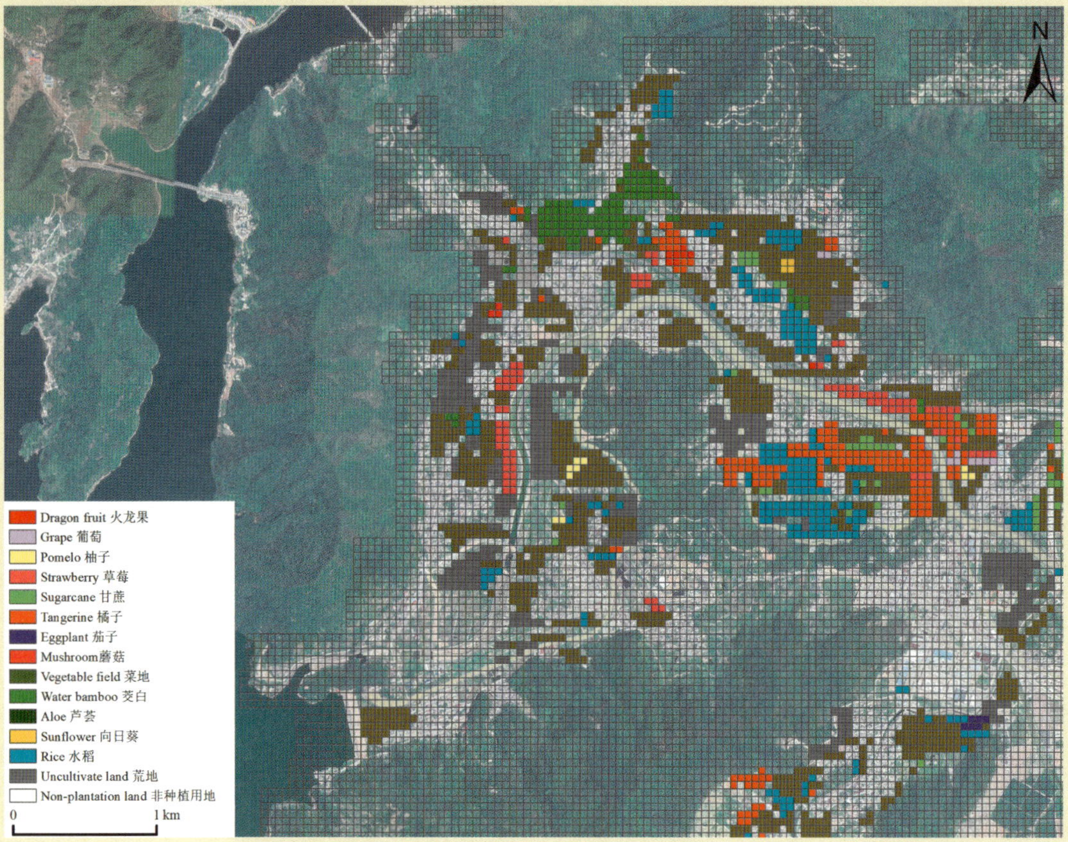

Fig. 13

GIS grid-based data analysis
Zheng Yang and Hongqing Li

GIS (Geographic Information Systems) and remote sensing serve as powerful tools in agricultural land use analysis, particularly in the context of crop distribution mapping across various regions.[15] Grid-based analysis based on GIS remote sensing data, supported by field data, can be applied as a method to achieve a comprehensive understanding of agricultural landscapes. The Urban-Rural Assembly project used it as a meticulous approach to the spatial analysis of farmland in the context of rural-urban transformation. By dissecting agricultural areas in Huangyan into a lattice of fifty by fifty-meter grids and more intensive farmland into finer twenty-five by twenty-five-meter grids, we were able to conduct a more granular and precise assessment of the types of crops on the farmland within each grid cell (Fig. 13). The results were verified and modified by field research, which ensured the collected data accurately reflected realities on the ground. Using the grid framework, we identified, photographed, and sampled each crop on selected agricultural land (see toolbox entry on biomaterial sampling). After collecting the data, we generated the grid-based map. We then used mathematical models and material flow analysis (see toolbox entry) to understand how nutrients move through different crops and how much biogas could be produced. This helped us see clearly how much energy we could extract from the crops within each field of the grid and how nutrients are currently used and recycled. Moreover, it revealed great potential for local application of small-scale biogas plants and composting facilities for bioenergy and organic fertilizer in Huangyan. This information has the potential to inform local energy optimization strategies and nutrient management plans, ultimately contributing to more sustainable agricultural practices and resource use in areas undergoing rural-urban transformation.

Location-Based Services analysis of commuting patterns in Taizhou

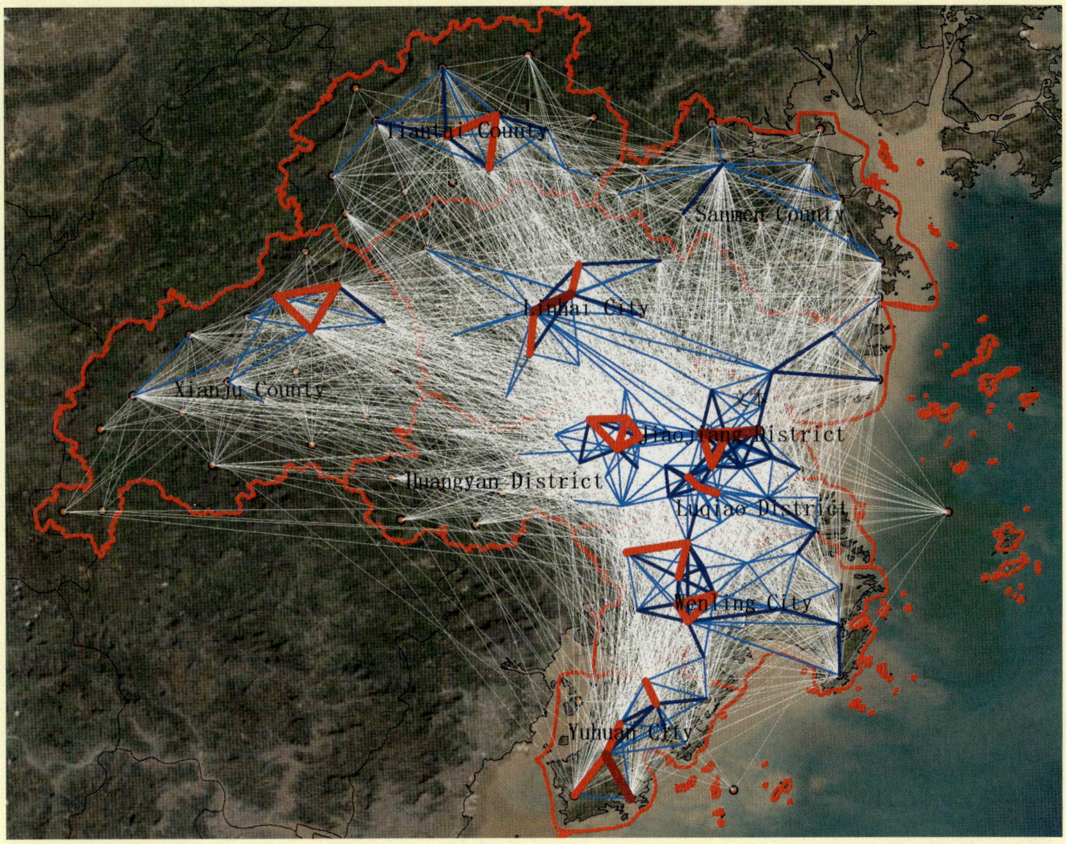

Fig. 14

Location-Based Services data analysis

Fengqing Li

Location-Based Services data refers to anonymized physical location data obtained from people's mobile phones, using GPS, public Wi-Fi, and MAC addresses. Location-Based Services data analysis is increasingly applied in urban-rural studies to look into urban transformation processes from the perspective of mobility.[16] From the registration information of mobile phone numbers, unidentifiable social data such as income, place of origin, workplace, and age group are related to location data to generate anonymized movement traces. By visualizing travel and commute behavior and cross-analyzing it with social tags over a continuous time frame, behavioral changes of different social groups are revealed. Thus, Location-Based Services data is regularly used in the analysis of urban spatial structures, regional and urban mobility patterns, work-commuting relationships, and everyday movements of various social groups.

In the Urban-Rural Assembly project, we used Location-Based Services data to analyze physical mobility patterns of different income groups to study socio-spatial inequalities in the process of rural-urban transformation (Fig. 14). The analysis revealed that higher income groups primarily moved between developed urban centers and traveled shorter distances. Conversely, commuting patterns of lower income groups were more geographically dispersed as they tended to live in peripheral areas (with more affordable accommodation) and commuted much farther distances to their workplaces (often located in industrial clusters outside urban centers). This suggested that income played a role in unequal mobility patterns at the level of the municipal region.

Location-Based Services can capture current data at any specific time window a study requires and can handle vast amounts of information within large population samples. However, we found limitations in location precision and a necessity to verify trends with field investigations. Moreover, Location-Based Services data only captures mobile (smart) phone users and is not universally accessible in every geographic context due to varying data privacy regulations.

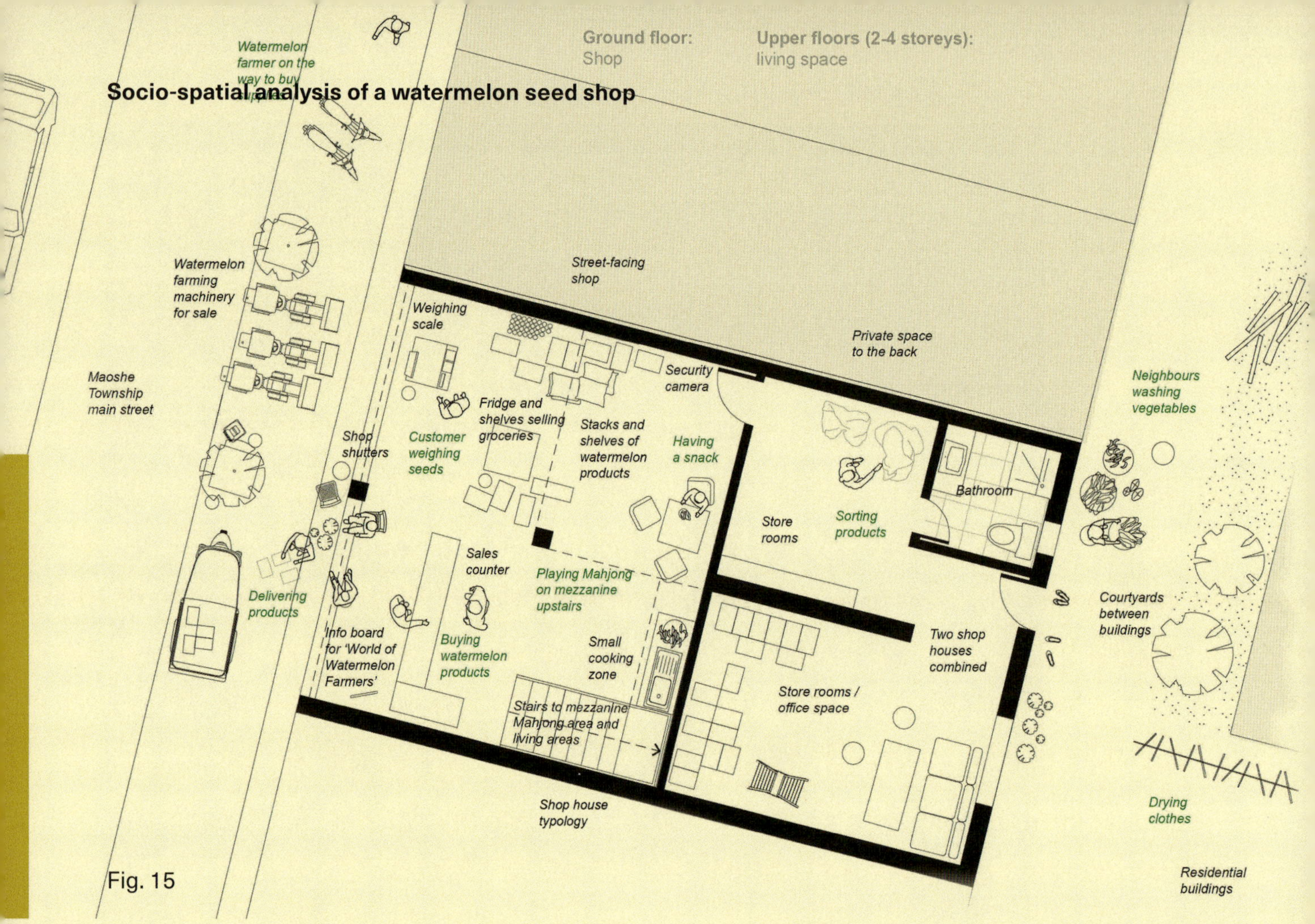

Fig. 15

Socio-spatial profiles

Gaoli Xiao and Ava Lynam

During rural-urban transformation, new everyday practices and spaces are produced through a dialectic relationship.[17] However, most spatial or architectural mapping methods are reductionist and fail to capture the richness of micro-scale empirical data which bring these social and spatial factors together. In the Urban-Rural Assembly project, we developed "socio-spatial profiles" to portray the social production of space in the process of rural-urban transformation. We illustrated profiles of local actors, spaces, and practices using a combination of qualitative data including architectural typologies, annotations, photos, quotes from interviews, and field notes from participant observation. The micro-scale mapping of spatial typologies and placemaking practices of social actors presented a visualization which brought the space to life and offered a detailed view of specific challenges and tactics employed to overcome them. This allowed us to draw out broader considerations of the underlying social, institutional, and economic forces that influence rural-urban transformation from an everyday perspective.

For example, the profile above (Fig.15) illustrates an important social group in Huangyan: watermelon farmers as circular migrants. In this profile, we mapped a typical watermelon seed shop in detail to demonstrate how villagers take part in the watermelon production chain, selling seeds and other supplies to translocal watermelon farmers who set out to farm in regions across China (and in some cases abroad). This shows how regional social and economic disparities trigger outmigration from underdeveloped rural areas.

This method accommodates a "deep dive" into specific socio-spatial profiles which requires highly contextual and localized qualitative data, generating smaller sample sizes. However, caution should be taken in generalizing with broad conclusions from such profiles without cross-referencing with other research methods. Rather, their value lies in providing detailed empirical "snap-shots" of actors, practices, and spaces, as well as their interactions at specific points in time during rural-urban transformation.

Material flows of rice fields in Huangyan

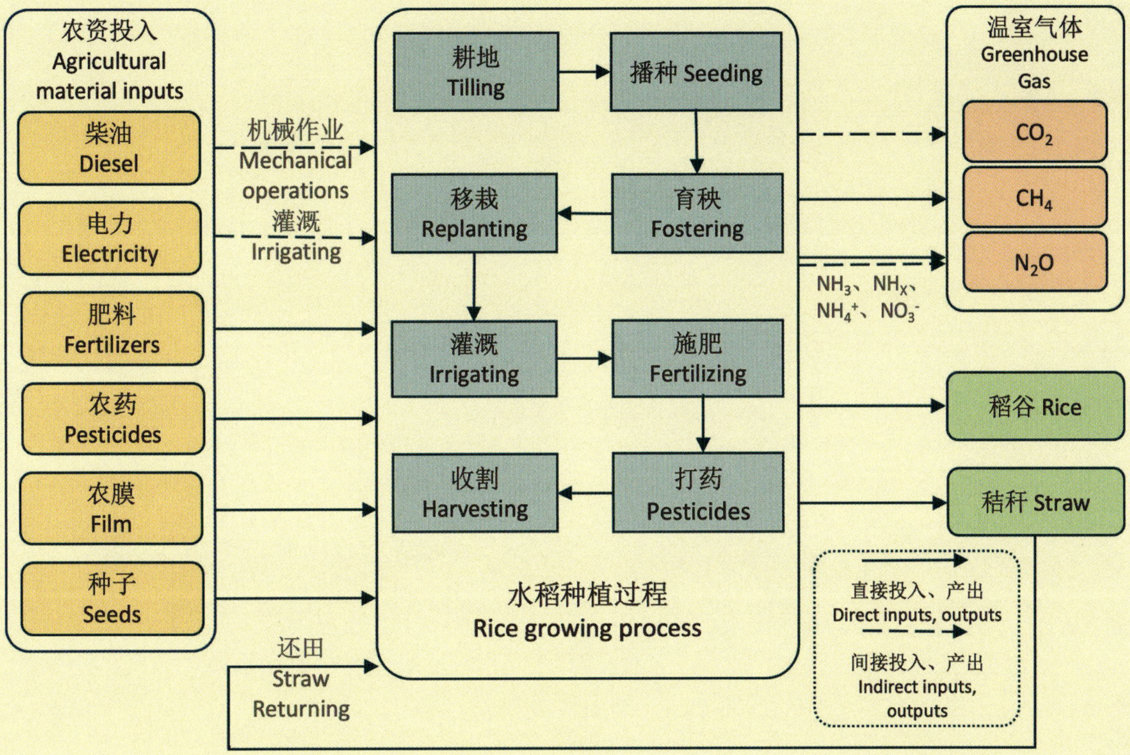

Fig. 16

Material flow analysis
Hongqing Li and Zheng Yang

Material flow analysis is a systematic assessment of the flows and stocks of materials within a defined system. It traces the journey of materials: where they come from, where they are going, how they are used, and how much is stored within a certain system. The aim is to monitor what impact they have on the environment, to better manage resources and waste while identifying important environmental protection interventions.

We used this method to provide valuable insights into how resources are consumed, transformed, and disposed of in the process of urbanization, as well as their impact on rural and urban areas. Based on our field investigations in Huangyan through sampling, interviews, and participant observation, we constructed a framework for the material flow analysis of rice field systems to track related rural-urban material flows (e.g., nutrients and energy (Fig. 16)). We considered the material flow of a growing season, from the developmental stage of the seed to the mature harvesting stage of the rice. Inputs mainly came from human activity systems (e.g., seeds, fertilizers, pesticides, energy fuels, and irrigation water) and natural systems (e.g., sunlight, rainwater, carbon dioxide, and nutrients taken from the soil). Meanwhile, outputs consisted of products (rice), bio-residues (straw), and associated greenhouse gas emissions and nutrient losses. We found that seeds, pesticides, fertilizers, and agricultural films come from local agricultural cooperatives. Diesel is bought from local gas stations and electricity comes from the national grid. Rice is sold to supermarkets in Taizhou, Hangzhou, and other provinces while straw is returned to the fields. The life cycle assessment of rice provides a scientific basis for developing solutions to reduce emissions and making rice production more sustainable.

While material flow analysis is valuable in developing more sustainable strategies for urban-rural resource management, it also faces challenges relating to data availability and quality, spatio-temporal boundaries, and limitations in capturing the complexity of rural-urban interactions.

Fig. 17

Dialogue

Urban-Rural Living Labs
Ava Lynam, Gaoli Xiao, and Kit Braybrooke

Urban-Rural Living Labs have been increasingly adopted as a means of facilitating sustainable urban-rural development through processes of participation, innovation, and iteration within real-life communities.[18] Urban and rural spaces are used as field "laboratories" in which "policymakers, researchers, businesses, service providers, citizens and other stakeholders work together to develop and test new ways to solve problems in a specific geographic region."[19] Through co-creation with local participants, Urban-Rural Living Labs foster collaborative experimentations and learnings that provide valuable references for potential adaptation to other locations undergoing similar challenges.

Urban-Rural Living Labs are a core element of the Urban-Rural Assembly project framework, with two in Huangyan, China, and one in Thuringia, Germany, serving as live sites for researching urban-rural development challenges and experimenting with potential solutions. The Urban-Rural Living Labs were identified through initial field investigations and consultation with local stakeholders with consideration of their relevance to the research design, strong local will for sustainable transformation, and potential for application of results elsewhere. The Urban-Rural Living Lab within traditional villages, fields, and forests in Thuringia provided a context from which to test methods before later intensively engaging with two Urban-Rural Living Labs at the urban-rural interface in Huangyan: one experiencing rapid urbanization and industrialization, the other undergoing revitalization through modern agriculture and rural tourism (Fig. 17). These Urban-Rural Living Labs with unique characteristics served as local anchors from which scientists, policymakers, and diverse local actors identified challenges and co-developed future visions for sustainable social and spatial transformation. In this way, they not only function as pilot sites of innovation but also allow for translocal knowledge transfer.

However, direct comparisons or transfers of findings and solutions should be avoided across

Fig. 18

Urban-Rural Living Labs with significantly different geographical, political, and cultural contexts. For instance, while some broadly similar challenges could be identified in Huangyan and Thuringia, such as the aging and hollowing out of rural villages, the drivers of migration and challenges to social inclusion are vastly different. Meanwhile, establishing and maintaining activities in Urban-Rural Living Labs requires significant resources in terms of funding, expertise, and time. Long-term commitment from stakeholders beyond the project duration is essential for sustained impact, particularly when translating results into policy and practice.

Multi-stakeholder workshops
Lukas Pappert

Multi-stakeholder approaches within planning processes aim to initiate dialogue and partnerships between relevant stakeholders from diverse fields including politics, administration, economics, NGOs, and civil society.[20] The goal is to build the trust and shared knowledge necessary for developing collective solutions to complex problems. Workshops can play a central role in stimulating creative dialogue among stakeholders through participatory formats.

The Urban-Rural Assembly research team utilized multi-stakeholder workshops as a central methodology to develop an "urban-rural co-visioning process" collaboratively with local stakeholders in Huangyan. This format facilitated cross-level and cross-sector exchange among various local stakeholders who may not typically interact. It also supported transdisciplinary exchanges between local stakeholders and the research team, playing a critical role in validating research data and bridging gaps through local knowledge (Fig. 18). The research team conducted

Fig. 19

a coordinated series of six multi-stakeholder workshops in Huangyan, with approximately fifteen to thirty stakeholders participating in each session. To promote cross-hierarchical dialogue, the workshop format alternated between roundtable and plenary discussions, transcending typical hierarchical room set-ups (Fig. 19). Additionally, the research team developed interactive workshop formats (see article by Maria Frölich-Kulik and Lukas Pappert on page 286) to structure discussions and promote open and creative discourse among participants. The aim was to support a results-oriented dialogue and maintain comparability across different focus groups on related topics. The workshops served as platforms for rich discussions among stakeholders and brought different perspectives to light for co-visioning regional "transformation-to-sustainability" pathways.

While six workshops were successfully conducted in Huangyan, the research team encountered various challenges during implementation. These included difficulties in translating individual ideas and demands into joint spatial strategies, related to language and cultural barriers between the international research team and participants. Participants also lacked experience with long-term visioning and spatial mapping processes. To enhance intercultural inclusivity, we employed simultaneous translators or conducted thorough briefings with native-language facilitators after each workshop session to avoid impeding immediate communication. Urban planning master's students supported the mapping process by spatially interpreting discussion points and illustrating them on maps.

As part of a duty of care to invited participants, attention must be paid to social hierarchies, power dynamics, and potential risks that may arise when assembling a diverse group of actors. Therefore, we opted to separate workshops in cases where cross-hierarchical set-ups would either not be accepted by participants or the discussions could potentially be strongly influenced by the presence of higher hierarchies. Nevertheless, the chronological order of the workshops from lower to higher hierarchies aimed to enable a bottom-up transfer of knowledge.

Urban-Rural Assembly (URA)
BMBF: 01LE1804A1-C1 (2019-2024)

URBAN – RURAL ASSEMBLY

URA Glossary

Urban-Rural Assembly (URA)
BMBF: 01LE1804A1-C1 (2019-2024)

URBAN – RURAL ASSEMBLY

Fig. 20

Urban-Rural Assembly Glossary

Li Fan, Jian Liu, and Anke Hagemann

Given the extent and speed of urban-rural transformation we have witnessed globally over the past ten or twenty years, it has become imperative to define (and redefine) terms associated with these processes. Concepts of "urban" or "rural" are not only constantly evolving but also hold diverse meanings in various global contexts. Moreover, projects dealing with urban-rural development integrating an interdisciplinary approach face obstacles in building a common discourse. Interdisciplinary collaboration is often considered more challenging than international cooperation because professionals in the same field typically share a common knowledge base and an understanding of the discipline's evolution.

The Urban-Rural Assembly consortium dealt with similar concerns as part of a collaborative Sino-German project which integrated manifold research perspectives, such as circular economy, ecology, landscape, socio-spatial practices, and migration. In an effort to establish a shared language across teams spanning different geographies, cultures, and disciplines, the team explored the use of a project glossary for frequently-used research terms as a collaborative, evolving document. The glossary provided a means of building a collective understanding of the varied and multiple concepts relating to urban-rural development across disciplines and nations captured within the Sino-German consortium (Fig. 20). Moreover, a glossary can also act as a tool to explore new terms, concepts, and interpretations of emerging spatial phenomena. While translating a term in itself can often be relatively straightforward, its interpretation may require a process of further exploration and consideration. For instance, how should we interpret terms like "urban-rural linkages" or "strategic spatial planning" in different global contexts? Moreover, how can terms which hold very specific meanings and allude to particular concepts and cultural or historical phenomena in their language of origin be interpreted in another language without losing their original meaning? For instance "*Raumbild*" in German, or "new villagers" (xin nongmin新农民) and "*hukou*" (户口) in Chinese.

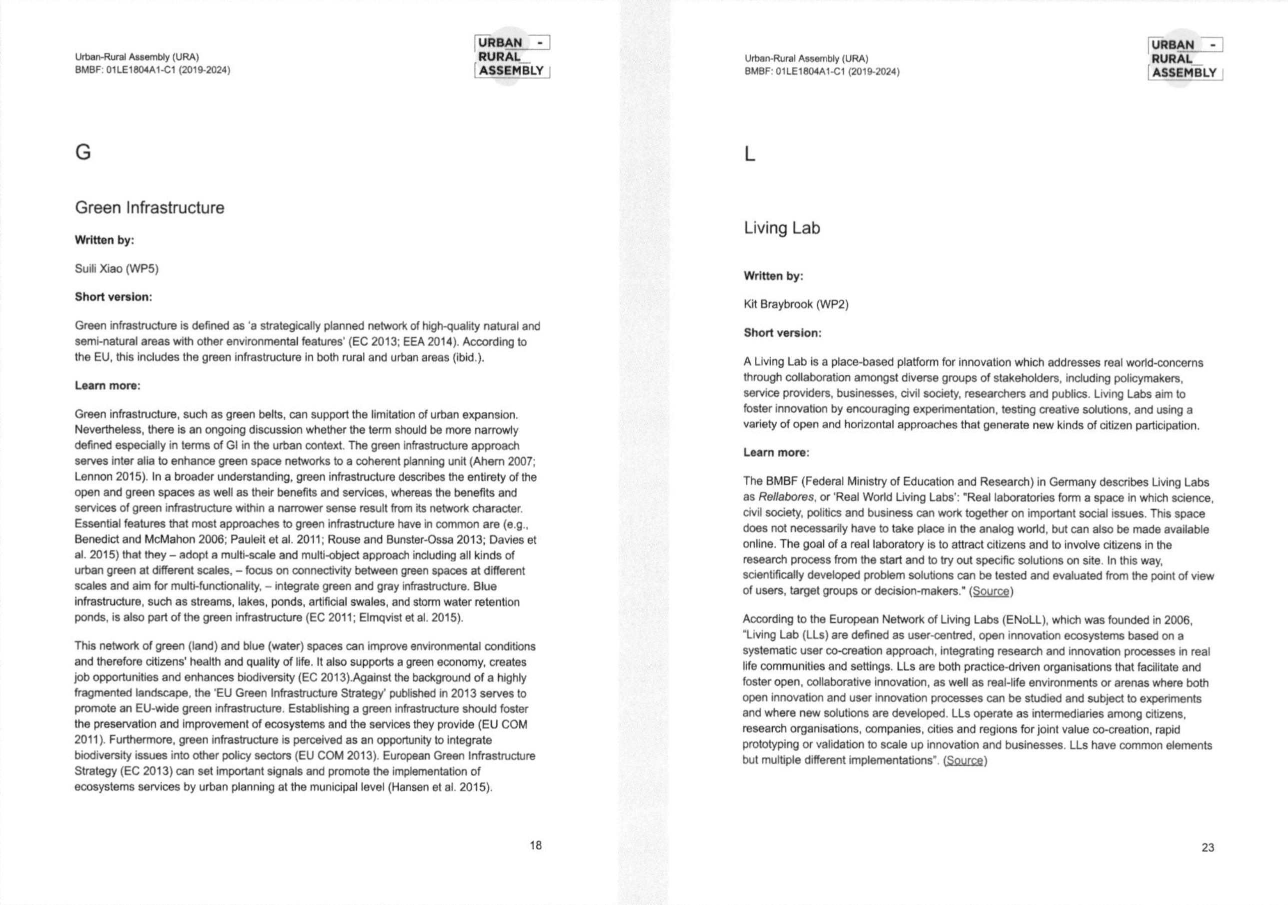

Urban-Rural Assembly (URA)
BMBF: 01LE1804A1-C1 (2019-2024)

URBAN - RURAL ASSEMBLY

G

Green Infrastructure

Written by:

Suili Xiao (WP5)

Short version:

Green infrastructure is defined as 'a strategically planned network of high-quality natural and semi-natural areas with other environmental features' (EC 2013; EEA 2014). According to the EU, this includes the green infrastructure in both rural and urban areas (ibid.).

Learn more:

Green infrastructure, such as green belts, can support the limitation of urban expansion. Nevertheless, there is an ongoing discussion whether the term should be more narrowly defined especially in terms of GI in the urban context. The green infrastructure approach serves inter alia to enhance green space networks to a coherent planning unit (Ahern 2007; Lennon 2015). In a broader understanding, green infrastructure describes the entirety of the open and green spaces as well as their benefits and services, whereas the benefits and services of green infrastructure within a narrower sense result from its network character. Essential features that most approaches to green infrastructure have in common are (e.g., Benedict and McMahon 2006; Pauleit et al. 2011; Rouse and Bunster-Ossa 2013; Davies et al. 2015) that they – adopt a multi-scale and multi-object approach including all kinds of urban green at different scales, – focus on connectivity between green spaces at different scales and aim for multi-functionality, – integrate green and gray infrastructure. Blue infrastructure, such as streams, lakes, ponds, artificial swales, and storm water retention ponds, is also part of the green infrastructure (EC 2011; Elmqvist et al. 2015).

This network of green (land) and blue (water) spaces can improve environmental conditions and therefore citizens' health and quality of life. It also supports a green economy, creates job opportunities and enhances biodiversity (EC 2013).Against the background of a highly fragmented landscape, the 'EU Green Infrastructure Strategy' published in 2013 serves to promote an EU-wide green infrastructure. Establishing a green infrastructure should foster the preservation and improvement of ecosystems and the services they provide (EU COM 2011). Furthermore, green infrastructure is perceived as an opportunity to integrate biodiversity issues into other policy sectors (EU COM 2013). European Green Infrastructure Strategy (EC 2013) can set important signals and promote the implementation of ecosystems services by urban planning at the municipal level (Hansen et al. 2015).

18

Urban-Rural Assembly (URA)
BMBF: 01LE1804A1-C1 (2019-2024)

URBAN - RURAL ASSEMBLY

L

Living Lab

Written by:

Kit Braybrook (WP2)

Short version:

A Living Lab is a place-based platform for innovation which addresses real world-concerns through collaboration amongst diverse groups of stakeholders, including policymakers, service providers, businesses, civil society, researchers and publics. Living Labs aim to foster innovation by encouraging experimentation, testing creative solutions, and using a variety of open and horizontal approaches that generate new kinds of citizen participation.

Learn more:

The BMBF (Federal Ministry of Education and Research) in Germany describes Living Labs as *Rellabores*, or 'Real World Living Labs': "Real laboratories form a space in which science, civil society, politics and business can work together on important social issues. This space does not necessarily have to take place in the analog world, but can also be made available online. The goal of a real laboratory is to attract citizens and to involve citizens in the research process from the start and to try out specific solutions on site. In this way, scientifically developed problem solutions can be tested and evaluated from the point of view of users, target groups or decision-makers." (Source)

According to the European Network of Living Labs (ENoLL), which was founded in 2006, "Living Lab (LLs) are defined as user-centred, open innovation ecosystems based on a systematic user co-creation approach, integrating research and innovation processes in real life communities and settings. LLs are both practice-driven organisations that facilitate and foster open, collaborative innovation, as well as real-life environments or arenas where both open innovation and user innovation processes can be studied and subject to experiments and where new solutions are developed. LLs operate as intermediaries among citizens, research organisations, companies, cities and regions for joint value co-creation, rapid prototyping or validation to scale up innovation and businesses. LLs have common elements but multiple different implementations". (Source)

23

Fig. 21

The Urban-Rural Assembly Glossary was used as a working tool but also carries the potential to develop more precise, accessible, and diverse descriptions of contemporary urban-rural transformation across geographic contexts. Thus, it could also act as a platform to communicate with different types of audiences, from planners and scientific researchers to policymakers and community members.

Film for transcultural communication

Maria Frölich-Kulik, Laura Henneke, and Lukas Pappert

When conducting multi-stakeholder workshops (see toolbox entry) in China, one of the biggest challenges was communicating our method for participatory planning to local stakeholders who may not be familiar with approaches originating in the German context. Therefore, we explored the production of audiovisual material as an engaging tool to capture attention while supporting transcultural communication and stakeholder engagement in the workshops. We developed a Chinese-subtitled documentary film aiming to facilitate understanding across different languages, cultural backgrounds, levels of education, and social status (Fig. 22).

The film introduced the key objectives and methods of our participatory planning process as applied in Nordhausen, Thuringia, as a practical reference. We showcased the film at the beginning of the workshops in Huangyan to establish a shared knowledge base and enable participants from diverse backgrounds

Fig. 22

to contribute meaningfully from the outset. This aimed to foster an inclusive environment, a context considered essential for effective co-visioning processes.

However, we observed that our first seventeen-minute film, densely packed with content, was also somewhat challenging for the audience to fully grasp. In light of this, we produced a shorter, simpler, two-minute film for the subsequent workshops which focused less on specific regional challenges or previous workshop results in Nordhausen. Instead, it focused on the atmosphere and practical set-up of the multi-stakeholder workshops. The short film was also distributed via social media to invite local stakeholders to participate in the events, an approach that received positive feedback.

1 William C. Adams, “Conducting Semi-Structured Interviews,” in *Handbook of Practical Program Evaluation*, eds. Kathryn E. Newcomer, Harry P. Hatry, and Joseph S. Wholey (Hoboken, NJ: Jossey-Bass, 2015), 492–505.

2 Joshua M. Bluteau, “Legitimising Digital Anthropology through Immersive Cohabitation: Becoming an Observing Participant in a Blended Digital Landscape,” *Ethnography* 22, no. 2 (October 15, 2019): 267–85.

3 Kit Braybrooke, Gaoli Xiao, Ava Lynam, “Living Lab, interrupted? Exploring new methods for postdigital exchange on WeChat with Urban-Rural Living Labs in China and Germany during COVID-19,” *JCOM* 22, no. 3 (2023).

4 Saara Vauramo and Heikki Setälä, “Urban Belowground Food-Web Responses to Plant Community Manipulation - Impacts on Nutrient Dynamics,” *Landscape and Urban Planning* 97, no. 1 (July 2010): 1–10.

5 Janice Morse and Peggy Field, *Nursing Research: The Application of Qualitative Approaches* (London: Chapman & Hall, 1996).

6 Roger Downs and David Stea, “Cognitive Maps and Spatial Behavior: Process and Products,” in *Image and Environments*, eds. Roger Downs and David Stea (Chicago: Aldine Publishing, 1973).

7 Millennium Ecosystem Assessment, *Ecosystems and Human Well-Being: Synthesis* (Washington, DC: Island Press, 2005).

8 Sigrun Langner, Yuting Xie, Maria Frölich-Kulik, Yuling Zhang, and Karl Beelen, *Between Land and Water*, (Berlin: JOVIS, forthcoming 2025).

9 Compton J. Tucker and Piers. J. Sellers, "Satellite Remote Sensing of Primary Production," *International Journal of Remote Sensing* 7, no. 11 (November 1986): 1395–416.

10 Alex de la Iglesia Martinez and S. M. Labib, "Demystifying Normalized Difference Vegetation Index (NDVI) for Greenness Exposure Assessments and Policy Interventions in Urban Greening," *Environmental Research* 220 (March 2023): 115-55.

11 Suili Xiao, Wolfgang Wende, Alexander Maximilian Haase, Wentao Yan, Hui Chen, Yuqiu Chen, Wei Hou, et al. "Ecosystem Services & Biodiversity Conservation in Huangyan, Taizhou, China" (Working paper, 2024).

12 Michel Callon, "Some Elements of a Sociology of Translation: Domestication of the Scallops and the Fishermen of St Brieuc Bay," *The Sociological Review* 32, no. 1 (May 1984): 196–233.

13 Bruno Latour, "On Actor-Network Theory: A Few Clarifications," *Soziale Welt* 47, no. 4 (1996): 369–81.

14 Cheng Chen, Jinlong Gao, and Jianglong Chen, "Behavioral Logics of Local Actors Enrolled in the Restructuring of Rural China: A Case Study of Haoqiao Village in Northern Jiangsu," *Journal of Rural Studies* 93 (July 2022): 223–33.

15 Javier Martínez, "The Use of GIS and Indicators to Monitor Intra-Urban Inequalities. A Case Study in Rosario, Argentina," *Habitat International* 33, no. 4 (October 2009): 387–96.

16 Axel Küpper, *Location-Based Services: Fundamentals and Operation* (Chichester: Wiley-Blackwell, 2014).

17 Henry Lefebvre, *The Production of Space*, trans. Donald Nicholson-Smith (Oxford and Cambridge: Blackwell Publishers Ltd, 1991).

18. Pia Laborgne et al., "Urban Living Labs: How to Enable Inclusive Transdisciplinary Research?," *Urban Transformations* 3, no. 1 (November 17, 2021): 1–18.

19 Rural Urban Europe, *Robust*, accessed May 16, 2024, https://rural-urban.eu/.

20 Adriane MacDonald, Amelia Clarke, Lei Huang, Mark Roseland, and M. May Seitanidi, "Multi-stakeholder Partnerships (SDG #17) as a Means of Achieving Sustainable Communities and Cities (SDG #11)," in *Handbook of Sustainability Science and Research*, ed. Walter Leal Filhon (Cham: Springer, 2018).

Fig. 1
Biomass and soil samples were collected in Beiyang Town for laboratory analysis.

Fig. 2
Quotes were obtained from semi-structured interviews conducted by the research team in the Xinqian community.

Fig. 3
Screenshots of photos shared by participants from the WeChat photo exchange group.

Fig. 4
Researchers in the process of collecting biomass and soil samples for laboratory analysis.

Fig. 5
A researcher observing and participating in assembling plastic products alongside elderly villagers.

Fig. 6
An example of a mental map drawn with a young factory worker.

Fig. 7 & 8
Distributing questionnaires on preferences for recreation and demand for ecosystem services in Huangyan.

Fig. 9
Socio-cultural landscape mapping of the Yongning River, exploring how local folk religion played a role in forming settlement patterns centered on temples implicitly tied to natural landscape elements.

Fig. 10
Normalized Difference Vegetation Index change in Huangyan during 1992-2020 shows a decrease in vegetation in urban areas and agricultural zones, and an increase in small forest areas and the old city center.

Fig. 11
Suggestions for ecological restoration in Beiyang Town based on a Normalized Difference Vegetation Index analysis and biodiversity assessment.

Fig. 12
Using Gephi software to generate a visualization of dominant and dependent "actants" and their interactions during rural-urban transformation in Huangyan.

Fig. 13
Results of GIS grid-based data analysis identifying local crops using a fifty-by-fifty-meter grid.

Fig. 14
An example of Location-Based Services analysis illustrating the intensity of commuting patterns between residential areas and workplaces in Taizhou in 2020.

Fig. 15
Socio-spatial analysis of a watermelon seed shop, illustrating the spatial manifestation of translocal watermelon production chains.

Fig. 16
Schematic illustration showing the material flows of rice fields in Huangyan.

Fig. 17
The Urban-Rural Living Lab in Xinqian served as a rich site for researchers to study local development challenges.

Fig. 18
Discussion during a multi-stakeholder workshop on ecological transformation pathways.

Fig. 19
Multi-stakeholder workshop in Huangyan.

Fig. 20 & 21
Excerpts from the Urban-Rural Assembly Glossary, showcasing a variety of explored concepts.

Fig. 22
Film stills showing scenes from a short documentary used as a tool to support transcultural communication and stakeholder engagement in workshops.

Chapter 3: Learning from the Hinterlands

Global hinterlands produced by processes of extended urbanization have become a major arena for future transformations regarding regional and regenerative supplies of energy, food, or building materials. At the same time, these regions can become vibrant places for everyday life and tourism by enhancing their specific rural qualities, such as rich nature or local heritage. There is much to learn from innovative—yet often overlooked—practices for sustainable rural development around the world. Chapter Three presents a wide range of cutting-edge approaches from Europe and China, including contemporary commoning practices, the revitalization of village public spaces, architectural acupuncture for rural placemaking, circular economy pilot projects in small towns, and the provision of bio-based building materials. These case studies all emphasize that the success of rural development projects depends heavily on the initiative and involvement of local people and key stakeholders.

Fig. 1

Architectural acupuncture: Reimagining Songyang County's rural identity

Eduard Kögel

The following article will address how architecture can significantly contribute towards the enhancement of an entire region on multiple levels. Case studies are used to illustrate developments in Songyang County, Zhejiang Province, China. This piece is a byproduct of many years of experience in the field, in cooperation with the district, the architect (Xu Tiantian), and the Aedes Architecture Forum in Berlin.

Xu Tiantian's vision: A rural renaissance in Songyang

Xu Tiantian is a Chinese architect who obtained a Bachelor's degree from Beijing's Tsinghua University in 1997 and a Master's degree from Harvard's GSD in 2000. In 2004, she became the first woman in China without a male partner to found her own office, Design and Architecture (DnA), in Beijing. In 2014, Xu Tiantian began working in Songyang County, Zhejiang Province, when the region was lesser known within wider China. At this time, it had only relatively recently been connected with wider infrastructure networks for the first time; however, the region consisted of old villages—most of which had heritage buildings that could potentially serve as local tourist attractions.

The district is topographically remarkable, with an elongated and fertile plain in its center; within this runs the Songyin River, its banks lined with several famous tea plantations and sugar cane fields. To the east and west of the region lie steep mountains peppered with small hamlets, villages, or farmsteads within their narrow valleys. Typically, only older residents remain in these settlements while most young people move to the cities as migrant workers. Sadly, many of the now empty local timber and rammed earth buildings have fallen into disrepair with little prospect of revitalization.

Sowing seeds of success: The Songyang development model

To encourage tourism potential in Songyang, the region had to endear itself to the collective memory of the young, urban, middle-class population. Within the existing radically vertical hierarchy, this required the support and leadership of political decision-makers—particularly the county's Party Secretary Wang Jun—

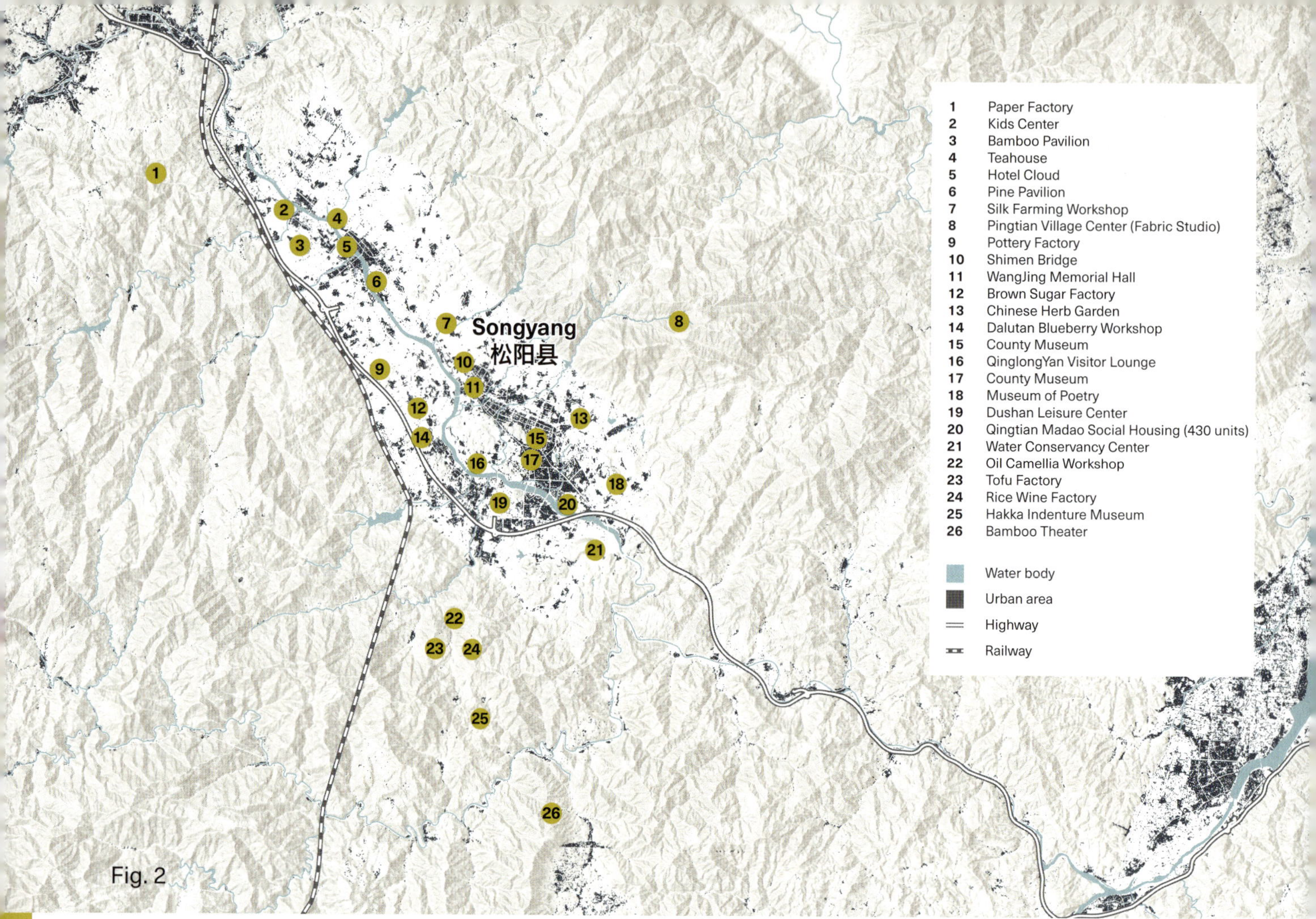

Fig. 2

alongside the "Culture Department" and other administrative units. However, autonomous village collectives in China are independent by nature in their decision-making, following their own values and rules; although the party secretary could propose new architectural interventions to drive rural development at his discretion, he must receive the unconditional support of village collectives. Therefore, Xu Tiantian was required to convince local village stakeholders of the pertinence of her strategy, a plan supported by the party secretary. She carried out the first dozen small interventions pro bono, partly on her own and partly on the initiative of the village collectives.

One of the first projects was in the village of Pingtian (2015), where the villagers and contractors sought to demolish an old rammed earth building. However, after persistent persuasion, the entire complex was repaired and has thus been regarded as a reference project showcasing adaptive reuse. In contrast, the initial situation was quite different for a new sugar factory in the village of Xing (2016); here, the working conditions for families were significantly improved while the community was given a meeting place for the first time. This was because sugar production can only occur in winter, with the building otherwise available for cultural and social purposes throughout the rest of the year. These first projects became important as examples, showcasing experiences that could be discussed in new projects.

After some initial successes, the village collectives approached Xu Tiantian with their ideas to utilize existing resources for future development. In addition, informal reports relating to the projects appeared on social media and briefly attracted attention. However, it was exhibitions outside of China—at the Aedes Architecture Forum in Berlin[1] and the Venice Biennale (both in 2018)—that first drew attention to the small-scale rural development and subsequently received heightened media coverage in China. Moreover, an international symposium organized by Aedes (2018) on site in Songyang further publicized the ideas developed there. Remy Sietchiping, Head of Policy, Legislation, and Governance in the Urban Practices Branch of UN-Habitat in Nairobi, attended the symposium. Sietchiping progressed the topic and developed the International Forum on Urban-Rural Linkages

Fig. 3

(IFURL) in collaboration with Songyang County, an event now held every two years in Songyang.[2]

The small-scale approach with local stakeholders developed by Xu Tiantian, in which architecture plays a key role, is now also being discussed in other regions worldwide. This positive yet complex development was only possible with the cooperation of the village collectives, party secretary Wang Jun, and international communication through Aedes that Xu Tiantian initiated. In June 2020, Wang Jun left Songyang on a rotational basis and now works at the provincial Ministry of Culture and Tourism. Since then, a second new party secretary has been appointed in the district who entirely shifted the regional focus to advancing industrial development.

Needlepoint vision: Xu Tiantian's strategic approach

Architect Xu Tiantian compared her concept of "small interventions" to the traditional approach of acupuncture; by applying a precise stimulus, it is believed that "self-healing powers" can be activated, triggering a momentum of their own in neighboring fields to advance development in rural areas. In the second year of Xu Tiantian's involvement in Songyang, she made an offer for an "acupuncture strategy" in the villages.[3]
As previously mentioned, in contrast to top-down planning in urban areas, village collectives are autonomous with projects only implemented in cooperation with them; therefore, each project has a unique dynamic, and progress can depend on numerous diverse factors. In any case, within Songyang it was not a smooth process as the villagers often had varying ideas about the appearance of new buildings. They typically either believed they should resemble the old temples that had just been demolished or take the form of miniaturized metropolitan architecture signifying an era of new glory. Initially, many disagreed that the new rural architecture could be inspired by the old local timber and rammed earth building culture, neglected for decades. Ultimately, it took numerous discussions and assertiveness from practitioners to dispel the fears and concerns of the local population and construction companies to make progress.

Each project required a different solution relating to its specific location; for example, the restoration

Fig. 4

of old rammed earth buildings and wooden structures, a new steel structure for a sugar factory, the wooden superstructures for a pedestrian bridge, or the translucent glass skin for a museum of poetry. These interventions are united by their scale, all oriented towards existing buildings; however, they all possess individual qualities that demonstrate how architecture can be inspired by long-established traditions without copying them.

Xu Tiantian completed about twenty-six adapted projects scattered throughout the main valley and mountainous side valleys, often stimulating entirely new economic opportunities in the process. For example, the sugar and tofu factories created new jobs, better working conditions, new income streams, and fresh marketing opportunities due to improved hygiene conditions. The same applies to a new rice wine factory that became a tourist highlight, attracting visitors with its show production, where they can observe the working process. Most of the projects are aimed at small-scale rural tourism; fundamental to this is the interplay between the traditional village and new constructions.

Community empowerment: Fostering equity in village revival

The success of Xu Tiantian's architectural projects demonstrated an alternative approach to the treatment of existing buildings, offering villagers new ideas and potential models to revitalize their structures and improve rural quality of life. Within several years, the positive outcomes of individual buildings grew, combining to become successful villages. One particular project in 2019 involved the transformation of the 600-year-old Shangtian Village into a collective business model where every resident automatically holds a share. In the past, urban entrepreneurs purchased individual homesteads for little money to market them profitably as boutique hotels after renovation.

In Shangtian, many of the old rammed earth buildings were empty without water and electricity. With the support of the local government, the village was completely renovated through simple means and now has thirty small, basic units to accommodate tourists. After a favorable start, China's Zero-COVID policy in response to the pandemic brought tourism in Shangtian to a standstill in 2020. Then, the village collective decided to work with a professional, private company that now pays local shareholders a fixed basic income. After the Zero-COVID policy was lifted in 2023, business developed well again.

Pandemic perspectives: Crisis, catalyst, or chance?

Before the COVID-19 pandemic, many families and collectives took part in positive village development, with at least 400 family-run bed-and-breakfasts, teahouses, and restaurants opening in traditional buildings. These enterprises were economically prospering in the first year and a half of the pandemic; however, by the winter of 2021/22, this progress had almost entirely stalled. China's Zero-COVID strategy was strongly implemented in most countryside regions through continuous lockdowns; this meant that tourism was detrimentally affected, with visitors from the large cities of Hangzhou and Shanghai unable to enter the region. It soon became clear that diversification of the rural economy would provide a more resilient solution. However, the tourism industry boomed again in 2023 with advance touristic bookings now essential.

Prior to the pandemic, more than 5,000 young people came to Songyang County to open their own company, with many leaving metropolitan areas in search of alternative living and business models. In China, rural

Fig. 5

regions appeal to this demographic as an escape from urban stress and economic pressures, combined with highly developed new digital marketplace opportunities. As a rural destination and remedy for these issues, Songyang undoubtedly has an advantage with its new architecture and positive branding. The administration established an office where returnees and newcomers can receive advice while the state provides grants for new businesses. Moreover, thanks to new technologies and the expansion of e-commerce, online sales in the district increased by more than 50% in 2021 alone. For example, young entrepreneurs have optimized the production of old beekeepers or invested in new pig farming and sold the products online. This new knowledge produces innovative ideas for untapped markets emerging in large urban centers.

Outlook and opportunities: Shaping the future of Songyang

In 2020, the COVID-19 crisis and new political leadership team provoked a realignment in priorities concerning the future development of Songyang County. As a result, some of the buildings already planned by Xu Tiantian—such as a new ceramics factory—could not be realized. Moreover, other projects already under construction were notably delayed, such as a local brick kiln museum expecting completion in spring 2024. In addition, other buildings are also affected, such as the Kids' Learning Field, a project primarily intended to impart information about rural areas to urban children. Despite the construction being completed, interior work and outdoor facilities were suspended during the pandemic as no operator could be found due to a lack of visitors. In 2023, a new operator took control of the facility, offering extracurricular learning opportunities to children from neighboring schools. Since many projects are initiated without a precise market analysis beforehand, there are almost always adjustments to be made during ongoing operations.

The urban renewal projects initiated during party secretary Wang Jun's term in office (until 2020) are also currently on hold. Xu Tiantian's plan to integrate agricultural aspects into urban development projects was intended to promote a new connection between rural and urban structures, for which new architectural ideas

Fig. 6

were also discussed. However, the new political leadership has focused more on diversifying the economy, with architecture playing little part in this drive. During Wang Jun's time in charge, Songyang's architectural development remained considerably avant-garde; despite the projects not being determined by him, the party secretary still provided the framework for robust governance through the autonomous village collectives. Today, these collectives have developed a stronger understanding of how to initiate projects, commission local architects to develop new bed-and-breakfast hotels, and stimulate the local economy with their ideas. The transformative approach to utilizing existing buildings encouraged by Xu Tiantian through the "acupuncture" strategy has thus become integral to the success of villages in the region.

Despite the numerous challenges in recent years, the development of Songyang remains positive. For example, the number and inherent quality of Xu Tiantian's fully realized projects alone show that, in only several years, small architectural interventions have succeeded in anchoring the region in the perception of the urban public in China. In addition, in 2022, Tiantian was

Fig. 1
The Rice Wine Factory, by architect Xu Tiantian, attracts visitors with its show production.

Fig. 2
Regional transformation through acupuncture: twenty-six projects by architect Xu Tiantian are scattered throughout the main and side valleys in Songyang.

Fig. 3
The Brown Sugar Factory in Xing Village of Songyang County, built in 2016 by architect Xu Tiantian.

Fig. 4
The Tofu Factory, by architect Xu Tiantian, stimulates new economic opportunities.

Fig. 5
The Shimen Bridge, designed by architect Xu Tiantian, was built on top of an abandoned 1950s viaduct over the Songyin River.

Fig. 6
Shangtian Village co-op housing consists of thirty small, basic units to accommodate tourists in renovated rammed earth buildings.

able to transform several old quarries in the neighboring Jinyun County that now serve as an ideal means of circulating visitor traffic. These successes are also tempered by the expectations of visitors who are pleasantly surprised by the rural development in Songyang, realized through contemporary architectural strategies. The completed projects illustrate how strongly architecture can influence social contexts with adequate political support and close consultation with people who use those spaces. The learning process through these interventions is significant for all stakeholders, perhaps reflected most acutely in the contemporary adaptation of village building traditions. The dynamics of development in the region can also be measured in numbers; by autumn of 2023, the district recorded exponential economic growth of 9.4%—a high figure for China, whose national economy grew by around half in the same year.

1 The Aedes Architecture Forum in Berlin is a globally recognized independent institution and exhibition space for the communication of contemporary architecture and urban design. For reference to Songyang see: Aedes, eds., *Rural Moves—The Songyang Story* (Berlin: Aedes Catalogue, 2018); Dunya Bouchi and Miriam Mlecek, eds., *Regions on the Rise: Culture and Architecture as Drivers for Rural Development* (Berlin: ANCB The Aedes Metropolitan Laboratory, 2019); Kristin Feireiss and Hans-Jürgen Commerell, eds., *The Songyang Story: Architectural Acupuncture as Driver for Rural Revitalisation in China* (Zurich: Park Books, 2020); Aedes, eds., *Xu Tiantian: Jinyun Quarries. The Quarry as Stage* (Berlin: Aedes Catalogue, 2022).

2 The first IFURL with the theme "Rural Revitalization through Innovations and Valorization" took place in Songyang County in November 2019. The theme of the second forum in October/November 2021 was "Integrating Health and Territorial Development for Sustainable Livelihoods." Due to travel restrictions caused by the coronavirus pandemic, the forum was held in a hybrid format. The third forum in 2023 had the theme "Enhancing Urban-Rural Connectivity for Better Livelihoods" and was again held in Songyang. https://urbanpolicyplatform.org/urban-rural-linkages/ (accessed January 8, 2024).

3 The idea of "urban acupuncture" was first used in 2006 as the title for an exhibition on architecture by Inge Roecker in Vancouver's Chinatown and medium-sized cities in southern Germany. See: Eduard Kögel, "Urban Acupuncture," in: *Inge Roecker / ASIR Architekten Stuttgart, ASIR Studio Vancouver, Urban Acupuncture, eds. Aedes* (Berlin: Aedes, 2006), 6–10. For an in-depth look at the idea of acupuncture in an urban context, see Jessica M. Hemingway and Alejandro De Castro Mazarro, "Pinning down Urban Acupuncture: From a Planning Practice to a Sustainable Urban Transformation Model?", *Planning Theory & Practice*, 23:2 (2022), 305–09.

Fig. 1

Thuringia as an urban-rural regional state and the IBA method

Marta Doehler-Behzadi

For more than one hundred years, international building exhibitions (IBA, short for Internationale Bauausstellung) have been a regular feature of the planning and building scene in Germany. The IBA label is not the preserve of any particular official institution and is instead based on self-appointment; hence, it has been suitably flexible throughout the decades. An IBA usually covers what is new with "Next Practice!"[1] looming large over them. The IBA is a formal declaration of a temporary state of emergency[2] and therefore promises to generate wide public and political attention.

An IBA is usually assembled over roughly a decade and hence requires tenacity and strategic thinking from all participants. IBA Thuringia has made urban-regional relations its central topic to contribute to a more integrated approach, linking urban and regional planning. This is to create more balanced development between urban centers and rural areas. Since 2012, IBA has initiated experimental projects throughout Thuringia with hundreds of partners, making it possible for the general public to experience a wide range of large and small-scale future scenarios. These include community-orientated economies and experimental building methods based on alternative organizational forms and approaches. Every trial undertaking is an attempt at sustainable spatial practice and provides a model for new lifestyles, different economic practices, and new design and procedural approaches.

Urban/rural Thuringia

Why should an IBA be concerned with the interrelation between urban conurbations and the wider surrounding rural areas? 90 percent of Thuringia is predominantly covered by countryside. According to one popular description of the region, it is possible to run into a village every three kilometers and a town every thirty. This seems like an apt portrayal, although not entirely based on scientific fact. Thuringian towns are small by national and international standards, with a population of 214,000 in its capital, Erfurt. More typical is the density of small settlements incorporated into areas of great natural beauty. While there is little urban sprawl, the cultural landscape is rich in history.

Fig. 2

Today, although the circumstances under which people live in Germany vary little by and large, conventional discourse often still centers on the fundamental dichotomy between urban and rural living. “Town” and “country” continue to evoke images of a vibrant city on one hand, contrasted with the “sleepy village” and its romanticized farming life on the other. This limited viewpoint misses the varied and nuanced ways of living and working that fall in between these stereotypes. For example, it omits many small towns, city perimeters, suburbias, conglomerations created by administrative reform, hidden regional economic champions, and successful small to medium-sized businesses that act as important economic drivers outside big cities without any cosmopolitan aspirations.

In addition, it also ignores the realities of modern-day industrial agrarian production. Moreover, discourse at professional and academic levels is often focused solely on politically well-organized urban centers, big cities, or metropolitan regions—an approach that no longer suffices. An inner periphery of gradually emptying residential spaces with an aging population has become common around cities—especially in East Germany—in the shadow of years of continual spatial concentration of people and institutions at urban centers. For the peripheries, public and private services are getting increasingly scarce and people are feeling left behind.

However, things are less clear-cut; while for many years bigger cities—with their attractive job markets, modern education opportunities, and wide range of urban amenities—registered significant population increases, much of the population aspired to live in the country or smaller towns outside cities. Moreover, many people moved into cities while continuing to dream of life in the countryside. The Berlin Institute, in conjunction with Wüstenrot Stiftung, recently conducted a survey titled “Landlust Neu Vermessen” (or, “Re-mapping Cottagecore”)[3]. They found that villages and smaller towns have recently benefitted from internal migratory trends, regardless of whether they are located centrally or peripherally.

The drivers of this included housing shortages and the COVID-19 pandemic, together casting a shadow on the “uplifting experience” of urban life. Hence, it is more than just wishful thinking to imagine there is more to

Fig. 3

these peripheral regions than merely existing as faded hinterlands with only an aging, left-behind population, rudimentary infrastructure, and memories of things past. This becomes even more relevant when considering the multiple crises and global challenges many suburban people face today. IBA's urban-rural approach was based on the observation that, in times of crisis and uncertainty, the countryside holds promise to become a refuge where life can be fulfilling even without the amenities of big cities. The country can maximize its potential and encourage people to visualize a promising future, thereby promoting its reputation for resilience, bolstered by unfettered access to unique resources and knowledge bases.

IBA as an instrument for transition

At its inception in 2014, IBA launched a broad public appeal for project ideas and proposals. A diverse range of applications were received by a variety of actors from various areas in the region, such as local authorities, departments within the housing sector, representatives from different professions, and sections of civil society. Each proposal was carefully examined to assess its relevance in the urban-rural approach, asking: where is the specific creative momentum? How can this be implemented in actuality? Who exactly is involved? The scale of structures ranged from small building conversions to complex new-builds and regional planning interventions.

The following are three examples: Representatives from the Schwarzatal Region were fatigued with complaining about the decline of their region. To engage with their concerns, their IBA-sponsored initiative created several projects and event formats. Previously, the region used to be an attractive tourist destination; however, after years of stagnation, a period of regeneration began (under the slogan "Summer Break"), which managed to galvanize people across the entire region and beyond. Real change was stimulated through measures such as revitalizing typical local architecture, the establishment of an annual festival called "Day of the Summer Break," and turning Schloss Schwarzburg into the foremost regional tourist destination through its gradual restoration and re-opening to visitors. Among the many agents who contributed were *Zukunftswerkstatt*

Fig. 4

Fig. 5

Schwarzatal and other local and regional community associations and authorities, tourist associations, the *Stiftung Thüringer Schlösser und Gärten* (Historical Monuments Foundation), the Association of Friends of Schloss Schwarzburg, the regional branch of LEADER (a network for the distribution of relevant regional EU funding), and numerous other cooperation partners.

The Protestant Church in Thuringia owns many buildings in the region, constituting about two thousand properties. In cooperation with IBA Thuringia, the Church conceived several trial projects for the adaption of existing buildings for new and extended uses in what became a model process. Examples included the historical St Anne's Chapel in Krobbitz (which was given a new lease of life as an art space), the project group called the "Family of Church Buildings," *Her(r)bergskirchen* in the Thuringian Forest (now offering community-hosted overnight stays), and the unusual "Bee Garden" Church in Rodlisleben—all of which have brought a "bounce" back to parishes in the region and attracted new visitors from abroad.

People resourcefully took matters into their own hands when it came to establishing their priorities for living and growing old peacefully, residing in a conglomeration of rural villages administratively joined under the banner of "Seltenrain." The aim was to keep the villages alive and ensure quality health care provision, especially for the elderly. Starting with an integrated concept for rural development, the project morphed into the *Stiftung Landleben* (or, "Living in the Countryside Foundation") and the non-profit organization *Landengel* ("Countryside Angel") to implement their aims. "We're doing this because no one else will do it for us otherwise," say the activists. With this in mind, their success has proven them right: they saved the local primary school and the lido from closure and have established a new low-barrier community housing at village centers with a community-based bus service. Moreover, IBA helped to open four community health centers and a multi-purpose town hall in a disused former village grocery store. Thus, the local experts of Seltenrain are now much in demand, even at a federal level.

The IBA method

An IBA is usually implemented when conventional regulations and routines no longer work or have become sub-optimal. IBA explores what is new on a defined terrain such as the Federal State of Thuringia. Its emphasis is on practical, project-driven work that could (ideally) establish new procedures and development instruments while making appropriate adjustments to existing rules and regulations. This particular IBA gained its insights from practical work carried out in the past. Moreover, considerable time was taken to allow multiple site visits and conduct serious theoretical discourse, with action taken not simply using impulse nor by writing potentially futile paperwork. Instead, any IBA acts from more than just an observer's perspective; it is also judged on the actual changes made. The advantage of acting practically (rather than academically) lies in the gains derived through actions that matter.

Throughout the decade since IBA's inception, the future of rural regions in Germany turned from being a virtually ignored concept into a highly relevant topic for current social debate. Demographic shrinkage and neo-liberal spatial practices have stimulated a decline within these regions, causing social friction which puts pressure on society as a whole. It has become increasingly evident that pitting town against country is no longer a viable approach, neither politically nor professionally. With its urban-rural approach, IBA Thuringia has made a unique contribution to current professional discourse, particularly as it focuses on the long-neglected prospects of rural areas. In previous decades, urban values, urban lifestyles, and urban spaces determined the era of liberalization and globalization.

As urban planners, our profession contributed towards an "urban logic" which culminated in the formation of the concept of the "European city,"[4] as defined in the Leipzig Charter for sustainable urban development. Against this background, IBA Thuringia has provided a new narrative on urban-rural matters—not against current urban development strategies but expanding and progressing from a dominant city-based focus. The pre-eminence of this metropolitan preoccupation emerged in Western Germany during the 1970s, largely determining policy in the East after re-unification in the 1990s. However, shrinkage and hard structural change after 1990, with the highest unemployment rates in the East, quickly revealed its limitations.

Focusing on rural areas suited well to settlement patterns in Thuringia has yielded new findings; for example, the previous urban focus negatively affected the "Hinterland," making it more varied demographically. It also contributed to a decline in infrastructure and public and private sector amenities in the region, with many variations of this development elsewhere. For example, these observations mirror similar developments across Europe and globally, a pattern we explored in the international conference "StadtLand: From Thuringia to a Planetary Perspective." This took place from May 4–6, 2023 in Thuringia and was organized in conjunction with the Urban-Rural Assembly project.

Fig. 6

Remy Sietchiping of UN-Habitat and Hilary Angelo from the University of California Santa Cruz (and many others) have criticized the prevalent city focus, describing it as merely "cityism." They believe that this approach focuses only on traditional conceptions of the city and its immediate environs while failing to consider other interdependencies with its extended perimeter.[5]

The end products of various interconnected IBA Thuringia projects and programs have borne fruit. Its incremental methods have proven their worth, fitting seamlessly into current relevant social discourse. Moreover, its extended urban-rural approach subverts conventional planning hierarchies pitting city centers against the wider perimeter, with rural areas usually losing out. In the future, systemic interconnections will become increasingly important—this will tackle the social dimensions of more equitable spatial planning policies. This could be achieved using building and infrastructure conditions of equal benefit for city and regional dwellers, countering inequitable development dynamics with poly-central models.

Relief for "over-stretched" urban centers could be provided by attractive targeted offers using incentives

Fig. 1 & 2
With the support of IBA Thuringia, collectives of professionals and activists are renovating old houses as "summer break" residences in the Schwarzatal region of Thuringia. Fig. 1: In 2022, a workshop was held in "Haus Döschnitz" with architecture students from TU Berlin. Fig. 2: Renovation work on the historical guesthouse "Haus Bräutigam" in Schwarzburg.

Fig. 3
The Schwarzatal is one of the rural project regions of the International Building Exhibition in Thuringia.

Fig. 4
The "Her(r)bergskirchen" initiative reuses underutilized protestant churches as overnight lodging and event venues for guests and residents of the Thuringian Forest; for example, in Neustadt am Rennsteig. The project was developed by studio etcetera, Berlin.

Fig. 5
A health kiosk in Blankenburg, in the village region of Seltenrain, helps to secure medical care in rural areas. The architecture was designed by PASEL-K Architects, Berlin.

Fig. 6
IBA's final exhibition took place in a landmark factory building (the Eiermann Bau) in Apolda from May to October 2023.

(for example, as in the housing sector with "depleted" regions). However, against the backdrop of rapidly advancing climate change, it is also about a completely new level of material and energy links and interdependencies. For example, where else should renewable energy and raw materials needed for an eco-transition in cities be sustainably "harvested," albeit in the country? Isn't it small, close-knit neighborhoods that are best suited for the implementation of circular models to use and recycle our resources? Thus, all the indications point towards the countryside hosting meaningful and well-paid work, offering progress and innovation. Once again, there will be good reasons for living in the country.

The success of an IBA depends on how it addresses central issues for social change, problems often initially based on speculation rather than scientific evidence or any political framing. If living labs, projects, and processes effectively get to the heart of contemporary issues, IBA will succeed in generating ample public interest for its themes. Ultimately, these gain prominence by "interfering" with the current built environment. IBA also takes the form of exhibitions; for example, IBA Thuringia concluded with a presentation of its results in a much-acclaimed showcase from May to October 2023 at the Eiermann Building in Apolda and all peripheral locations throughout the Free State. The show was confidently titled "UrbanRural – Learning from Thuringia." The reflections and results of IBA processes have also been published in two volumes focusing on the projects themselves, as well as offering more general reflections derived from the practical work on new urban-rural relationships (e.g., "StadtLand – Projekte"; "StadtLand – Perspektiven," available in German only). As of 2024, the Thuringian Stiftung Baukultur (Foundation for Building Culture) will take over the communications legacy of IBA. Overall, it is clear that the International Building Exhibition is a very suitable instrument for creating new and next practices.

Translated from German by Jörg von Stein

1 An IBA does not cover only "good practice" or even "best practice," it always wants to create the new and "next practice."

2 See No. 7 in "Ein Memorandum zur Zukunft Internationaler Bauausstellungen." 2017, accessed May 7, 2024, https://www.internationale-bauausstellungen.de/iba-memorandum/.

3 Berlin-Institut, Wüstenrot Stiftung, Eva Eichenauer, Sabine Sütterlin, Frederick Sixtus, and Catherina Hinz, "Neu im Dorf. Wie der Zuzug das Leben auf dem Land verändert," (2023), accessed May 7, 2024, https://www.berlin-institut.org/fileadmin/Redaktion/Publikationen/Neu_im_Dorf_online.pdf.

4 "Neue Leipzig Charta: Die transformative Kraft der Städte für das Gemeinwohl," 2021, accessed May 07, 2024, https://www.bbsr.bund.de/BBSR/DE/veroeffentlichungen/sonderveroeffentlichungen/2021/neue-leipzig-charta-pocket-dl.pdf?__blob=publicationFile&v=3.

5 Hannes Langguth and Remy Sietchiping. "Lokal verankert, global vernetzt – die transformative Kraft einer territorialen Stadt-Land-Governance." in IBA Thüringen. StadtLand Perspektiven, edited by IBA Thüringen, 2023, 157–66.

Fig. 1

Fig. 2

Townization driven by circular economy principles: The practice of Kongcun Town

Jian Liu

China has suffered for a long time from remarkable urban-rural disparities, largely due to the dual urban-rural system gradually established in the 1950s under its planned economy. The effects of this system had contributed towards the stagnation of rural development, increasing prosperity in urban development and resulting urbanization processes. Rural development has accelerated since the "opening-up" of China and its economic reforms in the late 1970s, propelling economic growth. However, this dilemma remains today.

To ensure the sustainability of socio-economic development and urbanization, in 2003, China's Central Government announced a scientific perspective for development highlighting the intention to synchronize urban and rural development as one of its key national strategies. Since then, a series of national policies and pilot programs on rural development have been conceived and implemented to improve the livelihoods of farmers, increase the productivity of agriculture, and modernize the countryside. These include the "Building of a New Socialist Countryside" policy of 2005, the "Building of Beautiful Countryside" policy of 2013, and the "National Plan of Rural Revitalization" of 2018. Various experiments were carried out in response to local conditions across China, each using economic development as a driving force in the urbanization process. Among them, the following case of Kongcun Town exemplifies an effort to achieve "townization" through the development of a circular economy and can be taken as an inspiring reference for others.

Kongcun Town and its cultural identity

Located at the southwestern corner of Jinan Municipality, Kongcun is a small town under the jurisdiction of Pingyin County, occupying a territory of about 100 square kilometers and with a population of around 40,000 people.[1] It could perhaps be considered mediocre in terms of population size among the 21,322 small towns in China. However, its level of economic development is notably higher than the national average.[2] The town has received several national titles since 2010, including being listed as one of China's "Key Towns" in 2014 and "Top 1,000 Towns" in 2021.

Fig. 3

Moreover, two features distinguish it from other small towns: one is its name relating to Confucius and the other is its development model structured on the circular economy concept.

Literately, Kongcun means "the village of Confucius." The town derived this name from the historical story that Confucius once carried out open lectures there about 2,500 years ago. These were reputed to have been held on the top of a small hill, Kongzi Hill (i.e., Confucius Hill), to the west of today's town center where a Temple of Confucius was built in remembrance. The town is also known for hosting the first CPC county committee in the southwest of Shandong Province, established in 1939; the residence of the Lian family built in the 1450s;[3] several catholic churches built by European missionaries at the turn of the twentieth century; and finally, several folk operas such as Yu-gu and Wang-pi. This tangible and intangible heritage lends the town a unique historic and cultural identity, supplemented by local resources enabling the development of cultural and creative industries supporting tourism.

Industrialization of Kongcun

As a town composed of a town center and forty-six villages, Kongcun has a favorable geographical location at the interchange of three regional transportation arteries, with distinct advantages in terms of land, water, and climate that can accommodate agriculture. Within policy frameworks established after China's "opening-up" and reforms—and based on the stable growth of the primary industry of agricultural production—the town commenced processes of industrialization in the late 1990s. As a result, the secondary industry focusing on the production of carbon products started to gradually dominate the local economy. The town witnessed an acceleration of socio-economic development in the twenty-first century thanks to the continued growth of the primary agricultural industry, the booming of the secondary industry, and the emergence of the tertiary industry in the service sector. Since 2006, the total GDP of Kongcun has almost doubled every two years while GDP per capita has remained stable at almost twice of the national average. By the end of 2020, GDP was over RMB 5 billion and GDP per capita was over RMB

Fig. 4

Circular economy processes in the primary agricultural industry

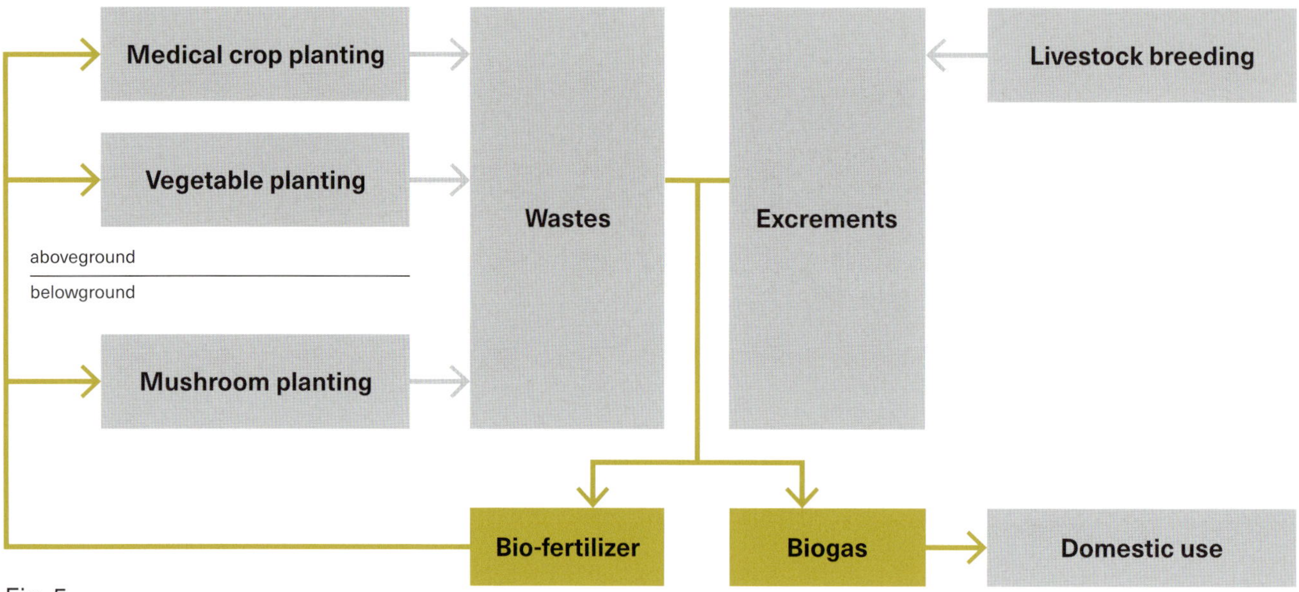

Fig. 5

120,000. In the same year, this ensured a fixed assets investment of RMB 780 million, a general public budget income of RMB 252 million, a disposable income per capita of farmers of RMB 20,000, and a collective income of over RMB 50,000 for each of the forty-six villages.[4]

"Townization"

Strong economic growth was the primary driver of urbanization within Kongcun, otherwise known as "townization" in the Chinese context. The booming of the secondary industry attracted many local rural residents to the town center, transforming themselves from traditional farmers working the fields to modern workers with better jobs and higher incomes in factories. In response to this rural-urban transformation, an industrial park was built to accommodate the agglomeration of factories and a new residential area of 84,000 square meters to accommodate about 600 rural families migrating to work there. By the end of 2015, twenty-two scaled enterprises were located in the industrial park. At the same time, new industries were introduced to extend the existing industrial chain, such as mechanical processing, organic fertilizer production, and warehousing and logistic services. New public facilities and civil utilities were built in the town center and the surrounding villages, including a kindergarten, an elderly care center, urban and rural roads, waste transfer stations, a wastewater treatment station, and a centralized heating system.[5] These facilities noticeably improved the physical environment and living quality within the town, resulting in a more densely populated town center accommodating half of all residents (Fig. 3).

Meanwhile, in the villages beyond the town center, agricultural modernization, new industry development, and farmland reclamation were strongly promoted by the town government. By the end of 2015, professional cooperatives and new farms of crop breeding, greenhouse planting, and standardized animal husbandry were established, with the mechanization rate of agricultural production elevated to 85%. New industries such as rural tourism, agrotourism, and creative activities were developed. As part of provincial pilot project, four villages were drafted for tourism and two farms for agrotourism. An area of over 1,400 hectares

Circular economy processes in the manufacturing of carbon products

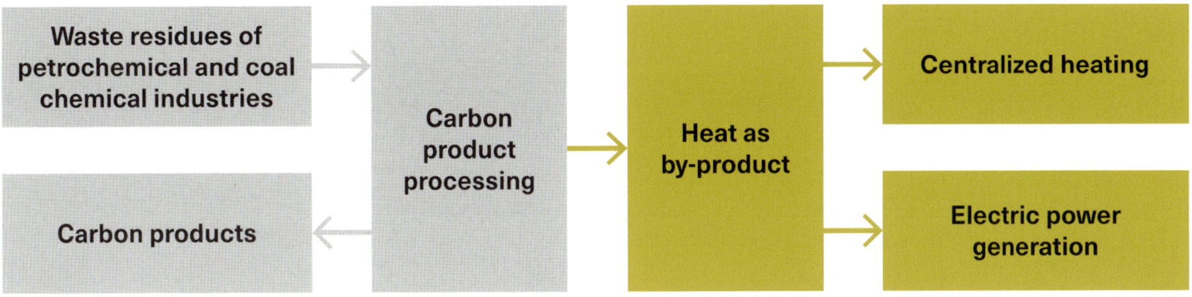

Fig. 6

was reclaimed from abandoned building land or waste land and converted into farmland. This was due to some farmers leaving the villages to relocate to the town center, accounting for 28% of its total farmland reserve at the time (Fig. 1, 2).[6]

Integrated circular economy

Apart from positive interactions between processes of industrialization and townization, the notable features of the three aforementioned industries and the emerging trend of the circular economy concept within Kongcun deserve further analysis.

Serving as the economic foundation of Kongcun, the primary industry of agriculture mainly consists of the cultivation of mushrooms, vegetables, and medicinal crops, alongside the breeding of livestock—both of which form a circular chain in terms of energy. Mushrooms are cultivated underground in the hilly topography to the west of the town center, leaving farmland on flatter plains for the cultivation of vegetables and medicinal crops to increase land use efficiency. Livestock excrement and organic waste from vegetables and medicinal crops are collected and processed into biogas for domestic use while bio-fertilizer is produced for crops (Fig. 5).

As a central economic pillar of Kongcun, the secondary industry is mainly characterized by the production of carbon products, such as prebaked anode and anode for aluminum electrolysis, with the annual productivity accounting for a quarter of the country's total and a half of the country's export volume. In 2020, the total output value of Kongcun's carbon production was RMB 6.1 billion while the foreign exchange value through export was RMB 1.4 billion.[7] The production of carbon products also forms a circular chain in terms of energy. On one hand, the raw materials used for carbon product processing are the waste residues from the production process of petrochemical and coal chemical industries (i.e., petroleum coke and pitch coke), implying the secondary utilization of energy. On the other hand, the deep processing of petroleum cokes and pitch cokes produces the by-product of heat. This is further transformed into the civil use of centralized heating in the town center and the surrounding villages, in addition to the generation of electric power (Fig. 6). By the end

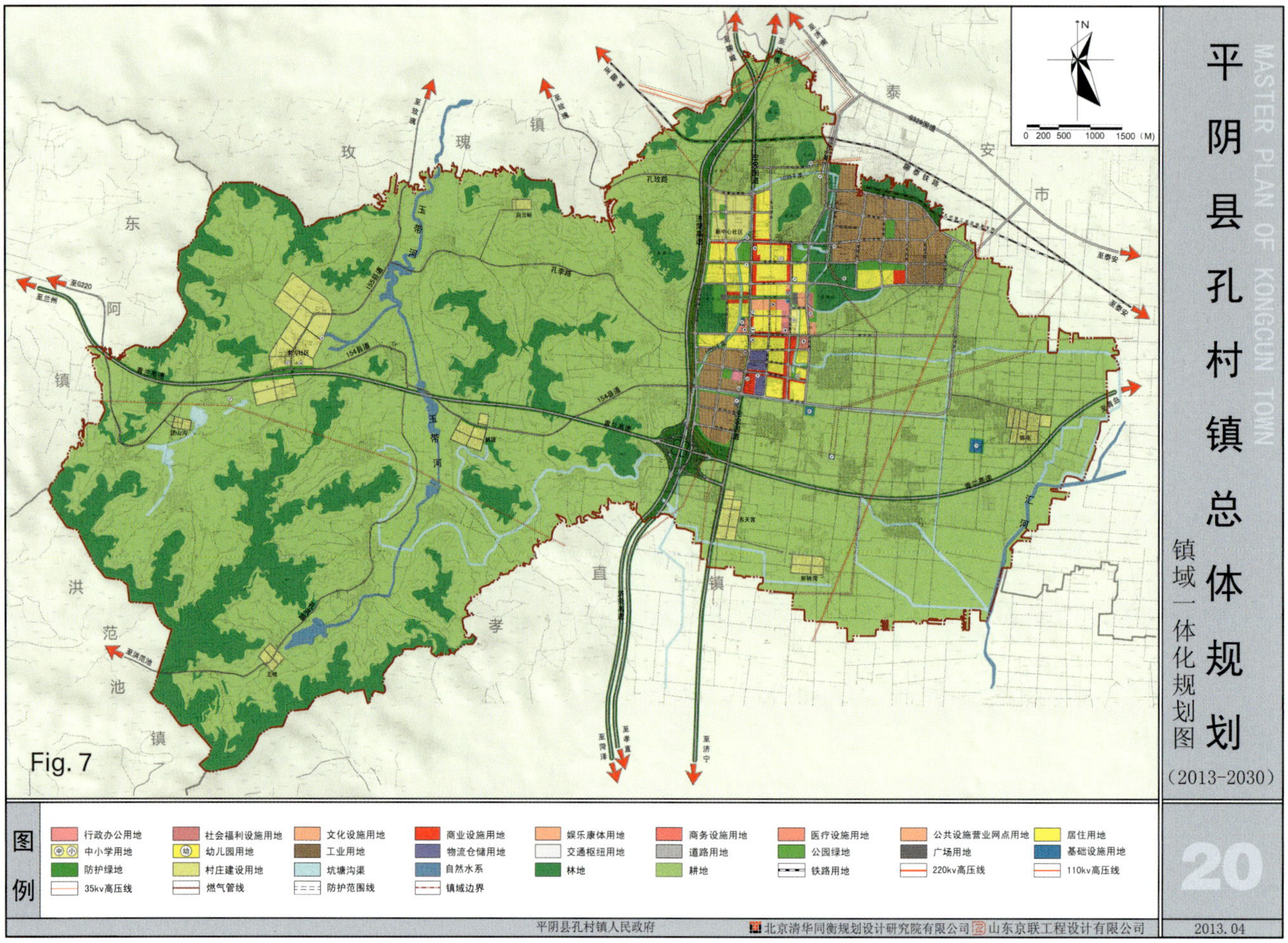

Fig. 7

Fig. 1 & 2
Farmlands and new farmer housing in the west of Kongcun Town.

Fig. 3
Kongcun town center.

Fig. 4
Industrial park for carbon products.

Fig. 5
In Kongcun's agricultural industry, livestock excrement and organic waste from vegetables and medicinal crops are collected and processed into biogas for domestic use while bio-fertilizer is produced for crops.

Fig. 6
Energy for the town center and the surrounding villages is produced as a by-product of petrochemical and coal chemical industries.

Fig. 7
Master plan of Kongcun Town (2013-2030), addressing urban-rural integration.

of 2015, the floor area of centralized heating in Kongcun reached 300,000 square meters. At the same time, great efforts were made to upgrade the technological level of carbon production to increase production efficiency and reduce negative environmental influences.

As a promising new economic industry in Kongcun, the tertiary industries of the town are principally characterized by modern services such as logistics and warehousing, rural tourism, agrotourism, catering services, and creative industries—all of which are either closely related to (or firmly based on) the primary and secondary industries. On one hand, the advantageous location of Kongcun at the interchange of three regional transportation arteries provided the town with substantial opportunities to develop logistics services, leading to the establishment of a logistic industrial park in southwest Kongcun's town center in the late 2010s. On the other hand, the rapid development of modern agriculture in various forms—combined with its cultural heritage—provides Kongcun with resources to develop new industries—particularly relating to tourism, recreation, and creative industries. The adaptive reuse of farmer housing and other unused facilities has contributed towards a slow transformation of the overall appearance of villages within the town. Moreover, the sustained development of new industries has also contributed towards a gradual updating of residents' mentalities. For instance, at Ligou Village in the hilly west of the town, the Pingyin Lux Louvry Painting Academy was established in 2010—an art institute engaged in the production of oil and watercolor paintings for export trade. It is based in the former middle school of Ligou Village, employing local residents (including people with health conditions or impairments) as painters after providing them with necessary training. In recent years, it has been developed further as an employment training center for people with disabilities, serving as a provincial base for primary and middle school studies. This has not only attracted outside visitors but also stimulated new ideas for development.

The role of planning

It is important to mention that the success of townization in Kongcun, driven by circular economy development, can be partly attributed to the guidance and support of the "Master Plan of Kongcun Town 2013-2030."[8] This policy document was formulated by the planning team from the School of Architecture at Tsinghua University in collaboration with a local planning institute and commissioned by the People's Government of Kongcun Town. Within just over one year, the planning process was shown to be an effective coordination platform upon which the opinions and requests of various stakeholders (e.g., the town government and its various departments, village collective organizations and their members, and key enterprises and their partners) were thoroughly discussed before final compromises and agreements were confirmed. This process highlighted the efficacy of developing a circular economy, the coordination of urban and rural areas, and the careful balancing of natural and manmade environments (Fig. 7). Ultimately, the experiences at Kongcun strongly justify the positive and significant role of thorough planning to effectively promote coordinated urban-rural development.

1 Department of Rural Socio-Economic Survey, National Bureau of Statistics of China, *China County Statistic Yearbook* 2022, Vol. of Towns: 280 (Beijing: China Statistic Press, 2022).

2 Ibid. Also according to the statistics issued by the National Bureau of Statistics of China, accessed February 27, 2023, https://www.stats.gov.cn/zt_18555/zthd/lhfw/2023/fjxsd/202302/t20230227_1918911.html.

3 The family is well known in China because of Lian Po, a great general of Zhao State during the Warring States Period from BC 476 to BC 221.

4 People's Daily Online, "The Way for Upgrading and Breaking-Through of China's Top Carbon Town," accessed February 27, 2023, https://baijiahao.baidu.com/s?id=1709029019165181348&wfr=spider&for=pc.

5 People's Government of Kongcun Town, *Annual Government's Working Report 2016*. 2016.

6 Op. cit.

7 People's Government of Kongcun Town, *Annual Government's Working Report 2021*. 2021.

8 People's Government of Kongcun Town, Beijing Tsinghua-Tongheng Urban Planning and Design Institute, Shangdong Jinglian Engineering and Design Company, *Master Plan of Kongcun Town 2013-2030*. 2013.

Fig. 1

Regenerative urban-rural systems

Philipp Misselwitz

The built environment is the elephant in the climate room. The so-called building sector has become the most important source of anthropogenic environmental pollution worldwide. At the same time, it has failed to fulfil the basic needs of billions of urban dwellers who continue to live in poor and undignified conditions. According to a recent report by GlobalABC,[1] the built environment accounted for 36% of global final energy consumption and 37% of global greenhouse gas emissions in 2020, despite a pandemic-related slowdown in construction activity. At the same time, resource consumption continues to rise inexorably: in the European Union, the construction sector is responsible for half of all materials extracted and more than a third of all waste generated.[2]

As planners and architects, we must admit that we did not foresee this drama, nor were we able to prevent it from coming to a head. Despite this, we must conduct extensive self-critical analysis. Today's crisis is, at least in part, a direct consequence of the deterministic modernism that still lingers—the paradigm of the functionally divided, car-oriented city we conceived and ingrained in our professional mindset has been consistently implemented. The "Athens Charter," promoted by Le Corbusier as part of the "Congrès Internationaux d'Architecture Moderne" (CIAM) in 1933, and Konrad Wachsmann's book *Wendepunkt im Bauen* from 1959, laid the foundations for an ethos prioritizing technological supremacy over nature. This ethos is exemplified, for instance, by events such as "Earth Overshoot Day." It marks the day humanity has used up all the natural resources the earth can provide within a year. In 2023, it fell on August 2. By demanding the disentanglement of production and consumption systems and consumption-orientated urban economies from surrounding natural ecosystems, cities became the laboratories of affluent society and its extractive, consumptive, and waste-producing logics. Advanced capitalism has embraced this separation by ignoring both the potential benefits and fragility of ecosystem services. This has occurred through cost-benefit analyses and externalization of the impacts of its extractive behavior. As a result, the "Anthropocene city"[3] exists and functions primarily as an antagonist towards natural biological systems and ecological landscapes.

Fig. 2

However, a pure *mea culpa* does not get us anywhere. While in Europe or North America, the call for a drastic restriction of building to its bare essentials or for conversion before new construction is understandable, this "building shame" falls short in a global context. By 2050, an additional two and a half billion people will be living in cities, primarily in Asia and sub-Saharan Africa—the latter of which is a region in which 80% of buildings are yet to be built. In addition, another two billion people should have the right to live in decent housing with access to essential public services infrastructure. Many urban areas require an upgrade through "strategic retrofitting," prioritizing the renovation of infrastructure and existing buildings. Thus, the unprecedented scale and pace of urban growth will create enormous demand for housing and urban infrastructure, potentially doubling the global building stock and the built footprint in the coming decades. Ultimately, the urbanization of the world previously considered a success now threatens to become a story of human failure.

So, what is to be done? Architects and planners are poor prophets of doom because optimism is inherent to their profession. A more socially relevant contribution would be to build on their self-criticism and reflection to develop a positive, post-Anthropocene utopia reflecting what a better future could look like within planetary boundaries. Can the built environment go from being a climate killer to a climate healer? How can we radically rethink and change the materials, means, and methods we use to construct our buildings and cities, in addition to reimagining how we organize, inhabit, and maintain them?

The global, interdisciplinary "think-and-do" tank "Bauhaus Erde" was founded by climate scientist Hans Joachim Schellnhuber to answer these questions. Based in Potsdam and Berlin, Bauhaus Erde refers to the famous German design school that, around a century ago, tried to use the opportunities of industrialization to build better homes and cities worldwide. Today, in the context of planetary crises, we again need a transdisciplinary effort to bring together leading thinkers, designers, and policymakers globally to formulate a new vision and action plans for systemic change. The basis of the concept developed by Bauhaus Earth is a call for a fundamental shift in perspective: instead of

Fig. 3

seeing city and countryside as opposites, human settlements of a post-Anthropocene must be seen as part of the surrounding and interpenetrating ecosystems and natural contexts. For example, this could be integrated into an overarching spatial system characterized by (limited) available material resources and flows, within which we are embedded and upon which we depend. Instead of continually extracting resources from this system ("extractivism") and polluting it with waste, our actions in the future must be geared towards restabilizing and strengthening human-nature interdependencies—i.e., making a positive or "regenerative" contribution. We therefore envision regenerative urban-rural systems to enable the following effects.

Climate restoration through recyclable and bio-based materials

Forests are often seen as balancing mechanisms in the climate equation. To limit global warming, it is of eminent importance to continue afforestation, facilitating the removal of carbon dioxide from the atmosphere. Subsequently, this will be permanently stored in above-ground and underground biomass in dead wood and bio-based building materials, such as wood, bamboo, hemp, or straw. However, the remaining global forest areas and other "natural sinks" are now too fragile to reduce the CO_2 content of the atmosphere to a tolerable level and thus stop global warming. Therefore, artificial—i.e., man-made—sinks must be utilized to help the system, which is precisely where construction could become a key lever. For example, replacing carbon-intensive building materials (e.g., cement) with bio-based materials (e.g., wood) can reduce greenhouse gas emissions and store the carbon dioxide (CO_2) removed from the atmosphere—an essential prerequisite for limiting global warming to below two degrees. Research has shown that buildings and cities constructed and maintained with bio-based and sustainably sourced building materials can be transformed into man-made carbon sinks.[4, 5] However, this transition will only be regenerative if the materials are sourced from certified and sustainably managed forests without compromising biodiversity and the ecosystem services forests provide humans. At Bauhaus Earth, this potential is analyzed using quantitative studies and global simulation

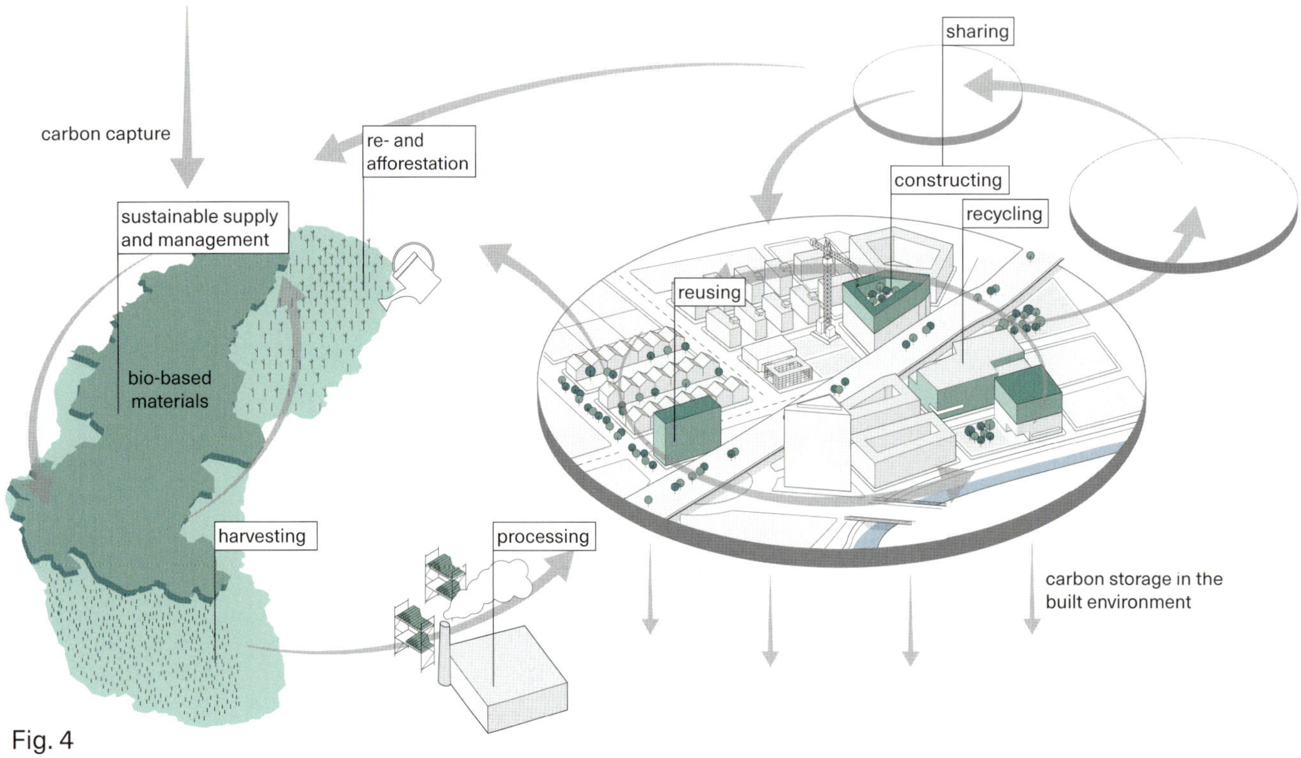

Fig. 4

models, ultimately to develop transformation scenarios and road maps for the global construction sector.

Concrete work on pilot projects that visibly and tangibly show new ways of building is also essential for Bauhaus Erde. To this end, Bauhaus Erde founded labs as collaborative spaces for experimentation, design, and implementation. A lab is currently being set up in Berlin's Marienpark—a former gasworks—and will enable prototypes of building elements and 1:1 models to be tested in collaboration with property developers, local authorities, and architects. The lab is set to become part of a global network of labs operated by an ever-growing group of experimenters found in various geographical regions worldwide. They all share the same view: a forest-building revolution can only succeed if we go beyond pure research and show what is already possible in the real world. For example, the "1,000 Bamboo Villages" project in Kalimantan, Indonesia, has developed a simple process for transforming bamboo—a fast-growing grass with high CO_2 storage potential—into modular building blocks such as panels. This can be used in a similar way as CLT (cross laminated timber) panels in Europe. Such approaches must be promoted in Africa for adobe construction or in South America with native plant species. Prototypes offer opportunities to increase visibility and thus create greater dissemination of this process. Bauhaus Earth actualized its first experiment in partnership with the Institute for Advanced Architecture Catalunia (IAAC) in October 2022. The "Mass is More" project explores the use of regenerative and decarbonizing architectural materials as part of a temporary installation at the Barcelona Pavilion (by Mies van der Rohe) and reveals the multi-layered processes behind the construction of built environments.

Re-regionalization through circular building practices

To date, the construction sector has largely been decoupled from the requirements and practices of the circular economy; however, the linear "extract-use-dispose" model is still common practice. While the supply chains of building materials currently span the entire globe and generate a gigantic ecological footprint through transport and logistics alone, thinking and acting in regenerative urban-rural systems could lead to greater re-localization or re-regionalization of production processes. For example, building materials—from production to recycling—could become elements of quasi-closed regional systems.[6] This would reduce energy consumption and CO_2 emissions while anchoring value creation gains regionally, reinvesting them in the stabilization of ecological systems. A regional, bio-based circular economy is considered an unattainable goal in the foreseeable future by many.[7] However, the optimization of existing material supply chains, intelligent product design, and production processes—as well as approaches for the reuse and further use of materials wherever possible—are important for more efficient resource usage, waste reduction, and re-evaluation of supposed waste products. A greater awareness of regional metabolisms and material flows has already developed concerning energy supply and nutrition in some urban-rural constellations. Moreover, the implementation of circular principles for a sustainable construction sector to close (construction) material cycles and the cascading use of buildings can also be organized regionally. Therefore, Bauhaus Earth understands the deeper urban fabric in the context of bioregions where forest reorganization plays a decisive role. It is not about traditional pines (and certainly not about old-growth forests) but rather about thinking openly about the future; for example, with fast-growing poplars, black locust trees, or various grasses.

Polycentric and green urban-rural systems

Extreme weather caused by climate change is already being felt in Central Europe and other continents. Moreover, the use of concrete and asphalt in urban areas has led to cities storing heat during the day and only releasing it slowly at night; in many regions, this means cities are barely habitable during heat waves. The cooling of cities depends largely on the integration of urban-rural constellations—i.e., the consideration of wind corridors or nature-based solutions such as green corridors or building greening—with the same applying to water and wastewater systems not designed for extreme weather conditions. Nature-based solutions, such as natural infiltration through unsealing and greening, reduce vulnerability to heavy rainfall and have cooling effects through evaporation. Moreover, the concept of the "sponge city," originally emanating from China, is now being used in many municipalities across the globe. This approach aims to keep rainwater as localized as possible to protect infrastructure, strengthen urban greenery and biodiversity, and

Fig. 5

Fig. 6

Fig. 1
The sawmill in Bralitz, Brandenburg, tackles the challenge of processing thirteen different types of regional hardwood for the Bauhaus Earth Lab. This effort is part of the "ProtoPotsdam" project, which aims to build a prototype using regional and bio-based materials.

Fig. 2 & 3
The agroforestry trial field at Eberswalde University for Sustainable Development combines conventional agriculture with regular rows of various hardwoods that counteract wind erosion and can be harvested as timber after 50-100 years. This initiative is documented as part of the "ProtoPotsdam" project.

Fig. 4
Supplying cities with renewable, bio-based building materials depends on circular and efficient urban-rural exchange relationships, along with the sustainable management of forests and agriculture.

Fig. 5
The project "Mass is More" (2022) examined the use of regenerative architectural materials through a temporary installation in Mies van der Rohe's Barcelona Pavilion, revealing the supply chains of the materials involved.

Fig. 6
Supported by the Bauhaus Earth Fellowship Program, the not-for-profit organization "Material Cultures" investigated the potential of rewetting peatlands in Brandenburg for producing regional bio-based building materials. Mock-ups of building components made from bio-based materials such as reed were presented in the exhibition "The Great Repair" at the Akademie der Künste, Berlin (2023-24).

exploit any positive effects such as evaporative cooling. Thus, nature-based solutions reduce environmental risks, serve as natural carbon sinks, promote the restoration of biodiversity and ecosystems,[8] and generate socio-economic and health benefits (e.g., by providing high-quality places to spend time). Therefore, the overarching urban structure can make a significant contribution to sustainability, with polycentric structures and urban-rural
constellations proving far better in this respect than monocentric urban typologies.[9] Therefore, a central endeavor should be to organize cities more efficiently in terms of their functional networks and regional-spatial structures, thus promoting the re-integration of urban and natural systems.

A focus on the symbiotic potential of urban and rural areas can form a robust foundation and starting point for model regions with regionally specific solutions to combat the global sustainability and climate crisis. Here, Next Practices[10] are used to create forward-looking proposals for prototypical and adaptable co-transformation approaches of urban-rural systems, land use, and the built environment—a framework in which the concrete use of local and bio-based building materials, the recycling of used building materials, and the closing of (building) material cycles could be tested. This would thus demonstrate new, visually, and haptically tangible ways of building within decentralized and climate-adapted urban environments. Funds from global development cooperation, or the "Loss and Damage Fund," initiated at COP27 (and first budgeted for at COP28), could be invested in a construction turnaround and sustainable transition. Several model regions could thus be brought together to form a global learning network. Despite the regional solutions we are finding for building transitions, the multiple crises of recent years—from the global pandemic and the conflict in Ukraine to the climate crisis—have taught us, above all, that local action must be grounded in a sense of planetary responsibility. Only through an unprecedented collective effort can the utopia of a regenerative built environment as a healing force for people and the planet become a reality.

1 GlobalABC/IEA/UNEP (Global Alliance for Buildings and Construction, International Energy Agency, and the United Nations Environment Programme), *GlobalABC Roadmap for Buildings and Construction: Towards a Zero-emission, Efficient and Resilient Buildings and Construction Sector*, IEA, Paris, 2020.

2 Edgar G. Hertwich, "Increased carbon footprint of materials production driven by rise in investments," *Nature Geoscience* no. 14 (2021): 151–55.

3 Cities dominate in the age of Anthropocene. Metaphorically, the term is used (independently of geological definitions) for the concept of an Earth shaped by man.

4 Galina Churkina, Alan Organschi, Christopher P. O. Reyer, Andrew Ruff, Kira Vinke, Zhu Liu, Barbara K. Reck, T. E. Graedel, and Hans Joachim Schellnhuber, "Buildings as a global carbon sink," *Nature Sustainability* 3, no. 4 (2020): 269–76.

5 Austin Himes and Gwen Busby, "Wood buildings as a climate solution." *Developments in the Built Environment* no. 4, 100030 (2020).

6 Hans Joachim Schellnhuber and Philipp Misselwitz, "Bauwende zur nachhaltigen Stadtentwicklung," in *Deutschlands Neue Agenda. The transformation of the economy and state into a climate-neutral and digital society | Climate change and digitalisation will change us*, eds. Veronika Grimm, Joachim Lang, Dirk Messner, Dirk Meyer, Lutz Meyer, Sigrid Nikutta, and Stefan Schaible (Berlin: Econ, 2021).

7 Jim Hart, and Francesco Pomponi, "A circular economy: where will it take us?, " *Circular Economy and Sustainability* 1, no. 1 (2021): 127–41.

8 Nadja Kabisch, Niki Frantzeskaki, Stephan Pauleit, Sandra Naumann, McKenna Davis, Martina Artmann, et al., "Nature-based solutions to climate change mitigation and adaptation in urban areas: perspectives on indicators, knowledge gaps, barriers, and opportunities for action." *Ecology and Society* 21, no. 2 (2016).

9 Yunfei Li, Sebastian Schubert, Jürgen P. Kropp, and Diego Rybski, "On the influence of density and morphology on the Urban Heat Island intensity," *Nature Communications* 11, no. 1 (2020): 1–9.

10 "Next Practices": Building and planning practices that have so far served as models but could become architectural routines in the near future.

Fig. 1

Regenerating public space in traditional Chinese villages: Lessons from Huangyan

Guiqing Yang

Alongside rapid urbanization in China and subsequent increases in rural-to-urban migration, rural areas have been neglected for several decades. It wasn't until the early 2010s that the "Beautiful Countryside" policy, aiming to improve the environment of Chinese villages, was promoted by the central government to narrow the gap between urban and rural areas (see article by Elena Meyer-Clement on page 82). This involved the modernization and renovation of building structures alongside the development of attractive public spaces considering local social needs. In 2017, a strategy of "rural revitalization" was highlighted at the Nineteenth National Congress in China. In line with efforts to enhance the beauty of the Chinese countryside, many towns and villages launched projects to improve physical conditions in rural areas. Since being invited by the local government in 2013, I have led a team of teachers and students from Tongji University to teach, research, and practice rural vitalization in Huangyan District, Taizhou City, Zhejiang Province. Through a joint effort between all parties, the results of these practices have received much public attention. In retrospect, our experience has provided valuable lessons for other regions in China and beyond concerning the revitalization of rural public space and on-site training in rural construction practices.

How can public spaces in rural areas be brought back to life?

Cultural cohesion is vital to underpinning a desirable rural community. This should be embodied not only in words but also in material space. With this in mind, rural public space is an important physical resource facilitating traditional cultural activities, bringing socio-economic benefits and a sense of belonging and pride to villagers. Rapid urbanization has greatly impacted the physical environment of traditional Chinese villages, alongside substantial changes to their social and economic structure. When revitalizing rural spaces, reconciling traditional functions and forms with contemporary demands presents a nuanced challenge.

As a result of the gradual decaying of village community spaces, there is typically a lack of appropriate locations for community activities, often negatively impacting cultural cohesion. Subsequently, the overall

Fig. 2

atmosphere within village communities is becoming increasingly indifferent, with villagers lacking motivation to participate in public affairs. Thus, the most effective way to renovate and renew villages while engaging local people is to develop their communal facilities and environment. With limited funds for initial construction, focusing on improving a civic site is the preferred route of practitioners. Based on my accumulated experiences practicing community space revitalization in Huangyan, Taizhou, I suggest following placemaking principles to design lively and high-quality community spaces in rural settings.

1. Find a suitable public location of a certain size and character

Firstly, the scale of public spaces should be appropriate to their specific context. It is necessary to adapt to local conditions and scale while acknowledging the existing built environment and the nature of land use in villages. For example, projects should not involve the demolition of old structures, the construction of large-scale residences for villagers, or the creation of urban-type plazas. The size of an open community space should be related to the size of villages and their diversity of topographical, socio-economic, and cultural characteristics. The selection of appropriate civic spaces should be given priority at the beginning of village planning. With these spaces typically located at the center of villages, the remaining open space of the village is planned around them. Walking paths connecting various cultural sites within the landscape should be linked into an open space network. By carefully selecting appropriate public spaces and organizing the different elements, it is possible to achieve twice the result with half the effort. A small amount of demolition of obstructing houses and villager resettlement may be necessary if the terms can be agreed upon by all parties.

2. Enrich the public space with local cultural characteristics

The planning and construction of each community space must be closely integrated with vernacular cultural characteristics. For example, public venues

Fig. 3

should fully reflect the historical and cultural connotations of local villages, focusing on specific cultural themes. If the venue does not have an obvious cultural theme, it may lack "spirit" of place and become like an empty shell. Therefore, to integrate local culture into any design, it is necessary to conduct in-depth field research and understand the historical and cultural connotations of the rural context, such as local stories, famous figures, and important historical events. For example, this could encompass red culture, historical heroes, and other themes. Moreover, the tangible and intangible cultural heritage of the countryside is an important resource for shaping the spirit of place in public spaces, such as ancient buildings, bridges, pagodas, trees, cultural relics and monuments, local handicrafts, theaters, and so on. Only by endowing the planning and construction of village venues with rural historical and cultural characteristics can the humanity and uniqueness of the village's physical space environment be fundamentally reflected. In this way, local people can regain pride in their village and thus in their homes.

3. Allow public space to play a leading role in rural culture and economy

Through creative transformation, public spaces can promote rural cultural and economic development by linking related activities: ancestor worship, temple fairs, or social dramas can be combined with art festivals, company team building, or special local product exhibitions. In this way, rural culture, reflected in the design of community spaces, is organically linked to tourism and employment provision. A growing tourism economy allows villagers to start businesses from home and raise their incomes while creating additional jobs and attracting young people to return to their hometowns as entrepreneurs. If the function of these public spaces is to reach their full potential as facilitators of a rural cultural economy, we must promote a two-way flow of urban and rural economic and social demands. For example, introducing the cultural and touristic needs of city dwellers into the countryside, such as safe hiking trails or hotel facilities, can provide numerous advantages for rural regions. Therefore, rural public space should take on new functions to accommodate a variety of activities

Fig. 4

to meet the multiple needs of villagers and tourists, from daily activities to the holiday pursuits of diverse social groups.

4. Build supporting facilities for this public space

The construction of supporting facilities for public spaces should be comprehensively assessed. This typically includes (1) easy access for pedestrians, with multiple access points to the main village footpath, facilitating daily use and organization of themed events; (2) a nearby car park for city dwellers with private cars and organizations arranging group buses; (3) public toilets within five minutes walking distance, with a layout and orientation combining with the overall functional requirements of the community space; (4) seats for rest and a rain shelter to support outdoor activities; (5) illumination such as night lighting to encourage evening activities and improve safety; (6) additional facilities such as rubbish bins, noticeboards, or guide signs.

All the above design principles can be found in Shatan Village, Huangyan District. The creation of a core public space in Shatan provides a central location for Huangyan villagers' ancestral worship and local belief activities, which helps to maintain family traditions, strengthen local belief culture, and enhance their cultural identity and sense of belonging. Ultimately, these factors bring about a new type of rural social cohesion. Additionally, Shatan's central public space is also a venue for interaction and communication between tourists and villagers, promoting the integration of the countryside into a novel urban-rural dynamic.

How can rural revitalization be mediated to students and administrations?

Rural revitalization faces the major challenge of lacking local knowledge and skills in planning, management, and implementation; therefore, in addition to encouraging and incentivizing talents from all walks of life to relocate to the countryside, the focus should be on nurturing local expertise. To achieve sustained success in rural revitalization projects, training activities can be institutionalized by establishing teaching and training centers on-site. "Tongji-Huangyan Rural Revitalization College" is the first of its kind in China to be inaugurated. Established in Shatan Village in 2018 as a cooperation between Tongji University Shanghai and leaders from Huangyan District, it has cooperated closely with local schools and implemented initiatives to train new talent for future rural development, reaping the benefits of Tongji University's faculty expertise. Moreover, the Rural Revitalization College has showcased the practical achievements of Huangyan's "Beautiful Countryside" policy drive and shared the results of local experiments. From this successful experience, I would like to give the following recommendations:

5. Capitalize upon the inherent advantages of colleges and universities

Collaboration between communities and universities is essential for rural revitalization as it leverages the skills and knowledge of faculty in relevant disciplines for on-site training activities.

In the case of the Tongji-Huangyan Rural Revitalization College, Tongji University is the main proponent of the educational side, developing the curriculum, preparing teaching materials, and organizing teaching staff. Meanwhile, the Huangyan government looks

Fig. 5

Fig. 6

Fig. 7

Fig. 1
A hiking path near Shatan Village, Huangyan County, created as part of the "Beautiful Countryside" government program to attract tourists to rural areas.

Fig. 2 & 3
The design of public spaces is a key feature in the revitalization of historical villages as it provides a backdrop for traditional festivals and contemporary events, serving the needs of locals and tourists equally Fig. 2: Lantern festival in Ningxi Town. Fig. 3: Theater activities in the central square of Shatan Village.

Fig. 4
In planning the revitalization of villages, central open community spaces should be integrated into a network of walking paths connecting various cultural sites and landmarks, supported by ancillary facilities such as parking lots, public toilets, and illumination. In this photograph, Guiqing Yang explains the visitor plan for Wuyantou Old Village.

Fig. 5
North campus of the rural "Tongji-Huangyan Rural Revitalization College" in a former health center, Shatan Village.

Fig. 6
Guiqing Yang conducts a training course in the lecture auditorium of the Rural Revitalization College, Shatan Village.

Fig. 7
The renovated main street of Shatan Old Village illuminated by lanterns.

Fig. 8
The South Campus of the college is located in Wuyantou Village, whose historical structure of courtyard houses has been largely preserved.

after enrollment, management, and logistic support for the training participants. Each thematic rural revitalization training course generally lasts three to five days. Participants learn the contemporary value of the rural revitalization strategy and gain an insight into the developmental history and practical achievements of Huangyan's implementation of the concept. Besides training activities, comprehensive cooperation encompasses research on the principles and legal side of rural revitalization, sharing the results and insights, and creating a pilot model of university-government collaboration. Moreover, universities can foster international exchange and research cooperation platforms to mutually share best practice experiences in rural development with partners from more economically developed countries who often face similar challenges. These practices could then be adapted and tested in other contexts.

6. Reap the potential of on-site training to impart practical knowledge

On-site training events link theoretical knowledge of rural planning, construction techniques, and project management with hands-on learning experiences and practical illustrations of pilot projects, which will guide future rural practices. In particular, comparing the old village before and after transformation vividly demonstrates how the rural revitalization concept can be physically implemented on the ground. It allows them to understand the working methods more directly and deeply while appreciating the charm of Huangyan's rural culture. The learning experience can be supported by identifying suitable unused public facilities in old villages and then renovating and transforming them into classrooms. Taking advantage of the faculty expertise of universities and based on rich practical experiences, these venues will condense the theoretical knowledge of village revitalization for the future and provide practical training materials. Subsequently, through the experience of "localized" training, the theoretical understanding of frontline cadres and administrative staff from local governments will be enhanced to implement innovative concepts in their respective home regions. Meanwhile, the capacity of rural construction projects will benefit from the practical training of local construction workers.

Tongji-Huangyan Rural Revitalization College is divided into two campuses located close to each other in regenerated historical villages: the North Campus is located in Shatan Village, Yutou Township. It is situated in an old, renovated building, formerly a health center that was later abandoned. As part of the conversion, two multimedia classrooms (with a capacity of 50 people) and an academic lecture auditorium (with a capacity of 120 people) were created. The South Campus is located in a renovated courtyard house in Wuyantou Village, Ningxi Township, which has been comprehensively preserved and restored in its historical structure. The South Campus serves dually as a teaching facility and a "Village Art Exhibition Center" for the public. It includes a multimedia classroom (with a capacity of 50 people) and an academic lecture hall (with a capacity of 80 people). The Academy's catering and accommodation facilities are accommodated in an old administrative building in the Wuyantou New Village site.

In summary, the key success factors for rural revitalization are related to the design principles outlined above. Emphasizing community space as an important starting point for village revitalization, repurposing historical buildings through renovation, and integrating new functions—such as culture or education. In particular, the revival of public space is integral to the rural revitalization concept as it provides a physical platform for the preservation and sustenance of traditional culture and built heritage while generating opportunities for economic development. Moreover, it promotes the two-way flow of urban and rural resources, and it improves socio-spatial dynamics between city and countryside. Rural vitalization requires a variety of skills; therefore, in the face of diverse, long-term challenges, it is necessary to provide different types of training to continuously improve the concepts and implementation of rural revitalization. Shatan Village offers a rich example of what can be achieved. However, not all villages have such potential; thus, policies should be adapted according to local conditions while village training facilities should be multi-purpose to generate sustained economic benefits. By doing so, these approaches hold the potential to be applied to other villages and different contexts in China and beyond.

Fig. 1

Contemporary commoning practices in the Alps: Co-creating spaces for imagination and action

Bianca Elzenbaumer

The Lagarina Valley in the Italian Alps is a region rich with practitioners striving to create physical and social spaces for imagination, action, and hope in times of environmental and social crises. This abundance of creative thinkers might not be immediately visible to the untrained eye; however, despite the valley's agricultural and industrial domination, limited public education system, and predilection for the population to conform to conventional consumerist lifestyles, a transformative paradigm shift is being cultivated in the region.

This valley, where biodiversity loss and climate crises are a fast-moving reality, is also where my feminist-oriented design research lab, the "*Alpine Community Economies Laboratory*,"[1] was established. It is in this valley, where rural and urban practices intermingle, that I strive to contribute to a dynamic assemblage of commoning practices showcasing how more caring ways of sustaining livelihoods are possible. I do so by contributing to the wider eco-social movement through design-led participatory methods, creating spaces with a caring mindset in the face of a non-linear tomorrow. My work aims to support various civic and public actors to achieve their goals for a more equitable and sustainable future.

What I would like to share in this text are some key working principles and community projects that underpin how I contribute to the collective, regenerative work already underway in the valley. I will introduce the working principles of "commons" and "community economies" that permeate my work, subsequently explaining how these principles manifest themselves as theory-practice relays (aka practical projects in a close and creative conversation with theory) within (and via) the community academy *La Foresta*[2]—a physical space and a collective that I co-founded.

Commons and community economies as working principles

The concept of the "commons," the first point of orientation in my contribution to the valley, has been defined as a "commonwealth" (i.e., land, water, houses, and other forms of wealth governed by a community of users) through processes of negotiation, care, and interaction (i.e., acts of commoning[3]). Personally, I think of com-

Fig. 2

mons as multispecies communities that interact with matter to regenerate and sustain their interdependent livelihoods in ways that allow all community members to thrive. This interaction should be conducted with care while benefitting living beings and ecosystems outside its boundaries.

When I first encountered the commons concept fifteen years ago, it became like a guiding star, allowing me and others to imagine and experience different ways of living. After investigating the connection between this concept and the Alps, much of what I had experienced as a child without understanding its value became clearer. For example, spending days in the forest near the village with my grandparents gathering firewood, watching my neighbors taking the cows home during a summer spent on the high alpine meadows, or hiking along the old irrigation channels while admiring their ingenuity—all these memories could be appreciated more fully by understanding the concept of the "commons." My desire now is to care for this Alpine heritage via art- and design-led engagements while "queering" it with feminist and post-humanist approaches; this will enable myself and others to live within an empowering kind of "commons-present" in the Alpine region. Moreover, it is hoped this will allow others in future to inherit a positive and sustainable commons culture and infrastructure with which to build their lives and activism within and around.

Community economies—my second point of orientation—can be defined as economies that care for the well-being of humans and more-than-human others, or those that foster sustaining interdependencies between living beings.[4] To me, the "community economies" approach is a powerful tool that fuels transformative imagination and action for several reasons. First, it defines the economy as "all the activities we do that sustain our livelihoods," encompassing diverse activities that are non-monetary, informal, and mostly side-lined or instrumentalized in service to "the real economy" by other economic theories.[5] Second, its intellectual standpoint is one of openness, curiosity, and indeterminacy; rather than looking for problems in a political system, it encourages individuals to seek out practices that defy the capitalist logic of profit, separation, and accumulation in the "here" and "now." Third, with its post-humanist stance, it strives to take other living beings (e.g., animals, plants, fungi, and bacteria) into account *with*—not *as*—resources merely existing for human use, but as co-creators of their livelihoods with agency, preserving the interdependent ecosystems that sustain life.[6]

La Foresta: A hybrid research assemblage relaying theory and practice

The community academy *La Foresta* is a hybrid research assemblage that emerged in 2015 out of community engagement, relationship building, and continual assessment of local needs in the Lagarina Valley. *La Foresta's* literal meaning in our local dialect is "the female foreigner"; however, it further acknowledges the forest as an ecosystem and a place to construct alternative futures. The practice itself is a self-governed assemblage of people, practices, spaces, materials, and ideas brought together in a 150-square-meter space within Rovereto train station. From 2017 onwards, *La Foresta*, steadily developed from a collective desire among its members to create a community resource connecting forward-looking changemakers in the valley; i.e., people actively contributing to the creation of alternative economies and practices of living that support the well-being of people and other living beings in the valley. The platform was intended to also be attentive to interdependencies with other localities.

Currently, within *La Foresta*, there are about fifteen people actively contributing to this collective effort daily, with another twenty-five engaging more informally. This dynamic group of people range in age from their early twenties to their mid-sixties and are knowledgeable in fields as diverse as agroecology, critical pedagogy, transformative social work, eco-social design, mental health, and herbology.

Sebastiano Moltrer, a human rights worker, artist, and inhabitant of *La Foresta*, believes a visual representation of the community academy and its organizational dynamics would be chaotic: "from bubbles to meteors, from circles to circumferences, from 2D to 3D figures to figures that are outside graphic representation but you know are there." In fact, each contributor has a slightly different idea of what *La Foresta* is and what it does. This diversity makes the space remain vibrant and empowering for our wide range of needs and interests. These include a desire to transition the valley into an agro-ecological landscape, find ways of supporting local mental health by treating it as a "commons," efforts to mitigate and adapt to climate change, actively including young people in the process of shaping the future of the valley, nurturing

Fig. 3

Fig. 4

improved biodiversity, creating spaces for people from diverse backgrounds to meet and support each other, and ensuring queer, working class, and migrant people have better access to affordable housing, among other endeavors.[7]

Chiara Bombarda, who contributed to *La Foresta* during a voluntary social year while searching for a purposeful profession, describes it as a relational space in which "you can test yourself, always supported by someone and always finding someone who opens a new door for you, allowing you to discover that there is more to the world than you have imagined." Her description grounds what *La Foresta* implicitly aims to achieve, namely, stimulating the imagination of people in the valley to see how life could be different (and much improved) if we collectively (re)organized our livelihoods. This could be realized through practices that allow life in its multiple forms to regenerate and thrive more naturally instead of focusing on competitiveness and maximizing the valley for profit.

Therefore, for most contributors at *La Foresta*, we must engage equally on a conceptual and practical level to explore how life could be positively changed in our valley and beyond, continuously relaying theory and practice. In the process, we must work together creatively and courageously to nurture ourselves and others, embracing the multiple ideas of a regenerative present and future.

Interdependence and enlivenment: Ways of fostering territorial futures

With our design and commoning practices in the Lagarina Valley, at *La Foresta* we often remind ourselves that we are committed to a marathon and not only a sprint; it typically takes years to develop a project from mere intuition and desire to realizing a concrete initiative. We are glad to have the privilege (and endurance) of being able to remain in one place, allowing relations between people to grow and become more complex and for efforts to solidify and build through more radical approaches. Personally (and as a collective), we believe in revolutionary world views, primarily those of interdependence[8] (i.e., that everything is connected as a pre-condition of being and that this is a beautiful thing to acknowledge and engage with),

Fig. 5

and enlivenment[9] (i.e., the idea that we can change our ways of living to contribute to our feeling of aliveness and that of other beings). Ultimately, this can be realized through implementing everyday practices that encourage life to thrive.

With our assemblage of activities experimenting with theory-practice relays, we desire to be actors fostering enlivened territorial spaces for the future. We are convinced that this rootedness and connectedness we experience daily through our work as a collective can support a different approach to how this region could be co-shaped to support the well-being of its multispecies inhabitants and their translocal connections. We are currently wondering how this process of multispecies grassroots engagement and transformation can be integrated into a pluralistic, regional, and long-term vision that should support as many actors as possible to co-shape this valley. We are exploring how we can "dance" with public administrators and local politicians to promote interdependence and enlivenment as a core organizing principle of territorial futures. Ultimately, we are working towards finding ways to use our experiences to contribute to enlivening how life in the valley is

Fig. 1
A Community Economies Retreat exploring traditional land-based commons.

Fig. 2
The Lagarina Valley in the Italian Alps.

Fig. 3
The La Foresta collective organizes an Eco Lab skills sharing workshop twice a week at the Rovereto train station.

Fig. 4
The Comunità Frizzante produces fizzy drinks while building the community.

Fig. 5
Children playing and learning outdoors as part of the *Sottobosco* education project.

governed and administrated and how we can invite others to open up to dynamic multispecies connections.

We acknowledge that there are many different modes of living and relating, of governing and administrating. Currently, these desires are actualized all too often with short-term thinking, such as focusing on individual well-being. This can become akin to a "private island" upon which people may take actions such as denying scientific facts, abstaining from voting in public elections, or voting but for "right" and "hard right" political parties. Those entities promise ways forward for humanity that avoid the process of change, implying that the problem is not the fault of the individual and their participation in Western imperial ways of life; instead, the blame is assigned to "others" (near or far) who are perceived as a threat. These shortcuts profoundly negate interdependence and enlivenment, thus worsening the situation through modes of practice that perpetuate disconnection between people, ultimately degrading the web of life that sustains us all. In this scenario, it is empowering to me and others within *La Foresta* to see ourselves as part of a genealogy of commoners keeping practices of commoning alive in this territory and elsewhere in the world, honoring the interdependence between all living beings. This allows us to feel connected with previous efforts cultivated for centuries in the Alps and worldwide through practices which are not only resisting the status quo but also thriving in spite of it.

1 Bianca Elzenbaumer, "Alpine Community Economies Laboratory," 2019, accessed April 25, 2024, www.alpinecommunityeconomies.org.

2 "La Foresta - Accademia Di Comunità," accessed February 23, 2021, https://laforesta.net/.

3 Massimo De Angelis, *Omnia Sunt Communia: On the Commons and the Transformation to Post-capitalism* (London: Zed Books, 2017).

4 Martina Artmann, "Human-Nature Resonance in Times of Social-Ecological Crisis – a Relational Account for Sustainability Transformation," *Ecosystems and People* 19, no. 1 (December 31, 2023): 2168760.

5 Community Economies Collective, "Community Economies Institute," accessed January 8, 2019, http://www.communityeconomies.org/about/community-economies-institute.

6 Community Economies Collective, "Community Economies Research and Practice," accessed April 13, 2020, https://www.communityeconomies.org/about/community-economies-research-and-practice.

7 August 31, 2023, https://laforesta.net/progetti/. The quotation by Sebastiano Moltrer is taken from a WhatsApp conversation with the author about La Foresta.

8 Arturo Escobar, *Designs for the Pluriverse: Radical Interdependence, Autonomy, and the Making of Worlds*, (Durham: Duke University Press Books, 2018).

9 Andreas Weber, *Enlivenment: Towards a Fundamental Shift in the Concepts of Nature, Culture and Politics*, Ecology Series, vol. 31 (Berlin: Heinrich Böll Stiftung, 2013).

Chapter 4: Co-Visioning Urban-Rural Territories

Planning urban-rural territories requires an integrated and collaborative approach that crosses administrative boundaries, sectors, and levels of governance while reaching out to local people. Chapter Four highlights the benefits of co-visioning practices in developing future pathways towards climate-friendly and people-centered urban-rural transformation. Contributions to this chapter feature large-scale planning and design approaches applied in Europe, China, and Vietnam that address landscape transformations in an integrated manner. They emphasize the engagement of a wide range of stakeholders from politics, civil society, and academia in urban-rural planning approaches, introducing relevant tools and steps toward collaborative planning and vision-building. The chapter also presents the co-visioning approach developed and tested in the Urban-Rural Assembly project and reflects on its potential to be explored, adapted, and developed further in different regional contexts worldwide.

Fig. 1

Perspectives on urban-rural vision building

Maria Frölich-Kulik, Sigrun Langner, and Lukas Pappert

The major global challenges we face today—climate change, resource scarcity, and increasing social polarization—demand the socio-ecological transformation of entire regions. Some transitions—such as shifting renewable energy supply or establishing resource-conserving and circular forms of production—urgently need to be implemented, making them unavoidable. Adaptation to climate change, including the conversion of forests and agriculture or flood protection measures, poses additional challenges. In this context, urban and rural development can no longer be viewed as separate entities. Rather, a change of perspective is required—one that recognizes the two spatial categories as permeable and interdependent. This new perspective must also examine the metabolisms in the extended region: the flow of people, goods, finance, and ecosystem services between urban centers and peripheries. Shaping sustainable and inclusive urban-rural relationships demands an overarching territorial and landscape-based approach. We now require tools and methods enabling a science-based, co-creative approach to regional planning practice—one which forges alliances and networks while linking urban and rural actors from different social groups and administrative sectors. Due to the intensity of these interactions and dependencies, the future of urban-rural territories can only be developed collaboratively, based on landscape-led strong spatial visions for the future.[1] The contributions in this chapter underscore the need to strengthen collaborative approaches in the governance and planning of urban-rural regions, highlighting the significance of spatial visions as a tool for co-creative communication and negotiation processes at the urban-rural interface.

Engaging with a landscape can serve as a starting point for developing sustainable urban-rural relations from an integrated, territorial perspective. Here, landscapes are understood as integral systems that allow us to comprehend the logics of urbanization and how its dynamics interplay with natural spatial conditions. A landscape-based perspective emphasizes the natural processes that underpin the formation of, for example, built structures, agricultural land, and open spaces. To better understand the interdependencies between natural processes and urbanization dynamics, it is first beneficial to decompose transformation systems using cartographic-interpretative methods[2] and

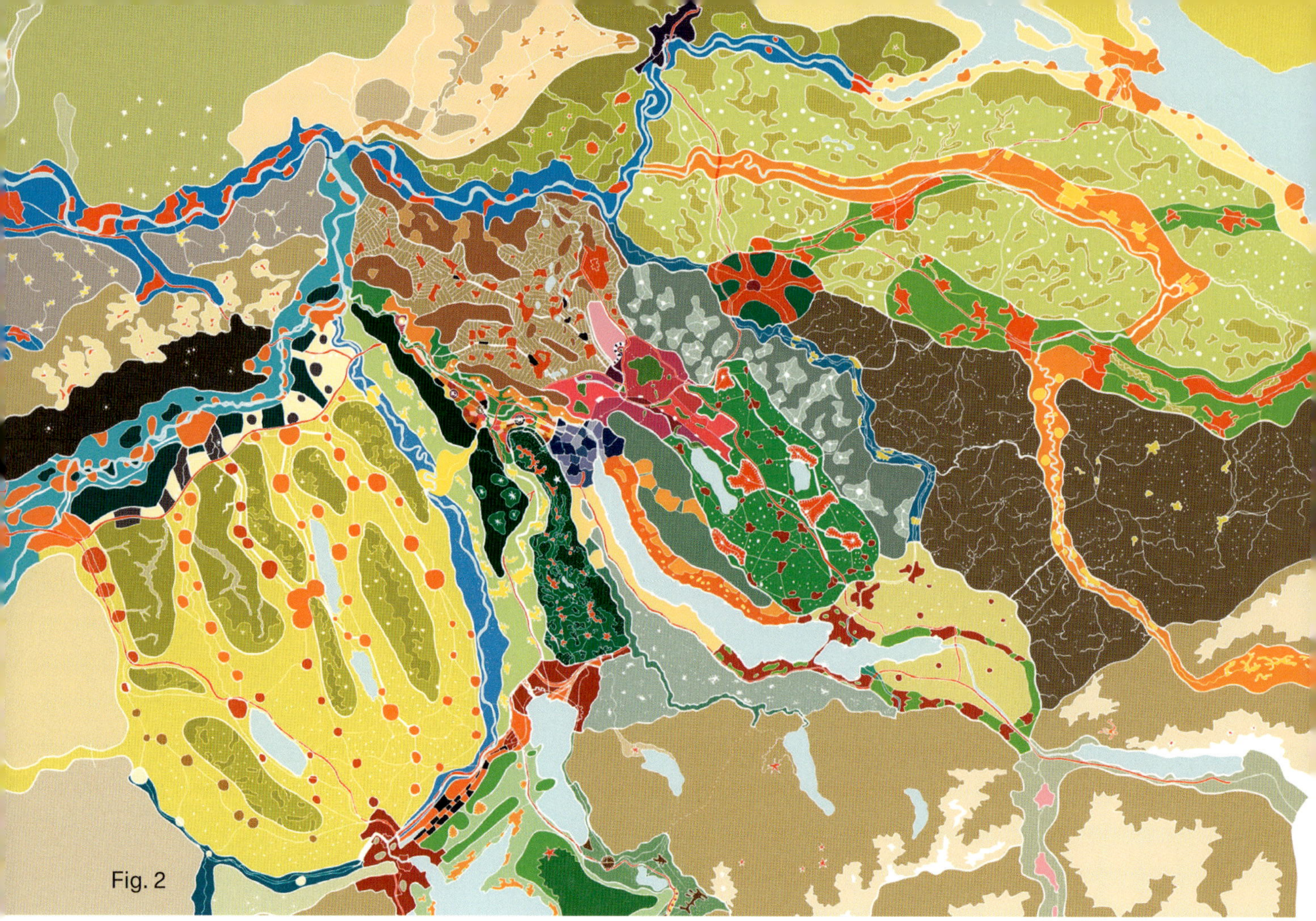

Fig. 2

to examine the relationships between different scales in space and time.[3] This opens up future questions of sustainable and landscape-based urban-rural transformation. The contributions in this book—by Steffen Nijhuis, Kelly Shannon, and Bruno de Meulder, and Christian Nolf, Yuting Xie, and Yi-Wen Wang—highlight the significance (and necessity) of landscape-based regional vision building. Nijhuis presents a compelling argument for the implementation of landscape-based regional design approaches, which he posits as a foundational strategy for the development of sustainable transformation. Nolf, Xie, and Wang provide illustrative examples of the development of territorial and landscape perspectives in the Yangtze River Delta. Meanwhile, Shannon and de Meulder present multi-scalar planning approaches based on thorough analyses of the Mekong River Delta, focusing on careful consideration of the intrinsic landscape-led and indigenous logics of the region. In the latter two cases, the particular context of the delta regions underlines the need for a holistic and systemic approach. The contributions employ mapping techniques, with the aims of carefully reading landscape contexts, uncovering their logics, and elaborating on urban-rural futures. (Re)reading and (re)configuring landscape relations through mapping facilitates the creation of landscape-based transformation pathways that guide us towards developing more sustainable urban-rural regions.

So-called "urban-rural regions" are characterized by shared spatial formations (such as river landscapes, forests, or mountain ranges) and functional systems (such as supply structures, commuting patterns, or natural resources) that link urban and rural areas. They also share common issues and challenges, as well as future potentials that transcend administrative boundaries, sectoral responsibilities, and administrative divisions. The inclusion of urban-rural linkages in regional planning systems can be a key factor in shaping sustainable social, economic, and ecological systems and their corresponding spatial transformation processes, accounting for the radius of people's everyday lives.

At a regional level, there is often a lack of tools beyond formal regional planning, which complicates the possibility of working on future prospects. Therefore, we must develop adaptive regional planning tools that help to identify and negotiate multi-layered spatial contexts—particularly those detached from administrative and sectoral boundaries—and to cooperatively work on regional visions building towards a sustainable future. It becomes clear that negotiation and collaboration between key actors play a crucial role in this kind of vision-building approach. This is why the UN-Habitat's "Urban-Rural Linkage Guidelines" place particular emphasis on the necessity of "an integrated governance approach" in its second principle[4] (see interview with Remy Sietchiping and Grace Githiri on page 66). Accordingly, it is essential to strengthen a governance structure that is multisectoral, multi-level, and multi-stakeholder to effectively deliver the Sustainable Development Goals and overcome conflicts and inequalities.[5]

Against this background, collaborative tools and methods that shape ongoing transformation processes are gaining attention in the European spatial planning context. In German-speaking countries, the so-called "Raumbild" (or "spatial image") planning approach is increasingly being used as an informal strategic planning instrument and communication tool at the regional scale.[6] In principle, spatial images aim to illustrate sustainable futures for regions through guiding visions[7] and to provide local stakeholders with orientation for cooperative regional sustainable transformations.

As informal strategic planning approaches, they supplement or prepare the formal instruments of regional planning and, above all, promote intersectoral and inter-municipal planning approaches.[8] Spatial image processes encompass formats that facilitate collective learning, co-productive knowledge generation, and collaborative visioning for the future of a region. As part of this process, transformation pathways are developed co-creatively with stakeholders so that they can identify with the established strategies. Consequently, the process fosters a networking and stabilizing effect on the stakeholder constellation, as the stakeholders develop a common basis for their actions.

The term "Raumbild" refers to the creation of spatial images—including interpretative maps, narrative metaphors, future images and scenarios, and other types of visualization that reveal and interpret existing socio-spatial relationships, raise future questions, and negotiate regional transformation paths. Therefore, "Raumbilder" are normally part of a collaborative and co-creative planning approach, typically developed in regions where overarching cooperation is especially important. This might be due to far-reaching processes of growth, shrinkage, and structural change, or in cross-border regions. Although the term "Raumbild" has already found its way into contemporary planning practice, there is still no common understanding of its meaning or application;[9] instead, it is often used in a broad sense to designate a range of working methods and results of regional vision building. The authors in this chapter use the English terms "spatial image" or "spatial vision" to address "Raumbilder" as tools and instruments to create platforms for communication and negotiating within "vision building" or "co-visioning" procedures. The proliferation of terms and imprecise definitions indicate that the practice of collaborative vision building at a regional scale is still in an experimental phase; at the same time, they are also an expression of the diversity of approaches converging from distinct methodological starting points.

This chapter examines various approaches to regional vision building, demonstrating how action-guiding spatial visions and images can be co-designed and how this, in turn, can strengthen cooperation across sectors and administrative boundaries in urban-rural regions. Spatial visions and images encompass a range of analytical techniques and planning tools, including exploratory and projective mapping approaches, future scenarios, and transformation strategies for implementation. These visions are characterized by concise narratives that vividly communicate the jointly developed visions of the future and transformation paths. The contributions by Schultz, Schmidt, and Langner in this chapter illustrate how collaborative approaches to regional planning can be promoted through vision building. For example, Schultz describes how spatial visions are developed and negotiated with the expertise of local stakeholders using various tools of image creation while Schmidt highlights the pivotal role played by future narratives in spatial planning processes. Meanwhile, Langner illustrates the potential of mapping strategies in these processes, particularly in uncovering and communicating the endogenous potentials and specific characteristics of a region.

Expanding on existing vision-building approaches, the Urban-Rural Assembly project developed the co-visioning methodology to foster an integrated, cooperative, and sustainable form of urban-rural transformation. The project initiated co-visioning in the urban-rural regions of Nordhausen, Germany, and Huangyan, China. In these regions, knowledge from science, politics, administration, and civil society was synthesized to collaboratively design sustainable spatial visions and transformation pathways. The aims of the project were twofold: first, to collaboratively produce knowledge about transformation processes in these specific areas; and second, to develop and test a planning methodology

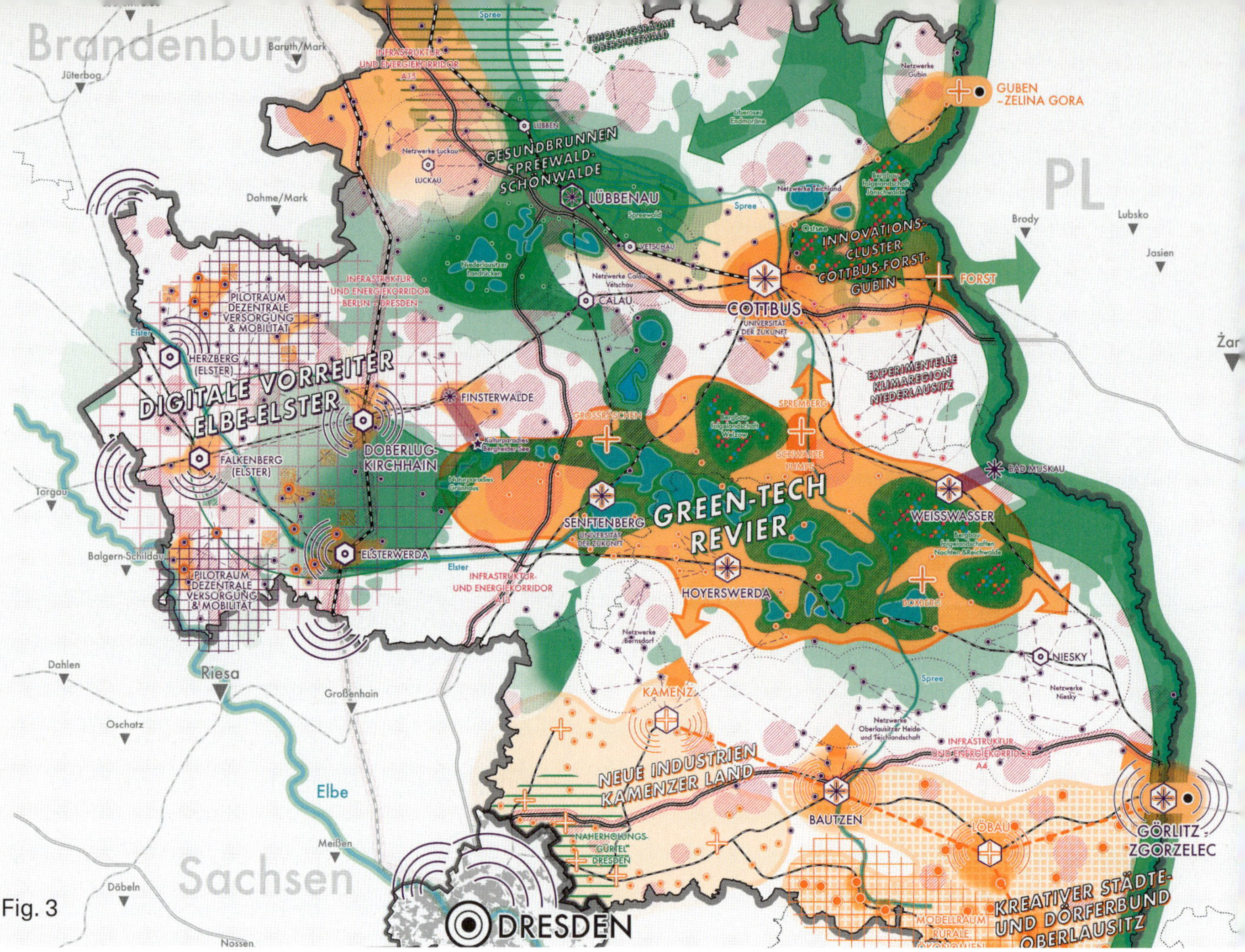

Fig. 3

that could be adapted to other contexts. The chapter concludes with an overview of the steps, methods, and results of the two co-visioning processes. It also reflects on various potentials and shortcomings, as well as open questions generated by the Urban-Rural Assembly co-visioning tool, to evaluate its transferability to other urban-rural regions.

The contributions in this chapter demonstrate how co-vision-building facilitates inter- and transdisciplinary knowledge production regarding complex landscape and social dynamics in urban-rural regions. They emphasize the importance of engaging and networking with local key players to strengthen their role in—and ownership of—sustainable regional transformation. This collaborative approach allows for the identification and localization of regional talents and the isolation of challenges related to sustainable transformation, considering these from various perspectives. Collaboratively designed spatial visions and spatial images illustrate what sustainable regional futures might look like and indicate the transformation paths that will guide us towards them. Connections between different scales, such as neighborhood, district, and regional levels can

Fig. 1
In a multi-actor workshop as part of the Urban-Rural Assembly "Raumbild" planning process in Nordhausen, collectively developed ideas were put together in a large format.

Fig. 2
The "Metrobild Zürich" is based on a morphological analysis of the area and identifies twenty-three sub-areas. The goal is for these areas to better recognize, complement, and support each other.

Fig. 3
From Lausitz to WOWsitz: The "Raumbild 2050" project for the Lausitz region illustrates the potential spatial effects of a socio-ecological transformation.

be revealed and enhanced, potentially serving as starting points for establishing and implementing jointly defined transformation paths. Thus, co-visioning can be a crucial approach for initiating and navigating processes that enable sustainable regional transformation involving multiple stakeholders and perspectives.

1 Valeria Lingua and Verena Balz, *Shaping Regional Futures: Designing and Visioning in Governance Rescaling* (New York: Springer, 2020).

2 James Corner, "The Agency of Mapping: Speculation, Critique, Invention," in *Mappings*, ed. Denis Cosgrove (London: Reaktion Books, 1999), 213–52.

3 Anuradha Mathur and Dilip Da Cunha, *Mississippi Floods: Designing a Shifting Landscape* (New Haven: Yale University Press, 2001).

4 UN-Habitat, *Urban-Rural Linkages (URL): Guiding Principles Framework for Action to Advance Integrated Territorial Development* (Nairobi: UN-Habitat, 2009; first published 2019).

5 The United Nations Sustainable Development Goals serve as a guide for sustainable development. See: https://sdgs.un.org/goals, accessed September 24, 2024.

6 Good-practice examples of "Raumbild" processes include: *Raumvision Südregion Luxemburg*, by Stein + Schultz, commissioned by Ministerium für Inneres und Landesplanung, Großherzogtum Luxemburg (2007); *Wasseratlas. WasserLand-Topologien für die Hamburger Elbinsel*, by Studio Urbane Landschaften, commissioned by IBA Hamburg (2008); *Metrobild Zürich*, by berchtoldkrass space&options, Studio UC, integral ruedi baur Zürich, commissioned by Metropolitanraum Zürich (2011); *Raumbild Mitte Thüringen*, by Stein + Schultz, Station C23, rabe landschaften, commissioned by IBA Thüringen (2016); *Raumbild Rheinliebe*, by rabe landschaften + Station C23, commissioned by IBA Basel 2020 (12/2017); *Raumbild Vorarlberg 2030*, by Amt der Vorarlberger Landesregierung Abteilung Raumplanung und Baurecht (2019); *Von der Lausitz zur WOWsitz* by Urban Catalyst, studio amore, brethdelacalle a.o. commissioned by Planungslabor Raumbilder Lausitz 2050 – *Nachhaltige Transformation entwerfen* (IÖR/IZS) (2021); *Raumstrategie Rheinisches Revier 2028+*, by Zukunftsagentur Rheinisches Revier (2022).

7 Detlev Ipsen, *Raumbilder: Kultur und Ökonomie Räumlicher Entwicklung* (Wiesbaden: VS Verlag für Sozialwissenschaften; Pfaffenweiler: Centaurus-Verlag, 1997).

8 Henrik Schultz, "Landluft macht frei? Informell Verhandeln mit Raumbildern," in *Rurbane Landschaften: Perspektiven des Ruralen in einer Urbanisierten Welt*, eds. Sigrun Langner and Maria Frölich-Kulik (Bielefeld: transcript, 2018), 321–40.

9 Nathalie Pszola, Frauke Morawski, Dominik Weiß, Theo Kötter, and Frank Lohrberg, "Raumbilder als Planungsinstrument für wachsende Stadtregionen," in *Stadtregionales Flächenmanagement*, eds. Sebastian Henn, Thomas Zimmermann, and Björn Braunschweig. (Berlin, Heidelberg: Springer Spektrum, 2022).

Fig. 1

Fig. 2

Landscape-based regional design as an approach towards sustainable urban development

Steffen Nijhuis

Urbanization is one of the greatest challenges of this century, alongside biodiversity loss and the effects of climate change (Fig. 1 and 2). It often occurs at the expense of fragile ecosystems that provide essential services (such as food and water) while increasing our vulnerability to flooding and drought. In turn, these challenges can exacerbate existing social inequalities. Achieving sustainable urbanization requires a landscape-based strategy that places the biosphere at the forefront of social and economic development (Fig. 3). A "landscape first" perspective binds people, themes, and scales in a spatially-minded and integrative approach. It considers landscapes complex systems—i.e., relational structures where urban, rural, and natural processes are interconnected—thereby helping to reconcile the rural-urban dichotomy. By considering landscape as the cornerstone for delivering more sustainable forms of urbanization, landscape-based regional design places design with nature, people, and history at the heart of its methodology. It employs knowledge-based spatial design as an integrative, multi-scalar, and transdisciplinary approach. Understanding landscape systems and their associated ecological and cultural logics is the starting point for spatial design across scales. Using this landscape logic, we can build nature-inclusive and climate-adaptive urban environments to ensure a healthy and safe living environment for all.

Landscape-based regional design

Landscape-based regional design uses the processes and functions of nature as a basis for spatial planning and design. Abiotic factors such as climate, elevation, soil, and water determine urban development opportunities while ecosystem restoration, management, and rehabilitation are employed as formative powers. At the same time, this approach recognizes that landscapes are socio-cultural constructs shaped by centuries of human interaction with the natural environment. Thus, learning from landscape history and vernacular practices while incorporating Indigenous and traditional ecological knowledge underpins this approach. As such, the physical landscape structure, with its associated natural and cultural processes, is leveraged to create favorable conditions for future development and to guide spatial transformations.

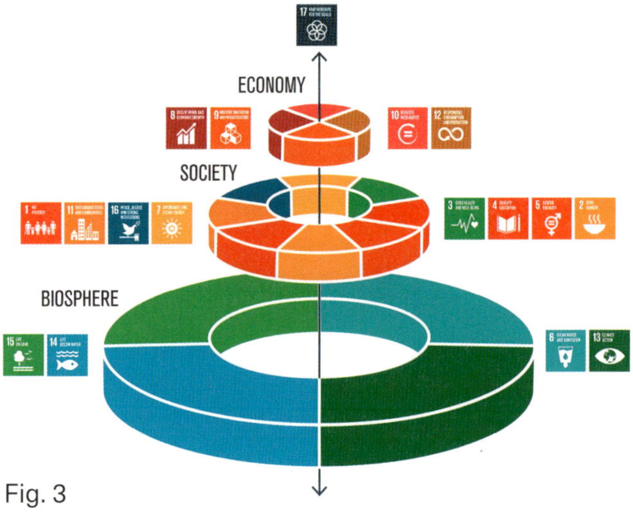

Fig. 3

Through the development of robust landscape structures, landscape-based regional design identifies and directs urban development towards the most advantageous places, functions, scales, and interrelationships. These resilient and adaptive spatial frameworks ensure the coherent development of the region (its long-term strategy) and at the same time create conditions and flexibility for local projects (as short-term interventions). Ultimately, the goal is to create and/or regenerate living landscape systems where (bio)diversity, cultural history, and multi-functionality lead to socially and ecologically inclusive water-sensitive urban landscapes.

Transdisciplinary design and co-creation

Balancing the relationship between experts, citizens, and authorities is essential for the success of landscape-based regional design (Fig. 4). Here, specialized knowledge and local expertise play vital roles in integrating sectoral activities, encouraging coordination, and achieving sustainable outcomes to benefit all stakeholders. This requires a process that extends beyond the domain of landscape architects, urban planners, and urban designers to actively involve other knowledge domains, such as data scientists, environmental technology, and urban studies. It also affects local residents, the business community, administrators, and other regional stakeholders. Through meaningful participation of all stakeholders in envisioning, designing, and policy-making, it is intended that the resilience and adaptive capacity of urban landscapes will be increased, not only in physical terms but also socioeconomically.[1] This strategy implies a shared understanding, often adopting a future-oriented, proactive approach where interactions among citizens,

Fig. 4

businesses, experts, and the government play a central role. From this perspective, the design process becomes an essential vehicle for collaboration and the co-creation of knowledge and ideas (Fig. 5).

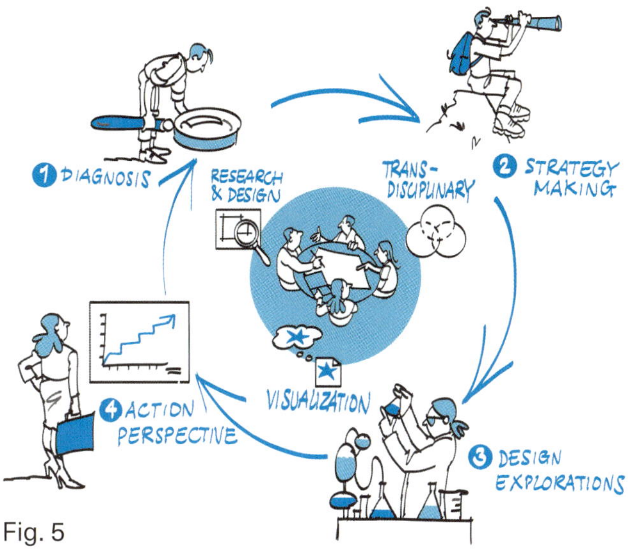

Fig. 5

Landscape in layers

Decomposing the urban landscape into layers according to the dynamic of change is a proven method to increase the understanding of the urban landscape system.[2] An urban landscape can be viewed as a complex system comprising subsystems, each within its own dynamics and rate of change (Fig. 6). Layers with a low dynamic of change are the substratum (e.g., topography, hydrology, or soil) and climate (e.g., precipitation patterns, temperature, or wind). These environmental factors are considered the most influential conditions for land use, termed “first-tier conditions.” Infrastructural networks for transportation, water management, and energy supply form another layer, termed “second-tier conditions.” Displaying quicker growth and change than the first-tier environmental conditions, these are also significant conditional variables for land use.

Together, these first- and second-tier conditions pave the way for the development of agricultural land use and urban settlements, resulting in the layer with the highest change and transformation dynamics. Thus, an understanding of urban landscapes is inherent to the concept of the layers and their relationships constituting the landscape system. The landscape is a relational structure connecting and influencing scales and spatial, ecological, functional, and social entities. As such, the landscape is not just a holistic system but also a scale continuum that we can only understand by looking at different spatial scales and their relationships.

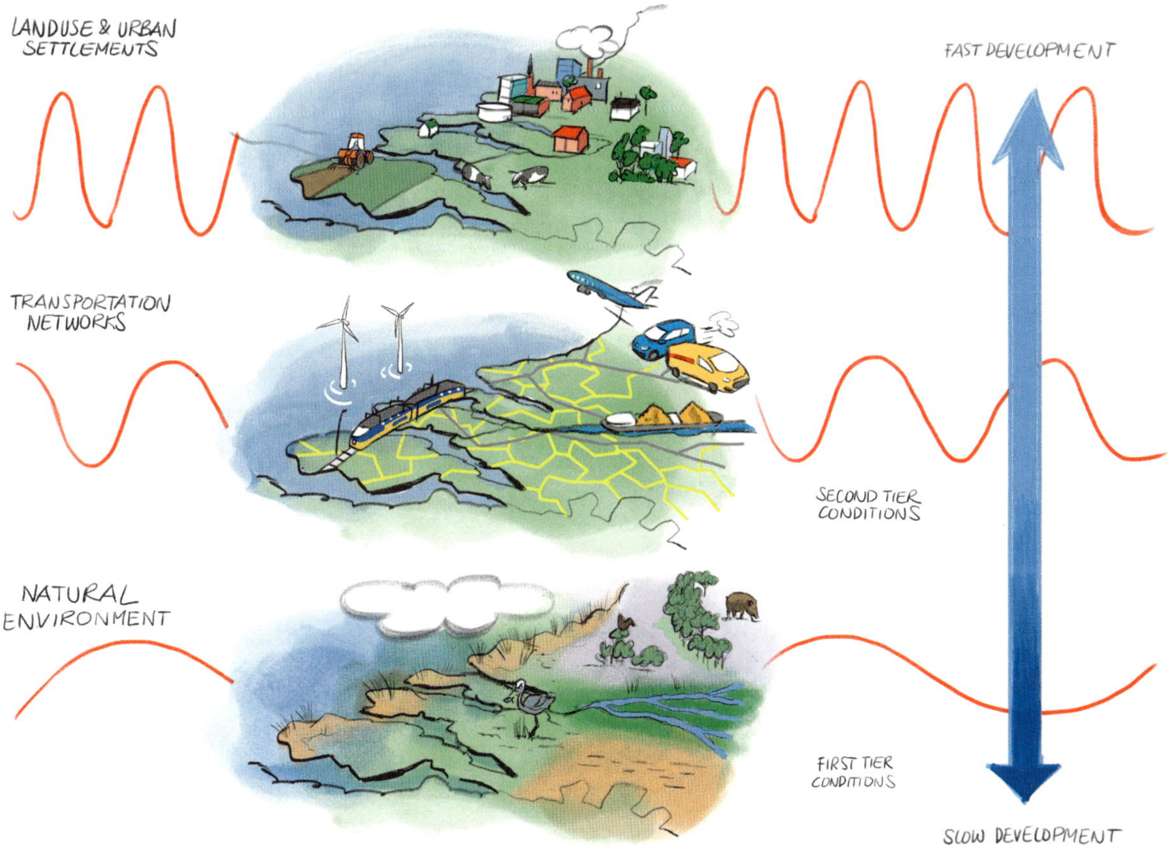

Fig. 6

Fig. 7

Strategy formation

Once knowledge of natural and urban systems has evolved into a solid and shared understanding of their functioning alongside the challenges and opportunities they present, the process of strategy formation and design explorations can begin (Fig. 7). Strategy formation involves making plans that guide long-term actions into the future;[3] one could say it is about outlining a path to get from "here" to "there." These outlines are typically broad, allowing details to emerge alongside them while providing flexibility. In this regard, strategy formation is a planning procedure to help guide design explorations and make plans accordingly.

Strategy formation also entails creating a long-term regional vision or perspective that utilizes knowledge of natural and urban systems to address identified challenges and potentials.

In this process, a regional design is developed to envision a desirable future, expressing what the urban landscape could or should look like. However, this is not a blueprint for the future. Instead, it provides strength and direction in spatial terms and gives meaning to what stakeholders want to achieve together, fostering a sense of focus and belonging when a vision is shared.

In the regional design process, scenario studies can be employed to better understand uncertainties related to spatial development. Scenario studies combine realism, prediction, and imagination to identify robust developments and "no regret measures."[4] In scenario studies, the emphasis is not so much on differences (expressing uncertainty) but on commonalities (most likely to occur); e.g., the structures, locations, and developments that appear in every scenario. Based on this understanding, the long-term regional vision is typically shaped and spatialized by developing adaptive regional design models, such as spatial arrangements that express the desired structure of an area.

Backcasting and adaptive design principles

Having established the long-term regional vision in the form of a regional design, the next question concerns what must be carried out today to achieve this vision and how to adapt to changing circumstances along the way. This question can be answered through a process of backwards reasoning, typically known as "backcasting," a method seeking to discover how a desirable future can be attained. This involves working backwards from the vision to the present, determining practical actions and considering what is realistic while charting the best possible approach in the right direction.[5] Adaptive design principles are a powerful means of guiding short-term actions and identifying solutions for actual problems. A "design principle" refers to a basic idea or rule that explains or controls how something occurs or works and can be identified by studying relevant cases. "Principles" represent generalized design knowledge detached from a specific context but applies to others.[6] Thus, design principles embody the essentials of particular proven design solutions in such a way that they can be applied and adapted to new contexts or changing circumstances while maintaining focus on the overall objective. In this way, adaptive design principles guide in substantiating the long-term vision in an open-ended process in which strategic projects and design explorations play a key role in achieving sustainable urban landscapes.

Design as knowledge production

Design aims towards inventions; i.e., finding spatial solutions and "making them possible." As such, spatial design translates abstract strategic notions into physical structures and layouts addressing several scale levels—a synthesizing activity that concerns putting things together rather than taking them apart. It is about integration instead of reduction; the relations between things and not the things alone.[7] In this respect, design explorations are used as a vehicle to make spatial problems visual, generate solutions, explore possibilities, and express cultural values through spatial form. Thus, design is regarded as a process or action geared towards exploring and producing.

In this process, knowledge from other disciplines, such as ecology, urban planning, cultural history, and water management is spatially translated and integrated. Designing, therefore, plays a role as a thinking-

Fig. 8

technical tool with which one thinks and acts in a structured way to generate ideas and explore possible solutions. This method is known as "research through design."[8] In this approach, goal-oriented searching is central to a process where thinking and producing go hand in hand while mechanisms of research and design are combined with imagination, creativity, and innovation. During this process, a conscious or unconscious synthesis occurs that precipitates into a visual form by drawing, mapping, or modeling with analog or digital media.

Design explorations

Research through design is an essential means to explore the possibilities of adaptive design principles and contextualize them, such as in "nature-based solutions," "water-sensitive design," "socially inclusive design," or "design with heritage." This requires a landscape-based regional design to operate at different scales—from regional to local—and to accommodate both general and more specific measures in rural and urban areas. In this process, the utilization of knowledge of the physical, biological, and cultural aspects of the landscape is inevitable. Therefore, design explorations become a powerful research method with which complex spatial challenges can be approached integrally and creatively (Fig. 8). A structured design process is employed, revealing important aspects as tasks are further translated and concretized in spatial terms. Moreover, adaptive design principles formulated in the strategy formation phase are adjusted and applied locally. Through these design experiments, knowledge is acquired by studying the effects of actively and systematically varying design solutions in a specific context.

Spatial design helps to identify challenges and potentials of the urban landscape and to suggest possible solutions. This is achieved by making matters explicit with drawings and sketching the context in which they can be fully realized. In this sense, the design explorations can also help to identify how stakeholders think about future developments at different scales. By visualizing ideas and programs of requirements and positioning them within the space, one can identify possibilities and limitations while formulating questions requiring further investigation.

Design results provide a context for conversations and observations about the importance of landscape structures and elements, facilitating discussion of any potential solutions and their spatial qualities. In landscape-based regional design, design explorations are used as a systematic search for possible solutions to a spatial problem. At the same time, the design exploration clarifies which landscape structures and elements should be preserved; for example, from an ecological or cultural-historical point of view.

Pilot projects as an action perspective

The identification of strategic pilot projects is crucial to fully realize the ambitions as formulated and mapped in long-term regional design. A pilot project is an initial and relatively small-scale implementation to prove the viability of the approach, principle, or idea, taking the form of a construction project, urban or landscape development project, or research project. The regional design usually entails many potential projects varying in scale and focus; however, these must translate ambitions into reality. Pilot projects can be based on local

Fig. 1 & 2
The landscape as an urban-rural continuum.

Fig. 3
Landscape as the basis for social and economic development.

Fig. 4
Co-creation of knowledge and ideas for the development of a region using a digital map table.

Fig. 5
Landscape-based regional design as a co-creative process for generating knowledge and ideas. The practical design process entails four key phases: (1) diagnosis, (2) strategy making, (3) design explorations, and (4) defining an action perspective. This process is supported by a combination of research and design, meaningful stakeholder involvement, and imagination.

Fig. 6
Landscape in layers based on the dynamic of change.

Fig. 7
The process of strategy formation and design explorations while utilizing knowledge of the natural and urban landscape, developing a vision, backcasting, and identifying adaptive design principles.

Fig. 8
Research through design to explore possible and desirable spatial developments for a future-proof urban region.

Fig. 9
Visualization of a pilot project that shows the potential of a landscape-based approach focused on design with nature, people, and history.

"bottom-up" initiatives, typically building on existing initiatives and networks. For example, these could be a neighborhood park, community gardens, housing project, or "top-down" projects that transcend locality and require regional coordination, such as river regeneration projects and "green-blue" infrastructure.

What the pilot projects have in common is that they contribute to realizing a long-term perspective through short-term actions and implementation. The purpose is to think together, contextualize the adaptive design principles through design, and implement the ideas in practice. Through the pilot project, designers, policymakers, citizens, academics, and industry are united in a "living lab" to experiment, co-create, and test concepts in a real-life environment delimited by geographical and institutional boundaries.[9] Experimenting together responsibly while monitoring and learning from mistakes creates an informal space in which innovation is key while everyone is equal.[10] This fits well with the social and political conditions needed to arrive at solutions on a policy and practical level. Pilot projects assume strategic value when they contribute to the realization of larger ambitions both in tangible and intangible ways, most notably when they build alliances of stakeholders, develop governance models that guide and facilitate implementation, and leverage innovative business models vital for gaining a realistic perspective on action (Fig. 9).

Landscape as the basis for sustainable urban development

In the above article, a regional design approach is presented that takes the landscape as the basis for sustainable urban development. At a time of complex challenges, the development of approaches such as this offers a pathway to realizing socio-ecological inclusive design processes and modes for collaboration among disciplines and stakeholders. As an inclusive design approach, landscape-based regional design establishes relationships between ecological and cultural factors, process and form, long-term and short-term developments, and regional strategies and local interventions. As such, landscape-based regional design is a powerful vehicle for guiding territorial transformations, creating local identity, and safeguarding regional relationships while simultaneously linking ecological and social processes to the development of urban form. Landscape-based regional design brings new operational power to spatial design as an integrative, creative activity and recognizes the regional rural-urban continuum as a significant field of inquiry that is context-driven, solution-focused, and transdisciplinary.

The text is based on material from: Nijhuis, 2022.[11] For an application of the approach in the Greater Bay Area in China see: Nijhuis et al., 2023.[12]

1 Jack Ahern, "From Fail-Safe to Safe-to-Fail: Sustainability and Resilience in the New Urban World," *Landscape and Urban Planning* 100 (2011): 341–43.

2 Steffen Nijhuis, "Landscape Authenticity: The Landscape as Living System, History and Spatial Experience," *Bulletin KNOB* 119, no. 4 (2020): 32–37.

3 Henry Mintzberg, *The Rise and Fall of Strategic Planning* (New York: Prentice Hall, 1994).

4 Ed Dammers *et al., Scenario's Maken Voor Milieu, Natuur en Ruimte: Een Handreiking* (Den Haag: Planbureau voor de Leefomgeving, 2013).

5 Karl-Henrik Robèrt *et al., Sustainability Handbook: Planning Strategically Towards Sustainability* (Lund: Studentlitteratur, 2012).

6 Steffen Nijhuis and Inge Bobbink, "Design-Related Research in Landscape Architecture," *Journal of Design Research* 4, no. 10 (2012): 239–57.

7 Dirk Sijmons, "Simple Rules. Emerging Order? A Designer's Curiosity About Complexity Theories," in *Complexity Theories of Cities Have Come of Age: An Overview with Implications to Urban Planning and Design*, eds. J. Portugali et al. (Berlin: Springer, 2012), 281–309.

8 Steffen Nijhuis and Jeroen De Vries, "Design as Research in Landscape Architecture," *Landscape Journal* 38, no. 1–2 (2019): 87–103.

9 Gabriela Schliwa and Kes McCormick, "Living Labs: Users, Citizens and Transitions," in *The Experimental City*, eds. James Evans, Andrew Karvonen, and Rob Raven (London: Routledge, 2017), 163–78.

10 Jack Ahern, op. cit.

11 Steffen Nijhuis, "Landscape-Based Urbanism: Cultivating Urban Landscapes Through Design," in *Design for Regenerative Cities and Landscapes*, ed. Rob Roggema (Cham: Springer, 2022), 249–77.

12 Steffen Nijhuis, Yimin Sun, Daniele Cannatella, and Guangyuan Xie, "A Landscape-Based Regional Design Approach for Sustainable Urban Development in the Pearl River Delta, China," in *Adaptive Urban Transformation: Urban Landscape Dynamics, Regional Design and Territorial Governance in the Pearl River Delta, China*, eds. Steffen Nijhuis, Yimin Sun, and Eckart Lange (Cham: Springer, 2023), 81–114.

Fig. 1

Accentuating Indigenous logics in regional vision building: Learning from Vietnam's Mekong Delta

Bruno De Meulder and
Kelly Shannon

The Earth is in extreme peril. A series of cascading crises are ever-more apparent, from the accelerating consequences of global warming to alarming ecological change and devastation with massive biodiversity loss. Along with this, humankind also has its challenges, from alarming systemic racism and social injustice to cultural elimination—as evidenced throughout the globe by increasingly repressive public policies and ongoing disastrous wars. The contemporary built environment is both a cause and effect of some of these crises, highlighting the urgent need for a paradigm shift towards balanced adaptation and the transformation of settled, productive, and "natural" landscapes. While traditional land use-based master planning was once heralded as a savior of the built environment, the illusion that everything could be planned has been subsequently questioned. There has been a reevaluation of planning approaches, with calls for strategic and collaborative planning gaining traction in recent decades. Concurrently, in the 1990s, landscape urbanism emerged in the United States as a response to a reduction of landscape architecture to mere gardening and the perceived failure of planning.[1,2] Many master plans were outdated before implementation while others contributed to "absent urbanism"—a form of urban development with no conscious attempt to foster a social sphere.[3]

Although discursive alternatives to (primarily monofunctional) land use planning have gained footing, it remains the default method and procedure for most municipal planning agencies worldwide. Scholars in Africa have gone so far as to label contemporary master planning as "persistent, pragmatic and prolific," particularly concerning transnational investment and the reigning institutional enthusiasm for control over nature.[4] Ultimately, land use is the modus operandi of neo-liberal economics since it fixes "value" and development rights to an ever-increasing system of private property. Fortunately, there are notable (yet marginal) efforts where the "common good" is regaining ground. Across scales, strategic urban projects endeavor to enhance the interplay of infrastructure, landscape, and urbanism. It is evident that engaged designers and thinkers, coupled with political will and financing, focus on locational assets and site qualities to redefine the interfaces between dualities of culture and nature, private and public, and architecture and urbanism.

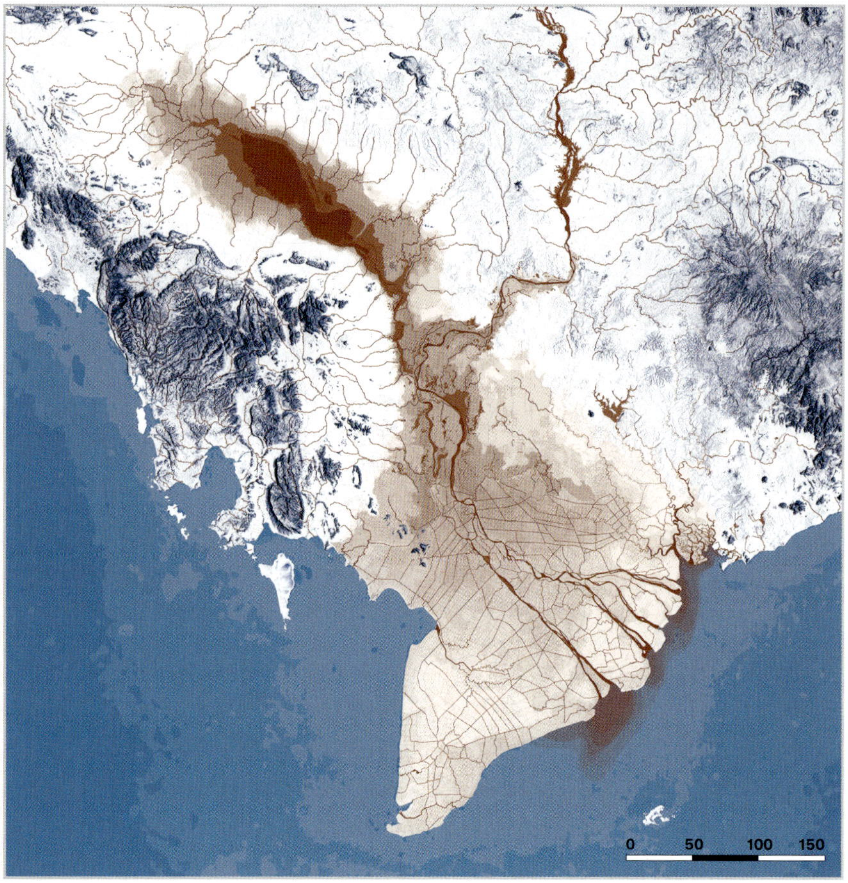

Fig. 2

This article will derive lessons for territorial-scale development from a case study in the transboundary Mekong Delta located in Vietnam and Cambodia. It will reveal a careful reading through interpretative mapping of landscape domestication over a *longue durée* in relation to contemporary challenges of urbanization and global warming. Moreover, it will focus on design research spanning over two decades through the co-development of the Vietnamese Mekong Delta Regional Plan (by Research Urbanism Architecture, an academic-based practice in Belgium,[5] in collaboration with the Southern Institute of Urban Planning based in Ho Chi Minh City) and ongoing research of the delta's evolution.

Landscape as urbanism: Desakota and agroecological regions

In the contemporary context, the interplay of landscape architecture and urbanism is the most effective way to engage with the territory and public realm. It allows a blurring of disciplinary boundaries and a focus on reconfiguring the city/nature relationship at a territorial scale. The process of landscape evolution means that territorial design is ever-changing, temporal, and indeterminate. Moreover, the notion of landscape as urbanism is particularly suited to the archetypal Southeast Asian settlement environment since there has been a long-standing rejection of the duality of nature and city in this region. The landscape itself—encompassing its hydrography, topography, and vegetation—has historically generated context-specific settlement patterns.

The Mekong Delta spans from the Khone Falls (north of Kratie in Cambodia) to the Tonle Sap Lake's tidal pulse system, eventually emptying through multiple distributaries into Vietnam's East Sea (Fig. 2). In the delta, the micro-topographies of the vast flood plain shaped both productive landscapes and settlement systems, which are embedded in various worldviews. Settling within and colonizing the delta quagmire necessitated the construction of (drainage) canals, along which military installations and human settlements were elongated—most often at the threshold between the water and land distinction generated by the excavated canals. They fundamentally defied Western notions of centrality and hierarchy.

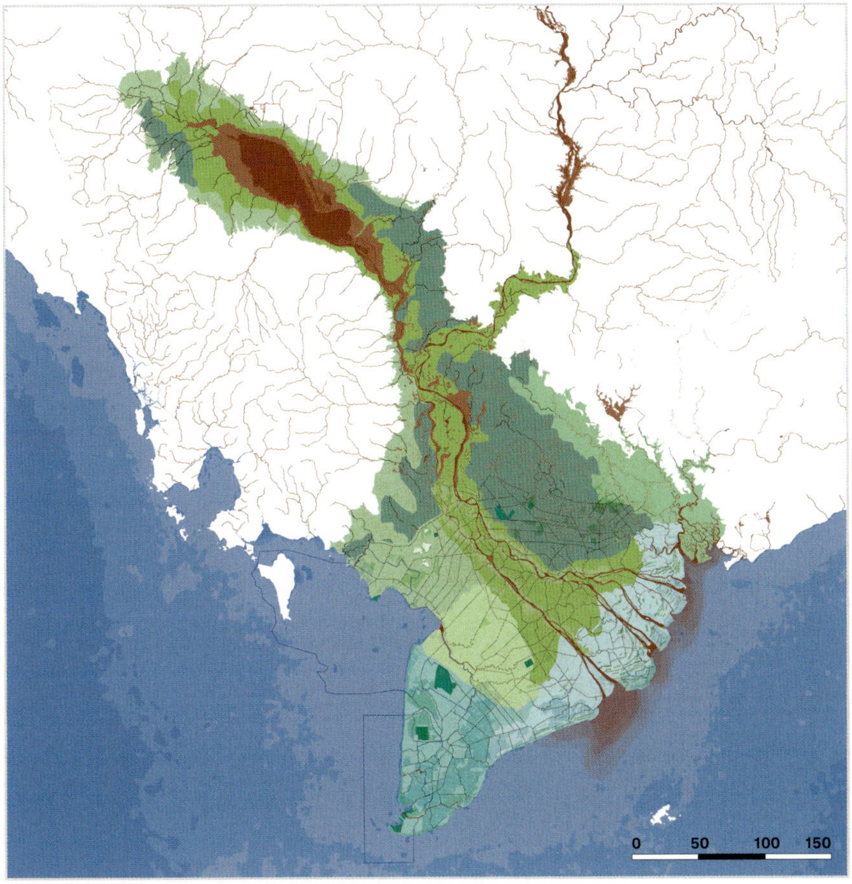

Fig. 3

Historically, in this vast quagmire, land and water were not necessarily opposites; settlements corresponded to the fluid deltaic culture of small, dispersed, and autonomous communities. Thus, everything oscillated between muddy waters and soggy mud. Degrees of wetness—forever shifting gradients of water and sediments—were pervasive. Simultaneously, the rich fertility of the land attracted farmers and generated massive population growth and development which led to more land-based, gridded, and densely concentrated settlements over time (and with significant colonial influence). Nonetheless, as in other Asian contexts, there was (and remains) the notion of "Desakota" ("Desa" for village and "Kota" for town),[6] where rural and urban socio-economic and cultural characteristics co-exist across territorial morphologies.

Despite there being various ethnic groups inhabiting the delta (Khmer, Vietnamese, Cham, and Chinese), a common territorial identity can be observed that remains tied to the interplay between land and water. More precisely, it relates to topography (including bathymetry), soil qualities (most broadly alluvia, saline, and acid sulphate), and salt and freshwater parameters. Geographers classify their recognition and accentuation of the delta's underlying geography into seven broad agroecological sub-regions [7] (Fig. 3). Today, from an anthropocentric point of view, the main asset of the delta is its enormous agri- and aquacultural potential. Yet, nuances in topography and bathymetry are often compromised for the mere profitability of the territory. In the process, age-old cyclic relations between humankind and the landscape are being replaced by linear and deleterious processes. Moreover, Indigenous knowledge systems and practices (IKSP)[8] and traditional ecological knowledge (TEK)[9] are disappearing (and/or being deliberately suppressed).

Landscape-led logics for the Lower Mekong Delta

Vietnam's Mekong Delta Regional Plan was commissioned in 2014 by the Vietnamese Government's Ministry of Construction. The plan by Research Urbanism Architecture and the Southern Institute of Urban Planning (based in Hồ Chí Minh City) sought to organize renewed landscape ecologies in harmony with the social, economic, and cultural dynamics of the

Water management units of watershed

- Ca Mau Peninsula
- Co Dong & Saigon-Dong Nai watershed
- Interfluvial Tien & Hau Rivers
- Long Xuyen Quadrangle
- Up Tien Rivers
- --- Sub-watershed boundary
- --- Sub-irrigation areas

Fig. 4

region. As opposed to contemporary development-as-usual, where land-consumptive and road-based urbanism unvaryingly blankets the territory, the regional plan began from the understanding of the delta's inherent landscape logics and the predicted consequences of global warming. Presently, the delta's enormous agri- and aquacultural potential is challenged by shifting rainfall patterns, saline intrusion, transnational deforestation, and upstream dam construction—not to mention large road and urban development projects. It was hypothesized in the design research that future alternatives for the delta could be grounded in the specificity of agroecological regions (of which there are six in the Vietnamese component of the delta) to reestablish the region's core identity. Their accentuation was developed to counterbalance the relative homogeneity of the region's regional urbanism and architecture, which has tended to "flatten out" due to processes of neoliberal economics.[10]

Therefore, the topography, soils, agroecological distinctions, and understanding of the delta's 120 water management units [11] (Fig. 4) were the primary qualifiers of the vision for 2050. In particular, the water management units were of strategic importance since water regulation (controlling quality and quantity of water allocation over time) defines the territory through engineering compartmentalization. At an even lower level, the drainage structure and parcel system define the fine-grained mesh of the mosaic landscape. Meanwhile, the water management units define the most important scale of differentiation in the landscape, in addition to the agroecological regions. Two new components of water management were introduced: firstly, a large monsoon rain catchment basin upstream was proposed for massive water storage and release into the delta's sophisticated water mosaic in the dry season. This intervention sought to reestablish the "Plain of Reeds" as a wetland, formerly a "back swamp" forming a large, inundated depression that has been massively drained since the 1970s. Secondly, massive coastal mangrove afforestation was proposed, coupled with rewilding of the islands in the Mekong River branches to attenuate sea level rise and combat erosion (Fig. 5).

Across the territory, the mobility infrastructure was reconceived in response to global warming challenges. There was an explicit move not to build new,

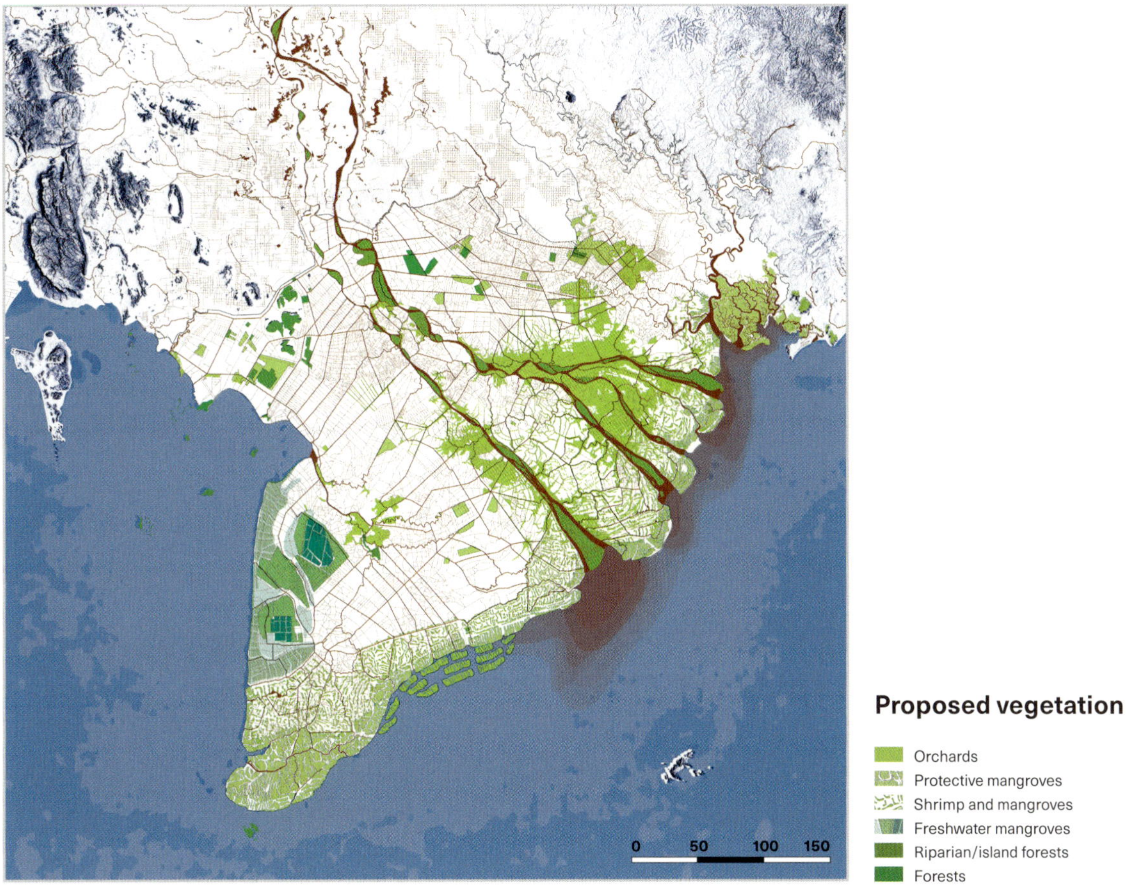

Fig. 5

extremely expensive road-based infrastructure in an area where there will be inundation; several highways previously planned by the Ministry of Transportation were not considered optimal investments since they would be flooded by 2050. Instead, the plan proposed connections, not as equal access or a homogenous grid across the territory but via a strategic selection of highways. This would be comprised of a main highway collector—a central spine located on guaranteed dry land in the center of the delta—and feeders or linkages to important socio-economic destinations (including Hồ Chí Minh City, ports, and transversals to Vietnam's border gates). The further from the spine, the more modest the profile of the feeders, combining with natural structures such as mangroves and water elements to take over as the primary structuring devices of the territory.

The feeders were intended to recuperate existing "national roads" that would be upgraded and modernized. Simultaneous upgrading and modernization of their parallel canals would occur: the canals and embankments, national roads and their respective interstices, and adjacent lands would literally superimpose a man-made framework that unites the territory. The mobility infrastructure could regain its "polytechnicity"—to use the term of Mumford, where infrastructural sections merge the "technical" with the "civic" and "economic" also with ecological performance.[12] The water and road mobility flows would articulate water and land relations (including the management, regulation, and protection of floodwaters) while systematic trees and forest planting would create a livable micro-climate. The overall configuration of the plan was governed by the landscape, determining where to build and—more importantly—where to *not* build (Fig. 6).

New morphologies and typologies based on Indigenous knowledge and practices

Aside from the agroecological sub-regions, the proposed plan defined three distinct morphologies and typologies for rural and urban development in the Plain of Reeds, Freshwater Alluvial Plain, and East Coast. These were developed as part of a system of wet and dry areas derived from soil types, sedimentation, erosion, and subsidence, as well as the 2050 predictions of inundation and saline intrusion. In all three typologies, the

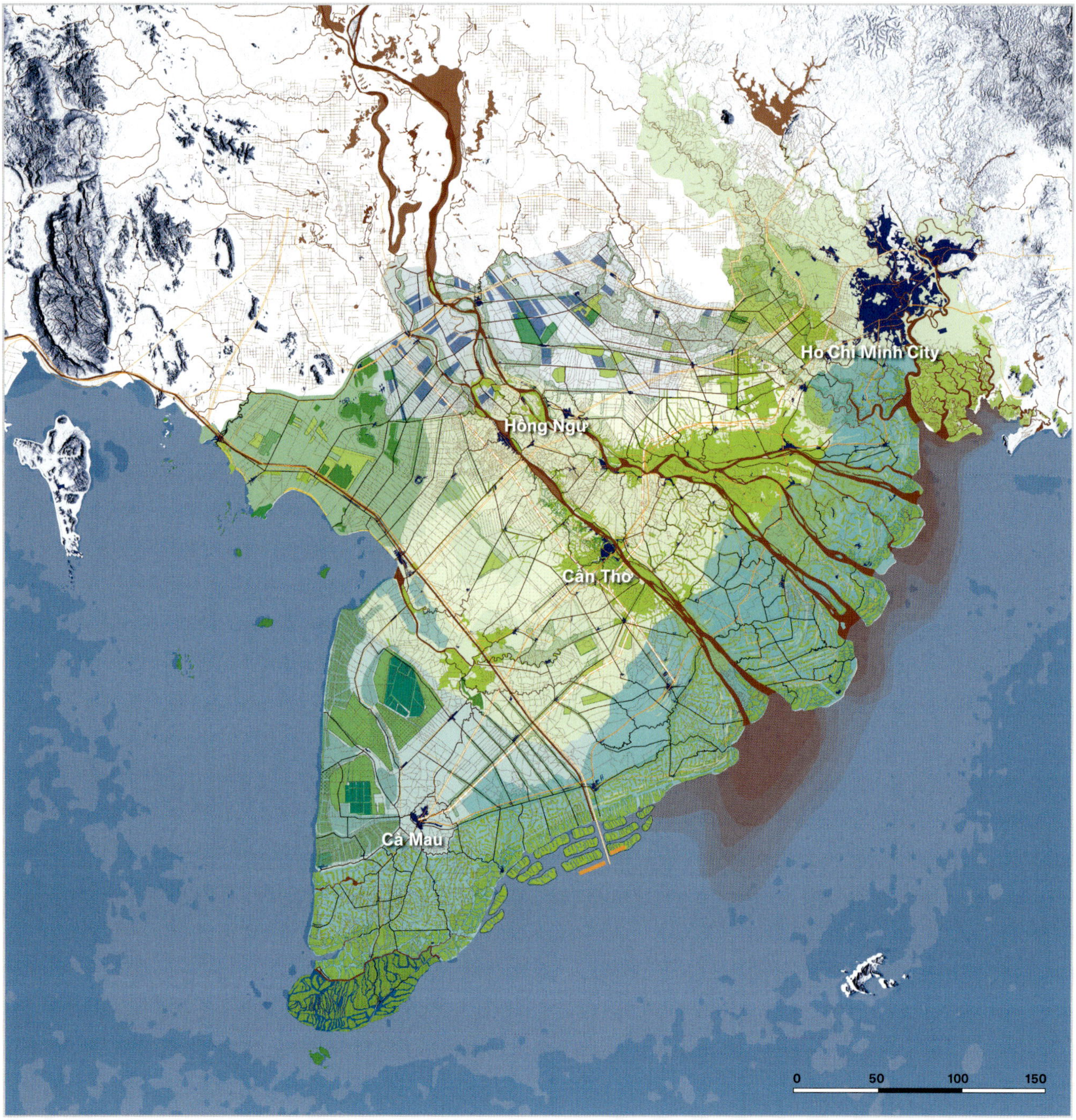

Mekong Delta regional plan 2030, vision to 2050

- Monsoon reservoir
- Reforestation
- Rice basket
- Urban clusters
- Regional airport/port
- Regional roads

Fig. 6

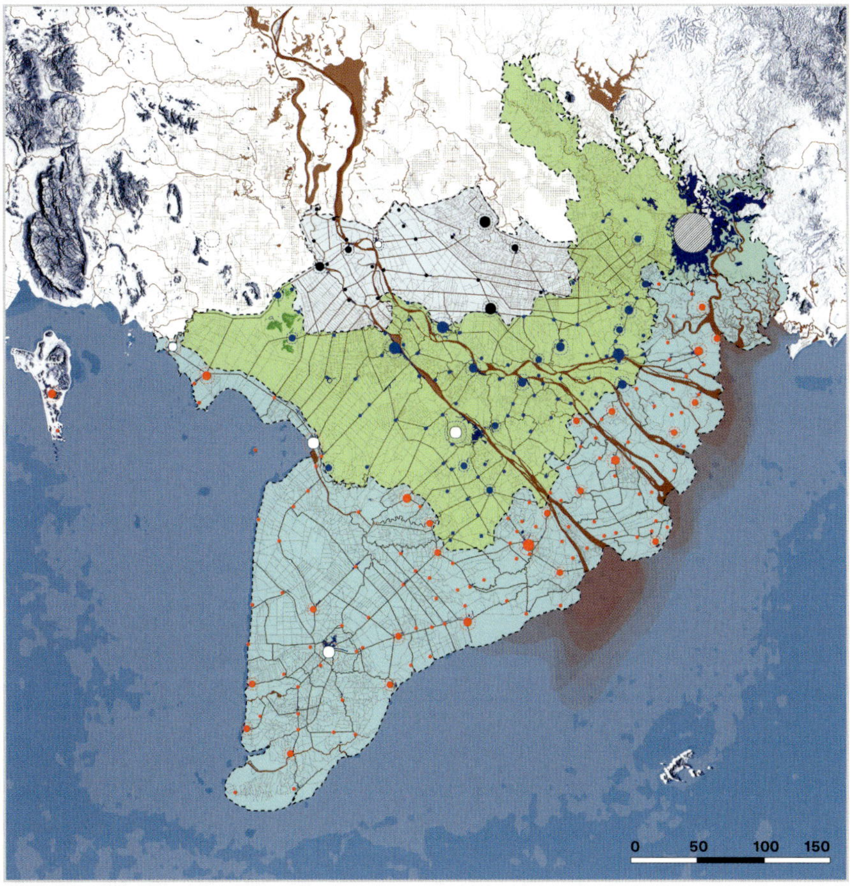

Three morphologies and typologies

Plain of Reeds
Freshwater Alluvial Plain
East Coast
Cities

Fig. 7

hierarchy of topography, infrastructure, and settlement was reconfigured in relation to the site-specific realities and future projections in the respective region (Fig. 7). Throughout the delta, villages can continue to be read as radically dispersed and heterarchical variations of elongated filaments—along canals, high alluvial (i.e., unsalinated) riverbanks, small and large dikes, sand ridges, linear floating and high-stilt settlements in rivers, and seasonally inundated wetlands (Fig. 8). The organized dispersal of the linear and clustered systems served as the inspiration for new development.

As well, both the morphologies and typologies in the plan were developed through lessons derived from extensive fieldwork, the interpretative mapping of Indigenous knowledge systems and practices, and traditional ecological knowledge. A host of local practices—often carried out in peripheral geographies—have either escaped the relentless "modernization" process, locally adapted, and/or intelligently subverted the imposed supra-order. Therefore, the development of the three types of morphologies and typologies was based on "Indigenous knowledge systems and practices" and "traditional ecological knowledge," which could serve as models for future development in the respective sub-regions.

In the low-lying Plain of Reeds, in the city of Hồng Ngự (of the Đồng Tháp Province, near the Cambodian border), and at the confluence of the Sở Thượng Canal and Mekong River, settlements would be inspired by the region's typical system of family compounds. Family clusters are organized across several degrees of wetness—from the dry area connected to the dike road to the riverbank wetlands and the open water of the canal itself. The houses closest to the dike are partly with foundations on terra firma and extend towards the river on stilts; they connect to river cage culture houses via floating planks and sampans (Fig. 9).

The cage culture houses are constructed on the water with durable hardwoods of high water resistance, allowing them to withstand the constant pressure of strong currents. Although there are problems related to the fish feed and its degradation of water quality, the floating houses—simultaneously productive and for inhabitation—are inspirational in a context that faces massive inundation in the years to come. In the Mekong Delta Regional Plan, an "extended Plain

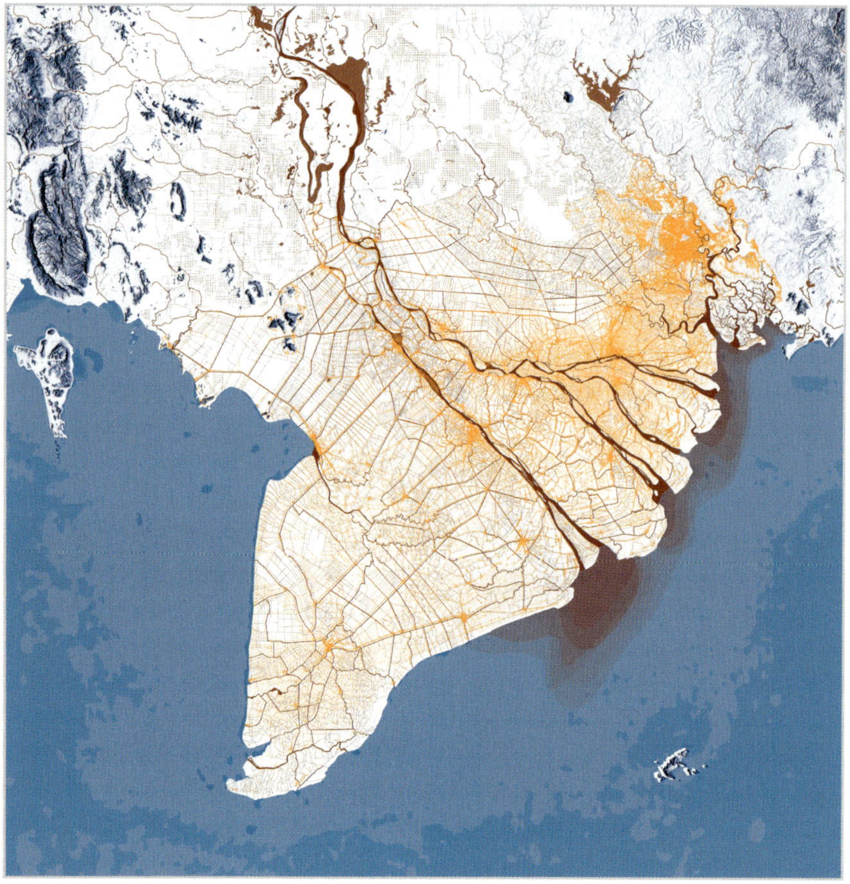

A web of linear settlements

Urban footprint

Fig. 8

Hồng Ngự family clusters

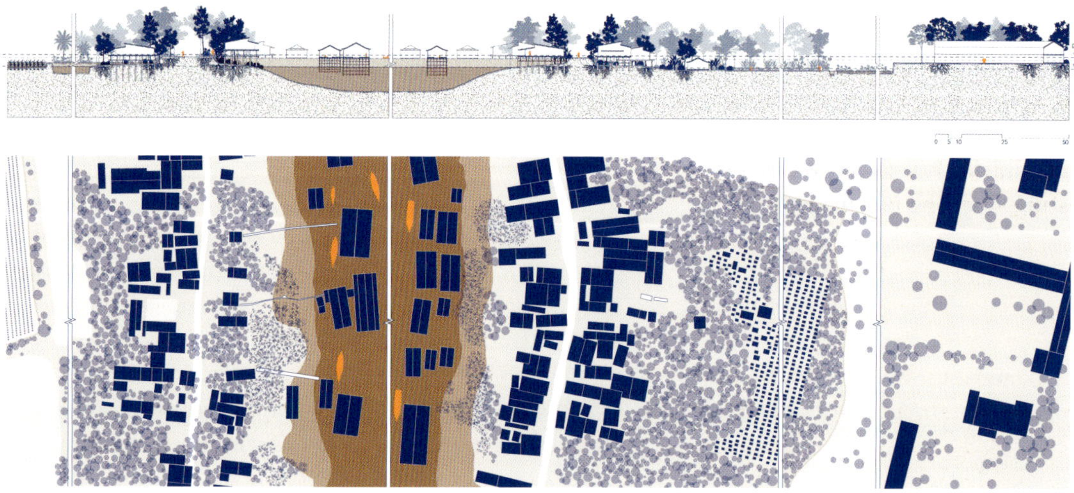

Fig. 9

Fig. 10

of Reeds" type would be developed for Đồng Tháp Mười and part of the Long Xuyên Quadrangle. Since the area is expected to be significantly inundated, the region could once again thrive with controlled flooding and water storage. As in Hồng Ngự, buildings could be on stilts and/or floating. As mentioned earlier, large monsoon collection basins could be inscribed into the existing canal and irrigation system and would be able to release freshwater into the delta during the dry season, as well as serve as an area for fish, indigo, and floating rice farming (Fig. 10).

Further downstream, in the city of Cần Thơ (situated in the Freshwater Alluvial Plain), is the Cái Răng Floating Market, existing since the late nineteenth century in the Cần Thơ River. It is located six kilometers southwest of the city center. Cái Răng and other floating markets thrived in the early development of the Mekong Delta, integrated into floating, aquaculture-based settlement systems prevalent in vast watery networks. During a period when a well-developed road and land-based market system was lacking, these floating markets served as efficient hubs for wholesale trading of aquaculture and agricultural products. In the Cái Răng market, boats moor in the river from pre-dawn until late morning while others maneuver through the water, with both selling their wares. Products are sourced from factories, plantations, farms, and orchards. The dynamics of the market and riverbank urbanization strongly contrast with other areas of the river, which has been rapidly transforming due to massive investment in bridge and road infrastructure (Fig. 11).

Along the northern banks of the Cần Thơ River and further from the city lies the rural district of Phong Điền, defined by the confluence of the Cần Thơ and Hậu Rivers. The elevation of Phong Điền is slightly more elevated than in the surrounding areas, providing higher grounds for orchards—the roots of which simultaneously strengthen the resiliency of the land and flood safety. The area is renowned for its extensive mosaic of orchards and the household level of "VAC" farming—a system of diversification and nutrient linkages of V (orchard), A (pond), and C (animal pens). The waste from one component becomes the input of another, increasing production and circumventing the need for chemical fertilizers and pesticides.

Cái Răng floating market

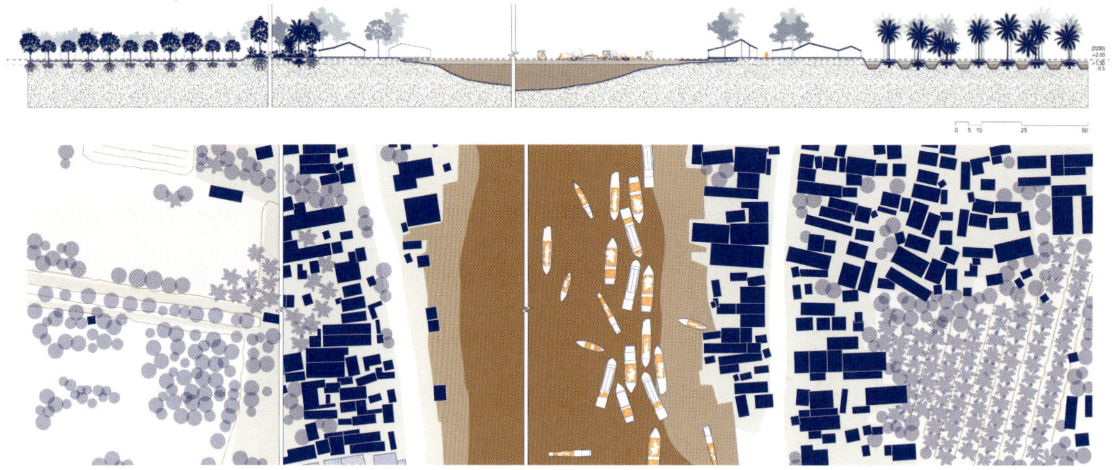

Fig. 11

Phong Điền orchard urbanism

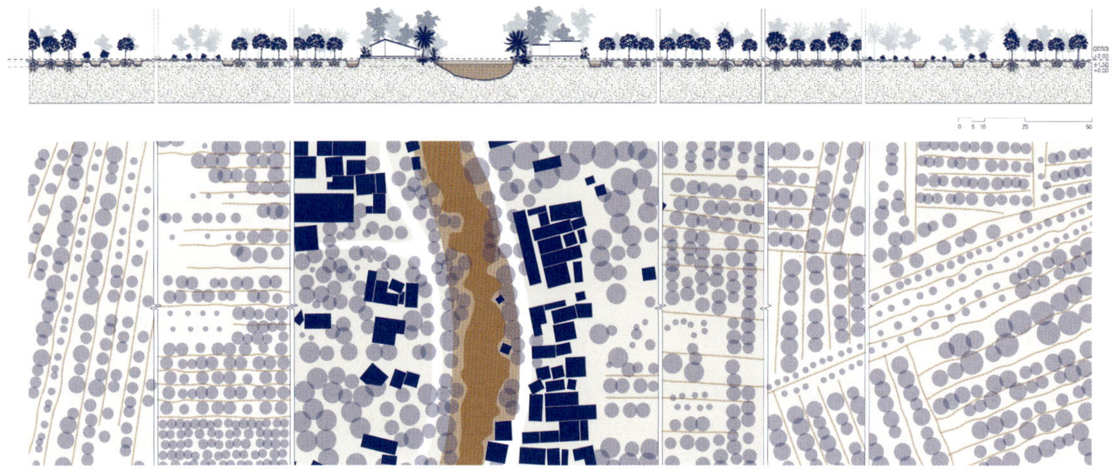

Fig. 12

Cà Mau aquaculture farms

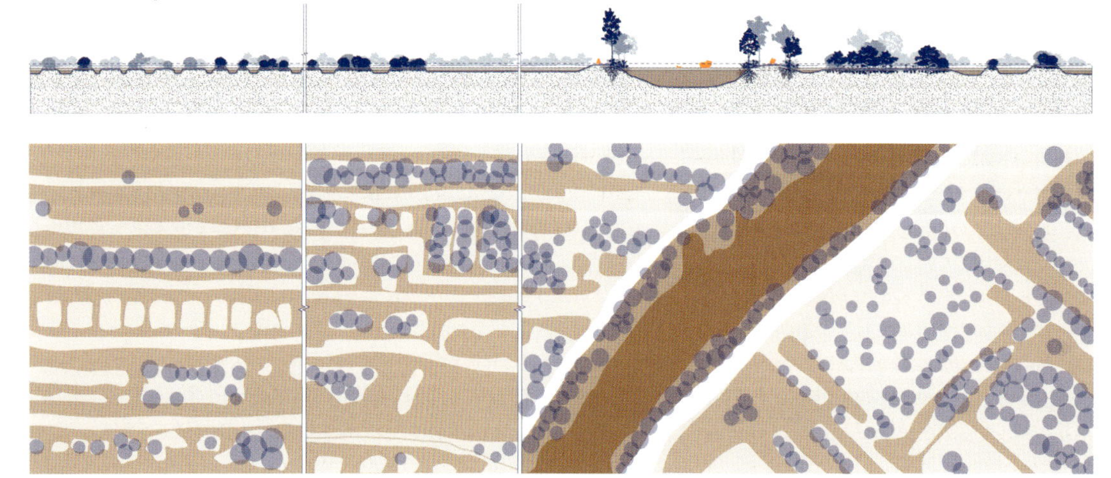

Fig. 13

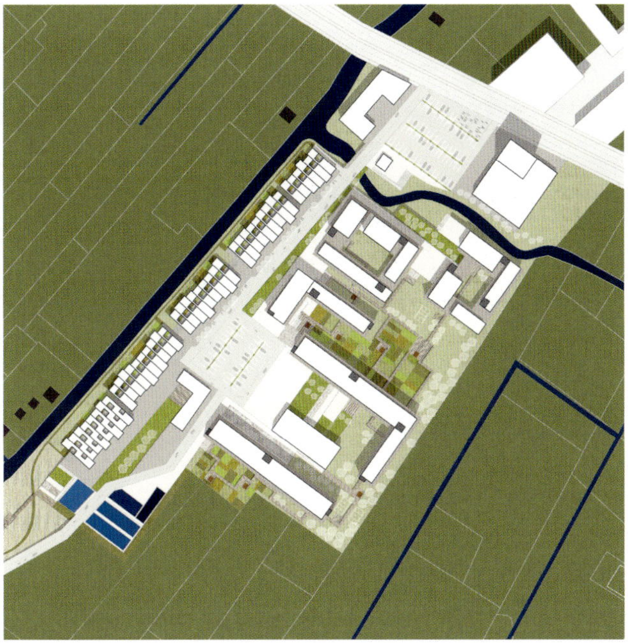

Fig. 14

Homesteads are included in the system, known as "VACB" (if biogas production is included) and "VACR" (if fish is stocked in the rice fields connected to the pond).[13] In Phong Điền, the degree of intensity/extensity of orchards and aquaculture input levels have been precisely developed in relation to the specific agroecological environment, geographical location, household context, and size of animal husbandry (Fig. 12). The area's unique ecology has developed a distinct form of orchard urbanism characterized by homes situated amid waterways and expansive gardens. This unique landscape holds significant economic value for the region as its orchards are worth roughly three times more per acre than the surrounding rice fields.[14] The waterways and orchards have become critically important for district-level identity and act as a structuring tool for urbanization.

For the delta's immense productive landscape, it is clear that such models—from times when the large-scale import of fertilizers or its production was out of reach—can be non-nostalgically upscaled, along with technological updates. The resilience of water-based activities and VAC farming is important from an economic and ecological perspective of ever-increasing territorial vulnerability. In the Mekong Delta Regional Plan, the "freshwater alluvial" type would be the most dense system developed for the Trans Bassac Depression and the Freshwater Alluvial zones. Here, a requalified system of urbanism on relatively high land would work together with a diversified productive landscape of rice, orchards, and vegetables. In addition, the existing settlement types could be modernized, densified, and clustered. Living with (and on) the water could densify the diffuse Desakota urbanization patterns that safeguard agricultural land, the main asset of the region; for example, as in the Cái Răng Floating Market, nestled amongst the productive landscape. Water transportation would be favored over road-based movement (Fig. 14).

Finally, settlements in the coastal areas could be developed to work with the East Coast's parallel and alternating rows of sand ridges, back swamps, successive peat layers, and subsiding lands of the Cà Mau Peninsula. They could learn from the existing system of aquaculture farms and dispersed settlement areas (Fig. 13). Directly along the coast, new settlements could be comprised of clustered, floating buildings that center on collective spaces in clearings of mangrove forests (Fig. 15). Aquaculture (fish and shrimp farming) would be interwoven into a rich mosaic able to withstand the tidal pulses from the East Sea and the Gulf of Thailand.

The Desakota principles would adapt to this new situation; the organized dispersal of floating settlements would respond to tidal pulses and sea level rise. Within this setting of new mangroves and water bodies, a new and complementary aquacultural economy could be built with greater emphasis on harvesting naturally renewable resources (there is significant potential for wind and tidal energy) and high-end specialized products, such as rare medical plants. As such, these additions, which would succeed in what was previously a largely monocultural economy, will strengthen the robustness of the economy and the sustainability of the development of the Mekong region while simultaneously rebuilding a biologically diverse environment.

Learning from the Mekong Delta

Design at the regional scale can contribute to the resilient transformation of urban-rural areas across administrative boundaries. The logics of landscapes—as agroecological (sub)regions with attendant water management units and vegetal mosaics—can guide strategies to restore ecologies, respond to sea level rise, mitigate flood and drought, address deep decarbonization, concentrate on food and water security, and create micro-climates and carbon sinks. However, none of the above strategies can be developed with mono-functional land use planning. The power of design to address the radical repair of deeply disturbed ecologies can be complemented with renewed respect for traditional forms of environmental stewardship and daily life practices. These thrive outside of the paradigm of late capitalism, extractivism, and endless growth.

Fig. 15

Fig. 1
Proposed re-mangroving in coastal areas.

Fig. 2
The Mekong and Sài Gòn-Đồng Nai Deltas converge into a vast mud plain spanning parts of Vietnam and Cambodia, with its floodplain delineated by a topographical line 16 meters above sea level.

Fig. 3
Agro-ecological regions in the Mekong Delta.

Fig. 4
The Vietnamese section of the Mekong Delta enables effective control over drainage and parcellation in distinct units.

Fig. 5
Proposed vegetation: protective landscapes and nature reserves.

Fig. 6
The Mekong Delta Regional Plan 2030, vision to 2050, combines multiple dimensions.

Fig. 7
Three distinct morphologies were developed: 1. coastal areas; 2. freshwater alluvial areas; and 3. extended floodplains.

Fig. 8
Linear filaments of urbanization traverse the entire territory in a heterarchical system of organized dispersal. These linear filaments are anchored predominantly to the water system defining the spatial register of the Mekong Delta.

Fig. 9
Family clusters develop perpendicular to the river, featuring boats, floating houses, stilt houses on riverbanks, and "land-based houses" along the embankment road. Gardens interweave with patches of paddy fields while tombs are embedded in the landscape.

Fig. 10
Massive inundation is predicted to increase progressively. Stilt buildings would be connected to dikes. Monsoon collection basins would release fresh water into the delta system during the dry season and also serve as aquaculture landscapes.

Fig. 11
Cái Răng hosts the region's largest floating market where the rich fruit produce of the area is traded. In recent years, it has been undermined by land-based markets. Cái Răng is presently being rebranded as a touristic site.

Fig. 12
Housing clusters are positioned next to the waterside, with tombs in back gardens, both on relatively higher land. Mosaics of regular planted orchards occupy the slightly lower land.

Fig. 13
The contemporary clearing of mangroves in the Cà Mau Peninsula generates a new and irregular water, land, and vegetational choreography suitable for many types of aquaculture (particularly crab farming).

Fig. 14
In the alluvial plain, existing settlement types would be modernized, densified, and clustered. Settlement would be on raised land (high and dry platforms) surrounded by a sea of low-lying rice fields.

Fig. 15
The new settlement strategy is comprised of "water clearings" within the systematically "re-mangroved" coastal area. These give space for organic aquaculture (fish, shrimp, crab, etc.) and accommodate small clusters of houses built on platforms that float seasonally.

Landscape can be reimaged as infrastructure and urbanism (once again) as a territorial, socio-ecological, and political project. Innovation involving the intersections of ecology and engineering, social policy, and political process are necessary to address the cascading crises of present times in the Mekong Delta and elsewhere. It is clear that the development of strategic visions across scales requires a collaborative and immersive process, from episodes of intensive fieldwork and participant observation to inter- and transdisciplinary perspectives and coalition-building. For the Mekong Delta Regional Plan, numerous sources of expertise were consulted (including Vietnam's Ministry of Construction [MoC], the Ministry of Agriculture and Rural Development [MaRD], the Ministry of Natural Resources and Environment [MoNRE], and the Ministry of Planning and Investment [MPI], among others). The plan was approved and signed by the Vietnamese Prime Minister in 2018.

Evidently, the immediate agency on the ground is scant. To date, there is not yet a legal mechanism for regional plans in the Vietnamese planning system; the highest level of plan implementation is that of provincial plans (of which there are thirteen in the Vietnamese Mekong Delta). Additionally, the Ministry of Planning and Investment took over spatial planning responsibilities from the Ministry of Construction. This was after the passing of the "Law on Planning" in 2017, which came into effect on January 1, 2019, only months after the Mekong Delta Regional Plan was approved. The law aims to unify and streamline the planning processes across different sectors, providing a more integrated and coordinated approach to national, regional, and local planning. However, this means that the approved plan from 2018, with its strong emphasis on agro-ecological balances, merely laid a basis for a series of iterations deeply ingrained in the cyclical Vietnamese planning system. In this system, plans are revised every few years. The 2018 iteration resonates in the ongoing critical debate in Vietnam on conventional land use planning, principles of mixture, sustainable agro- and aquacultural practices, local knowledge, and suitability that were part and parcel of this first-ever exercise in regional planning in Vietnam.

1 Charles Waldheim, *The Landscape Urbanism Reader* (New York: Princeton Architecture Press, 2012).

2 James Corner, "Recovering Landscape as a Critical Cultural Practice," in *Recovering Landscape: Essays in Contemporary Landscape Architecture*, ed. James Corner (New York: Princeton Architectural Press, 1999), 1–26.

3 Richard Marshall, *Emerging Urbanity: Global Urban Projects in the Asia Pacific Rim* (London: Spon Press, 2003).

4 Sylvia Croese et al., "Persistent, pragmatic and prolific: Urban master planning in Accra, Dar es Salaam and Lilongwe," *Land Use Policy* 133, (2023): 106832.

5 The authors are the founders of this design research and urbanism practice, Research Urbanism and Architecture (RUA).

6 Terry McGee, "The Emergence of Desakota Regions in Asia: Expanding a Hypothesis," in *The Extended Metropolis: Settlement Transition in Asia*, eds. Norton Ginsburg, Bruce Koppel, and Terry McGee (Honolulu, University of Hawaii Press, 1991), 3–25.

7 For over thirty years, the International Institute for Applied Systems Analysis (IIASA) and the Food and Agriculture Organization of the United Nations (FAO) have been developing the notion of agroecological regions/zones to assess agricultural resources and potential. AEZs are geographical areas exhibiting similar climatic conditions that determine their ability to support rainfed agriculture. At a regional scale, AEZs are influenced by latitude, elevation, and temperature, as well as seasonality rainfall amounts and distribution during the growing season.

8 IKSP (Indigenous knowledge systems and practices) is a term that is commonly used in The Philippines (https://www.ilo.org/manila/publications/WCMS_764036/lang--en/index.htm). It is similar to TEK (traditional ecological knowledge), a notion conceptualized in anthropology but with a strong focus on everyday customs and practices.

9 Melissa K. Nelson and Dan Shilling (eds.), *Traditional Ecological Knowledge: Learning from Indigenous Practices for Environmental Sustainability* (Cambridge: Cambridge University Press, 2018).

10 Kenneth Frampton, "Towards a Critical Regionalism: Six Points for an Architecture of Resistance," in *The Anti-Aesthetic: Essays on Postmodern Culture*, ed. Hal Foster (Seattle: Bay Press, 1983), 16–30.

11 Southern Institute of Water and Resource Planning (SIWRP), Hồ Chí Minh City: Master Plan in the Mekong Delta for Impact of Climate Change – Sea Level Rise (2012).

12 Lewis Mumford, *Technics and Civilization* (New York: Harcourt, Brace & Company, Inc., 1934).

13 Kieu Nhan Dang et al., "Development of "VAC" integrated farming systems in the Mekong Delta, Vietnam: A view of a system and a participatory approach," in *Development of integrated agricultural farming systems in the Mekong Delta*, ed. Ryuichi Yamada (Tre Publishing House, 2005), 101–25.

14 Roel H. Bosma, et al., "Agriculture Diversification in the Mekong Delta: Farmers' Motives and Contributions to Livelihoods," in *Asian Journal of Agriculture and Development 2*, no. 1 & 2 (2005): 54.

Fig. 1

Jiangnan Park: A territorial vision for the Yangtze River Delta megacity region

Christian Nolf, Yuting Xie, and Yiwen Wang

Jiangnan Park represents a territorial vision for the cultural landscape located at the heart of the Yangtze River Delta megacity region of China. At the hinterland of Shanghai, Suzhou, and Hangzhou, this area is often overlooked in spatial and development plans; however, it has the potential to evolve into a unifying core reflecting the multiple identities of the region. The concept of Jiangnan Park was developed through a five-year, incremental research-through-design initiative led by a multidisciplinary team of academics, students, and local experts. This chapter specifically highlights the role of collaborative pilot projects in shaping territorial visions within the context of China's "Ecological Civilization Construction" strategy.

A megacity region shaped by its cultural landscape

The Yangtze River Delta megacity region stands as one of the most economically prosperous and densely populated areas globally. This density reaches its pinnacle within the alluvial and marshy plains of the Taihu Basin. Although covering only 0.4% of China's landmass, the basin hosts 4% of its population and contributes to an estimated 11% of GDP[1]. This exceptional concentration of human activity is not recent and owes its existence to the region's very fertile soil and centuries of water management systems. Commencing with the completion of the Grand Canal in the early seventh century to facilitate grain export to the northern capital, the entire delta territory was meticulously tamed using a sophisticated network of canals and polders. Over centuries, this polder system underwent several adaptations, gradually densifying the productive territory into a continuous rural fabric interspersed in relative harmony with various towns and cities.[2]

However, since the 1950s—and especially following the economic reform of 1978—this balance has been disrupted by the acceleration of urbanization. Supported by centralized and mechanized water management systems and an extensive transportation network, the urbanized area within the Taihu Basin expanded up to tenfold from 1983-2015.[3] While this exponential growth has consolidated the region as an economic powerhouse, it has also generated serious environmental issues that threaten the region's sustainability,

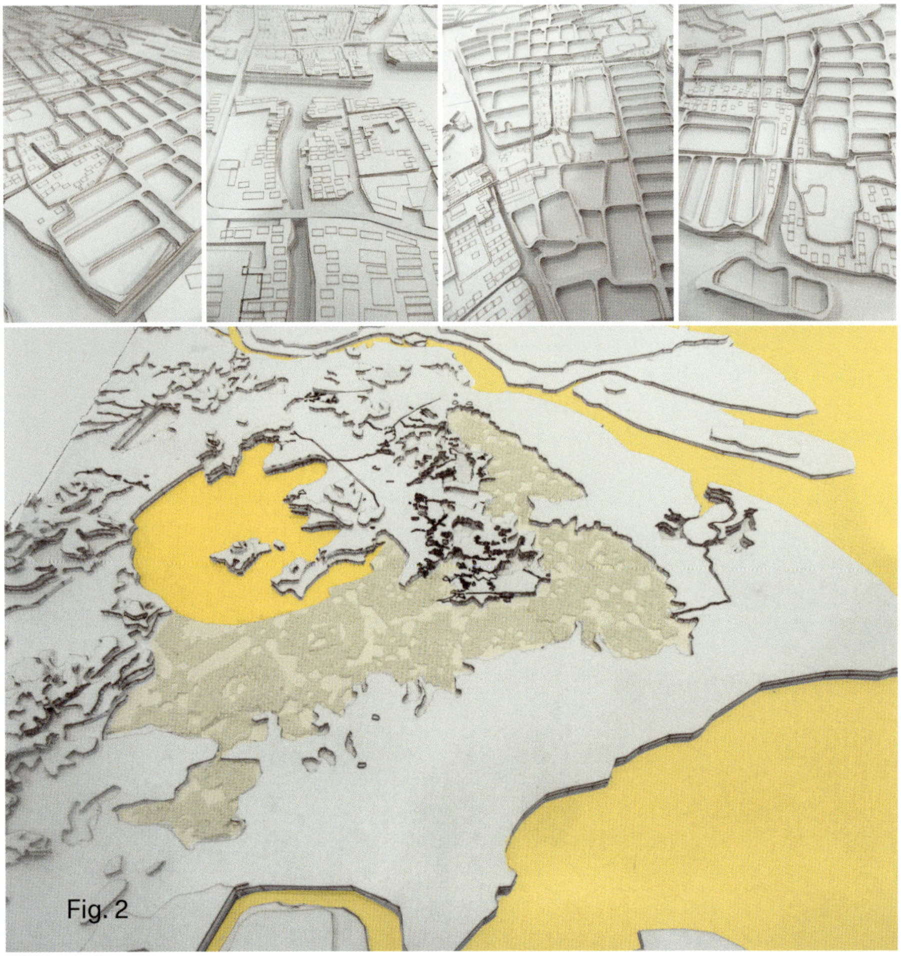

Fig. 2

including the alarming depletion of natural habitats, fresh water, and cultivable land resources.

A test bed for China's Ecological Civilization Construction

In response to these threats, a national-led program for the "Integrated Regional Development of the Yangtze River Delta" was launched in 2019.[4] Alongside economic, transportation, and energy aspects, the Yangtze River Delta integration plan introduced quantified objectives for permanent farmlands, ecological spaces, and water quality.[5] These objectives echo the priorities of the national strategy of "Ecological Civilization Construction" and the new territorial planning system of China. The creation of the new "Ministry of Natural Resources" confers upon it the responsibility of implementing the "Three Red Lines" policy, which pertains to the protection of permanent farmland, vital ecosystems, and the establishment of urban growth boundaries.

If these planning reforms suggest a more balanced and sustainable spatial development of the territory, they nonetheless adhere to a functionalist logic. This tends to contrast an urban model of compact, hyper-connected cities with a modernized rural alternative focused on agricultural and ecological performance. Within this productivist and dualist perspective, the cultural and inhabited dimensions of the rural landscape are often neglected. In numerous instances in the Yangtze River Delta, entire villages are demolished, their populations relocated to larger "super villages," and the historical polder landscape is reconfigured into regularly gridded fields to maximize agricultural output.

However, interestingly, a growing awareness of the characteristic Jiangnan culture has resurfaced in the Delta region in recent years. Jiangnan directly translates as "south of the river" and thus embodies a cultural significance associated with a lifestyle—half urban and half rural—centering on water. This idea is expressed in regional architecture, craftsmanship, music, painting, literature, and gastronomy. Moreover, the renewed interest in Jiangnan culture is evidenced in the ongoing joint applications of several water towns for inclusion on the World Heritage List.[6] However, spatially confined to several protected heritage sites, this interest has

Strategies at the regional scale: Framing, articulating, characterizing

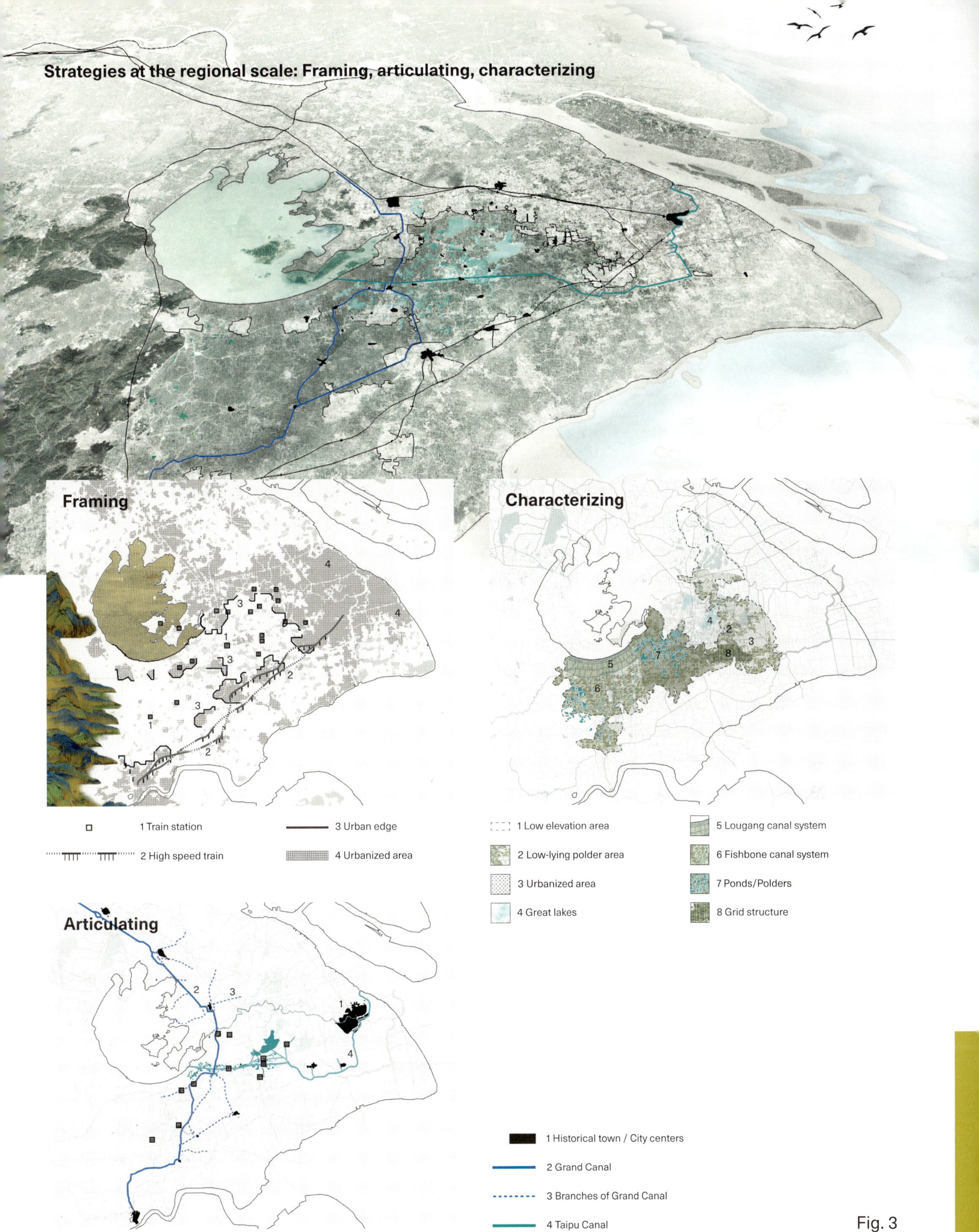

Fig. 3

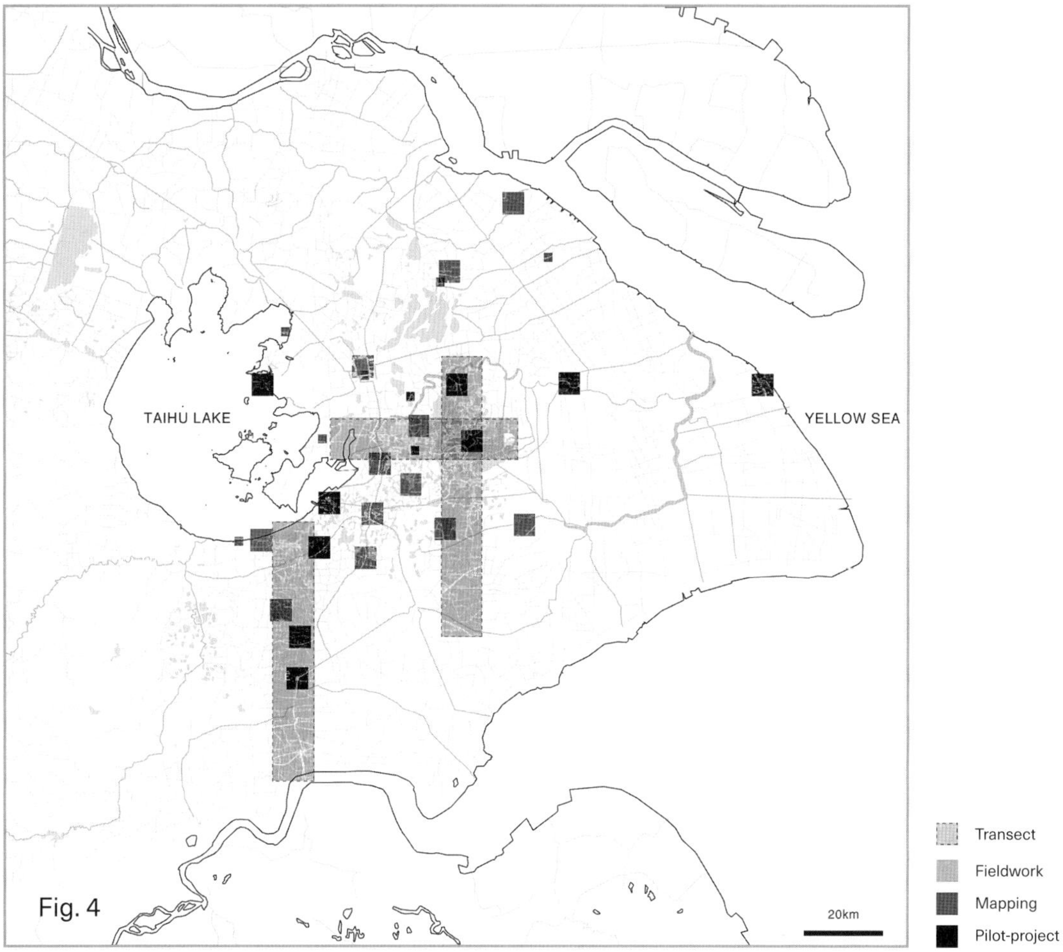

Fig. 4

yet to encompass the surrounding polder landscape.[7] Consequently, the modernization of rural areas promoted by the Ecological Civilization Construction strategy continues in the Yangtze River Delta without fully acknowledging the historical and cultural value embedded in the productive landscape.

Jiangnan Park: Objective and methods

The vision of Jiangnan Park focuses on the low-lying polder area at the heart of the delta. Situated at the intersection of Jiangsu, Zhejiang, and Shanghai Provinces—and until recently sparsely connected by roads and rail—this area has escaped the rapid urbanization that has transformed the rest of the delta region. Thanks to its isolation, the area has preserved its characteristic mosaic of fields, ponds, basins, lakes, canals, and a lacework of linear villages and water towns that constitute the Jiangnan polder landscape (Fig. 2). Typically overlooked as the hinterland of Shanghai, Suzhou, and Hangzhou, this area has the potential to evolve into a unifying core representing the diverse identity of the region. Employing the metaphorical concept of a "park," the territorial vision aims to regenerate this central rural area in its multiple productive, ecological, and socio-cultural dimensions, complementing the megacity.

Led by a multidisciplinary team of academics and students in spatial planning, urban design, and landscape architecture, the vision of Jiangnan Park crystalizes an incremental process that employed a variety of methods over several years (2016-2021). Initially, at the regional level, a descriptive and interpretative mapping exercise was conducted to identify the distinctive landscape features of the region and its evolution.[8] This mapping process suggested three complementary strategies for the Jiangnan Park area: first, framing it by defining its boundaries; second, articulating the area with key structures; and third, characterizing the region by emphasizing the diverse types of polder landscapes it encompasses (Fig. 3).

Each of these strategies at the regional scale was then explored in greater detail in representative sites through workshops and design studios. One studio focused on requalifying urban-rural edges as active interfaces to frame Jiangnan Park.[9] Two parallel studios

Fig. 5

delved into the structuring potential of the Grand Canal and the Taipu Canal to articulate the area.[10] Finally, a series of pilot projects were conducted in collaboration with local stakeholders in various sites to develop regeneration strategies tailored to distinctive landscape features (Fig. 4).[11]

Hunan Village as a pilot project

One of these pilot projects took place in Hunan Village, situated within the Tongli Township, south of Suzhou. Positioned in the delta's lowest area, Hunan serves as a quintessential example of traditional villages and the contemporary challenges they encounter. Functioning as a fishing village adjacent to a lake, Hunan Village comprises six distinct polder units. Each unit is encircled by an outer perimeter dyke, safeguarding it from the varying water levels of the surrounding lake and canal system. Within each polder unit, terraced sub-basins guide water toward a central drainage ditch. The houses are arranged atop the perimeter dyke and occasionally linked to neighboring homes in another unit via a bridge spanning the canal in between.

Fig. 1
Polder landscape and waterfront villages in Wujiang District of Suzhou.

Fig. 2
The central region of the Taihu Basin plain in the Yangtze River Delta is characterized by a landscape system of polders, whose micro-topographic structure continues to influence the morphology of the productive and inhabited territory.

Fig. 3
At the regional scale, three complementary strategies are proposed to define Jiangnan Park as a unifying core within the megacity region: framing, articulating, and characterizing.

Fig. 4
Map of detailed study areas (gray) and pilot projects (black) that were conducted in collaboration with local stakeholders to regenerate their characteristic productive landscapes.

Fig. 5
Images from the pilot project in Hunan Village converting rice paddies and fish ponds into a constructed wetland circuit. This project received a first prize from the Urban Planning Society of China in 2018.

Originally designed for rice cultivation, many villages of this type were adapted in the late 1980s, repurposing former paddy fields into fish and shrimp farming ponds. This shift to a more lucrative activity brought economic prosperity to the villages and resulted in water pollution from animal food, waste, and antibiotics. Presently situated in the middle of a new surface water collection zone supplying Shanghai's drinking water network, the village must cease its fish farming activities to prevent any risk of water pollution. While numerous similar villages in the area have been completely demolished and their residents relocated to larger communities, Hunan Village stands out for its potential for regeneration due to its charm, lakeside location, and proximity to transportation hubs.

Throughout the summer, we collaborated with local residents to devise a regeneration strategy for the village (Fig. 5). Following a diagnostic phase involving several days of fieldwork, including interviews and collaborative workshops with villagers, a proposal emerged: to repurpose the fishing village into a nature-based water treatment facility. This transformation involved converting the paddy fields and ponds into a constructed wetlands circuit, utilizing phytoremediation techniques to enhance water quality across the entire region. In doing so, the characteristic terraced structure of the polder area was repurposed to serve a new function while the surrounding fields and village houses were adapted to accommodate agroecology and agrotourism activities, aligning with the expertise and aspirations of the local community.

Awarded a first prize by the Urban Planning Society of China, the project for Hunan Village is less a definitive spatial solution than a replicable regeneration strategy. Together with other pilot projects, it exemplifies how leveraging characteristic cultural landscape features and community participation can offer a sustainable solution in the dynamic context of a megacity region.

Learning from Jiangnan Park

The territorial planning of China is at a new turning point. Several decades of rapid urban growth saw hundreds of millions of people migrate to cities, resulting in the disappearance of a significant portion of natural habitats and agricultural land resources. Thus, a new balance between urban and rural areas must be found. The "Ecological Civilization Construction" strategy, coupled with recent planning system reforms prioritizing ecosystem and farmland conservation under the guidance of a centralized Ministry of Natural Resources, marks significant and promising progress. However, adopting a simplistic approach that juxtaposes compact cities against modern countryside for the sake of efficiency could diminish the territory's richness, complexity, and diversity. Moreover, excessive focus on the ecological and agricultural performance of rural spaces at the expense of their inhabited and cultural dimensions poses the risk of homogenizing and anonymizing the productive landscape, which is nevertheless the essence of Chinese civilization.

The vision of Jiangnan Park, focused on the polder landscape at the heart of the Yangtze River Delta megacity region, illustrates a potential path of transformation for these landscapes. Developed through an extensive cartographic process and refined in local-scale workshops, it explores how to steer regional development toward a balanced and culturally rich future, highlighting the cultural dimension of productive landscapes in the evolving urban-rural dynamics. Initiated as a research-through-design project, the Jiangnan Park vision primarily aimed to identify context-specific elements, raise awareness, and explore alternative spatial planning methods. Through a series of publications, conferences, and exhibitions, we hope this endeavor has had a lasting impact, inspiring local and regional authorities to envision the future of the region. We invite researchers, educators, and local stakeholders to continue this mission in the Yangtze River Delta and comparable regions.

The authors would like to acknowledge the contributions of Chang Liu and the Master's students in Urbanism and Strategic Planning at KU Leuven under the guidance of Bruno De Meulder, Stefanie Dens, Racha Daher, and Christian Nolf in analyzing the region; Han Mengyi, in mapping model developments of the region; as well as the support of Dr. Sheng Zhong, Shengxi Xin, Xiang Zhou, Yannan Luo, Siyu Lu, Qi Wang, and Mengchuan Liu in conducting the pilot project in Hunan Village.

The research was facilitated by the following project funds: Evaluation Method for Blue-Green Infrastructure Connectivity in the Polder Areas: A Case Study of the Demonstration Zone for Integrated Ecological and Green Development in the Yangtze River Delta, Nature Science Fund of Zhejiang Province (No. LQ21E080016); Exploring the Spatial Implications of Integrated Water Management in the Suzhou Metropolitan Area, Jiangsu Province Program of Science and Technology (No. BK20151244); Towards Spatially Integrated Water Resource Management in the Yangtze River Delta Metropolis, The Research Development Fund of Xi'an

Jiaotong-Liverpool University (No. RDF 14-03-23); Integrating Spatial Planning and Water Management in Urbanised Deltas: A Comparison of Instruments in the Yangtze (CN) and Scheldt-Meuse-Rhine (EU) River Delta Regions, Young International Scientist Program of the National Science Foundation of China (No. 51550110235); Jiangnan Park: Designing a Metropolitan Landscape, Zhejiang University Education Foundation — Sun Xiaoxiang Landscape Architecture Education Fund (No. 317000-11103/001).

1 Christian Nolf, Yuting Xie, Florence Vannoorbeeck, and Bing Chen, "Delta Management in Evolution: a Comparative Review of the Yangtze River Delta and Rhine-Meuse-Scheldt Delta," *Asia-Pacific Journal of Regional Science* 5, no. 2 (2021): 597–624.

2 Yuting Xie, Christian Nolf, and Florence Vannoorbeeck, "Towards Integrated Water Management and Spatial Planning: Historical Review and Prospects for the Yangtze River Delta," *Landscape Architecture* 29, no. 2 (2022): 39–45.

3 Wenhui Kuang, "70 years of Urban Expansion across China: Trajectory, Pattern, and National Policies," *Chinese Science Bulletin* 65, no. 23 (2020): 1970–74.

4 "Outline of the Integrated Regional Development of the Yangtze River Delta," Central Committee of the Communist Party of China and the State Council, December 1, 2019, accessed April 1, 2024, http://www.gov.cn/zhengce/2019-12/01/content_5457442.htm.

5 Department of Natural Resources of Zhejiang Province, "Masterplan of Territorial Spatial Planning for the Demonstration Zone for Integrated Ecological and Green Development in the Yangtze River Delta (2021–2035)," February 21, 2023, https://zrzyt.zj.gov.cn/art/2023/2/21/art_1289955_59014874.html.

6 "The Ancient Waterfront Towns in the South of Yangtze River," UNESCO, accessed April 1, 2024, https://whc.unesco.org/en/tentativelists/5328/.

7 Yi-Wen Wang, John Pendelbury, and Christian Nolf, "The water heritage of China: the polders of Tai Lake Basin as continuing landscape," *Planning Perspectives* 38, no. 5 (2023): 949–74.

8 Yuting Xie, "Time, Space and Cultural Landscape: Morphogenesis of a Metropolitan Delta Landscape," in *Restructuring Cultural Landscapes in Metropolitan Areas: Characterization, Typology and Design Research*, ed. Yuting Xie (Singapore: Springer Nature Singapore, 2022), 65–106.

9 Christian Nolf, Yuting Xie, and Weishun Xu, "China's Urban Growth Boundaries: Towards a Context-Responsive Method," *The Evolving Scholar, International Forum of Urbanism (IFoU) 14th Edition,* November 2021, TU Delft (NL).

10 Yuting Xie et al., "Taipu Canal as a Regional Spine: A Prototypical Approach to Territorial Planning," *Landscape Architecture Frontiers* 8, no. 4 (2020): 114–25.

11 Christian Nolf and Yuting Xie, "Positioning Regional Design in Chinese Territorial Spatial Planning: An Exploratory Project in the Yangtze River Delta Megacity Region," *Landscape Architecture Frontiers* 8, no. 1 (2020): 92–107.

Fig. 1

Fig. 2

Mapping as a navigational practice within spatial vision processes

Sigrun Langner

Urbanization processes in Europe and worldwide produce complex dynamic relations between urban and rural areas. Considering socio-economic and ecological interrelationships goes beyond viewing space in the usual categories of "urban" and "rural." This relational notion of urban space allows us to think of it as a continuous "urban fabric" that extends across the land, woven sometimes more densely and sometimes more loosely.[1]

Urban-rural landscapes are shaped by the dynamic interplay of socio-economic and ecological processes that we must become more familiar with if we are to influence them productively and enhance the quality of "rurban" landscapes.[2] Many of today's urgent questions concerning the future of such rurban landscapes—such as, tackling the effects of climate change and the limitations of natural resources, challenges of demographic change in both growing and shrinking regions, questions of the quality of daily life, and issues of mobility—can only be addressed within regional landscape dimensions and regional planning and design approaches. In spatial design disciplines, one can recognize a reawakened interest in such large-scale thinking.[3,4] Large-scale landscape designing within complex systems involves special challenges, such as coping with the unpredictability of nonlinear processes, working within long-term time horizons, and ensuring the participation of multiple stakeholders with differing interests. To address these challenges, we must develop methodologies to read, reveal, interpret, and communicate the multifaceted interrelationships and processes shaping contemporary rurban landscapes. The complexity of urban-rural relations requires design approaches that aid in understanding shifting conditions; therefore, to effectively position and reposition oneself within these circumstances, one must carefully read and perceive existing situations. In this sense, designing in rurban landscapes can be likened to navigating risky and unchartered waters.

When navigating at sea, maps are a helpful tool for comparing observations, registering them, determining one's position, and checking the course forward. In this context, the focus is less on the map as a mere representation of the environment and more on how it aids in locating oneself in a given situation. Design-led mapping aligns with this situational use of maps; it is less concerned with what a map represents and more interested in how the mapping process can generate spatial ideas and knowledge. Mapping, as a long-standing cultural practice of understanding and "finding our way in the world,"[5] has been closely connected with navigating —(re)positioning oneself within dynamic spatial contexts. In large-scale design, there has been an increase in the use of atlases and mappings to understand complex space-generating processes. Thus, mapping practices have been proven useful for positioning within multilayered conditions of transformation processes while facilitating reflection on their impacts,[6] ultimately supporting ideas and knowledge creation in spatial vision processes.

Exploring rurban landscapes

Maps are usually used at the beginning of thc design process to "appropriate" unknown terrain. First impressions and perceptions can be important idea generators in the design process—maps are helpful instruments in this intuitive process. An initial approach decodes the landscape "from a distance," using a topographical map or aerial photograph. Specific structures from the map are read, worked out, interpreted, and the first theses and questions about the project area can be formulated. Subsequently, entering the project area, becoming part of the landscape, and perceive it from a ground-level perspective are critical steps. Here, the body actively engages as an instrument to sense, identify, and mark the social, political, and informational forces in the landscape. In these cartographic "approaching exercises," more refined hypotheses about the area and research questions are formulated while perception and sensitivity are heightened regarding how certain spatial structures in the project area have developed. Thus, the initial investigation framework for a focused view and study of the project area is created. By employing the map as a "spatial key," an approach to the design area opens up; or, as a "visual aid," it produces new perspectives on things that might seem familiar.

Reading and Revealing intrinsic logics of a landscape

In a deeper research phase, maps can serve as a tool for orientation within and understanding of the complex relationships of landscapes. *Understanding* a spatial nexus is a prerequisite for developing ideas for (re-)configuring it. Designing is structured by an interactive process of understanding, in which ideas and knowledge emerge through various methods of spatial perception and representation.[7]

From a landscape-oriented perspective of urban development, it is initially interesting to observe and comprehend the reciprocities between the natural spatial conditions of a landscape and its urban development. The aim is—with the help of maps—to uncover the internal mechanisms of a landscape, read their underlying structures, and reveal and understand their significance and historical origins. This approach of uncovering the existing logics of landscapes forms a basis for reformulating reality.[8]

Such maps contain analytical information while also allowing for interpretative readings. Using maps in this way goes beyond merely representing existing spatial attributes. The goal is not to present available knowledge in more legible ways but to use the maps to reveal previously unrecognized relationships, thus generating new knowledge about rurban landscapes that inform future actions. Maps can inspire new perspectives on landscapes, where new ideas emerge by making previously unseen nexuses visible.

(Re)interpreting and (re)configuring rurban landscapes

In that sense, maps are more than mere representations of relationships in rurban landscapes. The way these associations are presented influences our perception of the space. As such, maps are not a neutral representation of a given reality but rather present a concept—or a construct—of space[9] and thus have the capacity to "build the world."[10]

Mapping in spatial vision processes utilizes the power and mechanisms of maps not only to (re)interpret and (re)present a landscape but also to transform and (re)configure it. The way a map portrays the specific features and characteristics of a landscape—while highlighting certain structures, spatial relationships, and themes—tells us a story about the landscape and communicates a perspective on it. This type of design mapping oscillates between describing the existing situation and designing a future image, encompassing both the descriptive and analytical aspects of a map as well as its suggestive and projective qualities. Through designled mapping, the existing raw material of a region is connected to potential future transformation paths.

Communicating and negotiating possible futures

The map, as a tool of negotiation, assists in examining and adjusting the course through a lively exchange with existing conditions. The capacity of maps to open perspectives for the future through the existing can reveal possible courses of action and make them communicable. By visualizing a particular viewpoint, a map becomes an argument within a process of negotiation. Wood and Fels see maps as arguments and cartographic propositions.[11] They are interested in the performative character of maps and how meaning is constructed and ultimately leads to action. Therefore, maps cannot claim to be absolute, precise representations of reality; instead, they are a hypothesis or a proposition of how space can be perceived, open to negotiation. In conclusion, mapping integrated into spatial vision processes serves as a navigational tool for exploring, revealing, understanding, (re)interpreting, and (re) configuring urban-rural relationships, as well as negotiating possible futures for a rurban landscape.

Spatial vision process "Rheinliebe"

How to work with cartographic spatial images as part of spatial vision processes can be illustrated by the project "Rheinliebe" (Rhinelove), which the author conducted as part of the planning team rabe landschaften/ Station C23 between 2012 and 2017.[12] The project was part of the "International Building Exhibition Basel 2020." The main goal of the exhibition was to establish a new cross-border planning culture and community of responsibility in the region spanning France, Germany, and Switzerland. The slogan of the exhibition was: "growing together" and "together growing" in this tri-national region. The river Rhine is the backbone of the region and plays a politically, economically, and ecologically important role, particularly concerning its identity. The project aimed to design a holistic cartographic spatial image of the region that highlights specific qualities of the urban agglomeration around Basel and the adjacent rural municipalities, raising questions about how the Rhine landscape can be conceived as a shared area of responsibility for the three countries.

The cartographic spatial image reinterpreted the specific character of the Rhine landscape between Bad Bellingen (Germany), Communauté des communes Portes des France Rhin Sud (France), and Möhlin/ Schwörstadt (Switzerland). The intention was to highlight different existing spatial qualities of the Rhine landscape and to discuss their future potentials based on four landscape typologies: "landscape of seduction" (river bank), "old love landscape" (former wetlands), "landscape of admiration" (vineyard-clad slopes along the alluvial plains), and "closed-off landscapes" (isolated industrial areas and infrastructural strips) (Fig. 3).

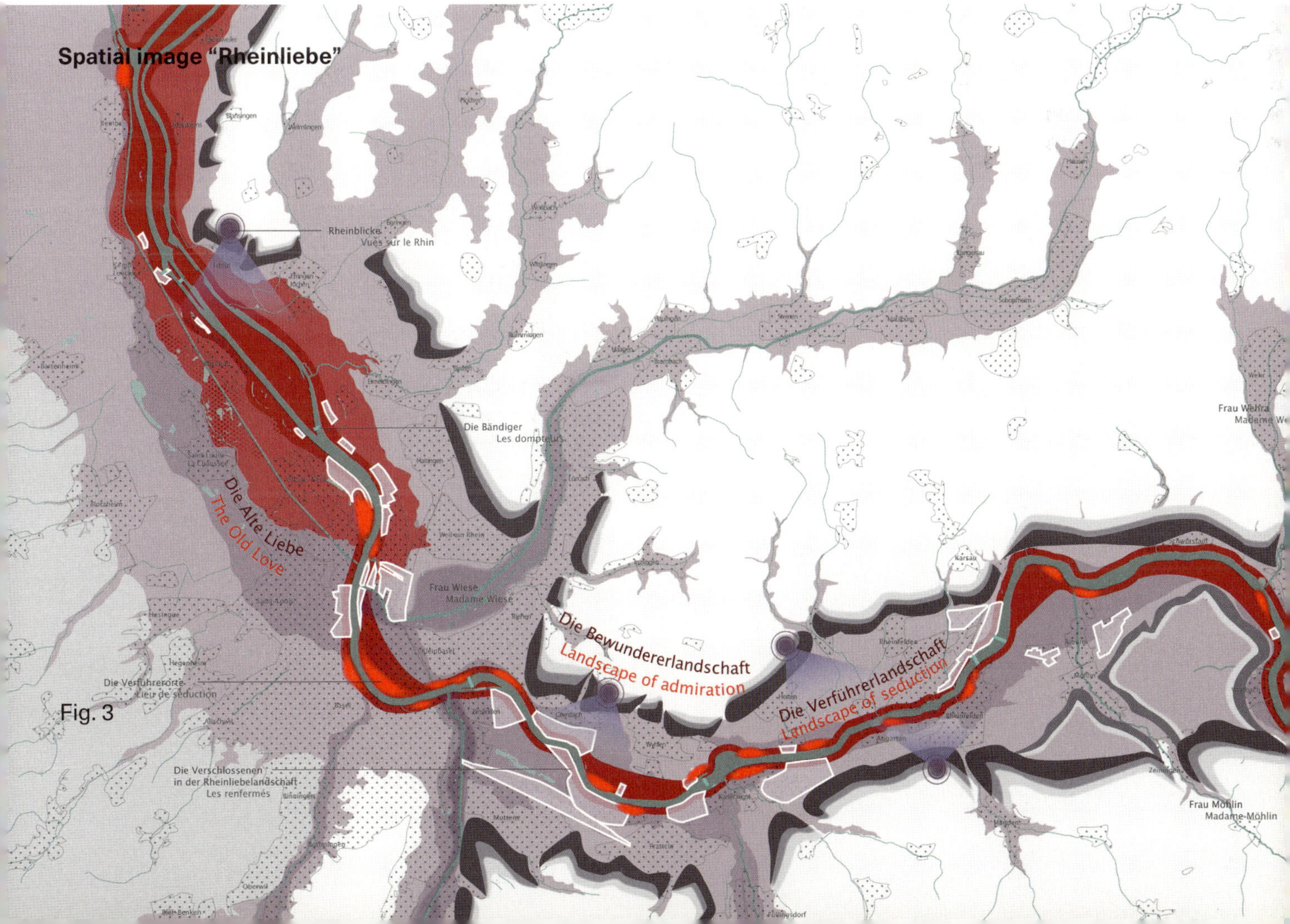

Fig. 3

Regional Landscape Park "Rheinliebe 2030"

Fig. 4

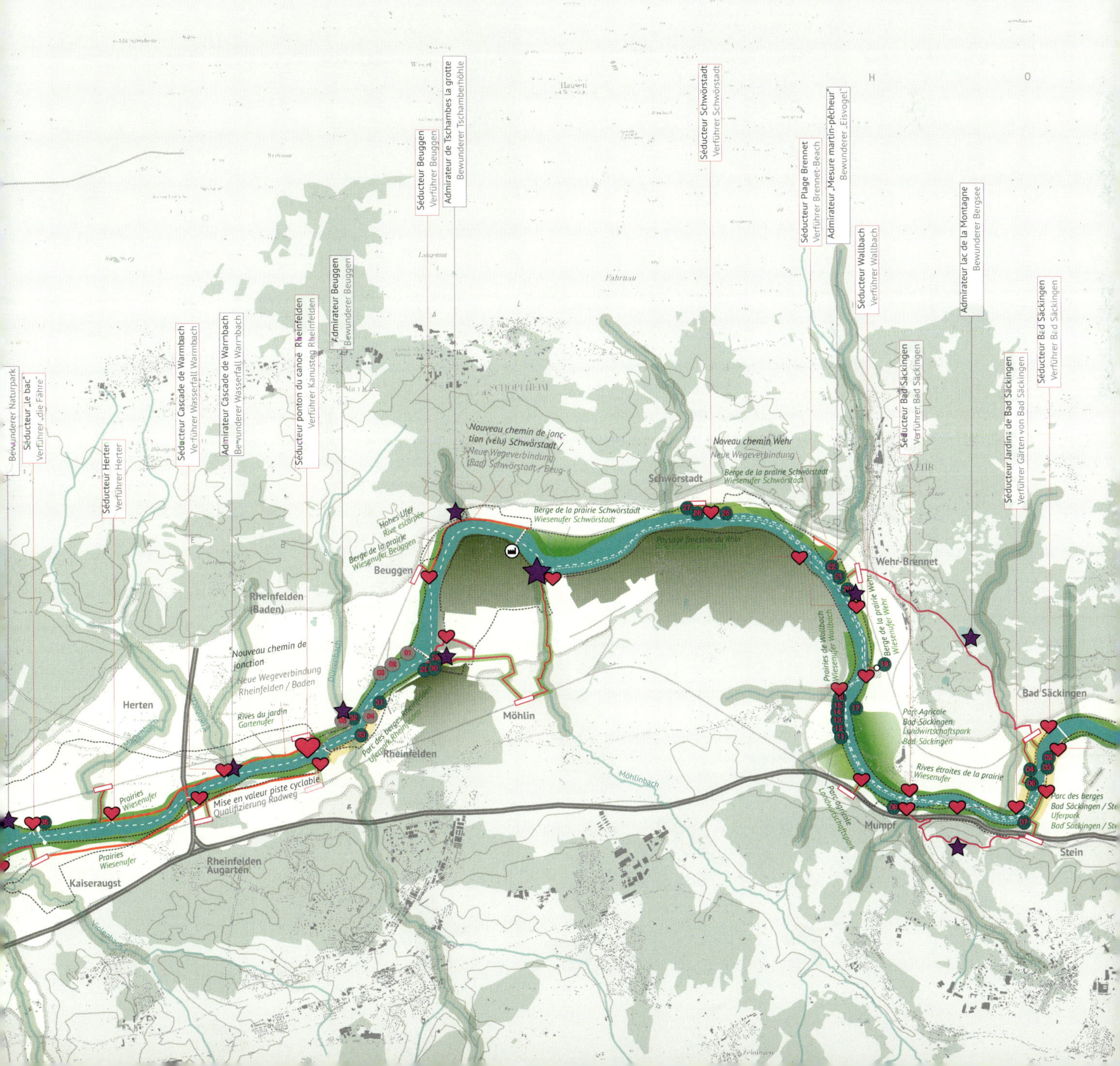

Bewunderer Naturpark
Séducteur „le bac"
Verführer „die Fähre"
Séducteur Herter
Verführer Herter
Séducteur Cascade de Warmbach
Verführer Wasserfall Warmbach
Admirateur Cascade de Warmbach
Bewunderer Wasserfall Warmbach
Séducteur ponton du canoë Rheinfelden
Verführer Kanusteg Rheinfelden
Admirateur Beuggen
Bewunderer Beuggen
Séducteur Beuggen
Verführer Beuggen
Admirateur de Tschambes la grotte
Bewunderer Tschamberhöhle
Séducteur Schwörstadt
Verführer Schwörstadt
Séducteur Plage Brennet
Verführer Brennet-Beach
Admirateur „Mesure martin-pêcheur"
Bewunderer „Eisvogel"
Séducteur Wallbach
Verführer Wallbach
Admirateur lac de la Montagne
Bewunderer Bergsee
Séducteur Bad Säckingen
Verführer Bad Säckingen
Séducteur Jardins de Bad Säckingen
Verführer Gärten von Bad Säckingen
Séducteur Bad Säckingen
Verführer Bad Säckingen
Nouveau chemin de jonction (vélo) Schwörstadt /
Neue Wegeverbindung (Bad) Schwörstadt / Beug-
Noveau chemin Wehr
Neue Wegeverbindung
Schwörstadt
Berge de la prairie Schwörstadt
Wiesenufer Schwörstadt
Hohes Ufer
Rive escarpée
Berge de la prairie
Wiesenufer Beuggen
Beuggen
Paysage forestier du Rhin
Wehr-Brennet
Prairies de Wallbach
Wiesenufer Wallbach
Berge de la prairie Wehr
Wiesenufer Wehr
Rheinfelden (Baden)
Nouveau chemin de jonction
Neue Wegeverbindung Rheinfelden / Baden
Rives du jardin
Gartenufer
Parc des berges Rheinfelden
Uferpark Rheinfelden
Rheinfelden
Möhlin
Möhlinbach
Herten
Prairies
Wiesenufer
Mise en valeur piste cyclable
Qualifizierung Radweg
Rheinfelden Augarten
Kaiseraugst
Parc Agricole Bad Säckingen
Landwirtschaftspark Bad Säckingen
Parc agricole
Landwirtschaftspark
Rives étroites de la prairie
Wiesenufer
Mumpf
Bad Säckingen
Parc des berges Bad Säckingen / Ste
Uferpark Bad Säckingen / Ste
Stein
Fahrnau
Hausen
Schopfheim

For each landscape typology, future-orientated questions were developed to enhance existing International Building Exhibition projects and reveal new project ideas. The cartographic spatial image served as an action-guiding framework within which to embed and enhance these projects and act as a communication platform for negotiating the long-term development of the tri-national border Rhine landscape.

The intention was, on one hand, to highlight the existing spatial qualities of the Rhine landscape and reveal future questions and topics about this landscape. On the other hand, it was intended to find a common language among the different planning cultures of the three countries involved, between planning professionals and local stakeholders, to discuss these qualities and future potentials (Fig. 5). The unusual language of "Rhinelove" stimulates the imagination. The cartographic spatial image is open to interpretation and further elaboration, providing an opportunity to think outside entrenched ways of thinking and the formal vocabulary of regional planning.

The cartographic spatial image of "Rhinelove" becomes a crucial instrument in the cooperative planning processes between three countries and also within intermunicipal discussions between Basel City and the more rural communities and small towns in Switzerland, Germany, and France. It was used in planning workshops and public communication as a way of discussing existing projects and new project ideas and how they contribute to this sense of common responsibility (Fig. 6).

The first outcomes from this process were (1) a catalog that included first and simple realizable measures to improve the accessibility and the experience of the "landscape of seduction" and "landscape of admiration"; (2) the identification of strategic key sites important as connecting sites for all three countries; and (3) a long-term master plan for developing the Rhinelove landscape (Fig.4). The first pilot projects have already been implemented as part of the International Building Exhibition Basel 2020.[13]

Conclusion

Cartographic spatial images play a significant role in spatial vision processes, helping to reveal and (re-)interpret the relational nexus of landscapes and open up new perspectives; for instance, as demonstrated by Rhinelove—the vision of a landscape of common responsibility across national borders and the urban-rural divide. Additionally, cartographic spatial images serve as a platform for communication and negotiation,

Fig. 5

Fig. 6

Fig. 1 & 2
Explorative walks of the working group "Rheinliebe" along the River Rhine.

Fig. 3
The cartographic spatial image of "Rhinelove" is based on four characteristic landscape typologies: landscape of admiration (steep slopes along the Rhine), landscape of seduction (river bank), landscape of "old love" (former wetlands), and closed-off landscape (inaccessible industrial and infrastructural landscape).

Fig. 4
Masterplan of the regional landscape park "IBA Rheinliebe 2030."

Fig. 5
In a workshop, the cartographic spatial image of "Rhinelove" is used to identify points of interest within the various landscape typologies.

Fig. 6
In the workshop "Rhinelove Date," representatives of municipalities along the Rhine and the IBA working group "Rhinelove" discussed about building up a common project "Rhinelove" within the tri-national Rhine landscape and identified implementation projects.

allowing for exchanges about transformation paths and development potentials. Such dialogue oriented processes highlight conflicts and synergies between different views and spatial perspectives. In this context, a cartographic spatial image is not a final, fixed representation but is open to a collaborative and co-creative process of knowledge and idea production.

In regional spatial vision processes with long-term planning horizons, there is a need for practices that facilitate the positioning and repositioning of individuals and communities within the complex and shifting conditions of rurban landscapes. This article has highlighted the potential of mapmaking within spatial vision processes for approaching and exploring unknown terrain, for reading and revealing the intrinsic logic of a landscape, for (re)interpreting and (re)formulating existing spatial configurations, for opening up perspectives, and ultimately for negotiating possible futures of rurban landscapes.

Thus, the understanding of cartographic spatial images is more performative than representational. The focus is on the impact of maps on concrete actions and how they promote context-dependent knowledge and idea production within collaborative regional vision building. Therefore, design-led mapping can become a key navigational practice for (re)positioning within the ever-changing, multifaceted conditions of rurban landscapes.

This article is based on: Sigrun Langner, "Navigating in Urban Landscapes - Mapping as a Navigational Strategy in Designing Landscapes," in Design Research for Urban Landscapes: Theories and Methods, *eds. Martin Prominski and Hille von Seggern (London: Routledge, 2019).*

1 Henri Lefèbvre, *Die Revolution der Städte* (Dresden: Dresden Postplatz, 2003).

2 The term "rurban landscapes" describes the intertwining of urban and rural realities, environments, and spatial structures. It is intended to focus on not only how the rural environment is being transformed by global urbanization processes but also how the "rural" is changing the "urban." It also questions what 'long-term, sustainable interactions between the "urban" and "rural" are conceivable and also desirable. Sigrun Langner, "(R)urban Landscapes: Navigating between the Urban and the Rural Perspective," in *Ruralism: The Future of Villages and Small Towns in an Urbanizing World*, ed. Vanessa Miriam Carlow (Berlin: JOVIS, 2016), 76–89.

3 Nancy Meijsmans, ed., *Designing for a Region* (Amsterdam: SUN Architecture, 2010).

4 Verena Elisabeth Balz, "Regional Design: A Transformative Approach to Planning," *Planning Practice & Research* 39, no. 1 (2024): 1-13.

5 Jeremy W. Crampton, *Mapping: A Critical Introduction to Cartography and GIS* (Chichester: Wiley-Blackwell, 2010).

6 Urs Primas, "Die Wirklichkeit der Kartografen," *StadtBauwelt* 24 (2008): 58–66.

7 Hille von Seggern, "Ohne *Verstehen* keine Entwurfsidee," in *Creating Knowledge: Innovationsstrategien im Entwerfen urbaner Landschaften*, eds. Hille von Seggern, Julia Werner, and Lucia Grosse-Bächle (Berlin: JOVIS, 2008), 212–51.

8 Kelly Shannon and Samitha Manawadu, "Indigenous Landscape Urbanism: Sri Lanka's Reservoir & Tank System," *Journal of Landscape Architecture* 2, no. 2 (2007): 6–17.

9 Martina Löw, *Raumsoziologie* (Frankfurt am Main: Suhrkamp Verlag, 2001), 68.

10 James Corner, "The Agency of Mapping: Speculation, Critique, Invention," in *Mappings*, ed. Denis Cosgrove (London: Reaktion Books, 1999), 213.

11 Denis Wood and John Fels, *The Natures of Maps* (Chicago and London: University of Chicago Press, 2008, xvi).

12 The study and spatial image for the joint development of the Rhine landscape is part of the "Internationale Bauausstellung Basel 2020" and was developed by rabe landschaften and Station C23 in consultation with Hille von Seggern and Henrik Schultz in 2012; the masterplan "Rheinliebe 2030" was developed by rabe landschaften, Station C23, and Genzmer in 2017.

13 International Building Exhibition Basel, ed., *Internationale Bauausstellung 2020: Gemeinsam Grenzen Überschreiten* (Munich: Georg – Media, 2021), 128.

Fig. 1

Using narratives in spatial vision design processes

Anke Schmidt

Spatial visions are an outcome of collaborative vision-building processes for entire regions, referred to as "Raumbild" in the German-speaking context (see article by Maria Frölich-Kulik, Sigrun Langner, and Lukas Pappert on page 230). They typically take a long view of the future of a landscape or region, building on complex interactions within a landscape to elaborate potential scenarios. They do not produce precisely outlined, legally sound proposals but instead examine the possibilities inherent within a landscape or region. Therefore, they outline possible alternative scenarios for the future development of regions and subsequently point to strategies for potential action. As such, they are an instrument for shaping long-term and large-scale transformation processes by visualizing potential approaches to the future of a region for discussion and negotiation.

"Spatial visions tell stories that link the past with the present and with potential trends and goals."[1] They tell us about the "what if ...?" and "what could be"? questions surrounding a landscape; for example, should certain decisions be made if certain people act accordingly, or particular qualities of a space are utilized? They encompass not only hard, quantifiable facts but also emotional levels of meaning, trends, and occurrences, as well as corresponding landscape processes.

Spatial visions are often elaborated in the context of spaces with complex interactions influenced by numerous different stakeholders. As a strategic instrument, spatial visions can help foster a cooperative, regional planning culture and facilitate communication across administrative boundaries and disciplines. By conveying spatial perspectives for a region's development, they help initiate dialogue between stakeholders from different disciplines and organizational backgrounds.[2]

Therefore, the elaboration of spatial visions requires processes and methods that can reveal knowledge of an area and the relationships and possible lines of development within it while facilitating dialogue between different stakeholders and users.

Spatial visions are developed in large-scale and long-term design processes in which potential paths of development are traced and elaborated based on knowledge of the interrelationships and specific characteristics of a region. In this process, new knowledge of the space is gained; for example, in the form of extensive geodata or through the findings of literature research into the region's historical development. It can also take the form of a variety of visits, such as tours using different means of transport or exploratory walks across the region. Conversations with local people and experts also provide valuable information for understanding the area and its relationships.

To ensure participants become more than just sources of implicit knowledge and can actively generate ideas and contribute to spatial visions, it is necessary to organize interactions and conversations in appropriate formats and settings that capture a wide range of individual perspectives. In co-creative processes, narrative practices help initiate conversations about a landscape and its possible future.

In their traditional representation as cartographic images, spatial visions are not usually narrative in the sense that they are rarely driven by protagonists or depict a storyline. Rather, they serve as an instrument for initiating the development of new narratives about a future way of inhabiting and working with a landscape, supporting the process of finding and agreeing on a common future scenario.

To describe how narratives and narrative practices can contribute to the design of spatial visions, the following section discusses the fundamental characteristics and features of narratives or stories, subsequently establishing their link to design. From this, we examine different fields of application for storytelling in spatial vision design processes.

The need for narration and stories in vision building

Narratives and storytelling are not exclusive to literary contexts. Telling stories is a fundamental human cultural practice for making sense of events and the processes that influence them. While fictions envision imaginary worlds, real-world narratives relate to the actual experiences of people. Through stories, we can reconstruct the past, reflect on the present, or "sketch out" the future. This narrative mode of thinking is deeply rooted in how people understand the world. Thus, stories are a form of "worldmaking" and structure our human perception of reality on both an autobiographical and cultural level: "narratives are at work in processes such as identity formation, ordering experience, remembering and negotiating values, and fabricating storied versions of 'the world'."[3]

Regardless of the narrative medium, stories are characterized by certain elements and principles that set them apart from reports, plans, or drawings. Most notably, they feature protagonists and places of action, have a temporal sequence of events and a defined beginning and end, and change in response to events and external influences. Integral to a story is also its setting in the material world. As such, narratives interweave events, people, and space; thus, they can depict complex relationships and processes understandably. A fundamental aspect of narratives is that they evolve; i.e., communicate processes of development and change. In addition to conveying the meaning and significance of a topic, stories can employ dramaturgical devices and suspense to entertain.

Narratives establish a communicative situation between the author and recipient in which the narrator guides the listener's field of perception. At the same time, the listeners construct the story as they link it to their own horizons of experience. Thus, storytelling can create shared zones of meaning and act as a channel for developing thoughts further. In addition, stories mediate between individual experiences and social conditions. Shared stories foster a sense of community, cohesion, and identity; at the same time, stories influence people by conveying ideas and values.

Before the invention of writing, the only repositories and conveyors of shared knowledge were memorized stories. Today, narrative knowledge is embedded in specific situations and contexts; Tim Ingold calls this "inhabited knowledge"[4] that can reveal—particularly the backgrounds and contexts of meaning. The organizational sciences have shown how such experiential knowledge can be tapped into through narrative methods to support shared knowledge processes.[5]

Unlike numerical and factual knowledge and actual events, stories always retain a certain vagueness that leaves room for a possible explanation.[6] This should not be regarded as a disadvantage but rather as having potential as it opens up possibilities for dealing with complex situations. Moreover, it makes stories receptive to different perspectives. However, narratives require intensive discourse before they can become productive sources of knowledge. In the context of the historical sciences, Hayden White has described the narrative as a "form of discourse."[7] The historian used narrative structures and plotlines to attribute meaning to historical facts; thus, the process of narration acts as a dimension of cognition alongside the history in which knowledge is bound. Therefore, narratives are not only "carriers of knowledge but also serve the production of knowledge."[8]

Narration and stories offer various interesting dimensions that can be used for spatial vision design processes; narration as a form of gaining knowledge unfolds between listening, presenting, and telling.

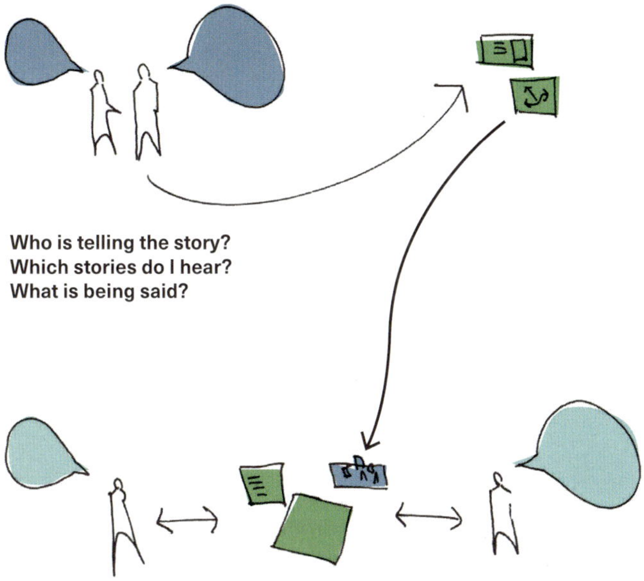

Fig. 2

These three modes can be assigned to phases in design, where design activities shift between perceiving (an existing situation) and generating ideas, representing and expressing ideas, and exchanging and reflecting concepts.[9] Vision building processes involve people from different backgrounds in the development process. For them to communicate equally and for citizens to have the same opportunity to participate, tools are required that transcend the language and perspectives of specialists. As such, stories and narratives offer a means of working and designing together across disciplinary boundaries.

Narrative practices and tools in spatial vision design processes

Narrative practices can be applied in multiple ways in spatial vision design processes: firstly, these approaches can be used to tap into local knowledge from people in the region and relate this information to places and activities; secondly, they can be used to develop visions for the future in a readily understandable form; thirdly, they facilitate dialogue with local stakeholders about future perspectives. These three applications each relate to different characteristics and after-effects of storytelling: storytelling as a perceptive practice (listening), storytelling as a communicative practice (sharing, exchanging), and storytelling as an inventive practice (creating).[10] Each practice can be implemented with a range of tools according to the situation and goal.

1. Storytelling as a perceptive practice: Listening

Traditionally, planners and architects use techniques and design tools that have evolved through years of architectural practice. They employ plans, drawings, and models to depict the structural and material dimensions of space. People and their actions only feature indirectly. Narratives provide a crucial perspective on the space in question when addressing complex and strategic development tasks. They capture the experiences of the people who live and work there, as well as the processes that occur within it. As local experts, people from the area are a primary source of information and stories about places. Discovering an area of study using narrative tools and formats, for example, through conversations with local people, in workshops, or through discussions with stakeholders, leverages the potential of narratives as a perceptive and cognitive strategy. Moreover, presenting places of personal importance, attributing meaning to them, and conveying changes in the landscape (e.g., through portraits of protagonists or spatial narratives) renders local (implicit) knowledge visible for the design process. Using the narrative practice of attentive listening and dialogue, it is possible to gain detailed insights into the perspectives of users in an area not previously documented.

2. Storytelling as a communicative practice: Visualizing, sharing, and exchanging

Alongside cartographic representations, narrative perspectives from stakeholders and protagonists within an area can help visualize stakeholder constellations, project ideas, and innovative spatial practices. In addition, narrative plot development techniques, such as storyboarding or novel and screenplay writing, can serve as techniques for developing action-orientated, process-based practices and for "playing out" scenarios. Such methods of mental rehearsal use storytelling as a means of sounding out spaces of possibility for long-term developments. Moreover, visualizing, sharing, and exchanging fictional stories simulate courses of action and possibilities for future development, depicting how new uses and practices can influence and change spatial

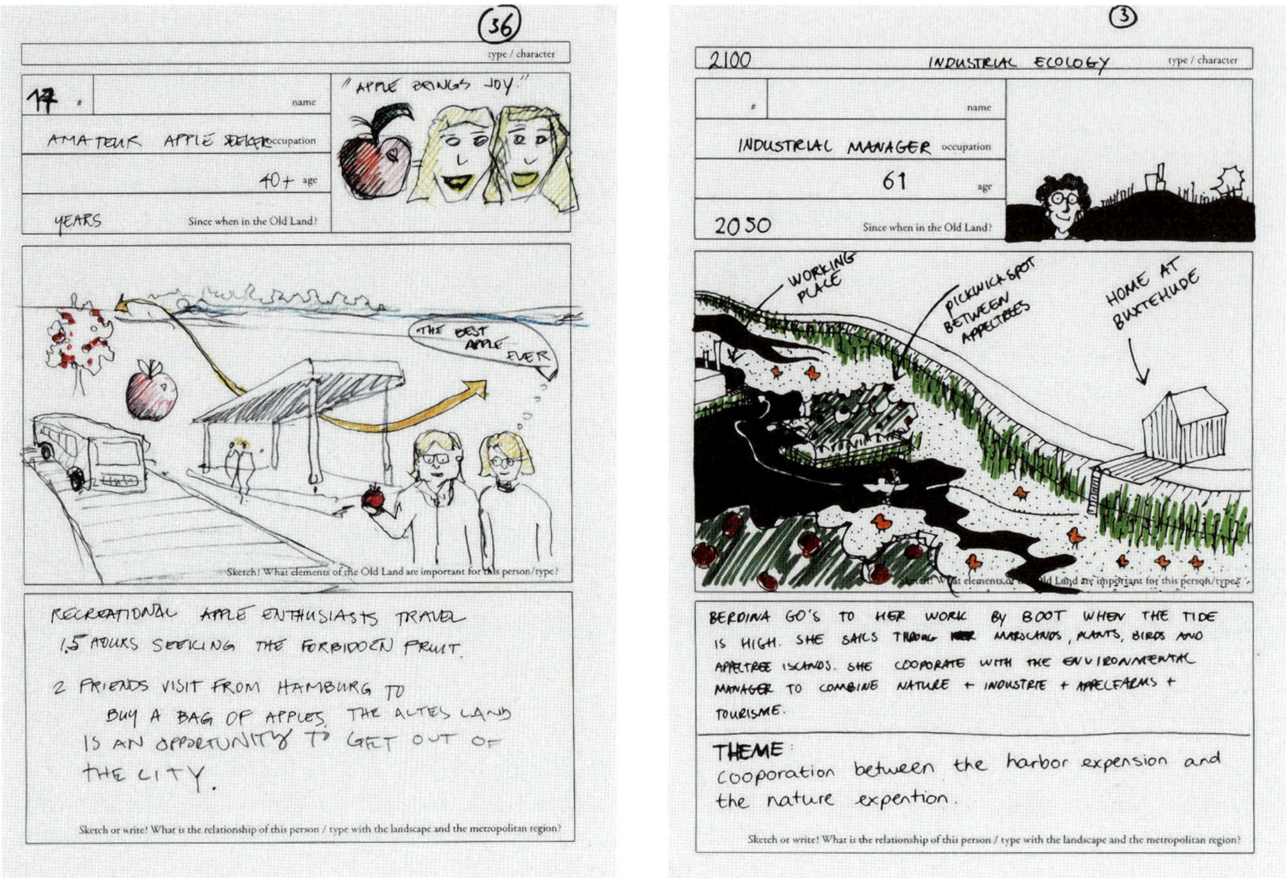

Fig. 3

contexts or reveal shifts in attitudes and motivations. They offer the opportunity to anticipate spatial adaptation strategies, new constellations of spatial practices, and the corresponding changes these bring about within the study area.

Fig. 1
Dialogue partners in the field.

Fig. 2
Narrative practices in spatial vision design processes.

Fig. 3
Stories of typical actors and their engagement with the landscape, local life, and potential futures found by students during a summer school.

3. Storytelling as an inventive practice: Creating and supporting dialogue

The openness of narrative structures—and the fact that stories can continue to be told—sets them apart from the clarity of a plan and its defined course of action. As dialogue-based tools, they can enrich communication in design processes through a joint cognitive process. In any ongoing dialogue concerning potential ideas and visions for an area, stories function as narrative anchors for a common vision for the future, within which a landscape can be found or elaborated upon discursively. This is because fictional stories about future changes often breathe life into abstract and long-term development plans. Moreover, they allow people to have a personal scope to these stories, empowering them to join the discussion. As such, narratives can be understood as a source of inspiration in processes of discourse and change, where future ideas conveyed through spatial visions are negotiated.

The impact of narrative tools in spatial vision processes

Narrative tools are well-suited for certain tasks, portraying the multi-dimensional nature of processes of development and change in a practical and relatable way. Narrative practices can be employed at different points in the design process to gain knowledge; as perceptive and research practices, they reveal topics and information about local contexts and their users relevant to its design. As "creative-inventive practices," they stimulate idea-finding processes for future developments; as "activating practices," they facilitate dialogue between spatial actors. As such, narrative tools can enrich co-creative design processes for spatial visions in several ways.

Narrative tools expand existing descriptive dimensions: stories and narratives expand the traditional descriptive dimensions of space by revealing social moments, the aspect of time, and how people interact with the physical space. Taking a narrative approach means adopting a change of perspective, allowing space and actions to be conceived and designed in an integrated manner. Dimensions that were previously separate—such as actors and space—can be considered in combination, and their interrelationships and contradictions are thus incorporated into spatial development processes.

Narrative practices contribute to designing as a dialogic practice: dialogue-based, "participatory" processes can significantly enhance design-development processes by fostering joint learning. This process requires trust on all sides and a revised understanding of the role of planners and designers. When effectively integrated, these processes—facilitated by suitable formats, tools, and visualizations—can enrich the design process and provide a source of inspiration.

Narrative approaches support co-creative processes: to be used in co-creative development processes, we need corresponding formal and procedural frameworks. By communicating the perspectives of users, everyday knowledge, and daily practices at the heart of the design process, narrative approaches support co-creative processes.[11] Storytelling is not about developing a "good story" to convince others; instead, it is an inventive practice that brings new perspectives into the picture. Motivating people to relate their own stories to practitioners means asking relevant questions, providing the space for others to tell their stories openly, and inventing stories that offer effective potential in narrative processes.

Planners are increasingly faced with the task of designing and organizing processes and communication.[12] At the same time, long-term spatial design processes entail thinking about a situation that lies in a more or less distant future but also needs communicating via illustrative examples. This challenges both the repertoire of design tools and planning instruments, as well as co-creative processes. The stimulating challenge we face today is to establish spatial visions as a viable instrument and to develop corresponding processes, methods, and practices for their creation.

1 Antje Matern, "Wozu ein Planungslabor Raumbilder Lausitz 2050?" in *Planungslabor Raumbilder Lausitz 2050*, ed. Leibniz-Institut für ökologische Raumentwicklung e. V. (Dresden: IÖR, 2021), 10.

2 Op. cit.

3 Ansgar Nünning and Vera Nünning, eds., *Erzähltheorie transgenerisch, intermedial, interdisziplinär* (Trier: WTV, 2002), 192.

4 Tim Ingold, *Being Alive: Essays on Movement, Knowledge and Description* (London and New York: Routledge, 2011), 145.

5 Gabi Reinmann and Rainer Totzke, "Der Umgang mit Geschichten in Organisationen – Beispiele und Kategorisierungsvorschläge," in *Erfahrungswissen erzählbar machen: Narrative Ansätze für Wirtschaft und Schule*, ed. Gabi Reinmann (Lengerich: Pabst Science Publishers, 2005), 71–89.

6 Alf Mentzer and Ulrich Sonnenschein, eds., *22 Arten eine Welt zu schaffen: Erzählen als Universalkompetenz* (Frankfurt am Main: Fischer, 2008).

7 Hayden White, *The Content of the Form: Narrative Discourse and Historical Representation* (Baltimore: Johns Hopkins University Press, 1990), 41.

8 Claudia Fahrenwald, "Erzählen zwischen individueller Erfahrung und sozialer (Re)präsentation," in *Erfahrungswissen erzählbar machen: Narrative Ansätze für Wirtschaft und Schule*, ed. Gabi Reinmann (Lengerich: Pabst Science Publishers, 2005), 36–51.

9 Donald Schön, *The Reflective Practitioner: How Professionals Think in Action* (New York: Basic Books, 1983).

10 Anke Schmidt, *Geschichten urbaner Landschaften: Formate des Erzählens für kollaborative Entwurfsprozesse* (Hanover: Leibniz Universität Hannover, 2018).

11 Op. cit.

12 Sigrun Langner, *Navigieren in urbanen Landschaften: Entwerfendes Kartieren als Navigationsstrategie* (Hanover: Leibniz Universität Hannover, 2013).

Fig. 1

Co-creative landscape design with spatial images

Henrik Schultz

Spatial visions will always sit in tension between practical implementation and the more ambitious goals they envision for the future. "Spatial visions" are understood here as representations, imaginative interpretations of the existing conditions and visions for future development (in the German planning context referred to as "Raumbild"—see article by Maria Frölich-Kulik, Sigrun Langner, and Lukas Pappert on page 230). These are expressed through the production of "spatial images" such as maps, illustrative drawings, or other visual material. Recent efforts in landscape architecture and urban planning address this inherent tension of spatial visions through concepts such as resilience building, co-creation, and transdisciplinarity. These are not mere buzzwords but rather approaches that reflect the dynamic interaction necessary for navigating between visionary futures and practical implementation.

This contribution illustrates and argues how "spatial images" can serve as common reference points for approaches that embrace resilience, co-creation, and transdisciplinary action in addressing today's climate crises. Avoiding steps too small and visions too disjointed for implementation, spatial images work through collaborative processes that highlight and/or omit landscape elements during design to vividly depict bold landscape futures while fostering the ideas required for their implementation.

It is argued that spatial visioning processes reveal the elements that should be prioritized in future to form a basis for resilient development. Arising from co-creative processes, spatial images have multiple authors dedicated to (and advocating for) their realization. They are enriched by the joint exploration of landscapes and the ensuing dialogues over images perceived by the various actors involved. The example of the transdisciplinary "Green Fingers Project" in Osnabrück shows that, when the influence of involved actors becomes visible, spatial images create a lasting impact—especially when working with scenarios.

Transformative resilience: A call for co-creation

Harald Kegler views climate resilience as a continuous transformational process of landscapes, emphasizing adaptability and various capabilities for change.[1] His definition aligns with a resilience concept that no longer relies solely on a return to the initial state (i.e., the "bouncing back") but emphasizes the adaptive and change capabilities of systems, hence focusing on the "bouncing forward." By placing the transformation process at the center, Kegler makes resilience a planning-cultural task. The question, "how can the transition to greater climate resilience in cities be shaped?" requires a process dimension that shows how dealing with disruptions can be cultivated and socially supported.

How can landowners, decision-makers, volunteers, and experts from planning-relevant disciplines collaborate in a way that allows for the design and, ultimately, the implementation or enforcement of resilient landscape transformations? Transformative planning, which aims to connect insights into landscape characteristics with multi-actor settings,[2] deals with this planning-cultural level.[3] In this sense, transformative planning is less about establishing binding frameworks and managing prescribed procedures than shaping a cultural process supported by many actors and determined by unpredictability. The objective is to harness the ideas and resources of a multitude of stakeholders in planning transformation and addressing the implementation deficit.[4,5,6]

This, in turn, calls for a transdisciplinary approach aimed at generating knowledge by integrating the scientific and non-scientific insights and ideas of various actors, including landowners, engaged community groups, and decision-makers.[7] What role can visual language play in this context? Can spatial images help design the "bouncing forward" to envision the future collectively, negotiate it, and align implementation strategies with these images?

From experienced images to negotiated images

Exploring landscapes on foot is a tried and tested practice for comprehending complex landscape transformations and gaining a comprehensive understanding of their attributes.[8] Walking draws from growing factual knowledge, such as understanding the functions of landscapes and experiential knowledge that can gradually accumulate during walks. Through this interplay of knowledge and experience, the conviction grew among the actors in the transdisciplinary research project "Green Fingers for a Climate-Resilient City" that the city's so-called "Green Fingers" (i.e., radially arranged green wedges extending from the city center to the city limits) should be preserved and enhanced. This would form part of Osnabrück's climate-resilient urban structure, serving as an essential part of the city's spatial vision.[9] As the evaluation of the walks in the Green Fingers project showed, the actors were active participants in this co-creative process. They became aware of the spatial qualities of the "Green Fingers" and interconnected spatial elements mentally and physically during their walks. Encounters, such as those with land users during the walks, led to a more acute perception of new perspectives and images (Fig. 2).

The goal of such explorations is to collectively uncover various peculiarities, challenges, and questions; i.e., insights that have not yet been captured in books or project reports but must be "mined" if landscapes are to be sustainably transformed. These walks are a means of unearthing the "treasure" from which good spatial images and thus good spatial designs grow. It is essential to make the tacit knowledge that arises during the walks explicit in the form of initial ideas, fuzzy images, and feelings. The images experienced during the walk must be translated into "conceived" images and become "negotiated" images in the process of co-creation.[10]

In the first step, it is crucial to put the experienced images on paper and let the images sink in. Reactions to those drawings can subsequently lead to a more comprehensive understanding.[11] Step by step, evolving into conceived images, those initial drawings on paper develop into inventive maps and pictures that begin to reveal visions and connections, albeit still in "sketchy" ways. However, this process of co-creation must remain open, where a "closed" and "finished" visual language can cause groups of actors to fall out of step and rebel. Only when ownership is created among the many groups involved in the transdisciplinary process do the sketches become negotiated images, serving as communication tools open to dialogue. They subsequently express spatial characteristics identified together and document interim results as part of a growing visual record.

The play of emphasis and omission

The creation of an image alone does not produce a spatial vision that different actors may see or apply as their own. This would require negotiation processes integrating the professional expertise of those creating the images and the knowledge of local actors. First drafts of spatial images are typically presented for discussion, revised, developed, and then reintroduced for further discussion. The more intense this process of iterative discussion, the more effective the spatial image becomes. However, spatial images do not get "built"; instead, they have a greater impact by becoming guiding principles for the many decisions made by actors in

"City of Green Fingers," a spatial vision for Osnabrück

Fig. 2

various project contexts, permeating the strategic orientation of a city or region. In the course of their joint search for images, participants develop a sense of the landscape and its potential which they can draw on in their assessments. In this way, the actors take a decisive step forward in the transformational process by developing a shared understanding of what "bouncing forward" might look like.

How exactly do these negotiated images come about? The co-creative work on image development toward a common spatial image can be described as a play of emphasis and omission. For example, which landscape elements appear central to the actors in landscape transformation? What elements are particularly sensitive? Which landscape element becomes the main "actor" in the image? Moreover, what elements appear less important and recede into the background? For example, in the context of flood events and biodiversity conservation, the group might agree that more weight should be given to rivers and their floodplains in landscape transformation. In this context, the centennial flood zone of the river might be highlighted in bright blue instead of the barely visible line of the river on the topographic map. This makes the river floodplain appear as a defining part of the landscape—in some places as a boundary for settlements, in others as a mandate to advance land swaps with farmers to replace farmland with grassland. Only when the river floodplain appears in the conceived image can a discussion take place about whether its influence on future landscape transformation is exaggerated, not powerful enough, or "just right." Hence, spatial images are subject to clarification and productive dispute, changing frequently in the co-creative process.

Spatial images are located between notions of "existing" and as part of an overarching vision. They are a representation and imaginative interpretation of the existing conditions. However, is assigning significance to a landscape structure already a vision? This question can only be answered by examining the impact of the images. For spatial images to have an impact, they must emerge during the process. Landscape architects are tasked with extracting, understanding, and translating the contributions of laypeople in these processes—whether sketches or verbal comments—into a professional visual language. When this interplay between

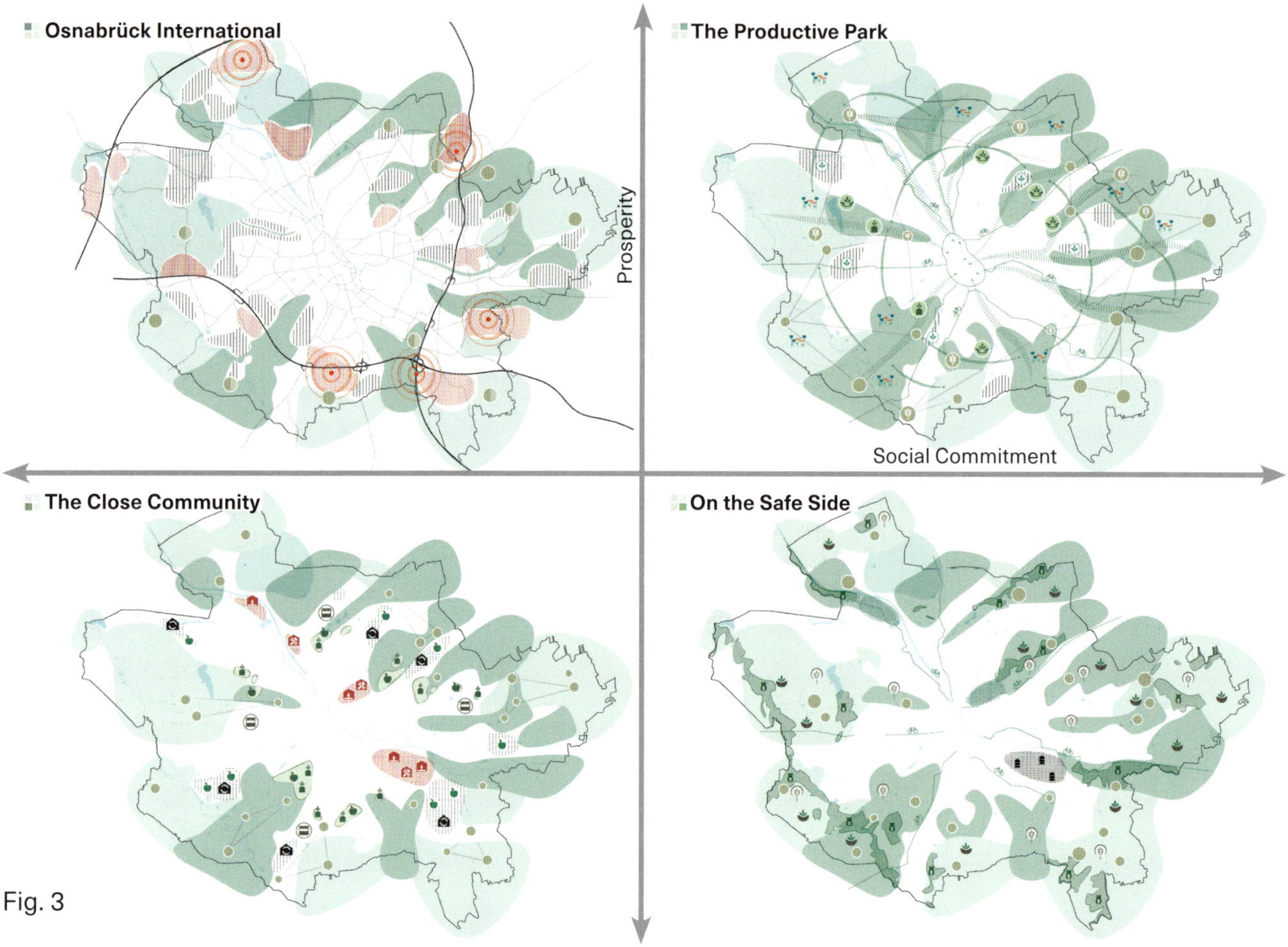

Fig. 3

professional image production and process design succeeds, spatial images can have a significant impact as the involved actors allow them to guide their everyday decisions.

Locating the actions of actors in spatial images

Spatial images have an impact when they guide action. In the Green Finger project, visual scenario unfolded their potential in workshops with key stakeholder groups and a political working group, illustrating four very different (and in some instances even extreme) futures for the city of Osnabrück in maps and stories. These sparked discussions around the question, "what kind of city do we want to live in?"—a query developed from research on the positioning of relevant stakeholders. These included the Chamber of Industry and Commerce, as well as stakeholders from agriculture and urban planning. Within the project, the scenarios aggregated the accumulated knowledge, highlighting the different aspects of each scenario (Fig. 3).

To ensure the scenarios could be understood by the various actors involved, the research team relied on

Fig. 1
The actors of the "Green Finger" project in Osnabrück were active participants in a co-creative process. They became aware of the spatial qualities of the "Green Fingers" and interconnected spatial elements—mentally and physically—during their walks.

Fig. 2
For the city of Osnabrück, a spatial vision was developed with the title "City of Green Fingers."

Fig. 3
The scenario "Osnabrück International" envisions a thriving city that grows significantly at the expense of the Green Fingers. The scenario "The Productive Park" depicts a city with multifunctional, interconnected green spaces whose form and maintenance are strongly influenced by societal groups. The scenario "On the Safe Side" describes an economically less prosperous city where the Green Fingers are protected but do not drive city development. Finally, the scenario "Close Community" portrays Osnabrück as focusing on sufficiency and local community gardens within a shrinking global economy.

storytelling and cartography. Following Anke Schmidt, storytelling can be a central component of design processes that aim to develop collaborative visions of the future on par with various stakeholders (see article on page 274). In the Green Fingers project, the stories used acting protagonists to describe what living in Osnabrück in the future would be like under different conditions. This encompassed considerations of who makes decisions and thus shapes resilient landscape transformation, in addition to what implications this has. Alongside the written story, each scenario was accompanied by mapping that highlighted the aspects and consequences described (see article by Sigrun Langner on page 266).

Working with the images revealed their accessibility even to those without a planning background. These individuals could relate to the characters in the stories and readily respond to questions regarding the actions required in each scenario from their perspective, as well as what measures would be necessary to enable or prevent a scenario. Inspired by the question, "what could be your role in the scenarios?," they vividly illustrated discussions about a landscape transformation towards a climate-resilient city of the future. Moreover, the involved actors could identify which "levers" make one scenario more likely than another. Their engagement was more proactive than reactive[12]—a typical quality criterion for co-creative processes.

In conclusion, in transdisciplinary, co-creative processes of landscape transformation, questions like, "which landscapes do we currently recognize?" or "in which landscape do we want to live?" often take center stage in discussions among different groups of actors. These discussions involve decisions about directions that cannot rely solely on the insights of a single scientific discipline but draw on a wide network of reasoning contexts as a reference precisely because they involve complex issues. Spatial images can stimulate—and certainly manipulate—the planning-cultural discourse. By emphasizing, omitting, and exaggerating landscape elements and structures, landscape architects design the "bouncing forward" of transformative resilience and present it in the form of spatial visions. When these visions are designed collaboratively, the stakeholders develop a sense of ownership for them. Moreover, they are likely to actively promote the strategic orientation associated with the spatial vision. The fact that stakeholders use the vision as a guideline for their everyday decisions is crucial because a spatial concept for a large-scale landscape will never be fully built as a whole. Instead, it serves as a concept and mindset for smaller projects.

1 Harald Kegler, *Resilienz. Strategien & Perspektiven für die widerstandsfähige und lernende Stadt* (Gütersloh, Berlin: Bauverlag, Birkhäuser, 2014).

2 Verena E. Balz, "Regional design: Discretionary approaches to regional planning in The Netherlands," *Planning Theory*, 17, no.3, (2018): 332–54.

3 Henrik Schultz and Hubertus von Dressler, "Grüne Finger für eine klimaresiliente Stadt – Wie lässt sich transformative Resilienz gestalten?" in *Resilienz als Strategie in Region, Destination und Unternehmen: Eine raumbezogene Perspektive*, eds. Harald Pechlaner, Daniel Zacher, and Elina Störmann (Wiesbaden: Springer Fachmedien, 2022).

4 Tony Bovaird and Elke Loeffler, "From Engagement to Co-Production: The Contribution of Users and Communities to Outcomes and Public Value," *Voluntas* 23, no. 4 (2012): 1119–38.

5 Taco Brandsen and Marlies Honingh, "Definitions of Co-Production and Co-Creation," in *Co-Production and Co-Creation: Engaging Citizens in Public Services*, eds. Taco Brandsen and Marlies Honingh (London: Routledge, 2018), 9–17.

6 Annaliesa Hilger, Michael Rose, and Andreas Keil, "Beyond Practitioner and Researcher: 15 Roles Adopted by Actors in Transdisciplinary and Transformative Research Processes," *Sustainability Science* 16 (2021): 2049–68.

7 Uwe Schneidewind, *Die große Transformation: Eine Einführung in die Kunst gesellschaftlichen Wandels* (Frankfurt am Main: S. Fischer, 2018).

8 Henrik Schultz "Designing large-scale landscapes through walking," in *Journal of Landscape Architecture* 9, no. 2 (2014): 6–15.

9 Hubertus von Dressler, Lea Nikolaus, Henrik Schultz, and Florian Eckhardt, *Osnabrück Stadt der Grünen Finger: Forschungsergebnisse des Forschungsprojekts Produktiv. Nachhaltig. Lebendig. Grüne Finger für eine klimaresiliente Stadt, Osnabrück*, accessed July 30, 2024, https://gruene-finger.de/wp-content/uploads/2023/09/2023_08_StadtDerGruenenFinger_Forschungsergebnisse_Gesamtbericht.pdf.

10 Henrik Schultz, "Erlebte, Konzipierte und Verhandelte Bilder – Wegbereiter einer transformativen Landschaftsforschung?" in *Interdisziplinäre Architekturwissenschaft*, eds. Karsten Berr and Achim Hahn (Wiesbaden: Springer VS, 2020).

11 Hille von Seggern, "Crossing Fields: Designing and Researching Raumgeschehen," in *Design Research for Urban Landscapes: Theories and Methods*, eds. Martin Prominski and Hille von Seggern (London, New York: Routledge, 2019), 8–32.

12 Markus J. Collier, Zorica Nedovic-Budic, Jeroen Aerts, Stuart Connop, Dermot Foley, Karen Foley, Darryl Newport, Siobhán McQuaid, Aleksander Slaev, and Peter Verburg, "Transitioning to Resilience and Sustainability in Urban Communities". *Cities, Current Research on Cities*, 32 (2013), 21–28.

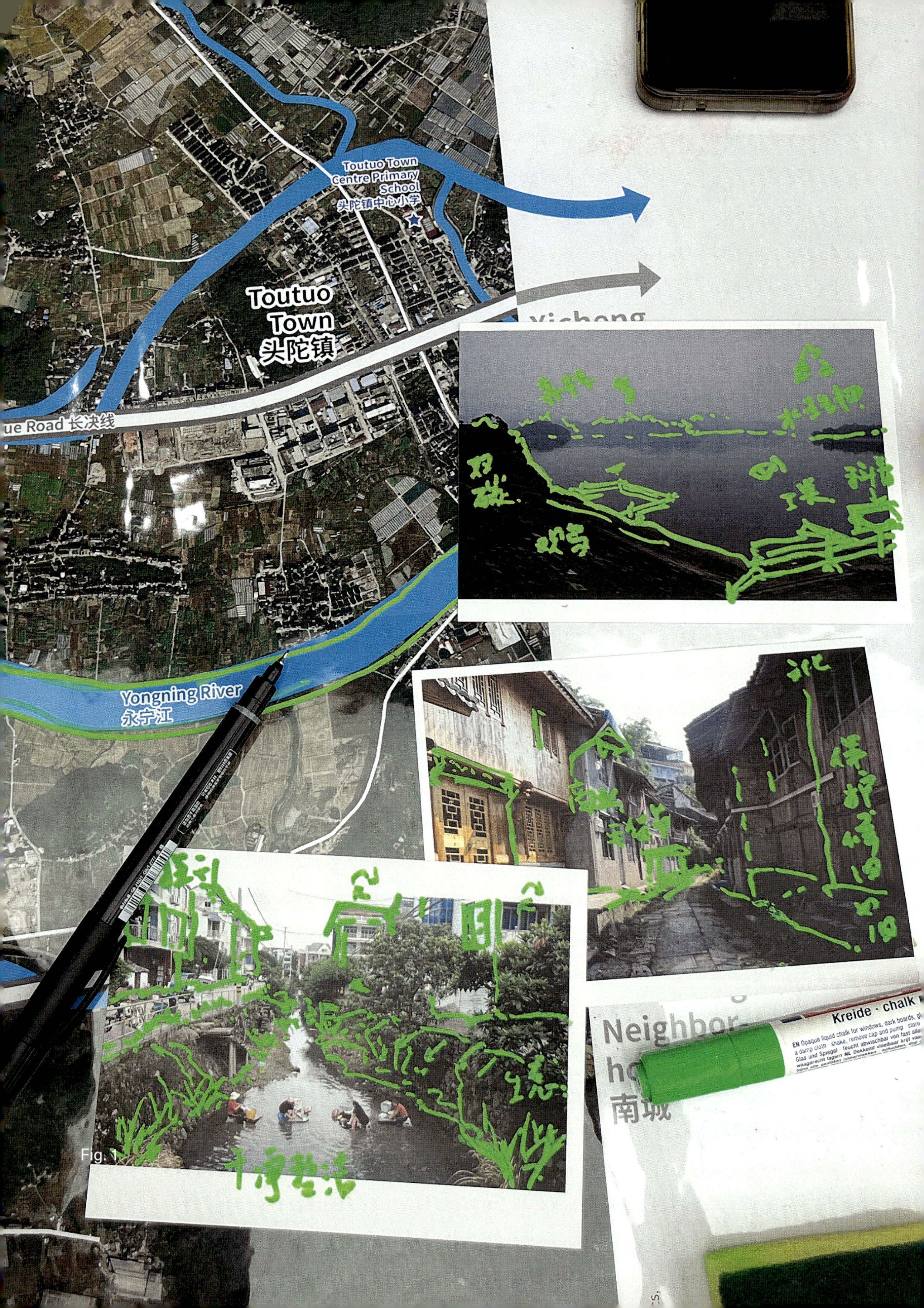
Toutuo Town
Centre Primary
School
头陀镇中心小学
Toutuo
Town
头陀镇
ue Road 长决线
Yongning River
永宁江
Neighbor-
ho
南城
Kreide · chalk

Fig. 1

Co-visioning urban-rural regions: Learning from living labs in Germany and China

Maria Frölich-Kulik and
Lukas Pappert

Sustainable change in urban-rural regions is achievable only through shared knowledge and close cooperation among actors from civil society, science, politics, administration, and business. Co-creative tools can facilitate exchanges between these actors regarding urban-rural futures, enabling the design of creative, resilient, and integrated approaches to sustainable regional transformation. The Urban-Rural Assembly research project focused on developing and testing such collaborative tools in the urban-rural regions of Huangyan (China) and Nordhausen (Germany), initiating what is termed "co-visioning" processes in both regions. These processes were based on close cooperation between scientists and local actors, working collaboratively on evidence-based and participatory frameworks for sustainable transformation in urban-rural areas. Co-visioning approaches were closely linked to ongoing specialized research that examined urban-rural relationships from various perspectives, including socio-spatial practices, material cycles, water landscapes, ecosystems, and migration and inclusion (see article on page 90). The co-visioning tool described here is the outcome of a joint learning process; it was developed, tested, and refined throughout the project. Methodologically, the tool blended approaches from transdisciplinary and transformative research, multi-stakeholder engagement, and regional design (Fig. 2).

From a transdisciplinary research perspective, the co-visioning approach was designed to develop and test formats and procedures that allow scientists and local stakeholders to collaboratively generate "socially robust knowledge"[1] for sustainable urban-rural transformations. The research conducted is thus not only transdisciplinary but also occupies a transformative research space, generating actionable knowledge (i.e., knowledge that contributes to shaping transformation).[2] To this end, co-visioning processes were initiated in "living labs" within two urban-rural regions, focusing on sustainable urban-rural transformation. The goal was to make existing and potential local sustainability approaches visible for a time horizon extending to 2040, scale them up to the regional scale, and assess their possible effectiveness.

Urban-Rural Assembly co-visioning approach

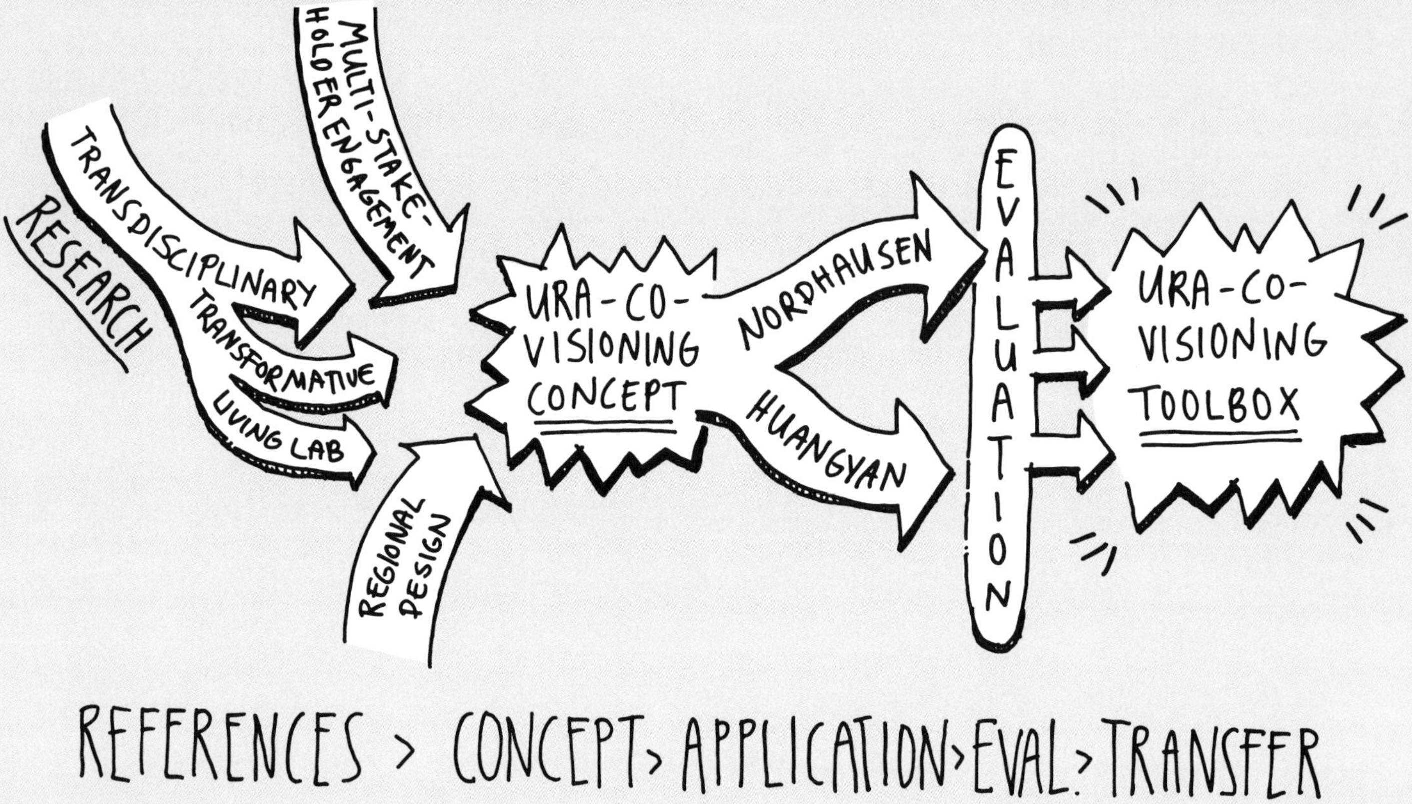

Fig. 2

Transdisciplinary and transformative research heavily relies on collaboration between scientists and local actors, making multi-stakeholder engagement a key foundation of the co-visioning approach in this research project. These multi-stakeholder engagement processes are structured and multi-stage, ensuring the involvement of diverse actors in a topic-specific manner.[3] Through a participatory and integrative approach, participants exchange different perspectives on set topics, strengthening mutual understanding and the development of shared positions and goals. Special attention is given to the roles of individual actors and the relationships and networks among them. This focus enhances both cooperation and the initiative of participants.

Regional design approaches,[4] particularly the so-called "Raumbild processes" in Germany (see Frölich-Kulik, Langner, and Pappert on page 230), have inspired a creative spatial methodology. These processes demonstrate how regional visions of the future can be developed, visualized, and communicated, in addition to how negotiation processes around these visions can be fostered. The multi-scalar and narrative approach, combined with an openness to integrating diverse subject areas, make Raumbild processes a suitable starting point for developing transdisciplinary and transformative tools for spatial planning at the urban-rural interface.

Using this as a foundation, the research project initiated two co-visioning processes in the urban-rural regions of Nordhausen and Huangyan between 2022 and 2024. The Nordhausen living lab was first established during the project period because joint research trips to China were not possible due to pandemic-related entry restrictions, delaying the commencement of the participatory process in Huangyan until 2023. In the Nordhausen living lab, co-visioning methods were initially developed and tested. After evaluation and adaptation, these methods served as the basis for the process design in Huangyan. The work in the Nordhausen living lab also allowed for a comparison of the two processes in China and Germany, providing early insights into the transferability of the procedures and methods. To implement collaborative co-visioning processes, the project team continuously developed various methods to facilitate

Collaboration in the co-visioning process

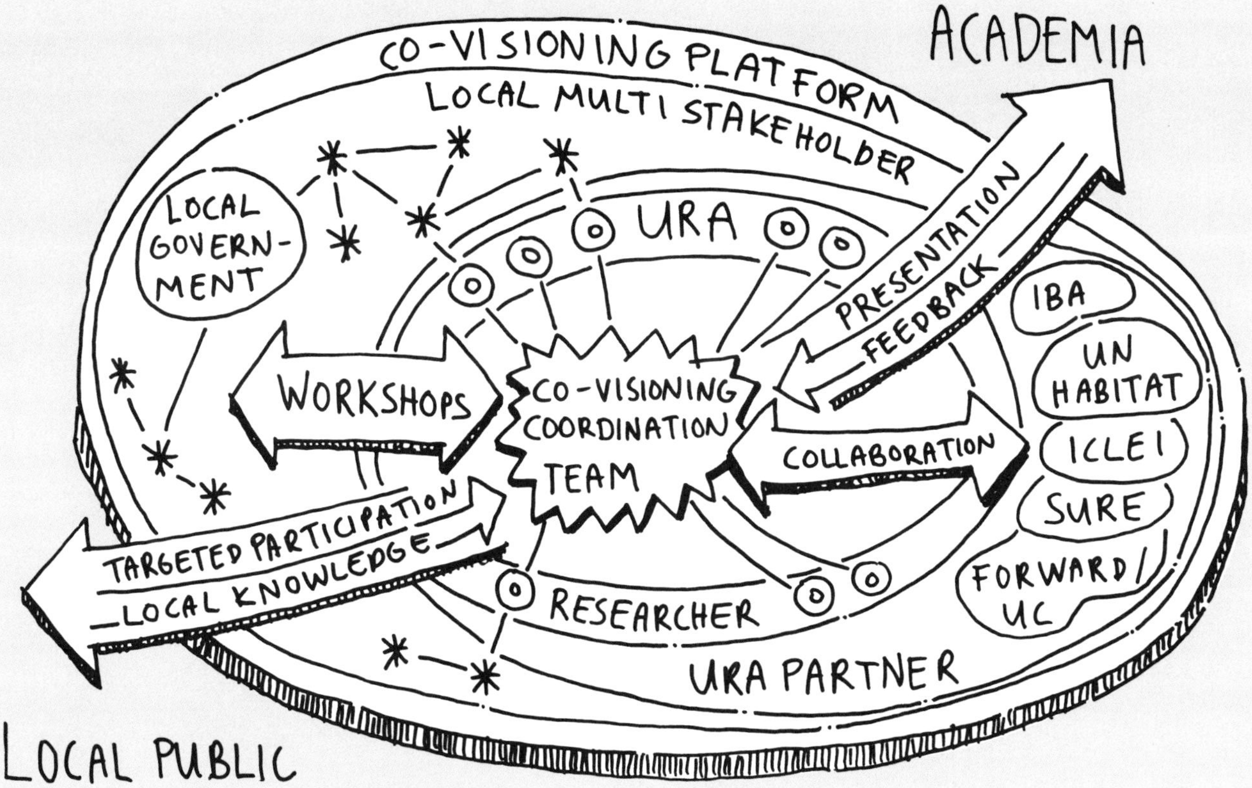

Fig. 3

communication between disciplines (sub-projects), local actors, and practice partners. Interim results were regularly prepared, communicated, and discussed at different levels (Fig. 3).

Co-visioning in the Urban-Rural Living Lab of Nordhausen

The first co-visioning process focused on the urban-rural region of Nordhausen, located in north Thuringia and extending into parts of the neighboring federal states of Saxony-Anhalt and Lower Saxony. Based on research and multi-stakeholder workshops, the project team identified four characteristic territories within the urban-rural region, each with common spatial and structural features, in addition to their opportunities and risks for the future. These four territories—*Harzland*, *Karstland*, *Regioland*, and *Salzland*—offer a new interpretation of the region (Fig. 8). In all of these areas the effects of climate change are already evident, necessitating urgent perspectives for a climate-friendly transformation.

Harzland in the north, encompassing the forested southern foothills of the Harz low mountain range, is suffering from widespread and unstoppable forest dieback. To the south lies *Karstland*, a small-scale gypsum limestone landscape and important biodiversity hotspot, increasingly threatened by natural gypsum extraction. *Salzland*, at the southern end of the Nordhausen urban-rural region, is characterized by the distinctive waste heaps from potash mining and mixed forests. It faces a projected population decline of over 20 percent by 2035 in some areas. Between *Karstland* and *Salzland* stretches *Regioland*, an agricultural valley crisscrossed by a network of rivers and streams increasingly affected by summer droughts. *Regioland* also includes the city of Nordhausen (population 41,339 as of 2022), which—situated within a system of supra-regional transport networks—serves as a hub for important functions for the surrounding villages and communities.

Although large sections of the urban-rural region are considered rural, the interrelationships within urban-rural systems remain omnipresent. The extensive mining of raw materials, such as gypsum, potash,

Fig. 4

Fig. 5

Fig. 6

Fig. 7

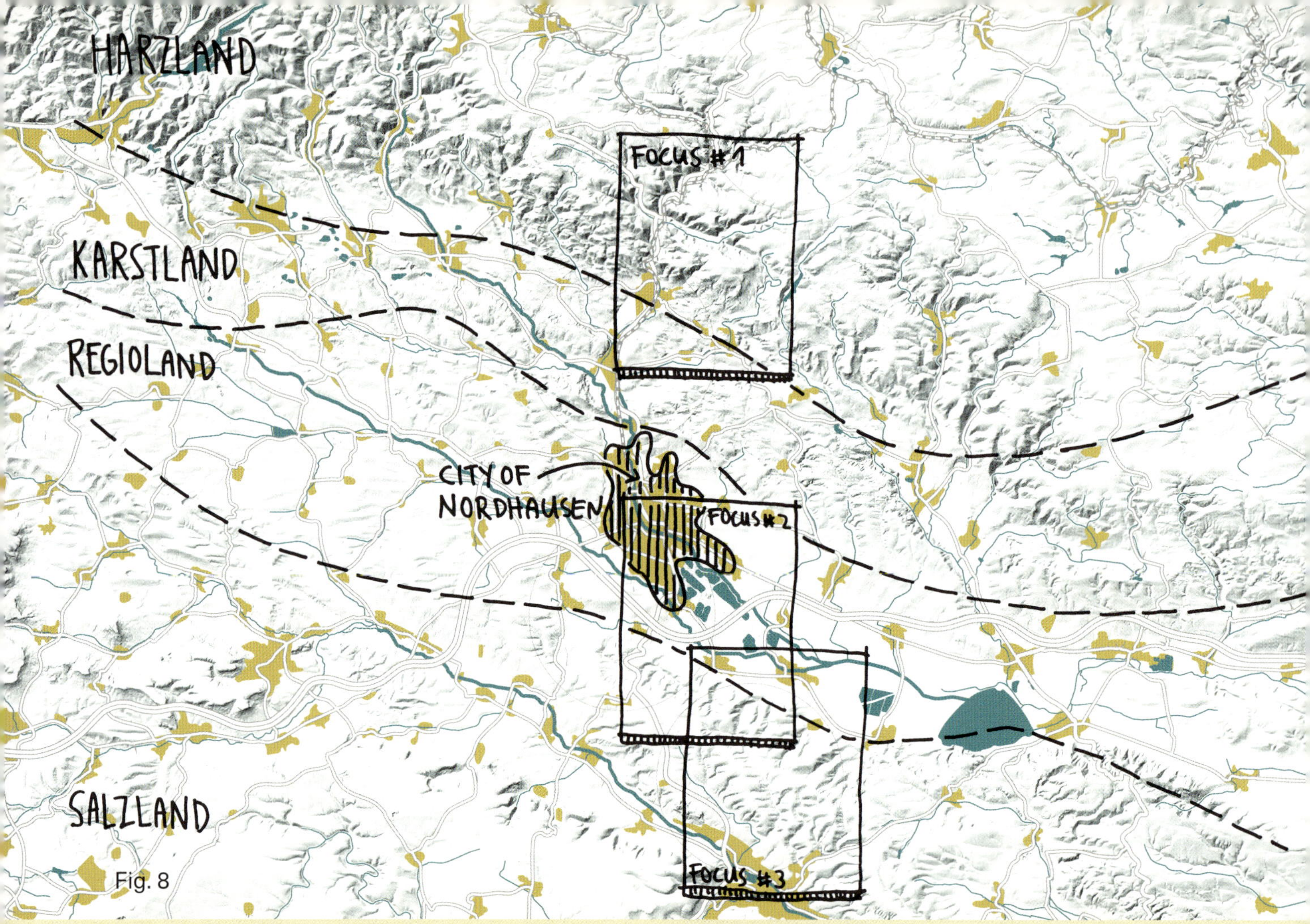

Fig. 8

and gravel, alongside large-scale agriculture and forestry, reflects a landscape where natural resources have become integral to global material and economic cycles. This raises questions about sustainable resources and local value creation. Over the past forty years, the Nordhausen urban-rural region has faced a gradual population decline accompanied by a loss of public service infrastructure and community facilities. These trends contribute to deprivation and increasing social and political polarization; thus, urgent questions arise regarding positive perspectives that promote sustainable forms of public services and enhance the quality of life in the urban-rural region of Nordhausen.

At the same time, competition for space is intensifying. Sectors such as agriculture, energy, raw material extraction, and environmental and nature conservation are vying for the limited resource of land. The challenge is to negotiate these competing claims cooperatively and design innovative models of landscape multi-coding. However, the urban-rural region benefits from strong cooperation and networks between municipalities, universities, and companies, as well as initial innovative planning approaches to address these numerous challenges effectively.

Built upon existing structures in the urban-rural region, the co-visioning process was divided into four successive phases: (1) "Exploring", (2) "Vision Building," (3) "Deepening," and (4) "Narrating," each representing a distinct step in "Vision Building". During the Exploring phase, the region was investigated through excursions (Fig. 9, 10). Initial technical analyses served as a foundation for identifying and mapping particular challenges, potentials, key players, and crucial spaces for sustainable urban-rural transformation. In the Vision Building phase, preliminary regional visions and transformation models were developed, focusing on the integrated themes of "energy," "everyday life," and "resources." The Deepening phase involved a more detailed examination of the approaches within these focus areas. Low-threshold future scenarios were created to describe the interplay of strategies, key players, and spaces, offering positive perspectives on the future of the urban-rural region. In the final Narrating phase, the results were

Fig. 9

Fig. 10

"It is an opportunity to focus on different areas and perspectives that are similarly affected and in need of solutions. The process of making the connections between them visible on maps and drawings is unique and has huge advantages in terms of public participation. It's good, something we haven't had here before." Marcel Hardrath, Department for Investments, Public Transport and Climate Protection, District of Nordhausen

consolidated into future narratives, with two central communication formats developed: a documentary film and a physical model for the closing exhibition of the International Building Exhibition Thuringia.

Throughout the four phases, the research team collaborated with a largely consistent group of local stakeholders, identified as key actors in a socio-ecological and circular-oriented transformation within the urban-rural region. This group included representatives from municipalities and districts, various interest groups (such as the Water Management Association or the Nature and Biodiversity Conservation Union), as well as farmers and foresters. The research project also benefitted from the support of the International Building Exhibition Thuringia, which shared a focus on urban-rural transformation.

Stakeholder involvement was most intense during three multi-actor workshops, each marking a transition between phases. These workshops allowed for discussion of the previous phase's results and collaborative preparation for the upcoming phase. Each workshop centered on focus group sessions that concentrated on specific topics, spaces, or strategies, bringing together actors from various administrative sectors and interest groups.

Interactive workshop formats were developed to facilitate co-creative work on sustainable transformation paths, regional visions, and compelling future narratives. For instance, in the first workshop, playing cards were used to represent actors, conflicts, and potentials of sustainable transformation, which were then located on spatial maps of the urban-rural region. In the second workshop, a voting format allowed stakeholders to evaluate the persuasiveness of developed ideas (Fig. 11). The resulting voting image then guided the selection and discussion processes at the workshop tables. The third workshop featured a game board where different components for implementing sustainable transformation models were linked (Fig. 12). The results from these focus group workshops were presented in plenary sessions at the end of each multi-actor workshop and compiled into a large synthesis model of the urban-rural region. This model highlighted dependencies, synergies, and conflicts between focus topics, facilitating collective discussion. Working with the characteristic

"Spatial envisioning creates awareness of things that may seem unrealistic at first but which will move the region forward in the future." Alexandra Rieger, former City Mayor of Nordhausen

Fig. 11

Fig. 12

territories developed for urban-rural Nordhausen enabled participants to identify, discuss, and further develop potentials, challenges, actor networks, and project ideas towards sustainable regional change, transcending administrative boundaries.

Co-visioning in the Urban-Rural Living Lab of Huangyan

The second co-visioning process was conducted in the urban-rural region of Huangyan, located on the east coast of China in Zhejiang Province. Huangyan is one of three urban districts (the other districts are Luqiao and Jiaojiang) within the metropolitan urban area of Taizhou, home to over six million people. As the largest and least densely populated urban district, Huangyan is inhabited by 707,453 people living across a variety of settlement typologies. The meandering Yongning River, which eventually flows into the Ling Jiang River, is a key feature that shapes the identity of this urban-rural region.

For a preliminary analysis, the urban-rural region of Huangyan was divided into characteristic territories based on spatial-functional features and future considerations, mirroring the approach used in Nordhausen (Fig. 13). The "urbanized river land" stretches along the Yongning River, which is predominantly agricultural in the west and industrial to the east. The historical core of Huangyan is also situated within this river land, nestled between Mount Jiufeng—a culturally significant landmark—and the Yongning River. However, the historical core now consists primarily of modern high-rise buildings, with only remnants of its original settlement structures.

The Changtan Reservoir, constructed in the 1960s by damming and straightening the Yongning River about twenty kilometers west of Huangyan's historical center, marks the beginning of significant urbanization and sometimes radical transformation of the region's spatial-functional systems. Some areas remain in the intermediate stages of urbanization, where old villages persist as relics of a rural agri-cultural past amidst modern industrial and residential developments.

Within this urbanized river land, two living labs—Beiyang and Xinqian—represent the dominant production sectors. Beiyang, located to the east of the

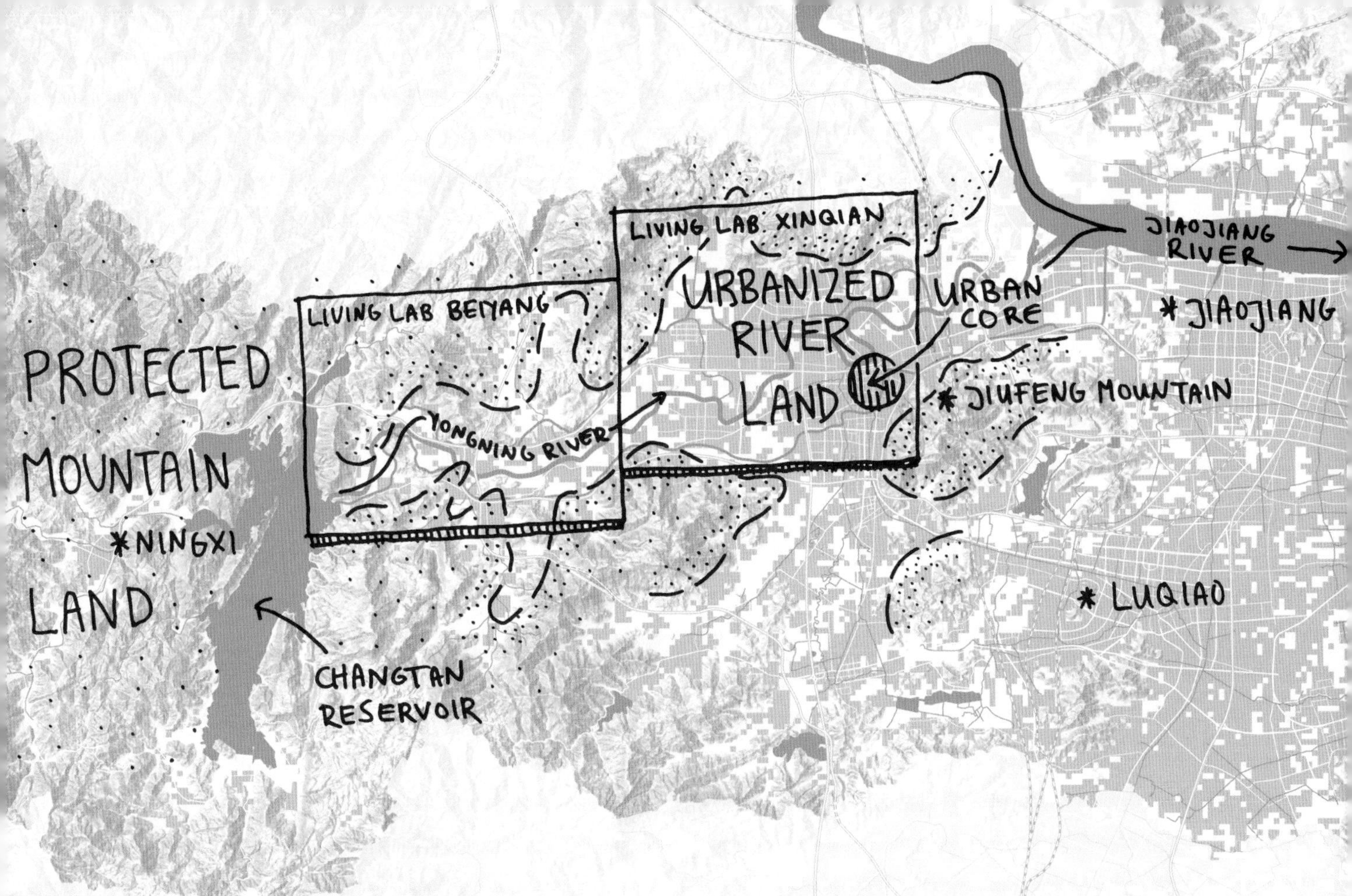

Fig. 13

Changtan Reservoir, is agriculturally focused, while Xinqian, west of the historical center, is dominated by industry. The research sub-projects centered on these two areas and the co-visioning process was deepened accordingly.

Due to the distinct characteristics of the Beiyang and Xinqian living labs within the urban-rural region of Huangyan, the co-visioning process addressed various transformation challenges specific to each area. In Beiyang, the process explored strategies for promoting ecological and circular agricultural practices, linking environmental protection with rural tourism. In Xinqian, the focus was on circular and resource-saving industrial transformation, addressing industrial waste management, recycling solutions, and the design of inclusive neighborhoods. These urbanization processes primarily concentrated on the river land, reflecting the diverse development dynamics across Huangyan's urban-rural landscape.

Another distinctive territory within the urban-rural region are the forested mountain ranges, defined as the "protected mountainous land." This area is characterized by its extensive ecological protection zones, particularly around the Changtan Reservoir, where strict regulations govern land use under the so-called "Ecological Red Lines." These measures aim to preserve the natural environment and also contribute towards challenges such as population decline, vacancy, and demolition in the sparsely populated villages scattered throughout the mountainous land.

Despite these challenges, some villages, such as Shatan or Wuyantou (see article by Guiqing Yang on page 214), have managed to survive and even thrive by becoming focal points for rural tourism, supported by China's current rural revitalization policy. The co-visioning process aligned with these developments, concentrating on strategies to reactivate and interconnect the villages and small towns within the protected mountainous land. Key areas of focus included exploring opportunities for rural tourism, developing new rural economic and production models, and establishing self-sustaining supply systems that could contribute to the sustainable transformation of these communities.

The co-visioning process in the urban-rural region of Huangyan was significantly influenced by the

Fig. 14

Fig. 15

Fig. 16

Fig. 17

Fig. 18

methodologies developed in the Nordhausen process. The research team adapted the procedures and workshop formats previously tested and refined in Nordhausen to create a tailored approach for Huangyan.

In the first phase, Exploring, the research project began by compiling and synthesizing the knowledge individual teams had gathered about the urban-rural region (Fig. 18, 19). To facilitate this, the coordination team designed specific formats that helped select, map, and relate experiences, data, and analyses for each research team.

In the second phase, Vision Building, the process moved forward with the proposal of eighteen transformation models, which were organized around three integrated focus topics: “Productive Huangyan,” “Attractive Huangyan,” and “Healthy Huangyan.” These models were visually represented through spatial sketches, providing a clear and tangible sense of potential future developments.

Finally, in the Narrating phase, these transformation models were further developed, interconnected, and unified into a comprehensive regional vision. This was then illustrated through photo annotations, which highlighted future development potentials and strategies for key prototypical locations within Huangyan (Fig. 21). Unlike the living labs established in Nordhausen, where spatial “deepening” occurred in a distinct phase, the Huangyan co-visioning procedure integrated this aspect concurrently with broader regional considerations, affirming a more cohesive and continuous exploration of spatial transformation throughout the process.

In the urban-rural region of Huangyan, sustainable transformation paths and spatial visions for the future were co-creatively developed by researchers and local stakeholders. To achieve this, the research team organized six multi-actor workshops—three during each of the two research trips in 2023 and 2024. On both research trips, a large workshop was conducted to address urban-rural relationships on a regional scale while two additional workshops focused on the living labs in Beiyang and Xinqian. In these cases, stakeholder selection required approval from the city government. Workshop participants primarily included specialist administrators, political representatives, and planning officers; however, farmers,

Compilation of research results on a digital platform

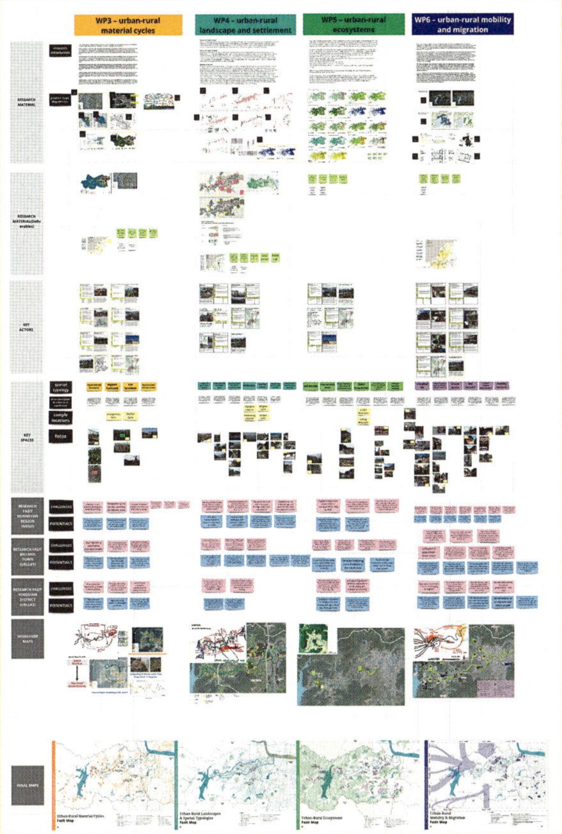

Fig. 19

"This is about describing the future; the usual procedures of state and regional planning are mainly regulatory instruments and contain few—if any—visions of the future that could inspire enthusiasm and guide action." Marta Doehler-Behzadi, Director, International Building Exhibition Thuringia

"Only when people think together about the future of a region and develop a shared vision of the future will they have a chance of finding solutions to challenges and managing the change that is already upon us." Cordelia Polinna, Forward Planung und Forschung, Berlin

industrialists, and other entrepreneurs also contributed, particularly at the living lab level.

The perspectives of other relevant groups, such as migrant workers and the Yongning River Sewage team, were incorporated into discussions through interviews and numerous informal talks during field research. The workshop processes were similar to those used in the Nordhausen project, alternating between plenary sessions and focus group discussions. In the focus groups, the project team utilized various mapping formats in all workshops to spatially record and overlay the results (Fig. 20). Other formats included "menu cards," which allowed participants to vote on their favorite ideas (Fig. 25), and photo annotations (Fig. 23) to directly visualize the jointly developed ideas spatially.

Learning from co-visioning processes

The Urban-Rural Assembly research project successfully carried out two co-visioning processes in urban-rural regions with different starting points and in diverse political and cultural contexts. In both regions, researchers collaborated with highly motivated actors and benefited from a strong interest in partnership. However, despite the completion of the co-visioning processes, several pertinent questions remain unanswered—particularly regarding the implementation of the results, the effectiveness of the processes, and the transferability of these methods to other urban-rural regions. Nevertheless, based on the experiences in China and Germany, initial conclusions can be drawn about the suitability of co-visioning methods for collaboratively generating knowledge on sustainable transformation processes at the urban-rural interface.

1. Visualizing and strengthening urban-rural relationships

Within the framework of the two co-visioning processes, the research project devised and applied methods to collaboratively generate and visualize socially robust, action-guiding knowledge on sustainable transformation processes in urban-rural relationships. The multi-stakeholder workshops, which

Fig. 20

“These are just ideas. They may need to be planned and implemented from top to bottom. As small, ordinary people, we can do very little. But what we have discussed in the workshop today can be fed back to the top, then implementation becomes possible.” Anonymous person, Xinqian Sub District, Huangyan

“I feel very honored to have attended two out of three workshops in the last few days. For me, exposure to these issues has broadened my perspective on them. I hope that this kind of exchange can be continued in the long term and on a more regular basis.” Lu Zhiyuan, Director of Agriculture Service Center, Xinqian Sub-District, Huangyan

Fig. 21

brought together a diverse range of actors and perspectives, played a crucial role in this process. These workshops made it possible to identify and discuss dependencies, synergies, and conflicts between the focus topics.

The transdisciplinary research approach added significant value, as the research findings were validated and adjusted based on local feedback. This resulted in research that closely aligned with specific local challenges and the potential for socio-ecological and circular transformation. Beyond grounding the research in local contexts, the co-visioning approach also facilitated interdisciplinary exchange among the research teams. This collaboration led to the development of integrated strategies for focus topics and encouraged interactions between the various research fields on sustainable urban-rural relations.

2. Opening spatial discourses on the future

The co-visioning procedures were modeled after the exemplarily integrated *Raumbild* processes. The research project simulated these planning processes in the urban-rural regions of Nordhausen and Huangyan, with the key distinction that these processes were not politically mandated nor embedded in the existing planning structures. Consequently, the focus of co-visioning was less on formulating concrete spatial planning proposals and more on using participatory approaches to integrated spatial development to generate transdisciplinary knowledge. Although these framework conditions limited the binding nature and immediate effectiveness of the results, they provided a protected space to test new formats for cooperative and integrated urban-rural transformation. With the time horizon set at 2040, co-visioning was able to complement regular planning periods which typically have shorter timeframes. By conducting the discussions based on characteristic territories rather than administrative spatial units, the process promoted open, integrated, and comprehensive debates among stakeholders. The extended time horizon and territory-based approach also affirmed that discussions did not become entangled in immediate conflicts of interest or obstacles to transformation.

Fig. 22

3. Mediating between complex research and local expert knowledge

The chosen transdisciplinary approaches relied heavily on intensive mediation and translation between scientific research findings and local expert knowledge on social-spatial and ecological issues at urban-rural interfaces. This exchange resulted in significant learning at various levels: on one hand, the scientific context offered the opportunity to benefit from a broad spectrum of findings; on the other hand, the scientific context provided a space for discussions and creative thinking beyond established modes of thought. The topics, processes, and terminology had to be tailored to each stakeholder, requiring careful preparation, implementation, and follow-up for the workshops. This included the ongoing challenge of managing interdisciplinary, transdisciplinary, interlingual, and intercultural translation services and structuring processes.

The mapping and workshop formats described above helped to present complex relationships in a way that was understandable for all participants, making them comparable across different subject areas. However, several researchers noted that the various translation processes sometimes led to information being lost or misinterpreted, necessitating additional efforts to correct these "translation errors." Despite the high level of effort required, the researchers emphasized the learning benefits of these translation processes. They gained a deeper understanding of different scientific and local perspectives and tested how to translate their research for a non-scientific audience. Local stakeholders, in turn, gained insights into transformation research and were able to contribute their local knowledge.

4. Identifying and networking changemakers

The participatory approach of co-visioning emphasized stakeholder participation over public participation. Key "changemakers"—such as climate protection managers, farmers, local politicians, foresters, or representatives of industrial companies—were identified and included, given their potential to be significant drivers of sustainable transformation. The aim

Fig. 23

"In Huangyan, we used a 'top-down' approach to invite workshop participants through government channels. This may have led to involuntary participation and introduced selection bias; both these issues could have affected the results we obtained from the workshops." Gaoli Xiao, researcher, Technische Universität Berlin

"Participatory processes and cross-level discussions can increase the motivation for two-way communication. However, most ideas for effective summaries come from discussions in Mandarin. As those who speak this language tend to be young or have a higher level of education or social status, the results are limited and subject to bias." Yulin Zhang, researcher, Bauhaus-Universität Weimar

was to represent as many diverse perspectives and roles as possible within the research fields. However, the selection of stakeholders greatly influenced which perspectives were integrated into the research and vision formation—and which remained underrepresented. These potential representational deficits, influenced by the project's research focus, were evident in both the Nordhausen and Huangyan processes.

In the Nordhausen living lab, the stakeholder research and invitation process had to be conducted quickly due to the short-term setup, resulting in some relevant stakeholders being overlooked. In Huangyan, the selective circle of stakeholders was influenced by the city government's requirement to approve all participants. Consequently, the selection and management of stakeholders play a crucial role in shaping co-visioning processes, raising sensitive questions about the inclusion and exclusion of specific actors and groups.

The implementation of relaxed workshop settings—with workshop tables instead of frontally oriented rows of seats—disrupted familiar structures, a change that was positively received by many stakeholders in both Huangyan and Nordhausen.

5. Scaling sustainable local practices regionally

The goal of co-visioning processes was to identify and visualize local sustainability approaches that could contribute to long-term, sustainable change while also discussing their potential effectiveness on a regional scale. Interestingly, in Huangyan, voting formats revealed that transformation strategies primarily focused on long-term resource protection were considered less important. Instead, strategies that appeared to be implementable in the short term were viewed as more relevant; for example, ecologically-based approaches like ecological buffer zones, stepping-stone biotopes, and soil-sensitive agricultural practices were critically discussed.

However, while these obstacles and conflicts were acknowledged, they were not dismissed. Instead, they were documented as system knowledge and integrated into the design of transformation paths as target and transformation knowledge.[5]

Fig. 24

"For co-visioning processes to work, resources must be allocated to implement, monitor, and evaluate the proposed activities and agreed plan. It can be challenging to sustain the co-visioning process, particularly where there is already an established and legal planning framework." Remy Sietchiping, Chief of Policy, Legislation and Governance Section, UN-Habitat

"The 'spiral of silence' observed in the workshops often prevents minority views from being expressed for fear of isolation. In addition, the reluctance of government representatives to discuss sensitive issues, such as environmental protection, leads to homogenized opinions." Yuting Xie, Peiwen Huang, and Ziying Chen, researchers, Zheijang University

Fig. 25

This method was positively received by stakeholders in both Nordhausen and Huangyan as it encouraged the exploration of new ideas that can be neglected in regular planning practices due to seemingly insurmountable obstacles. This highlights the living lab nature of the approach.

To better sensitize stakeholders to the benefits of long-term, sustainable strategies, it may be necessary to clearly demonstrate the long-term consequences of unsustainable practices and compare them with the added value of sustainable, long-term approaches.

Although the results of the co-visioning process are not binding, they can still have a significant impact on numerous levels. In the short term, they allow actors to reflect on ongoing planning processes with a focus on sustainability aspects. In the medium and long term, particularly compelling approaches can inspire the design of sustainable transformations. The obstacles to transformation identified during the process provide valuable starting points for critically reflecting on dysfunctional regulations, structures, and procedures. Moreover, the results can offer stakeholders a scientifically sound basis for argumentation in political and planning discourses—particularly in underrepresented areas such as material cycles and migration, which must receive greater attention in regional planning in light of major global challenges.

6. Promoting trust in international cooperation

The interactive formats were designed to make the workshops engaging and open while actively involving and motivating both stakeholders and the international research team. Tools such as mappings and photo sketches, where discussed ideas were visualized directly at the workshop tables, proved particularly effective. Researchers assisted the moderators by sketching spatial concepts on maps or photos. Additionally, playful elements like playing cards, building blocks, and large models encouraged open discourse among participants. In both Nordhausen and Huangyan, participants were able to influence the direction and focus of discussions through voting formats and mood pictures. Various film formats provided

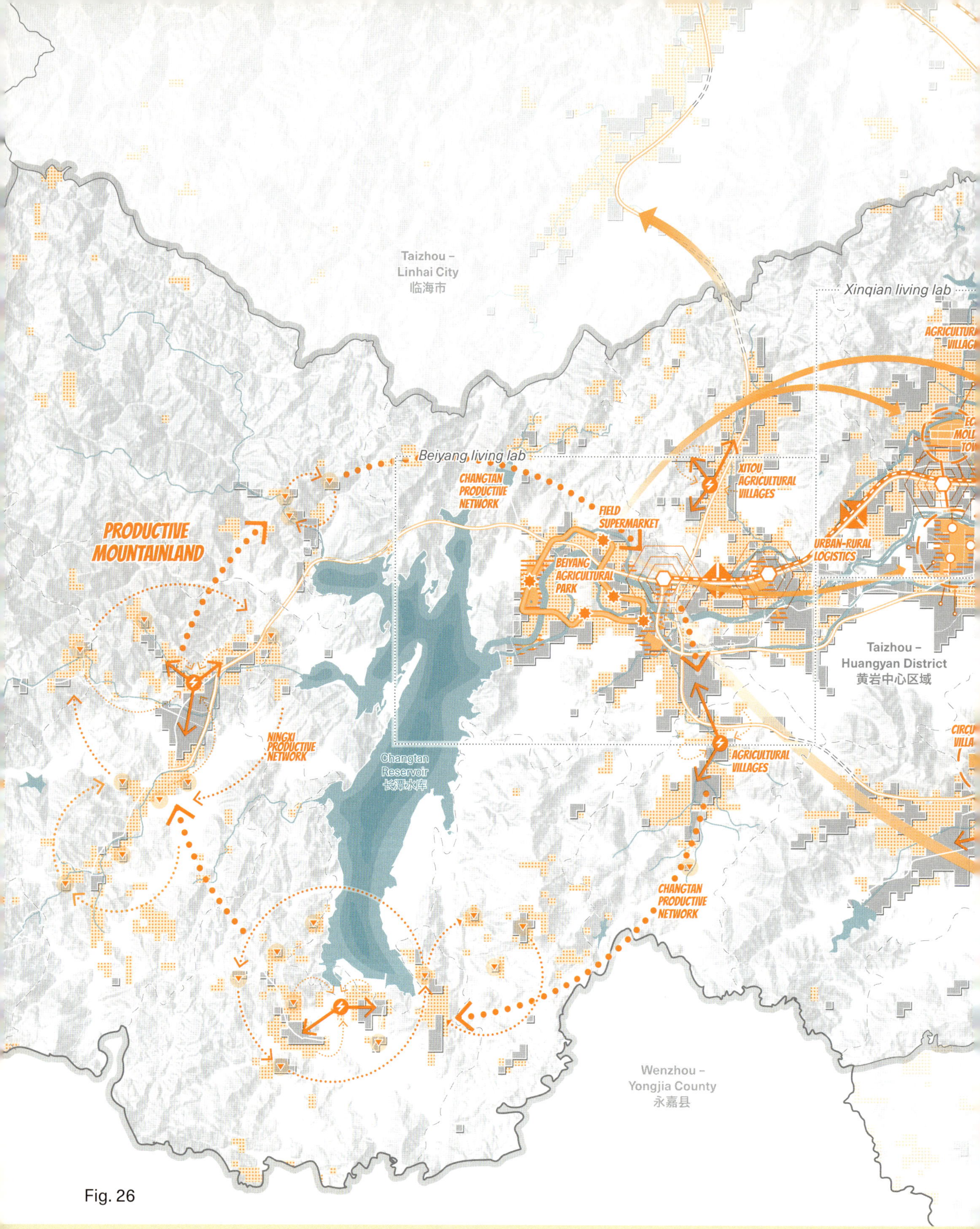
Taizhou –
Linhai City
临海市
Xinqian living lab
Beiyang living lab
CHANGTAN PRODUCTIVE NETWORK
FIELD SUPERMARKET
XITOU AGRICULTURAL VILLAGES
PRODUCTIVE MOUNTAINLAND
BEIYANG AGRICULTURAL PARK
URBAN-RURAL LOGISTICS
Taizhou –
Huangyan District
黄岩中心区域
NINGXI PRODUCTIVE NETWORK
Changtan Reservoir
长潭水库
AGRICULTURAL VILLAGES
CHANGTAN PRODUCTIVE NETWORK
Wenzhou –
Yongjia County
永嘉县
Fig. 26

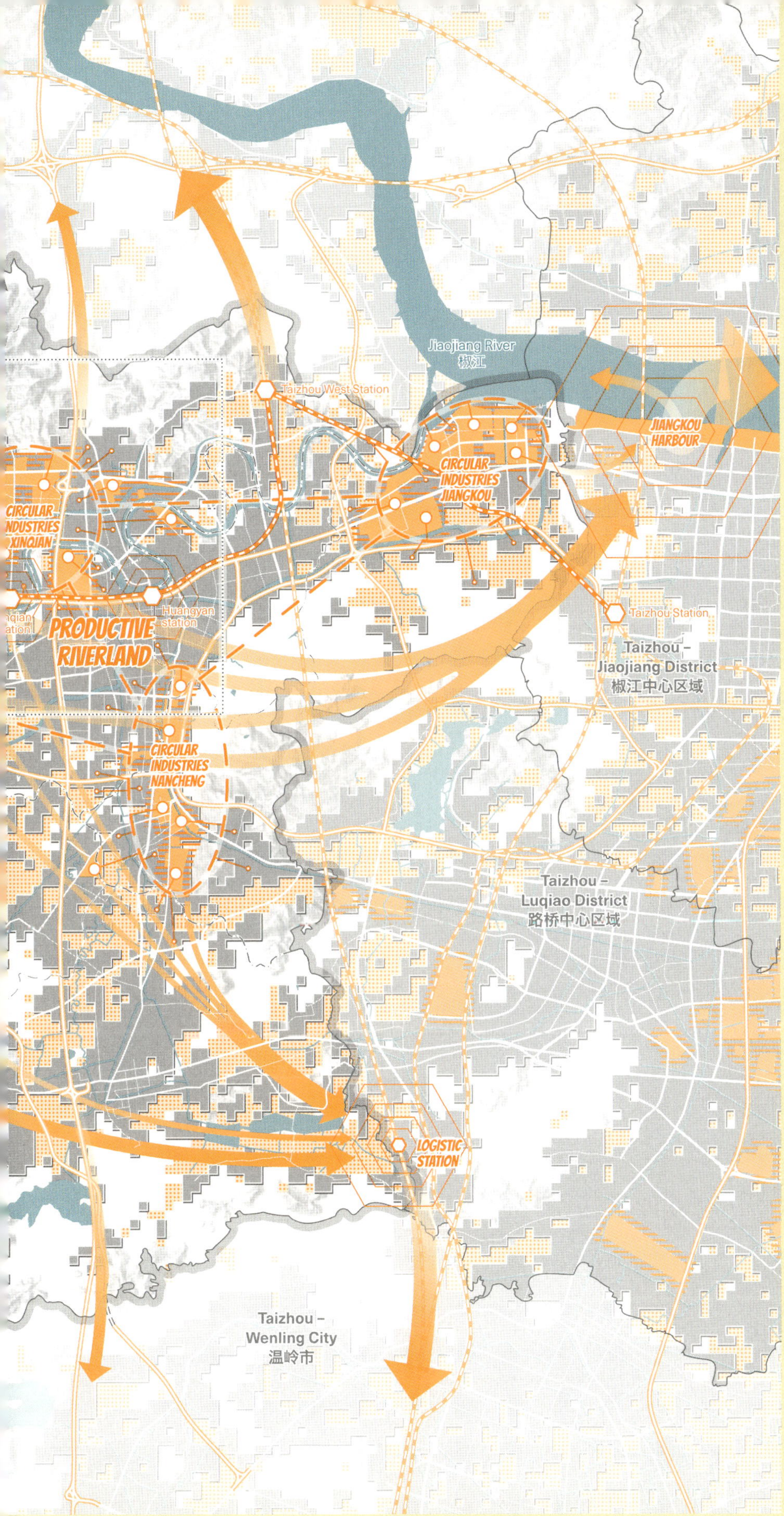

The “Productive Huangyan”

“Productive Huangyan” addresses the various productive fields in Huangyan and outlines paths for their sustainable transformation. A primary focus is on its industrial areas, where sustainable energy, water, and material cycles are being established. These circular systems include not only large factories but also numerous small workshops, which benefit from new approaches to, for example, waste management. Another focus is agriculture, where soil-sensitive and ecological forms of agriculture are being expanded to ensure the long-term cultivation of fertile soils. A key project here is the ecological agricultural park in Beiyang Town, which connects different farms and landscapes while simultaneously serving as a model for other agricultural regions. In the farming villages, the potential for local energy production based on agricultural residues is being explored. Additionally, local crafts and digital work in the villages will be strengthened. To promote local urban-rural integration, existing infrastructure (such as the new light rail) will also be used for logistics and new systems (such as a mobile field supermarket) will be introduced.

Sustainable industrial zones
Links between industrial areas and neighborhoods
Circular industrial networks
Circular factories
Circular workshops
Urban-rural logistics
Soil-sensitive agricultural zones
Circular rural networks
Productive mountainland villages
Local energy production and composting
Beiyang Agricultural Park
Flows of goods
Highways
Railways
Urban-rural logistic light rail
Railway stations

Water bodies, rivers
Settlement areas
Streets
Administrative borders

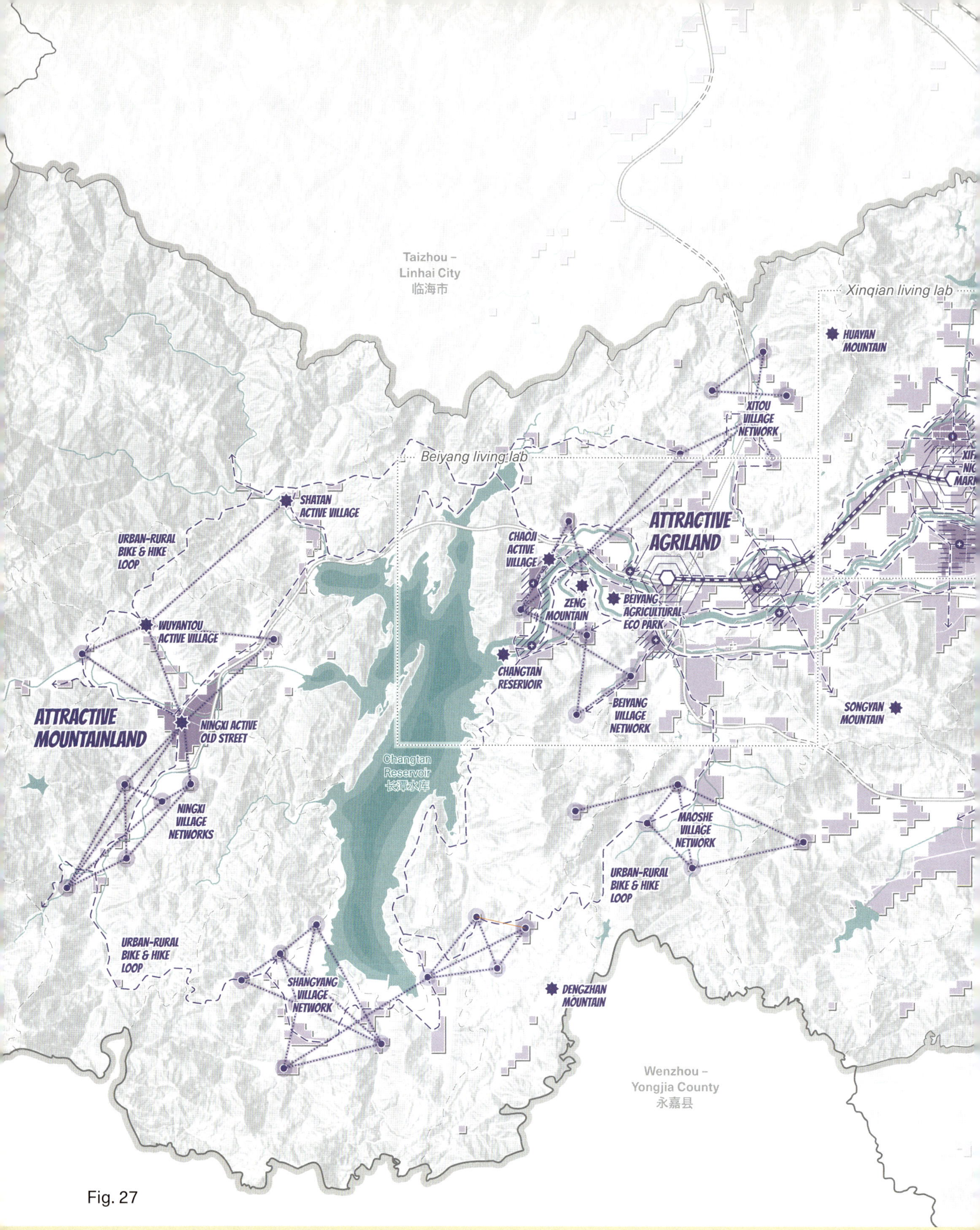
Taizhou –
Linhai City
临海市
Xinqian living lab
HUAYAN MOUNTAIN
XITOU VILLAGE NETWORK
Beiyang living lab
SHATAN ACTIVE VILLAGE
URBAN-RURAL BIKE & HIKE LOOP
ATTRACTIVE AGRILAND
CHAOJI ACTIVE VILLAGE
ZENG MOUNTAIN
BEIYANG AGRICULTURAL ECO PARK
WUYANTOU ACTIVE VILLAGE
CHANGTAN RESERVOIR
BEIYANG VILLAGE NETWORK
SONGYAN MOUNTAIN
ATTRACTIVE MOUNTAINLAND
NINGXI ACTIVE OLD STREET
Changtan
Reservoir
长潭水库
NINGXI VILLAGE NETWORKS
MAOSHE VILLAGE NETWORK
URBAN-RURAL BIKE & HIKE LOOP
URBAN-RURAL BIKE & HIKE LOOP
SHANGYANG VILLAGE NETWORK
DENGZHAN MOUNTAIN
Wenzhou –
Yongjia County
永嘉县
Fig. 27

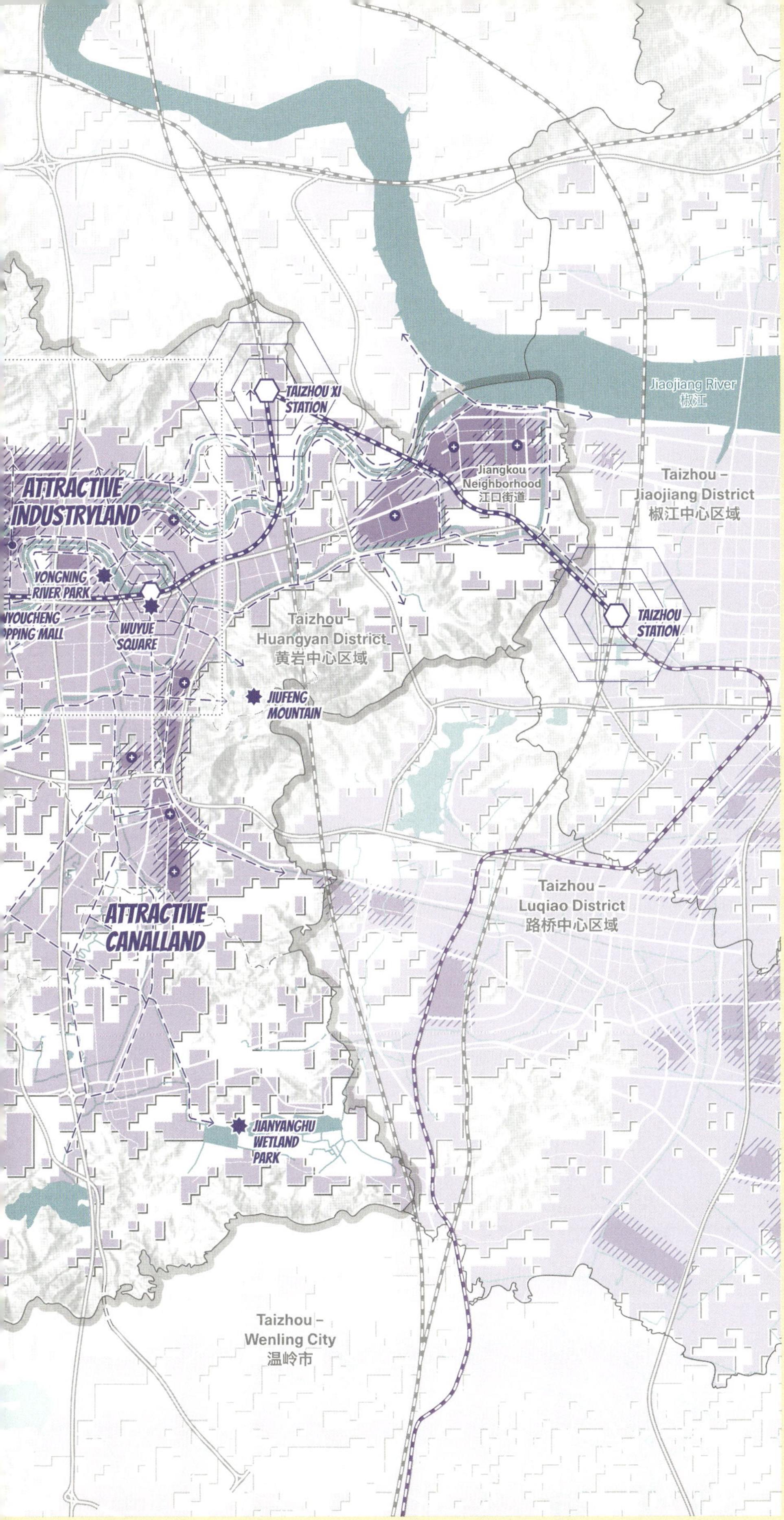

The "Attractive Huangyan"

"Attractive Huangyan" combines strategies for sustainable tourism and mobility with inclusive local neighborhood development. The key zones of this initiative are diverse; for example, it focuses on neighborhoods surrounding Indigenous regions in the urbanized river country, aiming to strengthen these areas as inclusive neighborhoods for different social groups. In the highlands, the initiative targets the villages that converge to form rural networks. This involves the joint development and operation of infrastructure that supports a degree of self-sufficiency, such as in energy supply. The preservation of village structures and the promotion of traditional crafts and local culture are intended to attract tourists and new residents. Between the river and mountain regions, the initiative plans to create a well-connected network of cycling and hiking trails, primarily oriented along landscape features like the reactivated pond-ditch system and mountain routes.

- Attractive settlement areas
- Attractive industrial zones
- Inclusive neighborhoods for industrial workers
- Attractive open spaces in industrial areas
- Attractive spots for locals and tourists
- Active villages
- Active village networks
- Mobility hubs
- Urban-rural light rail
- Urban-rural hiking and biking routes
- Water bodies, rivers
- Streets
- Highways
- Railways
- Administrative borders

Taizhou –
Linhai City
临海市
BUDAI MOUNTAIN
Xinqian living lab
HUAYAN MOUNTAIN
Beiyang living lab
Jiangbei Canal
POND-DITCH SYSTEM 2.0
Mao'erkeng Reservoir
猫儿坑水库
BEIYANG FIELD SUPERMARKET
ZENG MOUNTAIN
BEIYANG ECO AGRICULTURAL PARK
Jiangnan Canal
江南渠
ECOREGIONAL NETWORKS
SONGYAN MOUNTAIN
MOUNTAIN-LAND
Changtan Reservoir
长潭水库
Foling Reservoir
佛岭水库
Shangyang Township
DENGZHAN MOUNTAIN
Wenzhou –
Yongjia County
永嘉县

Fig. 28

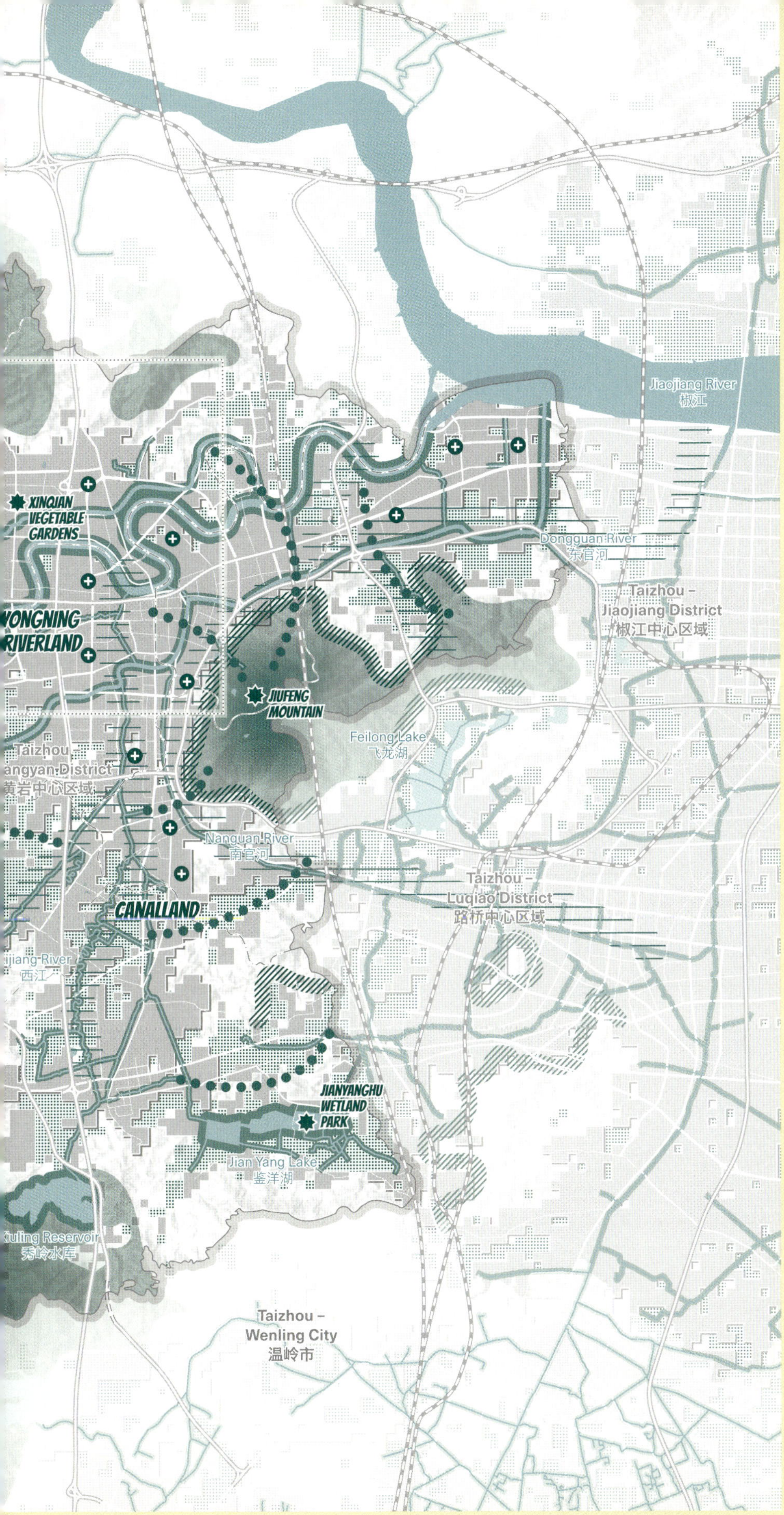

The "Healthy Huangyan"

"Healthy Huangyan" describes transformation pathways to strengthen healthy soils and water, ultimately aiming to protect and link biotopes in Huangyan and beyond. The goal is to develop an ecoregional network linking large-scale forests, flood-resilient water bodies, and small-scale biotopes in urban areas. The edges of forests are considered key zones, often located at the foothills of mountains. Here, buffer zones are established between settlement and landscape areas, reducing urbanization and constructing infrastructure to minimize water pollution. These infrastructures are part of a network of small-scale blue-green arrangements in the river country that build on historical pond-ditch systems and promote decentralized water management. In the industrial areas, small networked biotopes are being created on unsealed surfaces, serving both as habitats for animals and as recreational zones for people.

BUDAI MOUNTAIN
Taizhou – Linhai City
临海市
Xinqian living lab
HUAYAN MOUNTAIN
XITOU VILLAGE NETWORK
Beiyang living lab
SHATAN ACTIVE VILLAGE
CHANGTAN PRODUCTIVE NETWORK
BEIYANG FIELD SUPERMARKET
BEIYANG AGRICULTURAL PARK
URBAN-RURAL BIKE & HIKE LOOP
WUYANTOU ACTIVE VILLAGE
CHANGTAN RESERVOIR
HUANGYAN ECOREGIONAL NETWORKS
SONGYAN MOUNTAIN
NINGXI ACTIVE TOWN
NINGXI PRODUCTIVE NETWORK
Changtan Reservoir
长潭水库
NINGXI VILLAGE NETWORKS
MAOSHE VILLAGE NETWORK
URBAN-RURAL BIKE & HIKE LOOP
URBAN-RURAL BIKE & HIKE LOOP
CHANGTAN PRODUCTIVE NETWORK
SHANGYANG VILLAGE NETWORK
DENGZHAN MOUNTAIN
Wenzhou – Yongjia County
永嘉县
Fig. 29

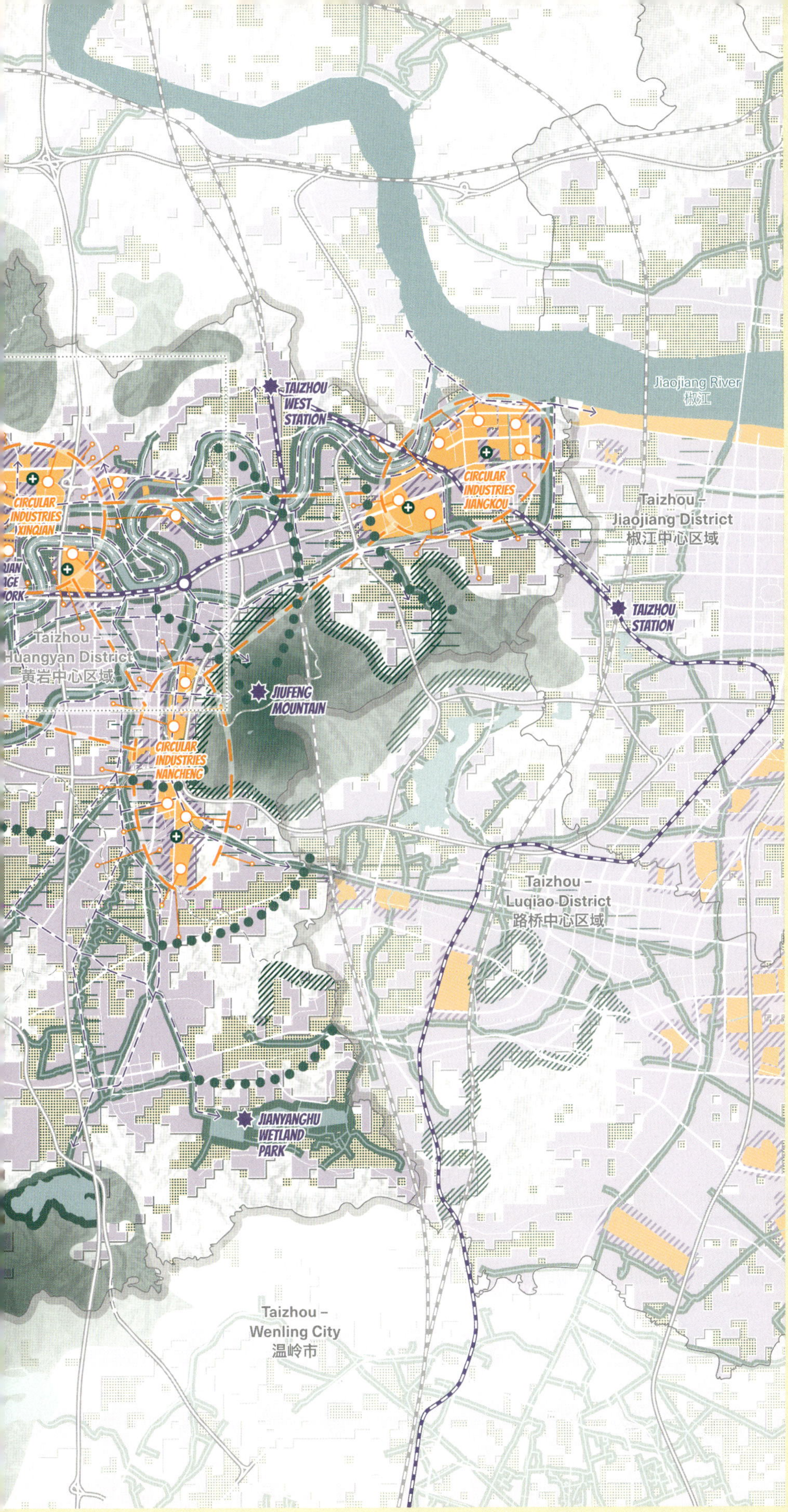

Integrated spatial vision

The integrated spatial vision illustrates how the transformation pathways of "Productive," "Attractive," and "Healthy" Huangyan work together. Key areas emerge that play a central role in a climate-resilient transformation from various perspectives. For example, the rediscovery and reactivation of the close-meshed pond-ditch system in the urbanized riverland strengthens decentralized water management systems and establishes biotope links simultaneously. This water network also provides an attractive framework for sustainable urban-rural mobility and soft tourism. Industrial areas and their neighborhoods serve as action points for different transformation pathways, combining social, ecological, circular, and economic objectives. In the villages, the spatial vision features a combination of small-scale approaches that can work together to markedly enhance local resilience.

Prototypical transformation in Xinqian

Fig. 30

an overview of the co-visioning procedures beforehand, helping participants understand what to expect. These and other formats made it possible to comprehend and clearly communicate particularly complex transformation processes in both urban-rural regions.

The participatory formats featuring playful approaches helped build trust between the research team and local actors, as well as among the stakeholders themselves during both processes. Since the group of participating actors remained largely consistent across all workshops, they became increasingly familiar with the methods, discussions, and exchanges, growing progressively more open-minded. While the presence of international researchers initially made some participants feel insecure, the international nature of the project, particularly in Huangyan, also served as a catalyst for experimenting with unfamiliar workshop settings and formats.

Organizing international multi-stakeholder workshops requires not only sensitivity and a willingness to experiment but also ongoing collaboration with local partners to fully explore the possibilities and limitations of implementing inclusive workshop settings. Ultimately, a long-term goal of multi-stakeholder participation is the development and consolidywation of structures for integrated urban-rural governance.

7. Developing strategies for urban-rural regions together

Urban-rural co-visioning is an effective tool for fostering mutual understanding and collaboratively designing transformation paths and processes at the urban-rural interface. The co-visioning approach, further developed in the Urban-Rural Assembly research project, is distinguished by its spatial and future orientation, participatory and co-creative nature, transdisciplinary approach, and narrative character. It can be applied at various spatial scales while always maintaining a systemic perspective on heterogeneous and interconnected urban-rural contexts. However, co-visioning processes cannot be directly transferred from one region to another; instead, they must be specifically tailored to each context, as planning systems, participation cultures, or data sensitivities can vary significantly.

"Attractive Huangyan" • Living Heritage

ACTIVE AND INTERCONNECTED VILLAGES

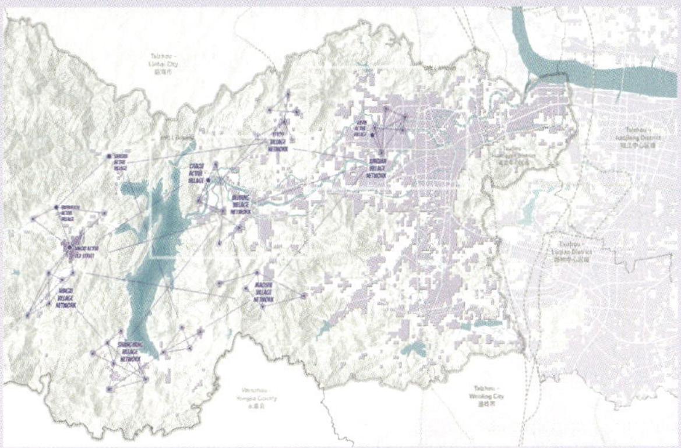

Images: Nicole Goymann

DESCRIPTION

Formerly active villages and old streets are now abandoned places in some parts of Huangyan; in some cases, they have even disappeared from the map. However, in the last ten years, the special architectural and cultural heritage of these historical villages has been rediscovered. Examples such as Shatan or Wuyantou demonstrate the future potential that lies in the revitalization of historical villages. With the help of new infrastructure, participatory formats, and local governance and management models, these villages can be strengthened as attractive and resilient neighborhoods while simultaneously being opened up for ecological tourism and new rural production.

GOALS

* Protecting villages from decay
* Attracting young residents
* Improving the living conditions and mobility in villages
* Strengthening rural tourism, productions, and ecologies

STRATEGIES

→ Continuation of revitalization
→ Strengthening participatory processes alongside forms of local governance and management
→ Construction of infrastructures for mobility, local energy production, water management, and others
→ Preservation and knowledge transfer of local crafts and culture

Case Study > > >

QINGSHAN VILLAGE, HANGZHOU, CHINA

Qingshan Village has significantly improved the quality of life in the region through innovative rural development practices. A key concern of the village community is the protection of local water resources. Projects such as the rehabilitation of the Longwu Reservoir, which supported local farmers in implementing environmentally friendly agricultural practices, have strengthened the ecological balance and improved the quality of drinking water for the villagers. The planning and implementation of the project also promoted the conscious and sustainable use of natural resources in the village community. Qingshan is also home to China's first non-profit library for traditional handicraft materials and various artisans who share their knowledge and create a unique cultural atmosphere. As a model of sustainable rural development, Qingshan impressively demonstrates the importance of community endeavor and environmental responsibility.

Fig. 31

Fig. 1
Working materials in a co-visioning workshop in Huangyan.

Fig. 2
Concept and derivation of the Urban-Rural Assembly co-visioning approach.

Fig. 3
Stakeholders and collaborations in co-visioning processes.

Fig. 4–7
Spatial typologies within the urban-rural region of Nordhausen.

Fig. 8
Characteristic territories identified in the urban-rural region of Nordhausen.

Fig. 9
Bicycle excursion to the Harz region.

Fig. 10
Researchers mapping their observations on an excursion in the Nordhausen region.

Fig. 11
Voting format of the multi-stakeholder workshop in Nordhausen.

Fig. 12
A "transformation kit" as an interactive format.

Fig. 13
Characteristic territories in the urban-rural region of Huangyan.

Fig. 14–17
Spatial typologies of the urban-rural region of Huangyan.

Fig. 18
Researcher workshop in the "Exploring" phase.

Fig. 19
Co-working on digital platforms.

Fig. 21
Photo annotations and collective mapping from the multi-stakeholder workshop in the Beiyang Town living lab.

Fig. 22
Compiling the results in a final discussion using a synthesis model.

Fig. 20, 23, 24
Joint mapping in the multi-stakeholder workshops at different levels, Huangyan.

Fig. 25
Menu cards as a voting format in the multi-stakeholder workshop in Huangyan.

Fig. 26
Regional spatial vision for the "Productive Huangyan" concept

Fig. 27
Regional spatial vision for the "Attractive Huangyan" concept.

Fig. 28
Regional spatial vision for the "Healthy Huangyan" concept.

Fig. 29
Integrated regional spatial vision for the urban-rural region of Huangyan.

Fig. 30
Spatial visualization for the transformation of a prototypical place in the Xinqian living lab.

Fig. 31
Transformation model "Active and Interconnected Villages" as a focus topic for the "Attractive Huangyan" concept.

The inclusive and integrated formats enable diverse perspectives from planning, science, civil society, and administration to be brought together in the context of regional transformation. These discussions occur within a protected framework, allowing for dialogue outside specific planning constraints. The transdisciplinary approach uncovers valuable transformation knowledge in urban-rural regions, including insights into resources, potential challenges and risks, and the identification of key areas and actors for sustainable regional transformation. The local anchoring of these processes allows for the localization of the Sustainable Development Goals[6] and fosters a common understanding of regional development aims and transformation paths among the involved stakeholders. This provides a framework for their actions and starting points for future regional cooperation and collaboration.

Moreover, the process offers a platform to identify and address conflicts of interests, goals, and spatial concerns among stakeholders, facilitating discussions on sustainable solutions for the scarce resource of "space." This approach sensitizes stakeholders with differing objectives and motivates them to pursue sustainable development cooperatively. Additionally, co-visioning processes can assist political decision-makers in the participatory implementation of transformation processes and promote the advancement of integrated governance structures.

Cooperative relationships between the "urban" and the "rural" in local and regional planning processes are crucial for designing sustainable urban-rural relationships and driving the associated spatial transformation processes. The long-term protection and management of urban-rural common goods—such as soil, water, stable social structures, fair resource distribution, and circular material cycles—are central to co-visioning processes aimed at strengthening functional urban-rural relationships across administrative boundaries. By developing selective, co-creatively engineered approaches, strategies can be crafted to protect resources in the long term and guarantee their fair distribution.

Evidence-based action strategies for sustainable transformation are formulated from an academic, scientific perspective; however, the greatest challenge lies in shaping these necessary paths for sustainable urban-rural transformation over the long term and in collaboration with strong alliances of actors. Thus, co-visioning processes can serve as a catalyst, fostering creativity, cohesion, and confidence in the future.

1 Uwe Schneidewind et al., *Pledge for a Transformative Science: A Conceptual Framework*, Wuppertal Paper No. 191 (Wuppertal: Wuppertal Institut für Klima, Umwelt, Energie GmbH, 2016).

2 Niko Schäpke et al., "Reallabore im Kontext Transformativer Forschung: Ansatzpunkte zur Konzeption und Einbettung in den Internationalen Forschungsstand," *IETSR Discussion Papers in Transdisciplinary Sustainability Research*, no. 1 (Lüneburg: Leuphana University of Lüneburg, Institute for Ethics and Transdisciplinary Sustainability Research, 2017).

3 UNDP, *Multi-Stakeholder Engagement Processes: A UNDP Capacity Development Resource* (November 2006), accessed July 23, 2024, https://www.undp.org/sites/g/files/zskgke326/files/publications/Engagement-Processes-cp7.pdf.

4 Verena Elisabeth Balz, "Regional Design: A Transformative Approach to Planning," *Planning Practice & Research* 39, no. 1 (2023): 1–13.

5 See, among others: op. cit. Uwe Schneidewind et al.

6 The United Nations Sustainable Development Goals (SDGs) serve as a guide for sustainable development. See https://sdgs.un.org/goals, accessed July 23, 2024.

Biographies

Sigrun Abels is the director of the China Center, managing director of the CDHK (Tongji University Chinese-German College, Shanghai) Berlin office—both at Technische Universität Berlin—and principal investigator in the Urban-Rural Assembly project. As a sinologist, her teaching and research activities cover the content of media development in China and Sino-German (higher) education cooperation.

Hillary Angelo is an associate professor of sociology at the University of California, Santa Cruz, and a former member of the Institute for Advanced Study in Princeton. Her work offers a social-theoretical perspective on socio-ecological questions through historical and contemporary research on urban greening, sustainability planning and policy, infrastructure, and climate change.

Kit Braybrooke was previously a senior researcher in the Urban-Rural Assembly team at Habitat Unit, Technische Universität Berlin. They are currently professor of transversal design, Institute of Experimental Design and Media Cultures, Fachhochschule Nordwestschweiz Academy of Art & Design, Basel. As a trans-media designer-researcher, their work asks how technological innovation can invite more-than-human networks (animal, vegetal, machine, and algorithmic) to walk together across new terrains.

Marta Doehler-Behzadi has a doctorate in urban planning and was managing director of the International Building Exhibition Thuringia from 2014 to 2023. Her research focuses on the intensive analysis of urban-rural relationships.

Bianca Elzenbaumer has a doctorate in design and is a social, environmental, and spatial activist. Her research and activities focus on supporting and creating community economies and commons in the Italian Alps.

Li Fan was a senior researcher at the Chair of Habitat Unit, Technische Universität Berlin, and coordinator of the Urban-Rural Assembly project. Her primary research area is urban and rural regeneration, as well as policy and governance of urban transformation.

Maria Frölich-Kulik is a senior researcher at the Chair of Landscape Architecture and Planning of the Bauhaus-Universität Weimar and part of the Urban-Rural Assembly team. She specializes in researching "rurban" landscapes, urban-rural transformation processes, and co-creative planning strategies from building to regional scale.

Grace Githiri is a program management officer at the Policy, Legislation, and Governance Section within the Urban Practices Branch of UN-Habitat. She task-manages the urban-rural linkages program, encompassing related work on urban policies and urban and territorial development.

Alexander Maximilian Haase was formerly a research assistant in the Urban-Rural Assembly project at Leibniz-Institute of Ecological Urban and Regional Development Dresden and a Master's student at Technische Universität Dresden. Through geoinformation technologies, his work focuses on ecological research, primarily biodiversity and land use changes using satellite data.

Anke Hagemann is acting professor at Habitat Unit, Technische Universität Berlin, and lead principal investigator of the Urban-Rural Assembly project. She researches and publishes on city-hinterland relationships, global commodity circulation and urban spaces, holiday architectures, and urban mega-events.

Laura Henneke is a researcher at Habitat Unit, Technische Universität Berlin, and part of the Urban-Rural Assembly team. Her research interests include infrastructures, global commodity chains, global corridors, and the use of visual methods to investigate socio-spatiality.

Huang Huang is a researcher within the Urban-Rural Assembly team and assistant professor at the Urban Planning Department, College of Architecture and Urban Planning, Tongji University. Her research concerns urban sociology and critical urban theory in projects relating to urban and rural community renewal and urban-rural integration.

Eduard Kögel is a curator and author with a doctorate in architecture and urban planning. He works on the development of architecture and urban planning in non-European countries, focusing on the topic of transformation in architecture and urban form.

Hannes Langguth is a PhD researcher in the "Urban Future-Making" research training group, funded by the German Research Foundation, at HafenCity University Hamburg. His current research investigates (trans-)local effects of China's global expansion within the context of the European green transition, with a particular focus on the deployment of large-scale projects in Eastern Germany.

Sigrun Langner is a professor of landscape architecture and landscape planning, Bauhaus-Universität Weimar, and one of the principal investigators in the Urban-Rural Assembly research project. Her research focuses on "rurban landscapes" as an expression of complex urban-rural interrelationships, incorporating mapping methods as practices of knowledge and idea generation in large-scale landscape planning and design.

Biographies

Fengqing Li is an associate professor of the Architecture Department at Shanghai University. Within and beyond the Urban-Rural Assembly project, he is primarily engaged in research on urban-rural mobility, urban social networks, and regional development through new technology and big data.

Hongqing Li is a PhD candidate of the Chair of Circular Economy and Recycling Technologies, Technische Universität Berlin, and is closely involved in the Urban-Rural Assembly team. Her research interests include resource metabolism and material recycling in rural areas, mainly focusing on the region of Huangyan-Taizhou, China.

Jian Liu is a professor of urban planning and design at the School of Architecture, Tsinghua University in Beijing. In her research, she particularly analyzes the integration of urban and rural development driven by economic growth in circular approaches.

Ava Lynam is a researcher within the Urban-Rural Assembly project at the China Center and PhD candidate at Habitat Unit, both at Technische Universität Berlin. Her research explores mobility, socio-spatial inequality, and the translocal production of space at globally connected borderland regions in China and Southeast Asia.

Bruno De Meulder is a professor of urbanism at Katholieke Universiteit Leuven, Belgium. He has had a long-standing focus on colonial and postcolonial urbanism, urban history, and urban design projects that intertwine urban analysis and projection. These have engaged with the social and ecological challenges that characterize contemporary times.

Elena Meyer-Clement is a sinologist and political scientist. She is an associate professor at the Department of Cross-Cultural and Regional Studies, Københavns Universitet. Her research focuses on China's governance system and state-society relations. In her current projects, she investigates urbanization, rural development, and land politics in China.

Philipp Misselwitz holds the Chair of International Urbanism at Habitat Unit, Technische Universität Berlin, and serves as executive director at the non-profit think tank Bauhaus Earth. He analyzes options for actor-based urban development and rural urbanization processes, as well as climate restoration in the building sector.

Steffen Nijhuis is a full professor of landscape-based urbanism and head of the landscape architecture section at the Faculty of Architecture and the Built Environment, Technische Universiteit Delft, The Netherlands. He oversees projects that address sustainable urban and landscape development and water-sensitive and social-ecological inclusive urban planning and design.

Christian Nolf is a lecturer in landscape architecture at Wageningen Universiteit and a guest professor of urbanism at Katholieke Universiteit Leuven, Belgium. His research explores the adaptation of cultural landscapes to environmental challenges and climate change, with a focus on water and urbanism.

Andrea Palmioli is an assistant professor in the Department of Architecture and Built Environment at the University of Nottingham Ningbo, China. His research investigates patterns and processes of spatial restructuring in China's extended metropolitan regions, with a particular focus on rural industrialization in the Yangtze River Delta.

Lukas Pappert is a researcher at Habitat Unit, Technische Universität Berlin. His scientific and practical activities focus on the investigation and further development of tools for the sustainable and cooperative transformation of urban-rural regions.

Anke Schmidt works as a professor of environmental and open space Planning at the Rheinland-Pfälzische Technische Universität Kaiserslautern-Landau. Her inter- and transdisciplinary research addresses questions relating to the design and planning of "blue-green" cities and landscapes, climate adaptation, and productive landscapes, with a focus on the relationship between space and people.

Henrik Schultz is a landscape architect and full professor for landscape planning and regional development at Hochschule Osnabrück. His research and publications focus on climate-resilient city structures, sustainable mobility, transdisciplinary planning processes, and walking as a creative practice.

Kelly Shannon is a professor of urbanism at Katholieke universiteit Leuven, Belgium. Her work focuses on the development of landscape urbanism in times of global warming and the development of strategies working with water, vegetation, and topography. Most recently, she has focused on design strategies concerning the consequences of global warming.

Remy Sietchiping is the chief of the Policy, Legislation and Governance Section within the Urban Practices Branch of UN-Habitat. He oversees the agency's programs, including national urban policy, legislation, governance, urban-rural linkages, and metropolitan development.

Jue Wang is a professor at the Chengdu University of Technology, China. Her research topics include regional sustainable development, human-land interactions, community resilience under climate change, and disaster risk reduction.

Ya Ping Wang is a professor at the School of Geography and Tourism, Shaanxi Normal University. He is also professor emeritus and a former chair of Global City Futures, Urban Studies at the University of Glasgow. His research focuses on housing, urban planning and development, and the living conditions of rural-to-urban migrants in China and developing countries.

Yi-Wen Wang is a senior associate professor and director of Cre8Place Research Lab at the Department of Urban Planning and Design, Xi'an Jiaotong-Liverpool University. She conducts research on heritage conservation and management, focusing on socio-cultural issues of heritage-led regeneration in both urban and rural contexts.

Wolfgang Wende is a professor and head of Research Area Landscape, Ecosystems, and Biodiversity at the Leibniz-Institute of Ecological Urban and Regional Development, Dresden. He is one of the principal investigators in the Urban-Rural Assembly project. His research strongly focuses on landscape planning, biodiversity offsets, and habitat restoration.

Gaoli Xiao is a researcher within the Urban-Rural Assembly team at Habitat Unit, Technische Universität Berlin, and PhD candidate at the Center for Development Studies, Universität Bonn. Her research engages with critical migration theories, neoliberalism, power, and social justice.

Suili Xiao is a researcher within the Urban-Rural Assembly team, Leibniz-Institute of Ecological Urban and Regional Development. In addition to her research activities on ecosystem services and biodiversity, she has also undertaken a range of environmental consultancy work for ecological protection and regional sustainable development in both Chinese and German cities.

Yuting Xie is the deputy director of the Institute of Landscape Architecture at Zhejiang University and a principal investigator in the Urban-Rural Assembly project. Her research focuses on regional design, flood risk management, and biodiversity conservation through blue-green infrastructure planning.

Guiqing Yang is professor and head of the Department of Urban Planning at Tongji University Shanghai and principal investigator in the Urban-Rural Assembly project. His current research concentrates on Chinese rural vitalization, with an interdisciplinary perspective of sociology and urban planning.

Zheng Yang is a PhD candidate at the Chair of Circular Economy and Recycling Technologies, Technische Universität Berlin. As a researcher within the Urban-Rural Assembly team, his research interests lie primarily in the integrated utilization of agricultural residues, employing mathematical models and material flow analysis as methods.

Yulin Zhang is a researcher in the Urban-Rural Assembly project and PhD candidate at the Chair of Landscape Architecture and Planning at the Bauhaus-Universität Weimar. Her research focuses on the decoding of the landscape transformation process in urban-rural areas from a constructivist view.

Yuqi Zhang is a student assistant within the Urban-Rural Assembly team at the China Center (CCST) while pursuing her Master's degree in urban and regional planning at Technische Universität Berlin. Her current research focuses on urban renewal and social-spatial practices in villages undergoing agricultural-industrial transition in China.

Image credits

Cover Gaoli Xiao (top), Maria Frölich-Kulik (bottom)
Flap front Atidh Jonas Langbein (top), Anke Hagemann (bottom)
Flap back Gaoli Xiao (top), Anke Hagemann (bottom)
1 Tino Imsirovic (Fig. 1)
2, 3 Anke Hagemann (Fig. 2)
4, 5 Gaoli Xiao (Fig. 3)
6 Jörg Gläscher (Fig. 4), Anke Hagemann (Fig. 5)
7–9 Anke Hagemann (Fig. 6–8)
10, 11 Gaoli Xiao (Fig. 9)
12, 13 Maria Frölich-Kulik (Fig. 10)
14 Tino Imsirovic (Fig. 11), Laura Henneke (Fig. 12)
15 Gaoli Xiao (Fig. 13), Filmproduktion: Fred Plassmann/OFFscreen.de (Fig. 14)
16–19 Anke Hagemann (Fig. 15, 16)
20, 21 Tino Imsirovic (Fig. 17)
22, 23 Lukas Pappert (Fig. 18–21)
24, 25 Maria Frölich-Kulik (Fig. 22)
26, 27 Jörg Gläscher (Fig. 23)
28 Tino Imsirovic (Fig. 24), Maria Frölich-Kulik (Fig. 25)
29 Anke Hagemann (Fig. 26), Jörg Gläscher (Fig. 27)
30–33 Gaoli Xiao (Fig. 28, 29)
34 Laura Henneke (Fig. 30), Anke Hagemann (Fig. 31)
35 Anke Hagemann (Fig. 32), Gaoli Xiao (Fig. 33)
36, 37 Anke Hagemann (Fig. 34)

CHAPTER 1

48 Anke Hagemann (Fig. 1)
51 From: von Thünen, Johann Heinrich, *Der isolirte Staat in Beziehung auf Landwirthschaft und Nationalökonomie, oder Untersuchungen über den Einfluß, den die Getreidepreise, der Reichthum des Bodens und die Abgaben auf den Ackerbau ausüben* (Hamburg: Perthes, 1826): Tafel I, Tafel II (Fig. 2)
53 Research and graphics by Milica Topalovic, ETH Zurich, Architecture of Territory, 2017 (Fig. 3)
54 Map by Giulia Altarelli, Elsa Beniada, and Martin Lepoutre, from: Gugger, Harry, Nancy Couling, and Aurélie Blanchard, *Barents Lessons: Teaching and Research in Architecture* (Zurich: Park Books, 2012): Map 2 (Fig. 4)
56 Philipp Deilmann (Fig. 1)
58, 59 Map by Nikos Katsikis, based on: European Commission Joint Research Center. *Global Human Settlement Layer*, 2016; Erb, Karl-Heinz et al., "A Comprehensive Global 5-Minute Resolution Land use Dataset for the Year 2000 Consistent with National Census Data," *Journal of Land Use Science* 2, no. 3 (2007): 191-224; National Imagery and Mapping Agency (NIMA), Vector Map Level 0 (VMap0) (1997); Halpern, Benjamin S. et al., "Spatial and temporal changes in cumulative human impacts on the world's ocean," *Nature communications* 6 (2015): 7615 (Fig. 2)
62, 63 Maps by David Bauer, Santiago Martinez Murillo, Yuliya Navatskaya, and Joseph Smithard, from: David Bauer and Philipp Misselwitz, eds., *Power, Flows, and Transformation* (Berlin: JOVIS, forthcoming) (Fig. 3)
64 Balazs Gardi (Fig. 4)
66 Julius Mwelu (Fig.1)
68 Julius Mwelu (Fig. 2)
69 Enabel Tanzania, from: Sietchiping, Remy and Grace Githiri, *Compendium of Inspiring Practices on Urban-Rural Linkages* (Nairobi: UN-Habitat, 2023), https://unhabitat.org/sites/default/files/2023/09/url_3rd_compendium_08.09.23_-_final_version.pdf, p. 63 (Fig. 3)
70 Makerere University/Mutumba Raymond (Fig. 4, 5)
71 Eol Chae (Fig. 6)
72 Ola Samarah, from: Sietchiping, Remy and Grace Githiri, *Compendium of Inspiring Practices on Urban-Rural Linkages* (Nairobi: UN-Habitat, 2023), https://unhabitat.org/sites/default/files/2023/09/url_3rd_compendium_08.09.23_-_final_version.pdf, p. 162 (Fig. 7)
74 Marcus Glahn (Fig. 1)
76 Map by Hannes Langguth, based on: Battery News, "Battery Atlas," accessed October 21, 2024, https://battery-news.de/en/battery-atlas/; and own research. (Fig. 2)
77–80 Marcus Glahn (Fig. 3–7)
82 Anke Hagemann (Fig. 1)
84 Elena Meyer-Clement, photo of local government leaflet by Chinese Communist Party (Fig. 2)
85 Elena Meyer-Clement (Fig. 3)
86 Anke Hagemann (Fig. 4)
87 Gaoli Xiao (Fig. 5)
90 Laura Henneke (Fig. 1)
92 Haoxun Zhang (Fig. 2)
93, 94 Laura Henneke (Fig. 3–6)
95 Gaoli Xiao (Fig. 7)
96 Gaoli Xiao (Fig. 8)
97 Map by Yulin Zhang, based on Sigrun Langner, Yuting Xie, Maria Frölich-Kulik, Yuling Zhang, and Karl Beelen, Between Land and Water, (Berlin: JOVIS, forthcoming 2025). (Fig. 9)
98 Haoxun Yang (Fig. 10), Gaoli Xiao (Fig. 11), maps by Maximilian Haase (Fig. 12)
99 Map by Zheng Yang and Hongqi Li (Fig. 13)
100–111 Maps by Lukas Pappert and Kateřina Marečková
112, 113 Laura Henneke (Fig. 14, 15)

CHAPTER 2

116 Maria Frölich-Kulik (Fig. 1)
118 Kateřina Marečková (Fig. 2)
122–128 Ya Ping Wang (Fig. 1–8)
130 Andrea Palmioli (Fig. 1, 2)
133 Map by Andrea Palmioli and Zhebin Chen, University of Nottingham Ningbo China, 2022, based on: Shanghai MetroData Tech Ltd. (Fig. 3)
134 Andrea Palmioli (Fig. 4)
135, 136 Map by Andrea Palmioli and the FoSE-URP research team, University of Nottingham Ningbo China, 2022, based on: National Earth System Science Data Center, National Science and Technology Infrastructure of China (Fig. 5, 6)
137 Model by Andrea Palmioli, Yifei Bian, Sihui Shen, Jie Qiu, Jiayu Chen, Shiming Chen, Yijia Yuan, Yingwen Zhu, Yirong Chen, Yuke Huang, Yundi Zhang, Yuyuan Chen, Haining Ding, Linde Ji, Xiao Chen, Zirui Zhang, and Yunkai Li, University of Nottingham Ningbo China, 2022 (Fig. 7)
138 Illustration by Andrea Palmioli, Yijia Zhang, and Yifei Bian, 2022 (Fig. 8)
139 Axonometric drawing by Andrea Palmioli and Yifei Bian, 2022 (Fig. 9)
140 Model by Yifei Bian and the FoSE-URP research team, University of Nottingham Ningbo China, 2023 (Fig. 10)
143–147 Jue Wang (Fig. 1–7)

152 Maria Frölich-Kulik (Fig. 2)
153 Gaoli Xiao (Fig. 3)
155 Anke Hagemann (Fig. 4)
156 Ava Lynam (Fig. 5)
158 Zheng Yang (Fig. 1)
160 Research and graphics by Zhelei Miu, Xiangning Chen, Jing Jin, Haoxun Zhang, and Rouhan Chen (Fig. 2)
161 Gaoli Xiao (Fig. 3)
162 Suili Xiao (Fig. 4)
163, 164 Ava Lynam (Fig. 5, 6)
165 Gaoli Xiao (Fig. 7), Hongqing Li (Fig. 8)
166 Map by Yulin Zhang, based on Sigrun Langner, Yuting Xie, Maria Frölich-Kulik, Yuling Zhang, and Karl Beelen, Between Land and Water, (Berlin: JOVIS, forthcoming 2025). (Fig. 9)
167 Map by Suili Xiao and Alexander Maximilian Haase, based on Landsat data (Fig. 10)
168 Map from: Xiao, Suili et al., "Ecosystem Services & Biodiversity Conservation in Huangyan, Taizhou, China," *Zenodo* (2024): 5; basemap: Esri, NASA, NGA, USGS (Fig. 11)
169 Map by Huang Huang, from: Lynam, Ava et al., "Capturing Socio-Spatial Inequality in Planetary Urbanisation: A Multi-Dimensional Methodological Framework," *Cities* 132 (January 2023): 104076 (Fig. 12)
170 Map by Bo Fu (Fig. 13)
171 Map by Fengqing Li and Liyuan Fei, based on Location-Based Services data (Fig. 14)
172 Ava Lynam (Fig. 15)
173 Zheng Yang and Hongqing Li (Fig. 16)
174 Gaoli Xiao (Fig. 17)
175 Anke Hagemann (Fig. 18)
176 Jiahui Jin (Fig. 19)
177, 178 Urban-Rural Assembly project (Fig. 20, 21)
179 Filmproduktion: Fred Plassmann/OFFscreen.de (Fig. 22)

CHAPTER 3

182 Ziling Wang (Fig. 1)
184 Graphics by Kateřina Marečková, based on map by DnA_Design and Architecture (Fig. 2)
185, 186 Ziling Wang (Fig. 3, 4)
187 handan (Fig. 5)
188 Ziling Wang (Fig. 6)
190 Matthew Crabbe (Fig. 1)
192–196 Thomas Müller, all rights reserved by IBA Thüringen, Stiftung Baukultur Thüringen (Fig. 2–8)
198–201 Courtesy of Kongcun Town People's Government (Fig. 1–4)
202–203 Jian Liu (Fig. 5, 6)
204 Map by Beijing Tsinghua-Tongheng Urban Planning and Design Institute (Fig. 7)
206–209 414films/Bauhaus Earth (Fig. 1–3)
210 Drawing by Johanna Westermann/Bauhaus Earth (Fig. 4)
211 Adria Goula/Bauhaus Earth (Fig. 5)
212 David von Becker/Bauhaus Earth (Fig. 6)
214, 216 Anke Hagemann (Fig. 1, 2)
217 Guiqing Yang (Fig. 3)
218 Anke Hagemann (Fig. 4)
219 Guiqing Yang (Fig. 5, 6), Jörg Gläscher (Fig. 7)
220 Anke Hagemann (Fig. 8)
222–227 Brave New Alps (Fig. 1–5)

CHAPTER 4

230 Jörg Gläscher (Fig. 1)
232 Map by berchtoldkrass space+options, Urban Catalyst, Integral Ruedi Baur (2011); commissioned by Verein Metropolitanraum Zürich (2011) (Fig. 2)
234 Map by Urban Catalyst, studio amore, brethdelacalle a.o., commissioned by Planungslabor Raumbilder Lausitz 2050 – Nachhaltige Transformation entwerfen (IÖR/IZS) (2021) (Fig. 3)
237 Milos Ruzicka, Alamy Stock Photo (Fig. 1), MEMEME, Alamy Stock Photo (Fig. 2)
238 Illustration by Stockholm Resilience Centre (Fig. 3), Steffen Nijhuis (Fig. 4)
239–241 Steffen Nijhuis (Fig. 5–8)
242 Illustration by Steffen Nijhuis, with OKRA Landscape Architects (Fig. 9)
244 Illustration by Superjacent, for: *Mekong Delta Regional Plan 2023: Vision to 2050*, commissioned by RUA, with consultancy by De Meulder and Shannon (Fig. 1)
246, 247 Map by Nhung Pham, from: De Meulder, Bruno and Kelly Shannon, *A World of Mud and People Passing By* (forthcoming) (Fig. 2, 3)
248–251 Map by Nhung Pham and Claudia Rojas Bernal, see credits for p. 246, 247/ Fig. 2, 3 (Fig. 4–7)
252 Map by Nhung Pham, see credits for p. 246, 247/ Fig. 2, 3 (Fig. 8, 9)
253 Illustration by Superjacent, see credits for p. 244/Fig. 1 (Fig. 10)
254 Map by Nhung Pham, commissioned by RUA (Fig. 11–13)
255 Map by Annelies De Nijs, Master of Architecture Thesis, KU Leuven (Fig. 14)
256 Illustration by Superjacent, see credits for p. 244/Fig. 1 (Fig. 15)
258 Christian Nolf and Yuting Xie (Fig. 1)
260 Studio Landscape Urbanism 2017, MaHS MaUSP, KU Leuven, under guidance of Bruno De Meulder, Stefanie Dens, Racha Daher, and Christian Nolf (top). Christian Nolf and Chang Liu (bottom) (Fig. 2)
261, 262 Maps by Christian Nolf, Yuting Xie, and Han Mengyi (Fig. 3, 4)
263 Illustration by Christian Nolf, 2017 (Fig. 5)
266–272 rabe landschaften / Station C23 (Fig. 1–5)
274 Maria Frölich-Kulik (Fig. 1)
277 Anke Schmidt, from: Schmidt, Anke, *Geschichten urbaner Landschaften: Formate des Erzählens für kollaborative Entwurfsprozesse* (2018): 165 (Fig. 2)
278 Student work, from: Summer school "Old Country for New Men" (Fig. 3)
280 Jacob Westphal, project Green Fingers, HOS (Fig. 1)
283, 284 Lea Nikolaus, project Green Fingers, HOS (Fig. 2, 3)
286 Laura Henneke (Fig. 1)
288, 289 Illustrations by Lukas Pappert (Fig. 2, 3)
290, 291 Filmproduktion: Fred Plassmann/OFFscreen.de (Fig. 4–6), Ava Lynam (Fig. 7)
292 Map by Lukas Pappert (Fig. 8)
293 Nando Reichard (Fig. 9) Tino Imsirovic (Fig. 10)
294 Till Pulst (Fig. 11), Urban Catalyst (Fig. 12)
295 Map by Lukas Pappert (Fig. 13)
296, 297 Lukas Pappert (Fig. 14), Maria Frölich-Kulik (Fig. 15), Lukas Pappert (Fig. 16, 17)
298 Lukas Pappert (Fig. 18)
299 Lukas Pappert (Fig. 19)
300, 301 Jiahui Jin (Fig. 20–22)
302, 303 Anke Hagemann (Fig. 23, 24), Kateřina Marečková (Fig. 25)
304–311 Maps by Lukas Pappert (Fig. 26–29)
312 Illustration by Yuliya Navatskaya (Fig. 30)
313 Maria Frölich-Kulik and Lukas Pappert (Fig. 31)

Imprint

This book is a result of the Sino-German research project "Urban-Rural Assembly" (URA, 01LE1804A-D), funded by the German Federal Ministry of Education and Research (BMBF) under the FONA program "Sustainable Development of Urban Regions." Urban-Rural Assembly is led by Habitat Unit, the Chair for International Urbanism and Design, Technische Universität Berlin, and carried out in cooperation with the Chair for Circular Economy and Recycling Technology, the Center for Cultural Studies on Science and Technology in China (both Technische Universität Berlin), the Chair for Landscape Architecture and Planning of Bauhaus-Universität Weimar, and the Leibniz Institute of Ecological Urban and Regional Development in Dresden, Research Area Landscape, Ecosystems and Biodiversity; together with research partners from Tongji University Shanghai, Shanghai University, Zhejiang University, UN-Habitat, ICLEI Local Governments for Sustainability, and Forward Planung und Forschung, Berlin.

Chief editor:
Anke Hagemann

Editorial team:
Ava Lynam, Gaoli Xiao, Wolfgang Wende, Li Fan, Sigrun Langner, Maria Frölich-Kulik, Laura Henneke, and Lukas Pappert

Copy editing:
Neil Insh and Cecilia Tricker

Proofreading:
Neil Insh and Bianca Murphy

Project management jovis:
Charlotte Blumenthal

Production jovis:
Susanne Rösler

Graphic design:
Till Sperrle

Lithography:
Bild1Druck, Berlin

Printed in the European Union.

Bibliographic information published by the Deutsche Nationalbibliothek
The Deutsche Nationalbibliothek lists this publication in the Deutsche Nationalbibliografie; detailed bibliographic data are available on the Internet at http://dnb.d-nb.de.

jovis Verlag
Genthiner Straße 13
10785 Berlin
www.jovis.de

ISBN 978-3-98612-092-4 (Softcover)
ISBN 978-3-98612-142-6 (E-PDF)

SPONSORED BY THE

Federal Ministry of Education and Research